Reading Psychoanalysis

A VOLUME IN THE SERIES

CORNELL STUDIES IN THE HISTORY OF PSYCHIATRY

Edited by Sander L. Gilman and George J. Makari

A list of the titles in the series may be found on the last page of the book.

ALSO BY PETER L. RUDNYTSKY

Psychoanalytic Conversations: Interviews with Clinicians, Commentators, and Critics (2000)

Psychoanalyses/Feminisms (2000) (ed. with Andrew M. Gordon)

Ferenczi's Turn in Psychoanalysis (1996) (ed. with Antal Bókay and Patrizia Giampieri-Deutsch)

Freud and Forbidden Knowledge (1994) (ed. with Ellen Handler Spitz)

Transitional Objects and Potential Spaces: Literary Uses of D. W. Winnicott (1993) (ed.)

The Psychoanalytic Vocation: Rank, Winnicott, and the Legacy of Freud (1991)

Contending Kingdoms: Historical, Psychological, and Feminist Approaches to the Literature of Sixteenth-Century England and France (1990) (ed. with Marie-Rose Logan)

The Persistence of Myth: Psychoanalytic and Structuralist Perspectives (1988) (ed.)

Ivan L. Rudnytsky, *Essays in Modern Ukrainian History* (1987) (ed.)

Freud and Oedipus (1987)

READING PSYCHOANALYSIS

Freud, Rank, Ferenczi, Groddeck

Peter L. Rudnytsky

CORNELL UNIVERSITY PRESS
Ithaca & London

First published 2002 by Cornell University Press
First printing, Cornell Paperbacks, 2002

Printed in the United States of America

Library of Congress Cataloging-in-Publication Data

Rudnytsky, Peter L.
   Reading psychoanalysis : Freud, Rank, Ferenczi, Groddeck / Peter L. Rudnytsky.
      p. cm. — (Cornell studies in the history of psychiatry)
   Includes bibliographical references (p. 285) and index.
   ISBN 0-8014-3777-6 (cloth) — ISBN 0-8014-8825-7 (pbk.)
   1. Psychoanalysis.   I. Title.   II. Series.
BF173 .R794 2002
150.19′5—dc21   2002009211

Cornell University Press strives to use environmentally responsible suppliers and materials to the fullest extent possible in the publishing of its books. Such materials include vegetable-based, low-VOC inks, and acid-free papers that are recycled, to-tally chlorine-free, or partly composed of nonwood fibers. For further information, visit our website at www.cornellpress.cornell.edu.

Cloth printing   10 9 8 7 6 5 4 3 2 1
Paperback printing   10 9 8 7 6 5 4 3 2 1

To Matthew S. Santirocco

Caelum non animum mutant qui trans mare currunt.
—Horace, *Epistles,* 1.11

Contents

Acknowledgments   ix

Preface   xi

1   Freud's Pompeian Fantasy   1

2   "Mother, Do You Have a Wiwimaker, Too?":
    Freud's Representation of Female Sexuality in the
    Case of Little Hans   22

3   "Does the Professor Talk to God?":
    Countertransference and Jewish Identity in the
    Case of Little Hans   35

4   *The Incest Theme* and the Oedipus Complex   58

5   Rereading Rank   86

6   Ferenczi's Turn in Psychoanalysis   107

7   The Analyst's Murder of the Patient   127

8   Groddeck's Gospel   141

9   Psychoanalysis and the Dream of Consilience   207

References   285

Index   303

Acknowledgments

That this book should appear in a series edited by Sander Gilman and George Makari has for me a feeling of inevitability. Like many others, I owe much of my good fortune in the academic profession to Sander Gilman. Not only did his approbation ensure the publication of *The Psychoanalytic Vocation*, but the first chapter of the present book had its origin in a National Endowment for the Humanities Seminar that he directed in the summer of 1991 at the Freud Museum in London. George Makari's review of *Freud and Oedipus* in the *Journal of the American Psychoanalytic Association*, which I remember saying to Jill Duncan was "as good as can be expected in this world," after I read it in 1989 in the library of the Institute of Psychoanalysis in London, buoyed my spirits at a crucial juncture.

It is a source of additional pleasure to me that this book is being published by Cornell University Press. John Ackerman was a paragon of courtesy in affording me the time I needed to complete my revisions. Catherine Rice and Teresa Jesionowski presided with sovereign grace over their domains of acquisition and production. The guidance I received from the report of the reader, whose identity I now know to have been Madelon Sprengnether, was indispensable in helping me to see the statue hidden in the stone. For a scholar of the caliber of Herman Rapaport to have been engaged as my chisel was a final stroke of providential benevolence.

I owe special thanks to those far-flung friends who inhabit the charmed circle of my obsession with psychoanalytic studies: Antal Bókay, Ernst Falzeder, Carlo Bonomi, Herbert Will, André Haynal, Michèle Bertrand, John Forrester, Patrick Mahony, Christopher Fortune, Judith Vida, John Kerr, Axel Hoffer, Paul Roazen, Paul Stepansky, Peter Swales, and Bernard Paris. Arnold Cooper, Bennett Simon, Patrick Casement, Robert Holt, and Robert Wallerstein model psychoanalysis for me both by their intellectual and by their personal examples. Asking Vera Camden to serve as my Coeditor was my first and best decision as Editor of *American Imago*. Daniela and Hubert Weitensfelder have seen to it that Vienna remains the city of my heart; Michael and Olga Bilynsky assure me I have a future as well as a past in Lviv. Kathie Plourde, Peter Greenleaf, and James Bednarz, together with their respective spouses, to say nothing of a certain classicist turned administrator and a taciturn Swede, make me think I can still make it in New York. Ted Spaeth connects me to Philadelphia. The late Sergei Tcherkasov, whose love for psychoanalysis outlasted the Soviet Union, took me to the circus in St. Petersburg.

I have been honored to present portions of this book at conferences organized by Judith Dupont, André Haynal, Keith Davies, Ludwig Janus, and Michèle Bertrand. Earlier versions of the following chapters have been previously published: chapter 1, in *Reading Freud's Reading*, ed. Sander L. Gilman et al. (New York: New York University Press, 1994); chapter 2, in *100 Years of Psychoanalysis*, ed. André E. Haynal and Ernst Falzeder (London: Karnac Books, 1994), and in *Psychoanalyses/Feminisms*, ed. Peter L. Rudnytsky and Andrew M. Gordon (Albany: State University of New York Press, 2000); chapter 3, in *Psychoanalysis and History*, 1 (1999); chapter 4, as the introductory essay to Otto Rank's *The Incest Theme in Literature and Legend*, trans. Gregory C. Richter (Baltimore: Johns Hopkins University Press, 1991); chapter 6, in *Ferenczi's Turn in Psychoanalysis*, ed. Peter L. Rudnytsky, Antal Bókay, and Patrizia Giampieri-Deutsch (New York: New York University Press, 1996); and chapter 7, in *American Imago*, 55 (1998).

Through it all, Cheryl has made everything possible—and worthwhile.

PETER L. RUDNYTSKY

Gainesville, Florida

Preface

As befits a work of psychoanalytic scholarship, the purposes of *Reading Psychoanalysis* are overdetermined. First, as the title suggests, the book examines the interfaces between literature and psychoanalysis by undertaking close readings of key psychoanalytic texts in a variety of genres as well as by reflecting on issues of theoretical importance to literary criticism. Second, the names in the subtitle—Freud, Rank, Ferenczi, and Groddeck—are intended to signal that this is simultaneously a study in intellectual history that maps the origins of contemporary relational theory in the lives and works of three of Freud's most brilliant and original disciples. Finally, and most ambitiously, the book articulates my vision of psychoanalysis as a discipline with the unique potential to conjoin science and hermeneutics, and that is thus—widespread reports of its demise notwithstanding—poised for an exciting period of growth and renewal in the twenty-first century.

Like any book of literary criticism, *Reading Psychoanalysis* should be judged by the passion and fidelity of its engagement with the works it discusses. I take it as axiomatic that if a text is to be considered as a piece of writing, it needs to be scrutinized in the original language. Accordingly, I have made it my practice to read Freud and the other early analysts in German. In furnishing my own translations, I nevertheless include references to permit the location of quoted passages in

English editions. All italics are found in the sources unless otherwise indicated.

One principle governing the structure of this book is temporal. The first three chapters take up two relatively early texts by Freud. Chapter 1, "Freud's Pompeian Fantasy," treats *Delusions and Dreams in Jensen's "Gradiva"* (1907), Freud's longest and most detailed exegesis of a literary work. Although *Delusions and Dreams* is a specimen of psychoanalytic criticism, it has become better known than the novella it dissects and can itself (by way of a postmodernist reversal) thus be deemed a primary text. Freud writes about the characters as though they were real people in a case history, just as he is surprised that his case histories should read like works of fiction. My excavation delves beneath the oedipal layer of Norbert Hanold's pathology to disclose both a conflict with a persecuting "bad mother" and a schizoid withdrawal that stems from a lack of love and the deaths of his parents. This pattern, as I argue in subsequent chapters, finds counterparts in the actual childhoods of Ferenczi, Groddeck, and Harry Guntrip. I take as my guiding thread throughout chapter 1 the multiple dimensions of transference exhibited in Freud's interpretation—to the characters of Norbert Hanold and Zoe Bertgang, to Jensen as an author, and to literature itself as the uncanny double of psychoanalysis.

Chapters 2 and 3 are both concerned with Freud's *Analysis of a Phobia in a Five-Year-Old Boy* (1909), the first recorded instance of child analysis and the only one of his five major case histories that has never, to my knowledge, been made the subject of a book-length study in English. I thus venture to hope that these chapters together represent an advance on the existing scholarship. As in my reading of *Delusions and Dreams*, I look critically at the case of Little Hans from a contemporary standpoint and uncover Freud's unacknowledged subjective involvement in his material. Chapter 2, " 'Mother, Do You Have a Wiwimaker, Too?': Freud's Representation of Female Sexuality in the Case of Little Hans," focuses on gender and argues that, despite being about a male patient, this text shows the emergence of Freud's views on *female* sexuality, which are codified in his notorious later papers. Chapter 3, " 'Does the Professor Talk to God?': Countertransference and Jewish Identity in the Case of Little Hans," shifts from gender to race and to Freud's neglect of environmental factors generally. I draw upon two texts by Max Graf, the boy's father—"Reminiscences of Professor Sigmund Freud" (1942) and an interview a decade later with Kurt Eissler—to document that Freud's identification with his young protagonist is far more extensive than has heretofore been appreciated. Freud's "shibboleth" of the Oedipus complex emerges from my reading as a defensive formation designed to efface the traces of his Jewish difference. Despite taking Freud to task in both chapters for his *a priori* thinking, I stress the acuteness and honesty of his clinical observations and the inexhaustible richness of the case of Little Hans as a literary work.

Besides being for the most part arranged chronologically, the chapters of this book also form an expanding spiral. Chapter 4, "*The Incest Theme* and the Oedipus Complex," begins a new sequence on Freud's disciples by situating Rank's *The Incest Theme in Literature and Legend* (1912) against the backdrop of Freud's quest between 1906 and 1912 to define the Oedipus complex as the nucleus of his theoretical system. Notwithstanding the developments that have transformed both literary and psychoanalytic studies in the nine decades since Rank published *The Incest Theme*, I argue that his emphasis on the roots of artistic creation in the unconscious fantasy of the artist remains compelling and that his anatomy of the endless permutations of the eternal triangle is the greatest single monument of psychoanalytic literary criticism. As in the case of Little Hans, I believe that my chapter on *The Incest Theme* may be the fullest exposition in English of this classic text. Chapter 5, "Rereading Rank," moves forward to the years 1924-1927 to consider anew my advocacy in *The Psychoanalytic Vocation* of Rank's writings in this interval between his orthodox Freudian and militantly anti-psychoanalytic periods. Although I still give Rank credit for being an originator of object relations theory, I now contend that he does not accompany his shift in emphasis from the oedipal to the preoedipal realms with a recognition of the interactive nature of the therapeutic relationship. For that reason, he has, in my judgment, less to offer contemporary analysts than does either Ferenczi or Groddeck.

In recent years there has been a dramatic revival of interest in Ferenczi, who, unlike Rank, never broke openly with Freud but came increasingly to criticize both his authoritarian tendencies and many of his theoretical assumptions. Chapter 6, "Ferenczi's Turn in Psychoanalysis," explores the biographical contexts for the innovations culminating in Ferenczi's final paper, "Confusion of Tongues between Adults and the Child" (1932). With the aid of the Freud-Ferenczi correspondence, now available in complete form, it is possible for the first time to follow not only the story of how, prior to World War I, Ferenczi found himself torn between his married lover Gizella Pálos and her daughter Elma, whom he had taken into analysis, but also the parallel story of his troubled relationship to Freud. It likewise becomes clear how Freud tendentiously distorts these crucial matters in his three published accounts of Ferenczi—a fiftieth-birthday tribute in 1923, an obituary in 1933, and, most egregiously, an anonymous clinical vignette in *Analysis Terminable and Interminable* (1937). Ferenczi's importance, I maintain, lies above all in his incarnation of an indubitably authentic psychoanalytic identity that cannot be called Freudian, while his greatness resides in his willingness to challenge Freud to live up to his own psychoanalytic ideals.

The Ferenczi renascence was launched by the publication in 1985 of his *Clinical Diary*, the private journal kept by Ferenczi in the year prior to his death. Chapter 7, "The Analyst's Murder of the Patient," uses the *Diary* to probe Ferenczi's conception of analysis as the reenactment of a reciprocal soul murder between mother and child, which can be healed only by mutual forgiveness. This idea, which Ferenczi worked out theoretically even as he enacted it both with his own patients and in his relationship with Freud, points up his affinities with Winnicott. Unlike Freud, moreover, who resisted the attempts of his analysands (including Ferenczi, Groddeck, and the American poet H.D.) to cast him in a maternal role, Ferenczi, like Groddeck and—on the intellectual plane—Rank, understood that the analyst had to play the part of the mother as well as the father. Despite their excesses, Ferenczi's experiments in mutual analysis with Elizabeth Severn and other patients in his final years grapple in a courageous way with the dialectical and intersubjective aspects of the analytic encounter.

In keeping with the spiral design of the book, my final two chapters are as long as the first seven put together. Chapter 8, "Groddeck's Gospel," backtracks chronologically to propose that the year 1923 constitutes (with 1897, when Freud abandoned his seduction theory) one of the two most important turning points in the history of psychoanalysis. Not only was Freud diagnosed with cancer of the jaw, thereby throwing into doubt the future of the psychoanalytic movement, but the same year saw the publication of *The Ego and the Id*. Crucially, however, in 1923 and 1924 the three other major figures I discuss also published landmark books; and I make the case that although Groddeck is less well known today among English-speaking analysts than Ferenczi or even Rank, *The Book of the It* (1923) may well be the greatest masterpiece in the psychoanalytic literature. Whereas *The Ego and the Id* was the fountainhead for ego psychology, I submit that Groddeck's work should be aligned with the contemporaneous texts by Ferenczi and

Rank—*The Development of Psychoanalysis, Thalassa*, and *The Trauma of Birth*—as the nucleus of a collective counterweight that inaugurated the rival relational tradition. That the relational paradigm has irreversibly superseded that of ego psychology is by now widely recognized. Going further, I polemically assert that *The Ego and the Id* is a book of the psychoanalytic past, while *The Book of the It* is a book for the future.

In the five sections of chapter 8, I first show how Freud's ambivalence toward Groddeck is reflected in his assimilation of the latter to both Stekel and Nietzsche—the former being his most despised disciple, and the latter his strongest precursor. I then proceed to look closely at *The Book of the It*, which, by virtue of its epistolary form, allows Groddeck to find an objective correlative for the clinical phenomena of transference and countertransference and to enact, as well as expound, psychoanalytic concepts. The real-life prototypes of the young woman who is Groddeck's (or rather Patrik Troll's) fictional addressee are not only Hanneliese Schumann and Emmy von Voigt, who became Groddeck's second wife, but also Freud himself. The third section takes off from Groddeck's experience with a patient, Miss G., whom he mentions in his initial letter to Freud in 1917 and credits in *The Book of the It* with transforming his understanding of the doctor-patient relationship, to sketch the history of mutual analysis from Jung to Ferenczi. Next, I delineate the autobiographical sources of Groddeck's exploration of the mother-child bond, and in so doing create a "composite photograph" that brings out the similarities between Groddeck's psychic landscape and those of both Winnicott and Freud. Finally, I justify my title of "Groddeck's Gospel" by taking seriously Groddeck's repeatedly drawn parallels between the teachings of Freud and Christ—his gnosticism makes him a kindred spirit less of the Swiss pastor Oscar Pfister than of the mystical H.D.—and using this as a springboard for a meditation on the many ways, both good and bad, in which psychoanalysis can indeed be compared to a religion. Given the paucity of commentary on Groddeck, I think it is safe to say that my chapter provides the most extensive reappraisal of his life and work in English since Carl and Sylva Grossman published their biography, *The Wild Analyst*, in 1965.

Chapter 9, "Psychoanalysis and the Dream of Consilience," radically expands the scope of the book and brings it into the present by comprehensively (though perforce selectively) surveying the contemporary state of American psychoanalysis. To do this, I also need to review its

history. A linchpin of my argument is that the relational turn inaugurated in 1923 made it possible not only to recognize the inherently subjective and interactive components of the analytic situation but also to
place psychoanalytic theory on a sound scientific foundation. Although
one of my concerns throughout this book is with the literary qualities of
psychoanalytic texts, I also consistently try (as Croce did with Hegel) to
sift what is living from what is dead in the thought of Freud and the rest;
and to do this it is necessary to hale them before the bar of science.
Thus, my first two ambitions in *Reading Psychoanalysis*—to examine the
interfaces between literature and psychoanalysis and to chart the intellectual origins of object relations theory—come together in my concluding attempt to expound a vision of how science and hermeneutics
can be synthesized within the interdisciplinary framework of psychoanalysis.

Like chapter 8, chapter 9 falls into five sections. The first briefly re-
views the testimony of expert commentators who concur that a paradigm shift has taken place in recent decades in American psychoanalysis. Although my focus is on the American scene, the reorientation
effected in the past twenty years or so by relational theory coincides
in large measure with that accomplished earlier in British psychoanalysis by the Independent tradition associated most notably with
Winnicott, about which I have written in *The Psychoanalytic Vocation*.
The second section, again briefly, outlines the range of possible positions on the science question and introduces my own conviction that
whereas psychoanalysis as a clinical practice is inescapably hermeneutic, its theory can and should be scientific. With Robert Holt, I maintain that the dead ends of Freud's metapsychology are a consequence
of his refusal to revise his thinking in a truly scientific manner, but
this does not mean that the ideal of psychoanalysis as a science has
been discredited.

The longer third section proceeds dialectically by critiquing those—
such as Kurt Eissler, on one hand, and Merton Gill, on the other—who
argue that psychoanalysis is either a purely scientific or a purely
hermeneutic discipline, and thus fail to do justice to its hybrid nature. I
likewise question Robert Wallerstein's claim that psychoanalysis is scientific in clinical practice, while its theories are metaphorical. This seems
to me to invert the true state of affairs. My use of the term "consilience"
is taken from Edward O. Wilson's 1998 book of that title, and in the
fourth section I juxtapose his magnificent conception of the unity of
knowledge with that of Gerald Edelman. Although Wilson's attitude

toward psychoanalysis is more critical than Edelman's, both seek to amalgamate Freud with Darwin. Both likewise accept that scientific disciplines are arranged in an intrinsic hierarchy of pairs, in which all the laws of the "lower" anti-discipline remain in effect in the "higher" parent discipline, though they are not sufficient to explain the latter. In addition to holding true within the sciences, I suggest that this principle can be extended to apply globally to the relations between the sciences and the humanities.

The last (and longest) section of chapter 9 is devoted to the convergence between psychoanalysis and neuroscience, which, in my judgment, subtends and complements that between psychoanalysis and attachment theory promulgated beginning in the 1960s by Bowlby. In keeping with the metaphor of a "dream" of consilience, I begin with a review of the current debates over the psychoanalytic theory of dreams. Because the meaning of dreams is a hermeneutic and not a scientific question, I contend that even if Freud's critics, such as J. Allan Hobson, were right about the biology of dreaming, this would not of itself refute his theories about how dreams should be interpreted. In fact, however, as reported by Mark Solms, recent research has tended to vindicate Freud even on a physiological level. By the same token, the use made by Morton Reiser of Eric Kandel's work, like that made by Arnold Modell of Edelman's work, attests to the potential for ongoing cross-fertilization between psychoanalysis and neuroscience. (Just as I rate *The Book of the It* more highly than *The Ego and the Id*, so I provocatively insinuate that present-day analysts have more to learn from two papers by Kandel and one by Harry Harlow than from the collected works of Lacan and Melanie Klein combined.) Taking off from Modell's redefinition of Freud's concept of *Nachträglichkeit* or "deferred action" in neuroscientific terms as "retrospective transcription," I conclude by offering this as a model for the dialectical interdependence between science and hermeneutics in psychoanalysis, citing the relation between the characters of Vergil and Beatrice in Dante's *Divine Comedy* as a literary analogue.

As a book that upholds the Enlightenment belief in the unity of knowledge and the attainability of truth, and that unabashedly seeks to interweave variegated strands of narrative into a single grand design, *Reading Psychoanalysis* is written against the spirit of a postmodern age. But if, as I am persuaded, psychoanalysis is poised for a resurgence in its second century, that is because a healing of the unfortunate rift (left over from the Romantic era) between the "two cultures" of science and hu-

manism is breathing new life into contemporary thought. By intertwining literary criticism with intellectual history, and never forgetting that
the theoretical is always also the personal, I hope by my backward
glances to provide a beacon for others to follow down as yet untraveled
roads.

Reading Psychoanalysis

1

Freud's Pompeian Fantasy

Delusions and Dreams in Jensen's "Gradiva" (1907a), although one of Freud's least famous works, is undoubtedly far better known than the novel it anatomizes, Wilhelm Jensen's *Gradiva: A Pompeian Fantasy* (1903). This reversal of the customary relation between primary and secondary texts invites the reader of Freud's reading of Jensen to assume a postmodernist stance. Despite its intricate web of themes and images, Jensen's tale of the archeologist Norbert Hanold's mysterious attraction to a relief depicting a young woman with an unusual gait is formally naive and employs the convention of an omniscient narrator. Freud's appropriation of Jensen's novel as a parable of psychoanalysis, by contrast, at once paradoxically throws open and reduces its meanings while imposing a subjective frame that transforms an unsophisticated text into a radically unstable and self-reflexive one. After Freud, every reading of *Gradiva* becomes a double reading in which there is no position of absolute knowledge or mastery, only a series of more or less adequate transferential investments in the reading and writing process.[1]

Delusions and Dreams—a title I shall use to distinguish Freud's *Gradiva*

---

1. On the tensions between deconstructive undecidability and metaphysical closure in Freud's reading of Jensen, see Kofman (1972). Despite her critique of Freud for reducing *Gradiva* to a "manifest text" for which he will uncover the definitive "latent content" (117),

from Jensen's—stems from the halcyon days of the psychoanalytic movement. Although it was almost certainly Wilhelm Stekel and not, as is generally believed, C. G. Jung who first drew Freud's attention to *Gradiva*, much of the confidence that Freud exudes in *Delusions and Dreams* derives from his having secured the support of a band of like-minded adherents, to which Jung was the latest and most distinguished recruit.[2] Basking in Jung's praise of the work as "magnificent," Freud expatiated in a letter on May 26, 1907: "This little book was written on sunny days and I myself derived great pleasure from it. . . . To tell the truth, a statement such as yours means more to me than the approval of a whole medical congress" (McGuire 1974, 51–52).

The frame of mind in which Freud wrote *Delusions and Dreams* is further attested by its opening words: "A group of men who regarded it as a settled fact that the essential riddles of dreaming have been solved by the author of the present work . . ." (1907a, 7). In the exaltation of a peak moment, Freud wraps himself in the mantle of third-person authority, asserts the findings of his *magnum opus* to be a "settled fact," and appeals for confirmation to the "group of men" who formed the nucleus of what in 1908 would become known as the Vienna Psychoanalytic Society. Thus, one crucial dimension of Freud's transference in *Delusions and Dreams* is to his followers in the psychoanalytic movement, and to Jung

---

however, Kofman claims that her own interpretation "takes into account the whole text. . . . Translated into the language of analysis, Norbert is born castrated" (104).

2. The assumption that Jung alerted Freud to *Gradiva* originates with Ernest Jones (1955, 382), and has been echoed by virtually all subsequent commentators. However, as William McGuire has observed, the Freud-Jung correspondence "casts no light" (1974, 45) on Jones's claim, which is rather placed in doubt both by the fact that neither Jung nor Freud ever indicates that Jung had mentioned the work to Freud and by the fact that Freud wrote *Gradiva* in the summer of 1906 before his first meeting with Jung. The case for Stekel's influence hinges on a passage in *The Dreams of Creative Writers* (1912, 14), in which he states that he had written to Jensen to ask whether he had been aware of *The Interpretation of Dreams* before writing *Gradiva*, and received a negative answer. In the final section of *Delusions and Dreams* (1907a, 91), Freud refers to an unspecified member of his circle who had posed this question to Jensen, adding that this was the same individual cited at the outset of the work whom he credits with having introduced him to *Gradiva* (9). This interlocking series of allusions warrants the conclusion that the colleague in question was Stekel rather than Jung. That Freud leaves him anonymous, moreover, is in keeping with his grudging attitude toward Stekel, whereas he would have had every reason to mention Jung by name. In a letter to Ferenczi of October 17, 1912, Freud disparages *The Dreams of Creative Writers* as "miserable trash" and Stekel himself as a "swine" (Brabant, Falzeder, and Giampieri-Deutsch 1993, 411); but this invective at the time of their rupture does not mean that Freud did not profit from Stekel's diligence in 1906.

in particular, and is marked by its appearance at a moment when the "sunny days" of collaboration were untroubled by the clouds of dissension that would soon dim the horizon.

A second transferential dimension in *Delusions and Dreams* arises from Freud's relation to Jensen's text, and by extension to literature as a whole. Just as in 1906 Freud began to gather the fruits of his heroic early labors and his professional life was at its most harmonious, so *Delusions and Dreams* shows him at the height of his optimism concerning the relations between psychoanalysis and literature.[3] *Delusions and Dreams* is Freud's first extended venture in applied analysis, and it remains his most ambitious and detailed exegesis of a literary work. In the same way that Freud's original 1901 title for the Dora case, *Dreams and Hysteria*, published four years later as *Fragment of an Analysis of a Case of Hysteria* (1905a), signaled his intention to synthesize his achievements in *Studies on Hysteria* (Freud and Breuer 1895) and *The Interpretation of Dreams* (1900), so too in *Delusions and Dreams* Freud consolidates his findings on dreams, sexuality, and the nature of the therapeutic process.

Extending a line of argument begun in *The Interpretation of Dreams*, Freud opens *Delusions and Dreams* by disdaining "the reproaches of strict science" and proclaiming himself "a partisan of antiquity and superstition" in upholding the meaningfulness of dreams (1907a, 7). Again referring to himself in the third person, he enlists imaginative writers as being "on the same side as the ancients, as the superstitious public and as the author [*Verfasser*] of *The Interpretation of Dreams*" (8).[4] In its championing of poetic as opposed to scientific truth, *Delusions and Dreams* is at the opposite pole from *The Future of an Illusion* (1927b), in which Freud aligns psychoanalysis with science in its fidelity to the reality principle and antipathy to all forms of illusion, aesthetic as well as religious. But since Freud had already announced to Fliess his ambition to found a psychology that could be a natural science in the *Project for a Scientific*

3. 1906, however, was also the year in which Wilhelm Fliess made public his well-founded accusation that Freud had divulged his ideas about bisexuality to Freud's patient Hermann Swoboda, who passed them on to Otto Weininger, who in turn gave them a prominent place in *Sex and Character* (1903). In a personal communication, Peter Swales has suggested that a somewhat earlier period, from the spring of 1902 through the spring of 1904, was a more truly tranquil interlude in Freud's life.

4. In Freud's German text, the word *Verfasser*, or scientific author, contrasts with *Dichter*, or creative writer. See *Gesammelte Werke*, 7:32. Where necessary, subsequent references to Freud in German will be indicated parenthetically by the abbreviation *G.W.* I have read Jensen's story in the German edition of Urban and Cremerius (1973).

Psychology (1895), this antimony reflects less an evolution from Freud's earlier to his later writings than a permanent dialectical tension in his thought.

Freud's enthusiasm for literature in *Delusions and Dreams* leads him to hail the creative writer as one who has "from time immemorial been the precursor of science, and so too of scientific psychology" (1907a, 44). Invoking one of his talismanic quotations from *Hamlet*, Freud affirms that the testimony of writers is to be "prized highly, for they are apt to know a whole host of things of which our philosophy has not yet let us dream" (8). So radically does Freud adhere to this conviction that he elevates *Gradiva* to the status of a case history. Conceding that he has proceeded as though Norbert Hanold and Zoe Bertgang "were real people and not the author's creations," Freud defends this apparent naïveté—akin to the Romantic tradition of Shakespeare criticism descended from Maurice Morgann—by arguing that "all [Jensen's] descriptions are so faithfully copied from reality that we should not object if *Gradiva* were described not as a phantasy but as a psychiatric study" (41). He adds: "Thus the creative writer cannot evade the psychiatrist nor the psychiatrist the creative writer, and the poetic treatment of a psychiatric theme can turn out to be correct without any sacrifice of its beauty" (44).

But if the psychiatrist and the creative writer cannot "evade" each other, and the latter can be clinically accurate, this carries the subversive implication that Freud's psychoanalytic study may be no more than a literary fantasy. In intimating this possibility, *Delusions and Dreams* evokes a specter that haunts all Freud's writings. As early as *Studies on Hysteria* he avers that "it still strikes me myself as strange that the case histories I write should read like short stories and that, as one might say, they lack the serious stamp of science" (Freud and Breuer 1895, 160); and the original title for his valedictory *Moses and Monotheism* (1939) was *The Man Moses: A Historical Novel*.

In reading Jensen's novel as a case history, Freud continues to rely on the paradigm of therapeutic action set forth in *Studies on Hysteria*. Zoe Bertgang's cure of Norbert Hanold's delusion "shows a far-reaching similarity—no, a complete agreement in its essence—with a therapeutic method which was introduced into medical practice in 1895 by Dr. Josef Breuer and myself" (1907a, 89). In *Studies on Hysteria* Freud had contended that, just as particular symptoms disappear after they have been abreacted through language, so "it is only with the last word of the analysis that the whole clinical picture vanishes" (Freud and Breuer 1895,

299). In *Delusions and Dreams*, despite his intervening recognition of the dynamics of transference in the Dora case, Freud writes of Norbert Hanold: "The disorder vanishes while being traced back to its origin; analysis, too, brings simultaneous cure" (1907a, 89). One may surmise that Freud, having experienced with Dora his first major setback as a therapist, which he chronicled in a narrative that he himself stigmatized as fragmentary, found in the closure provided by *Gradiva* a reassuring coherence that harked back to the optimism of his earliest psychoanalytic work. In both *Studies on Hysteria* and *Delusions and Dreams* Freud uses the word "vanishes" (*schwindet*; *G.W.*, 1:304; *G.W.*, 7:118) to convey his magical belief that when the analysis reaches its "last word" the "clinical picture" disappears, as it were, in a puff of smoke.

The impossibility of distinguishing between literary and clinical writing links *Delusions and Dreams* not only to *Studies on Hysteria* but also to both the Schreber case and the monograph on Leonardo. Although he believes his interpretations of *Gradiva* to be well founded, Freud nonetheless muses whether it is not "rather we who have slipped into this charming poetic story a secret meaning very far from its author's intentions" (1907a, 43), and admits that it might be so. Similarly, at the end of the Schreber case Freud leaves it to the future to decide "whether there is more delusion in my theory than I should like to admit, or whether there is more truth in Schreber's delusion than other people are as yet prepared to believe" (1911, 79). In *Leonardo da Vinci and a Memory of His Childhood*, Freud confesses that even his supporters may deem that he has "merely written a psychoanalytic novel," adding that "I am far from over-estimating the certainty of these results" (1910a, 134).

Freud rings every possible change on the permutations of fiction and case history in *Studies on Hysteria*, *Delusions and Dreams*, *Leonardo*, and *Psycho-Analytic Notes on an Autobiographical Account of a Case of Paranoia*. In *Studies on Hysteria* he writes case histories that read like short stories; in *Delusions and Dreams* he reads Jensen's novel as though it were a case history; in *Leonardo* he writes a psychobiographical novel about a historical figure; and he bases his so-called case history of Schreber on his reading of the latter's *Memoirs of My Nervous Illness* (1903). (The Schreber case might thus be more accurately described as a work of literary criticism.) Any attempt to maintain a sharp distinction between "pure" and "applied" analysis breaks down in the face of Freud's own highly equivocal practice. As Roy Schafer has argued, "it would be just as warranted to recommend viewing clinical analysis as a form of applied analysis as to continue viewing applied analysis as parasitic on clinical analysis" (1988, 180).

That *Delusions and Dreams*, *Leonardo*, and the Schreber case arise out of a continuous process of reading and writing can be further documented thanks to the fortunate circumstance that in all three instances the Freud Museum in London possesses the original books on which Freud relied, with markings in his hand. Although an exhaustive analysis of Freud's marginalia to *Gradiva*—to say nothing of the other sources in question—is beyond my scope here, some brief observations will suffice to make my point.[5]

On the penultimate page of his copy of *Gradiva*, which is heavily annotated throughout in green pencil, Freud notes that the word "*Verschüttung*" (burial) is the "*symbolischer Kern*" (symbolic core) of the whole story. In his discussion of psychotherapy in *Studies on Hysteria*, Freud had previously used "*verschütten*" to warn the physician lest he inadvertently "bury" a memory that the patient is seeking to recall (Freud and Breuer 1895, 292; *G.W.*, 1:297). Thus, when he encountered the same word in Jensen, it must have been with a tremor of recognition, which triggered his grandiose assertion that *Gradiva* shows a "complete agreement" with the methods of *Studies on Hysteria*. Echoing Jensen but also his own earlier formulation, Freud reiterates in *Delusions and Dreams* that there is "no better analogy for repression, by which something in the mind is at once made inaccessible and preserved, than burial [*Verschüttung*] of the sort to which Pompeii fell a victim" (1907a, 40; *G.W.*, 7:77).[6]

Like "*verschütten*," the phrase "*symbolischer Kern*" is charged with significance. In *Studies on Hysteria*, Freud had striven to penetrate to the "core of the matter" (*Kerne der Sache*; Freud and Breuer 1895, 126; *G.W.*, 1:186) in the case of Katharina; and he asserts in the chapter on psychotherapy that memories are organized around a "pathogenic nucleus" (*pathogenen Kern*; 289; *G.W.*, 1:292). During the period 1907–12, Freud embarked on a quest to find a *Kernkomplex*—a core or nuclear complex—of the neuroses, which culminated in his apotheosis of the Oedipus complex in *Totem and Taboo*: "We have arrived at the point of regarding a child's relation to his parents, dominated as it is by incestuous longings,

---

5. A preliminary assessment of Freud's marginalia to *Gradiva* is offered by Edward Timms (1988). The edition in Freud's library is Wilhelm Jensen, *Gradiva* (Dresden: C. Reissner, 1903).

6. The word "*Verschüttung*" occurs also in Freud's comparison of repression to the "burial" of Pompeii in the case of the Rat Man (1909b, 176; *G.W.*, 7:400).

as the nuclear complex of the neuroses" (1912–13, 17).[7] In annotating his copy of *Memoirs of My Nervous Illness* (1903, 45), moreover, Freud again employs *"Kern der Sache"* to gloss Schreber's fantasies of emasculation. Wherever he comes across a passage explaining the etiology of Schreber's delusions, Freud scribbles *"Quelle"* in the margins, just as he does in *Gradiva* with respect to Norbert Hanold's delusions. Thus, whether he is reading fiction or autobiography, Freud's method of analysis remains the same, and the texts he produces reflect this indeterminacy.

The principal subtext for *Leonardo da Vinci and a Memory of His Childhood* is Dmitry Sergeyevich Merezhkovsky's *Leonardo da Vinci: A Biographical Novel from the Turn of the Fifteenth Century*, published in Russian in 1902 and read by Freud in a 1903 German translation.[8] Because Freud based his study of Leonardo on a fictionalized treatment, his admission that he may have written only a "psychoanalytic novel" places his work in its proper generic context. What is more, Freud's notorious mistranslation of the Italian word for "kite" (*nibio*) as "vulture" in his exegesis of Leonardo's childhood memory has its origin in the German translation of Merezhkovsky, a symptom of the problems that plague Freud's narrative because of its remoteness from historical reality.

Although Freud's copy of Merezhkovsky has no annotations, but only occasional lines penciled in the margin, it remains revealing to see which passages attract Freud's notice. Of only three marked with double lines, all occur in Chapter 11, "The Wings Will Come." Two have to do with Leonardo's mother and her smile; the third recounts his memory of the bird that visited him in his cradle. I quote the first passage:

> Leonardo remembered his mother. Especially vivid to him was her tender, mysterious [*geheimnisvolles*], and roguish smile, which stood out oddly from her sad, severe, beautiful face. One day in Florence in the museum of the Medici garden of San Marco he found a small copper statue of Cybele, the ancient goddess of the earth, which had been excavated from a small Etruscan city in

7. I return to Freud's search for a core complex in chapter 4. In German, the word *Kern* can mean both "core" and "nucleus," and in the compound *Kernwaffen* means "nuclear weapons."

8. Freud had read the novel by 1907, when he named it as one of ten "good books" in response to a questionnaire from the publisher Hugo Heller. For some useful comments on Freud and Merezhkovsky, which leave open whether Freud had "already chosen Leonardo as the subject of a psychological biography when he opened the novel, or . . . [Merezhkovsky's] work help[ed] determine Freud's decision," see Rose (1998, 99). As I argue in the text, I think it is clear that Freud's reading of Merezhkovsky was decisive in crystallizing his interpretation of Leonardo.

Arezzo. The features of its face showed the same smile that belonged to the young peasant woman from Vinci, his mother. (Merezhkovsky 1903, 366; my translation)

As Paul Ricoeur has remarked (1970, 173–74), the most dubious aspect of Freud's procedure in *Leonardo* is that he moves from the known (the smile of the Mona Lisa) to the unknown (speculations about Leonardo's childhood memories). In Freud's words: "we begin to suspect the possibility that it was his mother who possessed the mysterious [*geheimnisvolle*] smile—the smile that he had lost and that fascinated him so when he found it again in the Florentine lady" (1910a, 111; *G.W.*, 8:183). As the iteration of "mysterious" attests, Freud's reconstruction of Leonardo's childhood again rests directly on his reading of Merezhkovsky, whom he cites in a note to this passage, although he acknowledges that the latter's depiction of Leonardo's childhood differs in key respects from his own, based on an analysis of the vulture fantasy.

Freud's assumptions in *Delusions and Dreams* are identical to those to which he adheres three years later in *Leonardo*. Not only does he regard Norbert Hanold and Zoe Bertgang as real people, but he traces the origin of Hanold's fixation on the statue of Gradiva to his putative childhood experiences: "For there can be no doubt that even in her childhood the girl showed the same peculiarity of a graceful gait, with her toes almost perpendicularly raised as she stepped along; and it was because it represented that same gait that an ancient marble relief acquired such great importance for Norbert Hanold" (1907a, 46). Merezhkovsky's account of Leonardo's discovery of a statue in a museum that reminds him of his mother's smile uncannily parallels Jensen's story, which opens with Hanold's puzzling attraction to a bas-relief he sees in a museum in Rome, of which he obtains a plaster-cast copy to hang on the wall of his study. Since Freud's knowledge about the historical figure of Leonardo is mediated by textuality and contaminated by fictional elements, it simply reverses the equation for him to look upon literary characters as though they were living beings and to impute to them an actual history.[9]

As befits the double reading required by *Delusions and Dreams*, Freud's

9. To give the matter one more twist, Max Schur quotes from a letter written by Freud to Martha Bernays in 1882: "You don't seem to know how observant I am. Do you remember how in our walk with Minna along the *Beethovengang* you kept going aside to pull up your stockings? It is bold of me to mention it, but I hope you won't mind." Freud adds that the foot of the Venus de Milo could cover two of Martha's. Schur comments: "Could the memory of this episode including the name *Beethovengang* (so similar to Bert-

conflation of real and fictional characters reenacts the central problem faced by Norbert Hanold in Jensen's story. Hanold is smitten by the bas-relief because it seems to have been taken "from life," and the grace of the represented movement gives the impression of "imparting life" (Jensen 1903, 4) to the relief. But when he seeks to find a contemporary woman with a gait resembling that of the statue, whose folded dress is pulled up slightly and trailing right foot touches the ground almost vertically, Hanold at first fails and regretfully concludes that this manner of walking "had been created by the imagination or arbitrary act of the sculptor and did not correspond to reality" (11). However, on one occasion, after awakening from a dream, he catches a glimpse of a woman walking in this fashion through the street of his northern German university town and, still dressed in his night clothes, rushes after her in vain. Finally, in the last sentence of the novel, after Hanold has recognized the apparition of Gradiva he encountered at Pompeii to be his childhood friend Zoe Bertgang and won her consent to marry him, she gratifies his desire and strikes the requisite pose: "raising her dress slightly with her left hand, Gradiva *rediviva* Zoe Bertgang, viewed by him with dreamily observant eyes, crossed with her calmly buoyant walk, through the sunlight, over the stepping-stones, to the other side of the street" (117–18). In his copy of Jensen, Freud annotates this passage: "*Erotik! Aufnahme der Phantasie-Versöhnung*" (Erotic! Assimilation of the fantasy-reconciliation).

Hanold's confusion between reality and fantasy is equally one between life and death. When he arrives in Pompeii on a journey unconsciously motivated, as he belatedly realizes, by a quest to find the woman of whom he thought he had caught a glimpse in his native town, and who he dreamt had been buried in the eruption of Mount Vesuvius in 79 A.D., he becomes convinced that dead spirits return to life at noon: "Then something came forth everywhere without movement and a soundless speech began; then the sun dissolved the tomb-like rigidity of the old stones, a glowing thrill passed through them, the dead awoke, and Pompeii began to live again" (Jensen 1903, 45). Precisely at noon, Hanold beholds the apparition of Gradiva, walking in her inimitable fashion, and addresses her first in Greek and then in Latin, before she wryly tells him he must use German if he wishes to be understood. After she disappears, Hanold is bewildered by the "physical manifestation of a

---

gang) and the comparison between Martha's foot and that of the Venus de Milo have been an added determinant for Freud's interest in the Gradiva story?" (1972, 248).

being like Gradiva, dead and alive at the same time, although the latter was true only at the noon hour of spirits" (64).

The theme of reality and fantasy again converges with that of life and death when Hanold buys a worthless brooch from the innkeeper at the remote Albergo del Sole—the name of which links it to the sun imagery throughout the story—in the belief that it had been worn by a young woman, the original of Zoe-Gradiva, one of a pair of lovers who had been buried together near the Forum by the eruption of Vesuvius.[10] Just then he sees in an open window of the inn an asphodel branch covered with white flowers—the same flower of death he had given at noon to Gradiva—and "without needing any logical connection, it rushed through his mind, at the sight of the grave-flower, that it was an attestation of the genuineness of his new possession" (78). Hanold's rash inference exemplifies Freud's original definition of transference in *Studies on Hysteria* as a "false connection" (Freud and Breuer 1895, 302); and in *Delusions and Dreams* Freud explains Hanold's error concerning the brooch by saying that he "transferred [*überträgt*] his conviction that Gradiva lived in the house to other impressions which he had received in the house" (1907a, 79; *G.W.*, 7:107). Subsequently, when Hanold recognizes the woman he has met in Pompeii as Zoe Bertgang, she observes that it is strange "that a person must die to become alive again, but for archeologists that is of course necessary" (Jensen 1903, 110).

The intertwined problems of distinguishing what is alive from what is dead and what is real from what is fictional, central both to Jensen's story and to Freud's analysis, bring *Delusions and Dreams* into close connection with Freud's later and far more famous paper, "The Uncanny" (1919b). Observing that the appearance of a living Gradiva in Pompeii initially bewilders the reader no less than it does Norbert Hanold, Freud notes that Jensen, "who has called his story a 'phantasy,' has found no occasion so far for informing us whether he intends to leave us in our world . . . or whether he intends to transport us to another and imaginary world, in which spirits and ghosts are given reality" (1907a, 17). He likens this uncertainty to that produced by Shakespeare's use of supernatural phe-

10. As Vitz (1988) has observed of Freud, "almost the only times that he expressed happiness and joy, the times in which he escaped his baseline mood of melancholy and even sorrow, was when he was in Rome or speaking about it. Only in Rome did the sun seem to break into his life" (78). That Vitz's reference to the sun fortuitously echoes the name of the Albergo del Sole points to the connection between Freud's affective investment in Italy generally and his analysis of Jensen's novella.

nomena in *Hamlet* and *Macbeth*. Similarly, in "The Uncanny," Freud states with reference to E. T. A. Hoffmann's "The Sand-Man" that "the writer creates a kind of uncertainty in us in the beginning by not letting us know, no doubt purposely, whether he is taking us into the real world or into a purely fantastic one of his own creation" (1919b, 230); and he again cites Shakespeare's exploitation of supernatural agents in *Hamlet* and *Macbeth*.

This parallel movement of thought suggests that *Delusions and Dreams* prefigures "The Uncanny," while "The Uncanny" retroactively glosses *Delusions and Dreams*. In "The Uncanny," Freud emphasizes the distinction between two causes of eeriness—repressed complexes and superseded thought processes. His paper is largely a polemical effort to debunk the second hypothesis, which he equates with Ernst Jentsch's derivation of the uncanny from intellectual uncertainty, though by the end Freud admits that "these two classes of uncanny experience are not always sharply distinguishable" and "an uncanny effect is often and easily produced when the distinction between fantasy and reality is wiped away, when something real appears before us which we have previously taken for fantasy" (1919b, 249, 244). Thus, this second definition of the uncanny, a suppressed element in his own text, returns to subvert Freud's ostensible argument. Although Freud nowhere mentions Jensen in "The Uncanny," his description of the confusion between fantasy and reality bears directly on the action of *Gradiva*.

The two sources of the uncanny—superseded thought processes and repressed complexes—find a theoretical counterpart in Freud's (1915) distinction between primary and secondary repression. Secondary repression wards off ideas and memories that could in principle be remembered and put into words, whereas primary repression cloaks infantile memories that people carry with them as inarticulate moods or states of being. In contemporary parlance, Christopher Bollas (1987) refers to these existential memories of maternal holding (or its lack) as the "unthought known."

This distinction between primary and secondary repression can in turn be applied to Jensen's *Gradiva*, where from the beginning Norbert Hanold is disoriented by moods he cannot understand. On the one hand, there is his mysterious attraction to the statue of Gradiva; on the other, he has a persistent sense of loss and something missing in his life. Seeing from his window a caged canary, which actually belongs to Zoe, Norbert was "moved by a feeling that he, too, lacked a nameless something" (1903, 20). Throughout his Italian journey Norbert is irritated by the billing and cooing of honeymooning couples from Germany, and upon arriving in Pompeii his mood is further soured by the houseflies he associates with these couples. "He felt that he was out of sorts because he lacked something without being able to explain what, and this ill-humour he took everywhere with him" (35); and again, "even nature was unable to offer him what he lacked in his surroundings and within himself" (36).

As in his commentary on "The Sand-Man," where he seeks to play down the importance of the episode involving the mechanical doll Olympia so as to sidestep Jentsch's derivation of the uncanny from uncertainty about whether or not something is animate, so in his discussion of Jensen's novel Freud concentrates on the oedipal level of repressed wishes but neglects to consider moods or states of being. (Freud, of course, is writing in 1906, but it is still revealing to see what he includes and excludes.) He brings out the sexual jealousy in Norbert Hanold's fantasy that Gradiva has been buried in the embrace of a rival, but these dynamics emerge most clearly in Freud's elucidation of Zoe's attraction to Norbert. Zoe was raised by her father, an absent-minded zoologist, and she found in Norbert Hanold a man who was similarly "absorbed by science and held apart by it from life and from Zoe. Thus it was made possible for her to remain faithful in her unfaithfulness—to find her father once more in her loved one" (Freud 1907a, 33).

Freud's oedipal analysis of the characters is convincing as far as it goes, but it leaves out important aspects of Jensen's novel. In particular, Freud glosses over the fact that Zoe has lost her mother, and he never mentions that Norbert is a double orphan. Jensen writes that Norbert Hanold "already at birth had been hedged in by the grating with which family tradition, by education and predestination, had surrounded him" as the only son of a university professor. He had "clung loyally" to the task of exalting his father's name "even after the early deaths of his parents had left him absolutely alone." He passed his university examinations brilliantly, but could take no pleasure in aesthetic objects or human emotions. "That beside these objects from the distant past, the present still existed around him, he felt only in the most shadowy way; for his feelings marble and bronze were not dead, but rather the only really vital thing which expressed the purpose and value of human life" (1903, 18–19).

If we follow Freud and heuristically imagine Norbert Hanold to be a real person, the confusions of life and death and of reality and fantasy in his attraction to Gradiva can be attributed to what Harry Guntrip (1968) would call his schizoid condition. His early parental losses and deficient nurturing are the root causes of his undefined feelings of lack and longing. As James W. Hamilton has written, "archeology, as the science which deals with the relics of the past, serves as a symbolic representation of the lost object which is incorporated and becomes a 'frozen introject'" (1973, 384), from which Norbert is unable to break free in order to invest his emotional energy in a living woman. In other words, his inner emptiness is due to an incomplete work of mourning.[11] Only after meeting Zoe, Hamilton continues, "with the prospect of recovering the lost object in the outer world," can he "begin to give up or decathect the internal representation or introject—archeology" (398).

Another aspect of Jensen's novel not dealt with by Freud is the aggression manifested in Norbert Hanold's irrational hatred of flies. There is likewise an incident in which he slaps Zoe's hand to see whether she is real. Insofar as Freud considers aggression at all, he regards it as an expression of "man's inevitable duty in love-making" (1907a, 38), as when near the end of the story Norbert uses an imaginary fly on Zoe's face as a pretext for pressing his lips on hers. But the aggression exhibited by Hanold has other sources than masculine sexuality. In particular, as John Bowlby has demonstrated, anger and longing are inevitable components of the reaction to a premature bereavement. Of a patient who had lost his mother at the age of five and could not express his grief, Bowlby writes: "although immobilized, both his love and his anger had remained directed towards the recovery of the dead mother. Thus, locked in the service of a hopeless cause, they had been lost to the developing personality. With loss of his mother had gone loss also of his feeling life" (1961, 56).

If we expand the perspective of classical analysis by putting on the lenses of object relations theory, we can distinguish three superimposed levels of pathology in Norbert Hanold's character: (1) oedipal sexuality, involving rivalry with other males and repressed desire for the woman; (2) a preoedipal hostility toward women and life, stemming from an internalized "bad mother" and manifested by an aggressive persecutory ego; and (3) a regressed or schizoid ego, reflecting the inner sense of

11. For a comprehensive reinterpretation of Freud's life in terms of the dynamics of death and loss, particularly in relation to his mother Amalie, see Breger (2000). Rand and Torok propose that "the premature death of his parents has led to an *illness of mourning* in Norbert" (1997, 67), though they appear unaware that theirs is not an original insight. Suzanne C. Bernfeld (1951) was the first to trace Freud's passion for archeology to his repeated experiences of loss, including being uprooted from his birthplace of Freiberg, in early childhood.

nonexistence due to the deaths of his parents and the absence of love.[12] From this final vantage point, *Gradiva* becomes an allegory of what Michael Balint (1932) would call the achievement of rebirth or a "new beginning" through psychoanalytic therapy. Both Zoe and Norbert are phantoms recalled to life through the power of love. As the happily united pair stroll hand in hand through the streets of Pompeii, "the whole excavated city seemed overwhelmed, not with pumice and ashes, but with pearls and diamonds, by the beneficent rainstorm"; and Zoe's eyes shone over "her childhood friend who had, in a way, also been excavated from the ashes [*Verschüttung*]" (Jensen 1903, 117; Urban and Cremerius 1973, 85).

Although the preoedipal dimensions of *Gradiva* highlighted by object relations theory go beyond Freud's oedipal reading, they do not contest his mimetic assumptions about character. Thus, as a counterpoint to the analyses governed by a metaphysics of presence, I would propose both a Lacanian and a Derridean approach to the text. Jensen's story is Lacanian in its stress on the etiological role of names and signifiers. Hanold's decision to bestow the name "Gradiva" ("the girl who steps along") on the statue is determined not simply by its appearance but also by his unconscious memory of the name "Bertgang." As Freud explains, "that very name turns out to have been a derivative—indeed a translation—of the repressed surname of the girl he had loved in childhood which he was supposed to have forgotten" (1907a, 38). Moreover, "Zoe" means "life," and her name is thus part of the ironic juxtaposition of life and death throughout the work. When Norbert Hanold encounters Zoe in Pompeii without recognizing her, he says that her name "sounds to me like a bitter mockery." She replies: "I have long accustomed myself to being dead" (1903, 71). As Maud Mannoni has insisted from a Lacanian standpoint, analysts should construe fantasy "not as the image or trace of an experience lived through, but rather as a word lost" (1967, 44).

Mannoni's reference to a "trace" leads us from a Lacanian to a Derridean reading of *Gradiva*. Norbert Hanold goes to Pompeii in search of traces of his beloved, "and that in a literal sense—for with her unusual gait, she must have left behind in the ashes a footprint different from all

12. The second level—that of the persecutory "bad mother"—is brought into prominence above all by Fairbairn (1952). Guntrip expressly presents his own exploration of the schizoid condition as an attempt to build on, while going beyond, Fairbairn's work, which itself radically extends and transforms the perspective of Freud.

the others" (Jensen 1903, 47). The motif of the trace is bound up with the collapse of the distinction between the original and copy in Jensen's novel. In his analysis, Freud draws attention to two notably implausible elements of the plot: first, the way Jensen "makes the young archaeologist come upon what is undoubtedly an ancient relief but which so closely resembles a person living long afterwards"; and second, "where he makes the young man meet the living woman precisely in Pompeii, for the dead woman had been placed there only by his imagination, and the journey to Pompeii had in fact carried him away from the living woman, whom he had just seen in the street of the town in which he lived" (1907a, 41–42). Although this second coincidence can be ascribed to chance, Freud continues, the first—"the far-reaching resemblance between the sculpture and the live girl"—seems "to spring from the author's arbitrary decision." But if the relief of Gradiva mysteriously resembles the living Zoe, the explanation is that Jensen—notwithstanding his aesthetic naïveté—has staged a postmodern reversal of the usual metaphysical relations between life and art, so that it is rather the living woman who imitates her inanimate double, as when in the final sentence she becomes "Gradiva *rediviva*." As Mary Jacobus has proposed, "the uncanny priority of the representation over what it represents" in Zoe's resemblance to the statue of Gradiva "parallels the priority of Freudian theory over the literary text" (1982, 91). Coming at this paradox from a complementary standpoint, Lis Møller observes that "the similarity between Zoe and Gradiva appears to be the mark of fictionality; it is the one feature that prevents *Gradiva* from being a 'perfectly correct psychiatric study'" (1991, 106).

Jensen's collapse of the distinction between life and art, original and copy, is strikingly glossed by a passage in "The Sand-Man," in which Hoffman's belatedly introduced narrator explains his reasons for having first presented his protagonist through a series of letters. "Perhaps, like a good portrait painter, I may succeed in depicting Nathanael in such a way that you will recognize it as a good likeness without being acquainted with the original, and will feel as if you had very often seen him with your own bodily eyes. Perhaps, too, you will then believe that nothing is more wonderful, nothing more fantastic, than real life" (1816, 196). Even life—Zoe—bears the impress of the signifier and cannot be known outside its traces. And Freud, in his clinical fictions, depicts likenesses we can recognize without being acquainted with the originals. Emulating Norbert Hanold, Freud hung a plaster cast of Gradiva (taken from the bas-relief in the Vatican Museum that he joyfully beheld for the first time in 1907) in his study, so that even today we can verify her appearance or purchase a simulacrum for our own walls.[13]

In both *Delusions and Dreams* and "The Uncanny," Freud insists on granting explanatory primacy to repressed complexes rather than to intellectual uncertainty and superseded thought processes. But despite his attacks on Jentsch, the latter sources are actually more crucial to understanding the uncanny. I suspect that this insight may have been resisted by Freud on subjective grounds, because he could not come to terms with his own magical belief in the omnipotence of thoughts. As I have argued in *Freud and Oedipus* (1987, 18–23), a dread of the power of his own thoughts was instilled in Freud by the premature death of his younger brother Julius—his first rival for his mother's love—when Freud was not yet two years of age. The effects of the fulfillment of Freud's infantile death wishes against Julius are exhibited in his preoccupation with the motif of the revenant. In *Delusions and Dreams*, Freud seeks to account for the "mental cobweb" that caused Norbert Hanold to believe that he was conversing at noon with the ghost of Gradiva—a delusion that, as Freud says, justifies Jensen's calling his story a "Pompeian fantasy." Acknowledging that "the belief in spirits and ghosts and the return of the dead . . . is far from having disappeared among educated people," Freud offers an exemplary anecdote:

A man who has grown rational and skeptical, even, may be ashamed to discover how easily he may for a moment return to a belief in spirits under the combined impact of strong emotion and perplexity. I know of a doctor who had once lost one of his women patients suffering from Graves' disease [exophthalmic goiter], and who could not get rid of a faint suspicion that he might have contributed to the unhappy outcome by a thoughtless prescription. One day, several years later, a girl entered his consulting-room, who, in spite of all his efforts, he could not help recognizing as the dead one. He could only frame a single thought: "So after all it's true that the dead can come back to life." His dread did not give way to shame till the girl introduced herself as the sister of the one who had died of the same disease as she herself was suffering from. The victims of Graves' disease, as has often been observed, have a marked fa-

13. To the spectrum of readings of *Gradiva* delineated in the text, I should add a feminist critique, since Gradiva's status as the fetishized object of a male gaze is taken for granted by Jensen's novel and remains unquestioned by any of the proposed modes of interpretation. The concept of the fetish applies to Hanold's obsession with his beloved's feet, but it can be understood not only in classically Freudian terms with reference to castration, but also as an attempt to cling to a fantasy of the prematurely lost mother, represented synecdochically by her breast.

cial resemblance to one another; and in this case this typical likeness was reinforced by a family one. The doctor to whom this occurred was, however, none
other than myself; so I have a personal reason for not disputing the clinical
possibility of Norbert Hanold's temporary delusion that Gradiva had come
back to life. (1907a, 71–72)

Freud presents his ideas not through exposition but through a compelling interpolated narrative, which is itself uncanny in the way that it
first solicits the reader's belief in spirits, then undercuts it, and finally
produces a genuinely eerie effect with the revelation that Freud is himself the guilt-ridden protagonist. In "The Uncanny," Freud returns to
experiences "associated with the omnipotence of thoughts, the prompt
fulfillment of wishes and with the return of the dead." He continues:

We—or our primitive forefathers—once believed that these possibilities were
realities, and were convinced that they actually happened. Nowadays we no
longer believe in them, we have *surmounted* these modes of thought; but we do
not feel quite sure of our new beliefs, and the old ones still exist within us ready
to seize upon any confirmation. As soon as something *actually happens* in our
lives which seems to confirm the old, discarded beliefs we get a feeling of the
uncanny; it is as though we were making a judgement something like this: "So,
after all, it is *true* that one can kill a person by the mere wish!" or, "So the dead
do live on and appear on the scene of their former activities!" and so on. (1919b,
247–48)

Freud's impersonal exclamations in "The Uncanny" echo his autobiographical confession in *Delusions and Dreams*, as the German originals of
both passages demonstrate: "*Also ist es doch wahr, daß man einen anderen
durch den bloßen Wunsch töten kann, daß die Toten weiterleben*" ("The Uncanny," *G.W.*, 12:262); "*es sei doch wahr, daß die Toten wiederkommen kön-
nen*" (*Delusions and Dreams, G.W.*, 7:99). Near the end of the story, Norbert Hanold reflects that he had "mitigating grounds for his madness in
for two days considering Gradiva a resurrection [*Rediviva*]" (1903,
109–10; Urban and Cremerius 1973, 81). Writing to Ferenczi on December 16, 1910, Freud portrays the defections of Adler and Stekel as reen-
actments of the rupture of his friendship with Wilhelm Fliess: "Adler is
a little Fliess *redivivus*, just as paranoid. Stekel, his appendage, is at least
called Wilhelm" (Brabant, Falzeder and Giampieri-Deutsch 1993, 243).
Freud's compulsion to view his life in terms of such repetitive patterns is
rooted in the death of Julius, the prototype not only of Fliess but of all

Freud's male friends and rivals.[14] In light of this history, Freud indeed had "a personal reason for not disputing the clinical possibility of Norbert Hanold's temporary delusion that Gradiva had come back to life."[15]

Freud's anxiety about dead people who come back to life is reinforced by two disastrous episodes from his medical practice. They are juxtaposed in his associations to the "specimen dream" of "Irma's injection" in *The Interpretation of Dreams*, which occurred on the night of July 23–24, 1895. The first is the death in 1891 of his idealized friend (and rival) in Ernst Brücke's laboratory, Ernst von Fleischl-Marxow, whom Freud had urged to inject cocaine in the misguided belief that this would wean him from an addiction to morphine. The other concerns a female patient named Mathilde, who perished after Freud had prescribed the toxic drug sulphonal, thinking it to be innocuous. Freud associates this patient's death to a "serious illness" of his eldest daughter, also named Mathilde, which seemed to him "almost like an act of retribution on the part of destiny. It was as though the replacement of one person by another was to be continued in another sense: this Mathilde for that Mathilde, an eye for an eye and a tooth for a tooth" (1900, 112).[16] Freud's infantile fantasy that his wishes had caused Julius's death is corroborated by these occasions when he was at least indirectly responsible for the deaths of two human beings and helps to account for the way he is

14. In his recent biography, Breger has persuasively suggested that the emotions Freud ascribed during his self-analysis to guilt at Julius's death were rather due primarily to "anger and rivalry" at the loss of maternal care resulting from Julius's birth (2000, 20). To the extent that Julius's death became an issue, moreover, it was because of the "atmosphere of mourning and depression" (12) pervading the family. Although Julius's death may not have been the ultimate cause of Freud's susceptibility to revenants, it remains heuristically useful as a guiding thread to his psychic life.

15. If one entertains the hypothesis (Swales 1982) that Freud had an affair with his sister-in-law, Minna Bernays, in 1900, moreover, then the fact that his autobiographical anecdote in *Delusions and Dreams* about the return of the patient who died of Graves disease involves two interchangeable sisters takes on an additional level of significance.

16. Wilcocks (1994, 227–80) assumes that Freud's allusion must be to a case of diphtheria not contracted by his daughter until 1897, and charges that this casts doubt on the veracity of Freud's entire account of the earlier Irma dream. Wilcocks's thesis has been given wide currency in the scholarly literature. As Peter Swales has demonstrated in his interview with me (Rudnytsky 2000, 336–38), however, it is based on a fallacy. Freud does not say that Mathilde had diphtheria before 1895, but only that she had a "serious illness" that "reminded" him of this dreaded disease. In a letter to Fliess on September 29, 1893, moreover, Freud reports that there was an "epidemic of throat infections" (Masson 1985, 56) in his family; and it is surely this episode that he is recalling in his exegesis of the Irma dream.

haunted by the motif of the revenant in *Delusions and Dreams* and "The Uncanny."

Freud's reading of Jensen's text, then, is filtered primarily through his identification with Norbert Hanold, the archeologist-protagonist in search of a lost object. Freud himself, of course, was an avid collector of antiquities and frequently compared to psychoanalysis to archeology in its task of making sense of the past.[17] But his transference to *Gradiva* occurs on multiple levels simultaneously. In reading the novel as a clinical case history, Freud proposes that it depicts not only the origins of Norbert's delusion but also its cure, a process in which Zoe Bertgang plays the part of analyst. Thus, Zoe-Gradiva provides a further magnet for Freud's identification, though she, unlike other analysts, is Norbert's predestined love object and thus permitted to gratify his transference love in reality. Despite its licit nature, the ending that Freud characterized as "Erotic! Assimilation of the fantasy-reconciliation" serves as a prototype of those cases of boundary violation in which what commences as a therapeutic relationship gives way to a compulsive sexual affair. In a reversal of the classic scenario, however, the male Norbert is the patient and the female Zoe the analyst. In this connection, it is noteworthy that Freud diagnoses Hanold's malady as a *"hysterical* delusion" (1907a, 45*n*) and assimilates Jensen's "imaginary case" to patients "medically treated in real life" by Breuer, Charcot, and Janet, as well as to his own Dora case (54). Freud does not draw attention to this inversion of conventional gender roles, but he took it for granted that women could be analysts and (as early as his lecture [1886] delivered to the Society of Medicine in Vienna six months after his return from studying with Charcot in Paris) refused to define hysteria as an exclusively female malady.

Beyond his identification with the two main characters, Freud exhibits a transference to Wilhelm Jensen as the author of this Pompeian fantasy. His attachment is, however, ambivalent, as the striking metamorphosis in Freud's estimation of Jensen's literary merits attests. In *Delusions and Dreams*, Freud reveres Jensen as a genius, in all seriousness comparing him to Shakespeare not only in his deployment of supernatural elements but also in the way he grounds his plot on an implausible premise, where the alleged resemblance is to *King Lear*. In Freud's first blush of enthusi-

17. As Møller points out, the archeological metaphor in Freud's writings expresses his belief in the possibility of an authentic reconstruction of the patient's past, an epistemological "discourse of mastery" that exists in tension with a postmodernist emphasis on the inescapable fictionality and unverifiability of his analytic constructions (1991, 26).

asm, Jensen can do no wrong. He "never introduces a single idle or un-intentional feature into his story" (1907a, 68), and even the dreams are wholly believable. By the time of his 1912 postscript, however, appended the year after Jensen's death, Freud has begun to have second thoughts. He refers condescendingly to writers like "our Wilhelm Jensen" who are "in the habit of giving themselves over to their imagination in a simple-minded [*naiver*] joy in creating" (1907a, 94; *G.W.*, 7:123). Finally, over a decade later, in *An Autobiographical Study*, Freud dismisses *Gradiva* as a story of "no particular merit in itself" (1925a, 65), notwithstanding its utility for his psychoanalytic purposes. If, in his euphoria at the burgeon-ing international recognition of the psychoanalytic movement and dis-covery of literary confirmation for his ideas, Freud at first overestimated the worth of *Gradiva*, his later disparagement seems correspondingly ex-aggerated. But this ambivalence, characteristic of every encounter with a double, attests that Freud's deepest transference is not to Jensen as an au-thor, but to literature as the uncanny twin of psychoanalysis.

Freud sent a copy of *Delusions and Dreams* to the elderly Jensen, who was flattered by his attentions, and followed it with a request for infor-mation that he hoped would corroborate his hypotheses about the bio-graphical genesis of *Gradiva*. After reading two other stories recom-mended by Jung, "The Red Umbrella" and "In the Gothic House," collected in *Superior Powers* (1892), Freud speculated in a letter to Jung on November 24, 1907, that either "Jensen actually had a sister who died young or . . . never had a sister and transformed a playmate into the sis-ter he had always longed for" (McGuire 1974, 100). Freud interpreted these three stories, culminating in *Gradiva*, as a cycle depicting the loss and refinding of an object. What Freud learned from Jensen, who, de-spite Freud's complaints in the 1912 postscript (due in all likelihood to his emotionally charged sense of disappointment in the author), an-swered his intimate queries with unfailing courtesy, impressively con-firmed his reconstructions: "No. I never had a sister or any other blood-relation. But 'The Red Umbrella,' to be sure, is woven together from my own memories of life: from my first youthful love for a dear girl friend of childhood who grew up with me and died of tuberculosis at age eight-een; and from the essence of a young woman with whom, many years later, I came into friendly relations and who likewise was snatched away by sudden death" (Urban and Cremerius 1973, 15; my translation). Thus, a dynamic of object loss and recovery indeed played a decisive role in Jensen's life, just as it did in Freud's. But Jensen neglected to add that he had lost his mother when he was thirteen and his father when he was eighteen (Hamilton 1973, 410). Hence Freud divined even more truly than he knew, and his reading of *Gradiva* lays bare the inexhaustible overdetermination of aesthetic creativity and our own transferential responses to it.

2

"Mother, Do You Have a Wiwimaker, Too?"
Freud's Representation of Female Sexuality in the Case of Little Hans

It has become commonplace to observe that Freud's case histories are themselves great works of literature that must be read with the sophisticated techniques of literary criticism.[1] Whatever one may think of Freud's ideas, there can be no doubt of his brilliance as a writer. Indeed, it is a testimony to Freud's genius that his works continue to be a source of instruction and inspiration for each new generation of readers, however much one finds in them to dispute.

The case of Little Hans—or, to give it its proper title, *An Analysis of a Phobia in a Five-Year-Old Boy* (1909a)—has a special place in the annals of psychoanalysis because it is the first recorded instance of a child analysis. Part of the distinctiveness of the case, moreover, is that the child in question, whose real name was Herbert Graf, was not analyzed by Freud himself (though he did see the child for a single consultation) but by his own father, the musicologist Max Graf, who belonged to the cadre of Freud's adherents that in 1908 became known as the Vienna Psychoanalytic Society. The complex narrative structure inherent in any case history, which must strive to capture the dynamics both of the treatment process and of the patient's life, is thus compounded by the way that

---

1. See Marcus (1974) for an early and exemplary demonstration of this claim with respect to the Dora case.

Freud's text contains extensive extracts of dialogue and other material reported by the father, punctuated by Freud's editorial comments. The effect is to create a multilayered text, much like a work of modernist fiction, in which Hans plays the part of the hero, the father of the unreliable narrator, and Freud of the omniscient narrator.[2] Underlying these formal intricacies is what by today's standards would be deemed the highly irregular transferential situation, in which the father combined the roles of parent and analyst and had in addition his own deeply invested relationship to Freud. Hans's mother, moreover, had herself been a patient of Freud's, and it was thanks to her that her husband had been introduced first to Freud's work and then to the man himself in 1900 (Graf 1942, 467). Rather than the therapy of an individual child, therefore, the case of Little Hans is better understood as an instance of family therapy, a precursor of Freud's own even more dubious experiment in commingling parental and professional roles in his prolonged analysis of his daughter Anna (Mahony 1992).[3]

In this chapter, I shall approach the case of Little Hans from a feminist standpoint. Precisely because it constitutes Freud's quintessential depiction of the crystallization of masculine sexuality and identity, I shall argue, this text likewise shows the genesis of his views on sexual difference and *female* sexuality, which are codified in his notorious later papers. It thus invites a critique along the lines laid down by Luce Irigaray (1974) in her brilliant dissection of Freud's chapter on "Femininity" in his *New Introductory Lectures on Psycho-Analysis* (1933a).[4] Accordingly, I

2. On the thematics of writing in Freud's text, see Mahony (1993). Whereas Mahony holds that "Freud's treatise is almost wholly based on the note-taking by Max Graf" (1245), I read Freud's narrative as a free-standing fiction.

3. Apparently, the experiments in unconventional analysis continued in the Graf household. In a letter to Jung of February 2, 1910, Freud writes: "I should have thought it impossible to analyze one's own wife. Little Hans's father has proved to me that it can be done. In such analysis, however, it just seems too difficult to observe the technical rule whose importance I have lately begun to suspect: 'surmount counter-transference'" (McGuire 1974, 291). One wonders what Freud made of this "technical rule" when it came to his own analysis of Anna. On the case of Little Hans as family therapy, see Strean (1967).

4. For other influential readings of Freud in the French feminist tradition, see Cixous and Clément (1975) and Kofman (1980), neither of which takes up Little Hans. Although written independently, my argument dovetails with that advanced by Chasseguet-Smirgel (1975). From a Kleinian standpoint, Meltzer indicts Freud's tendency to "diminish the significance of the boy's femininity in favor of the role of his masculine castration complex in the formation of his Oedipus conflict" as the "chief weakness in his interpretative work" (1978, 47). Meltzer hails Freud's exposition of Hans's treatment as "the most delightful

shall probe Freud's confused and misogynistic attitudes toward female sexuality in the case of Little Hans in order to lay bare their connection to his phallocentric perspective; in a brief coda, I shall contend that the work also reveals a heterosexist bias.

The first words of Little Hans to be reported by his father and quoted by Freud in the case history, spoken by the child before the age of three, and occurring two years before the outbreak of his phobia, are: "'Mother, do you have a wiwimaker [*Wiwimacher*] too?'" (*G.W.*, 7:245; *S.E.*, 10:7).[5] Like the initial communications by a patient entering analysis, this question acquires an ever-increasing resonance and can by the end of the process be seen to have held the key to the entire mystery. Strictly speaking, Hans's "analysis"—if we deign to refer to the didactic interest taken by his father in Hans's condition by this term—has not yet commenced; but insofar as Hans's analysis now exists only in the form of Freud's written record, everything that is contained therein may be said to belong to it.

The question of whether or not women possess a penis is no less urgent for Freudian theory as a whole than it is for Little Hans's analysis. Indeed, if we regard all of Freud's writings as fragments of his interminable self-analysis, it is not difficult to surmise that the prominence of this leitmotif is determined chiefly by Freud's own preoccupations. When, fifteen years later, Freud in "The Infantile Genital Organization" codifies his conviction that initially "for both sexes, only one genital, namely the male one, comes into account" by the interpolation of the phallic phase into his libido theory (1923c, 142), he does so by appealing to the case of Little Hans.[6] Pursuing the same line of thought, he accounts for fetishism (1927a) in exclusively phallic terms (ignoring its potential to serve as a bulwark against traumatic separation from the mother) as a means of warding off castration anxiety, allegedly triggered

---

piece of writing in the whole of psycho-analytic literature" (48), a tribute with which I would be tempted to concur were it not for Georg Groddeck's *Book of the It* (1923).

5. All quotations from the case history in this chapter are my own translation. For ease of reference, volume and page citations will be provided to both the *Gesammelte Werke* and the *Standard Edition*. Strachey's translation of *Wiwimacher* as "widdler" is inspired, but to preserve the link to the verb form "to make wiwi," I prefer a more literal rendering.

6. In his notes to "The Infantile Genital Organization" in the *Standard Edition*, Strachey draws attention to Freud's allusions to the case of Little Hans in his intertwined claims that boys look for a penis not only in all living creatures but also in inanimate objects, and that they ward off threats of castration by convincing themselves that girls do possess a penis, but a small one, which will grow bigger (1923c, 142*n*1, 144*n*1).

by the boy's glimpse of the female genitals, a substitute for the dis-avowed missing penis of the mother.

If we examine the presentation of sexual difference in the case of Little Hans, we find confusion perpetrated at every turn by adults—by Little Hans's parents and above all by Freud—and the child doing his best to sort things out for himself. To Hans's repeated queries about whether she has a wiwimaker, his mother answers "'of course'" and "'naturally'" (*G.W.*, 7:245, 247; *S.E.*, 10:7, 10).[7] Like his parents' promulgation of the fable that the stork is responsible for bringing his baby sister Hanna, this misleading account of the female genitalia deserves to be branded a lie. Allied to sexual difference is the distinction between what is animate and inanimate, and here again the wiwimaker comes into play. At three and three quarters, Hans sees a locomotive from which water is being re-leased and says it is "'making wiwi.'" He wonders where its wiwimaker is located. He adds on reflection: "'A dog and a horse have a wiwimaker; a table and a chair don't.'" Freud comments: "So he has gained an essen-tial characteristic for differentiating between the animate and the inani-mate" (*G.W.*, 7:246–47; *S.E.*, 10:9).

The confusion into which Hans is led by those who should know bet-ter is not only anatomical but also semantic. Indeed, in the interplay be-tween biological and linguistic frames of reference in the term "wi-wimaker," we can observe the penis in the process of becoming the phallus or transcendental signifier in the strict Lacanian sense of this term. Although by "wiwimaker" Hans most obviously means "penis," the word itself refers to an organ for urination, which women of course do possess. Thus, in one sense Hans's mother is correct to say that she does have a wiwimaker, though not in the disingenuous way that she im-plies. That Hans is concerned not simply with whether women have a penis but with how they urinate is made clear when he asks his father: "'But how do girls make wiwi if they don't have a wiwimaker?'" His fa-

---

7. Under his real name of Little Herbert, Little Hans likewise figures as an exemplar of sexual curiosity in Freud's "The Sexual Enlightenment of Children" (1907b), written when the boy was four years old and prior to the outbreak of his phobia. Mahony ob-serves (1993, 1245–46) that the only passage of dialogue reported by his father to diverge materially from the version in the case history concerns Hans's question about the female wiwimaker. Instead of "'Of course. How come?'" ("'*Selbstverständlich. Weshalb?*'") in the case (*G.W.*, 7:245; *S.E.*, 10:7), Hans's mother is quoted in the paper as having replied, "'Naturally, so what did you think?'" ("'*Natürlich, so was hast du denn gedacht?*'") (*G.W.*, 7:23; *S.E.*, 9:134). "Naturally" occurs two pages later in the case history, but the rest of her answer corresponds only vaguely to "How come?" Freud's interest in the child's point of view seems to diminish as he appropriates his story for his own theoretical purposes.

ther gives him an evasive answer: "'They don't have a wiwimaker like yours. Haven't you seen when Hanna has been given a bath?'" Moments earlier, however, Hans's father had told him that "'girls and women don't have a wiwimaker'" (*G.W.*, 7:267; *S.E.*, 10:31). These statements do not cohere. The father uses "wiwimaker" ambiguously to say both that women possess an anatomy unlike Hans's and that they do not have a penis. He thus simultaneously defines women in terms of a lack when measured against a male norm and adumbrates the possibility of regarding the two sexes as different but equal, although the word "wiwimaker" retains an androcentric bias that forever precludes this possibility from being realized.

Freud, as I have indicated, far from mitigating Little Hans's bewilderment, actually exacerbates it. His casual acceptance of the equation between the female and the inanimate is especially disturbing. (As one of my students at the University of Florida exclaimed, "I guess I'm a table!") In the final section of his narrative, Freud reiterates that Hans "discovers that on the basis of the readiness-to-hand [*Vorhandenseins*] or absence of the wiwimaker one can differentiate between what is living and lifeless" (*G.W.*, 7:341; *S.E.*, 10:106). By treating this hypothesis as a "discovery" on Hans's part, instead of as a childish error, Freud remakes Hans in his own image as a phallocrat. Of course, Hans uses his own body as a basis for comparison and wonders how his mother and other females are different. But the point of his questions is precisely to clarify *how* they are different, not to assume that they must be identical. That is *Freud's* mistake, not Hans's. He writes of Hans's displays of affection toward boy as well as girl playmates: "Hans is homosexual, as all children may well be, completely in accordance with the not to be overlooked fact that he only *knows one kind of genital*, a genital like his own" (*G.W.*, 7:344–45; *S.E.*, 10:110). By employing the collective noun "children" (*Kinder*) instead of the gender-specific "boys" (*Knaben*), Freud elides the situation of girls, who presumably also take their own bodies as a point of reference even though, according to his theory, they too only know one kind of genital—that belonging to males.[8] How girls,

8. In 1923 Freud appended a footnote to this passage in which he directs the reader to "The Infantile Genital Organization" and asserts that Hans finds himself at the period of sexual development that "is quite generally characterized through its acquaintance with only one genital—the masculine. In contrast to the later period of maturity, it consists not in genital primacy, but in the primacy of the phallus" (*G.W.*, 7:345; *S.E.*, 10:110). Hans himself commits a linguistic error comparable to Freud's when he declares, "'And all men have wiwimakers'" (*G.W.*, 7:269; *S.E.*, 10:34), using the generic word for people (*Men-*

who, according to Freud, know only genitals *unlike* their own could conceivably become lesbians remains mysterious in this account.

Freud's insistence on the primacy of the phallus is allied to his conviction of the centrality of the castration complex to the discovery of sexual difference. The case of Little Hans provides the prototype upon which he bases this claim; not coincidentally, the term "castration complex" is introduced with reference to it.[9] In a pattern that Freud does not hesitate to call "typical for the sexual development of the child" (*G.W.*, 7:245; *S.E.*, 10:7), Hans is first threatened by his mother with castration as a punishment for masturbation and later catches sight of the genitalia of his baby sister, which brings home to him the reality of this threat. The structure of retrospective signification linking these two events exemplifies the distinctively psychoanalytic mode of temporality. As Freud remarks, "it would be entirely the typical procedure if the threat of castration now came to effect through *deferred action [nachträglich]*" (*G.W.*, 7:271; *S.E.*, 10:35).

In order to realize how deep an impression the case of Little Hans left on Freud's thinking, it suffices to quote the following passage from "Femininity" in the *New Introductory Lectures*:

> In [boys] the castration complex arises after they have learnt from the sight of the female genitals that the organ which they value so highly need not necessarily accompany the body. At this the boy recalls to mind the threats he brought on himself by his doings with that organ, he begins to give credence to them and falls under the influence of fear of castration, which will be the most powerful motive force in his subsequent development. (1933a, 124–25)

Although Freud does not appeal to the analysis of Little Hans for corroboration, he has clearly relied on it here as a precedent. Not only is there an identical sequence of events—a verbal threat followed by a vi-

---

schen) in place of the restricted word for males (*Männer*). This universalization of the masculine perspective reaches its apogee in Freud's invocation of the Oedipus myth in *The Interpretation of Dreams*: "It is the fate of all of us, perhaps, to direct our first sexual impulse toward our mother and our first hatred and our first murderous wish against our father" (1900, 262), where, again, the subject-position of girls (as well as nonheterosexual boys) is elided.

9. Although Strachey identified in a note what he believed to be the first appearance of this term (10:8*n*1), he later acknowledged that Freud had previously used it in "On the Sexual Theories of Children" (1908b, 217*n*1). But since Freud is here summarizing material from Hans's analysis, the castration complex retains its connection with this case. Strachey's self-correction is pointed out by Lindon (1992, 377–78).

sual glimpse—but Freud's emphasis on the gaze that defines the female genitalia in terms of absence is crucial to the case. The primacy of the phallus thus has as its corollary the primacy of the gaze, and both define female sexuality simply as the negative of the male. The above-quoted passage from "Femininity" continues: "The castration complex of girls is also started by the sight of the other sex" (125).[10]

Hans's father's equivocations about the female genitalia are efforts to implement the advice of Freud. In order to rid Hans of his desire to see his mother's genitals and set him on the "way to sexual enlightenment," Freud counsels, his father should inform him at a propitious moment that "his mama and all other female beings—as indeed he could know from Hanna—do not possess a wiwimaker at all" (G.W., 7:264; S.E., 10:28). The problem here again is that of defining women in terms of privation. As Jules Glenn has observed, "Hans was to be told that a girl has no penis, thus indicating that she is deficient," and not that a girl "has a vulva (including the clitoris), vagina, and uterus" (1980, 125).[11] Although it might not have been necessary to enter into such encyclopedic detail with Little Hans concerning the female anatomy, it surely ought to have been possible to present the facts of life to him in a less distorted way. When Freud writes that "the enlightenment . . . that women truly do not have a wiwimaker can only have shattered his self-confidence and awakened his castration complex" (G.W., 7:271; S.E., 10:36), he assesses accurately the traumatic effects on Hans of his father's lessons, but Freud is wrong to dignify such misinformation by calling it "enlightenment."

Despite Freud's recommendation that Hans be told that women do not have a wiwimaker, moreover, the boy's father persists in using this word. "'You know, don't you, how Hanna's wiwimaker looks?'" (G.W., 7:297; S.E., 10:62), he asks later in the analysis; and he doggedly insinuates (notwithstanding his son's denials) that Hans has seen his mother's genital area: "'Perhaps black hair by the wiwimaker, when you were curious and looked'" (G.W., 7:302; S.E., 10:67). Thus, just as Hans's mother leads him into confusion by her affirmative answers to his question about

10. "*The gaze is at stake from the outset.* Don't forget what 'castration,' or the knowledge of castration, owes to the gaze, at least for Freud" (Irigaray 1974, 47). "It is the boy who looks and is horrified first, and . . . the little girl merely doubles and confirms by reduplication what he is supposed to have seen. Or not seen" (49).

11. "The pleasure gained from touching, caressing, parting the lips and vulva simply does not exist for Freud. . . . Just as he will never refer to the pleasure associated with the sensitivity of the posterior wall of the vagina, the breasts, or the neck of the womb" (Irigaray 1974, 29).

whether she has a wiwimaker, so his father undercuts such accurate information as he does impart about the difference between the sexes by continuing to speak of girls and women as possessing wiwimakers.

In keeping with its function as a transcendental signifier, the word "wiwimaker" is used by Hans's parents with a range of connotations—penis, urinary organ, genital organ, and genital area—and their failure to disentangle these meanings exacerbates his dilemmas. Because the primary definition of "penis" cannot be escaped even when the metonymic reference is more general, however, the word, as I have already indicated, inevitably carries a sexist overtone.[12] Freud's semantics prove even slipperier than those of Hans's parents. In a lengthy footnote near the beginning of the narrative, which expatiates on Hans's alleged inability to credit his perception that his baby sister does not have a wiwimaker, Freud adds that "behind the error a piece of correct recognition is hidden. The little girl to be sure also possesses a little wiwimaker, which we call the clitoris, even though it doesn't grow, but remains stunted" (*G.W.*, 7:249*n*1; *S.E.*, 10:12*n*3). In this version, his contention is not that women don't have penises, but that they have vestigial ones. To the other meanings of wiwimaker, therefore, we must add that of the clitoris. The best retort to Freud's demeaning view of this organ is provided by Jodi Bray, one of my students at the University of Florida, who has remarked that the clitoris "grows to the size necessary to perform its very useful functions" (1992, 8). Indeed, the clitoris grows larger as the child matures and undergoes tumescence during sexual activity. Little Hans seems to have grasped this truth more securely than Freud, for to his father's statement that when Hanna grows up her wiwimaker will not look like his, he replies: "'I know that. It will be the way it is, only bigger'" (*G.W.*, 7:297; *S.E.*, 10:62).

In view of Freud's obfuscation of the complexities of the female genitals, it is ironic that he should remark: "The child naturally lacks an es-

---

12. Although Freud says nothing about it in this case, the male genitals consist of a scrotum and testicles as well as a penis. In a footnote to a passage in "The Infantile Genital Organization" that refers back to Little Hans on how the penis serves as a criterion for distinguishing the animate from the inanimate, however, Freud remarks on "what a small degree of attention the other part of the male genitals, the little sac with its contents, attracts in children. From all one hears in analyses, one would not guess that the male genitals consisted of anything more than the penis" (1923c, 142). But given the belief of many children that the scrotal sac contains urine and the emphasis on "making wiwi" in the case of Little Hans, it may be Freud himself, and not his young patient, who has forgotten about the testicles in this analysis (Silverman 1980, 114–15).

sential piece in the understanding of sexual relations as long as the female genital is undiscovered" (*G.W.*, 7:323; *S.E.*, 10:87). That children of both sexes lack any knowledge of the vagina is an integral premise of Freud's phallocentric perspective. What makes this contention most outrageous in context is its irrelevance to the foregoing conversation between Hans and his father, which has to do not with the female body but with Hans's doubts about the father's role in procreation and how he can "belong" to the latter when it is his mother who has brought him into the world.[13]

Just as Freud insists on children's ignorance of the vagina, so he refuses to believe that boys can envy women their procreative power. Notwithstanding Freud's denials, however, Hans on numerous occasions voices a desire to give birth to children as his mother has done. To his father's assertion, "'You would like to be the Daddy and be married to Mommy, would like to be as big as I am and have a moustache, and would like Mommy to have a child,'" Hans replies: "'Daddy, and until I'm married I'll only have one when I want to, when I'll be married to Mommy, and if I don't want to have a child, God doesn't want it either, when I've gotten married'" (*G.W.*, 7:328; *S.E.*, 10:92). The confused syntax captures the child's primary process thinking, but what comes through clearly is that Hans, despite his father's Freudian promptings, desires not simply to marry but to *be* Mommy. The child's identifications are multiple, maternal as well as paternal. Most strikingly, Hans has introjected his mother's ambivalence about becoming pregnant, since his declaration, "'if I don't want to have a child, God doesn't want it either,'" alludes to her words in an earlier quarrel with his father (*G.W.*, 7:327; *S.E.*, 10:91). Ignoring all this empirical evidence, Freud protests in

13. The German text of this dialogue indicates a slippage in Hans's mind between the awareness that "'a boy gets [*kriegt*] a girl and a girl gets a boy'" and his father's reply that "'A boy doesn't get [*bekommt*] children. Only women, mommies get children.'" Hans is struggling with the connection—and the distinction—between having sex and having children, but obtains no help from his father. Similarly, just as "wiwimaker" can refer either to the urinary or genital organs possessed by members of both sexes or to the masculine penis, so Hans asks how he can "belong" (*gehören*) to his father when his mother has given him birth. The concept of "belonging" is no less ambiguous than that of the wiwimaker, only here the norm is female rather than male. Hans's father, again, makes matters more obscure by telling Hans: (a) that Hans "belongs" both to him and Hans's mother; (b) that Hanna "belongs" only to Mommy and not to Hans; and (c) that Hanna belongs at once to him, Mommy, and Hans. The concept of "belonging" has been attenuated to encompass any kinship tie, leaving Hans to sort out how being a sibling differs from being a mother or a father (*G.W.*, 7:322–23; *S.E.*, 10:87).

a footnote: "There is no necessity here to ascribe to Hans a feminine trait of longing to have children" (*G.W.*, 7:328; *S.E.*, 10:93).[14]

Further proof of Hans's awareness of the female anatomy is his mockery of the hypothesis that his sister Hanna was brought by the stork. When Hans tells his father that until the preceding year, when the newly born Hanna accompanied the family by train on their summer holiday to Gmunden, "'*But always before that she travelled with us in the box,*'" the "box," as Freud interprets in a footnote, "is naturally the womb" of the mother (*G.W.*, 7:304; *S.E.*, 10:69–70).[15] Freud continues: "What can the assertion that the preceding summer Hanna already travelled to Gmunden 'in the box' mean other than his knowledge of the pregnancy of his mother?" (*G.W.*, 7:305; *S.E.*, 10:71). Just as absurdity in dreams, according to Freud, often signals mockery in the latent dream thoughts, so Hans's seemingly nonsensical replies to his father's questions are a way of saying, in Freud's paraphrase: "*If you can expect me to believe that the stork brought Hanna in October, when I already noticed mother's big body in the summer when we travelled to Gmunden, then I can require you to believe my lies*" (*G.W.*, 7:305; *S.E.*, 10:70–71). Hans likewise grasps the concept of a fetus when he tells his father: "'She was already in the world a long time, even when she wasn't there yet'" (*G.W.*, 7:308; *S.E.*, 10:73).

In addition to noticing his mother's pregnancy, Hans conveys a child's comprehension of sexual intercourse through two fantasies involving himself and his father. In the first, as he says, "'I was with you in Schönbrunn near the sheep, and then we crawled under the cord, and we told the guard at the entrance of the garden about it, and he packed us up'" (*G.W.*, 7:275; *S.E.*, 10:40). In the second, "'I was travelling with you on the train, and we smashed a window, and the guard took us away'" (*G.W.*, 7:276; *S.E.*, 10:41). Freud sums up Hans's conception of sexual intercourse near the conclusion of the case history:

It must have to do with an act of violence, which one carried out on the Mama, with a smashing, a creating of an opening, a forcing into an enclosed space, the

14. What is more, the theory expounded by Hans's parents that "children grow in the Mommy and then, when great pains come, are brought into the world by being pressed out like a 'lumpf,'" not only strengthens his anal fixation but also fuels his fantasy that pregnancy is something of which he too is capable (*G.W.*, 7:323; *S.E.*, 10:87).

15. Just prior to this he says in another footnote that both the box and the bathtub are for Hans "representations of the space in which babies are found" (*G.W.*, 7:304; *S.E.*, 10:69).

impulse to which the child could feel in himself. But although he was on the way, aided by the sensations in his penis, to postulating the existence of the vagina, he still could not solve the riddle [*das Rätsel nicht lösen*], because to his knowledge no such thing existed as his wiwimaker needed; much rather did the conviction that his Mama possessed a wiwimaker like his own stand in the way of the solution [*Lösung*]. (*G.W.*, 7:366; *S.E.*, 134–35)

As so often, Freud is at once incontrovertibly right and alarmingly wrong—right in his interpretation of Hans's fantasies and wrong in his assertion that Hans is ignorant of the existence of the vagina. For what is the "enclosed space" into which Hans imagines forcing himself, that opening he longs to penetrate, if not the vagina, the reality of which he is more than dimly aware, just as he intuits his mother's possession of the womb in which she carries his baby sister?

What is mysterious in all this is not the mentation of Little Hans but how Freud could persist so resolutely in not seeing what lay before him in plain sight. Time after time, Freud introduces evidence that demonstrates womb envy or an accurate picture of the female sexual organs on the part of Little Hans, yet disregards it and insists on his own biased theories of the maternal penis and female castration.[16] Although a biographical investigation of the origins of Freud's phallocentrism is beyond my scope here, scholars have linked this blind spot to his conflicted relationship with his preoedipal mother (Roith 1987; Sprengnether 1990). But I hope to have made it clear that a feminist perspective is no less relevant to reading the case history of Little Hans than that of the more celebrated heroine Dora. With the benefit of hindsight, it is salutary to contrast the obsolescence of Freud's views on gender with the percipience of Karen Horney, the first and still one of the most trenchant of his feminist critics. She writes:

On the one hand, of course, a boy will automatically conclude that everyone else is made like himself; but on the other hand his phallic impulses surely bid

16. When Hans laughs at the sight of Hanna's wiwimaker, Freud claims that this is "the first time that he acknowledges the difference between the male and female genital in this way, instead of denying it," but earlier he had quoted Hans's declaration, after his mother had given birth to Hanna, "'But out of my wiwimaker there comes no blood'" (*G.W.*, 7:257, 248; *S.E.*, 10:21, 10). Hans has pinpointed a key difference between male and female genitalia, but Freud is unable to give him his due. On the marginal place of menstruation in psychoanalytic theory, see Lupton (1993).

him instinctively to search for the appropriate opening in the female body—an opening, moreover, that he himself lacks, for the one sex always seeks in the other that which is complementary to it or of a nature different from its own. (1932, 140)

Although not referring to Little Hans, Horney's remarks are a far more adequate interpretation of his sexual fantasies than Freud's claim that "to his knowledge no such thing existed as his wiwimaker needed." Equally pertinently, though again without appealing to Little Hans for confirmation, Horney challenges Freud's one-sided preoccupation with penis envy by observing that "in boys of the same age, we meet with parallel expressions in the form of wishes to possess breasts or to have a child" (1933, 151).[17] Without indicting Freud by name, Horney intimates the personal origins of his theoretical blindness: "If the grown man continues to regard woman as the great mystery, in whom is a secret he cannot divine, this feeling of his can only relate ultimately to one thing in her: the mystery of motherhood. Everything else is merely a residue of his dread of this" (1932, 141).

As a coda to this discussion, it cannot be overlooked that Freud evinces an attitude toward homosexuality no less prejudiced than that toward female sexuality. As Roy Schafer has observed, "it requires no great leap in reasoning to conclude that, if the psychology of women is problematic, then that of men, from which it purports to be derived, must be equally problematic. . . . [O]n this expanded critical basis, one readily sees that there is much to question about Freud's views on gay and lesbian sexuality, for, at bottom, these views have been derived from his phallocentric approach to the psychological development of both sexes" (1994, 237). An outpouring of recent work in gay and lesbian studies has extended the intellectual revolution wrought by feminism, while providing a salutary reminder that the dynamics of gender and sexuality need to be analyzed separately.[18] In their preoccupation with issues of

17. "Why not *also* analyze the 'envy' for the vagina? Or the uterus? Or the vulva? Etc. The 'desire' felt by each pole of sexual difference 'to have something like it too'?" (Irigaray 1974, 52).

18. For an outstanding synthesis of gay and lesbian scholarship in Shakespeare studies, see Traub (1992). Traub defines "sex" as "those anatomical, biological distinctions by which cultures differentiate between males and females"; "gender" as "the culturally prescribed roles and behaviors available to the two 'sexes'"; and "sexuality" as "erotic desires

gender difference, in other words, feminists are in danger of eliding equally important issues of *sexual* difference.

I cite three instances of Freud's heterosexist bias in Little Hans, all from the first section of the case. Right at the outset, after introducing Hans's question to his mother about whether she has a wiwimaker, Freud reports that Hans saw a cow being milked and said that milk was coming out of its wiwimaker. Invoking his own earlier findings in the Dora case, Freud assures the reader that "one does not need to be unduly shocked if one finds in a female being the idea of sucking at the male member," since it has an innocent origin in the experience of sucking at the mother's breast, and the cow's udder provides a ready visual link between the breast and the penis (*G.W.*, 7:245; *S.E.*, 10:7).[19] But why should Freud limit his exculpation to women, since fellatio is manifestly an act performed also by men? The answer can only be that he is thinking exclusively in heterosexual terms. Several pages later, Freud describes the four-year-old Hans's verbal and physical displays of affection toward a male cousin of five, and exclaims: "Our little Hans seems to be truly a paragon of depravities!" (*G.W.*, 7:252; *S.E.*, 10:15). He lauds Hans for refusing to renounce his desire to sleep with the fourteen-year-old Mariedl, despite his mother's threat that he would have to leave the house: "Our little Hans conducted himself like a real man in the face of his mother's challenge, in spite of his homosexual proclivities" (*G.W.*, 7:254; *S.E.*, 10:17). Homosexuals, therefore, must not be real men.

These remarks are all admittedly lighthearted in tone, but precisely their casual nature allows us to catch Freud off guard, as it were, and to glimpse the bourgeois prejudices that remain veiled in his more circumspect theoretical pronouncements. That Freud's disparagement of homosexuality, no less than of female sexuality, is seriously disturbing cannot, I think, be doubted, and it should be deplored by all those who are drawn to psychoanalysis as a means not of oppressing but of emancipating the human spirit.

---

and practices, including but not limited to the direction and scope of erotic preference (i.e., object choice)" (21).

19. In the Dora case, despite deploring other writers for giving way to their "personal repugnance" and his admonition that "we must learn to speak without indignation of what we call the sexual perversions" (1905a, 50), Freud goes on to assert that "this excessively repulsive and perverted phantasy of sucking at the penis has the most innocent origin" (52). Even in a heterosexual context, the idea of fellatio appears to have been deeply disturbing to him.

3

"Does the Professor Talk to God?"
Countertransference and Jewish Identity in the Case of Little Hans

One of the most valuable contributions of the extensive feminist literature on the Dora case has been to point out the degree to which countertransferential factors hampered Freud's treatment of his renowned female patient.[1] Although there is a danger of anachronism in these critiques, since Freud in 1901 was just beginning to consolidate his concept of transference and the term "countertransference" does not appear in his published writings until 1910, the basic point that Freud was in various unconscious ways both libidinally invested in and identified with Dora, and that his failure to recognize the extent of his own subjective involvement in the therapeutic process had much to do with its unsuccessful outcome, is surely valid.

In this chapter, I propose to extend this line of argument to the case of Little Hans, which, like its nearly contemporaneous adult pendant, the case of the Rat Man, can in large measure be viewed as an attempt on Freud's part to recover from the self-confessed debacle of his first major venture in clinical writing.[2] Although Freud's countertransference

1. See especially the essays by Moi, Hertz, and Sprengnether in Bernheimer and Kahane (1985), as well as Mahony (1996).
2. According to Mahony (1993, 1246), Freud's participation in Hans's father's treatment of Hans's phobia ran from approximately January 10, 1908, to May 2, 1908; his pro-

toward Dora was negative, whereas that toward Little Hans and the Rat Man was positive, the danger of subjective distortion is as great in either instance. Indeed, it is an obvious but nonetheless important point that the gender of his patients played a decisive role in orienting the direction of Freud's countertransferential responses.[3]

In addition to taking place in the aftermath of his setback with Dora, the case of Little Hans occupies a crucial place in Freud's elaboration of the theory of the Oedipus complex. For this text, published in 1909, is a bench mark in the odyssey extending from Freud's letter to Fliess of October 15, 1897, in which he first broaches his interpretations of *Oedipus Rex* and *Hamlet*, to *Totem and Taboo*, where he holds that "the beginnings of religion, morals, society and art converge in the Oedipus complex" (1912–13, 155), which itself originates in a primal patricide purportedly committed at the dawn of humanity. Even these terminal points are not absolute. Freud's investment in the Oedipus myth can be traced both further backward to the circumstances of his family constellation, in which his forty-year-old father was twice the age of his mother at the time of their marriage and already had grown children from his first marriage—thereby creating a situation in which Freud's kinship ties were doubled, just as they were for Oedipus as a result of his incest with Jocasta—and further forward at least as far as *The Ego and the Id* (1923b), where Freud introduces the concept of the negative Oedipus complex. Not by chance, Freud's first published use of the term "Oedipus complex," like that of "countertransference," occurs in 1910, one year after the case of Little Hans, and grows directly out of his experiences both in this case history and that of the Rat Man.[4]

By bringing countertransference together with the Oedipus complex, I mean to suggest a revision in the way that the story of Freud's intellec-

---

cess notes on the Rat Man case extend from October 1, 1907, to January 20, 1908. As I have suggested in chapter 1, a desire to rebound from the Dora case also animates *Delusions and Dreams in Jensen's "Gradiva"* (1907a).

3. Freud's choice of the pseudonym "Hans" is striking in light of the fact that the real name of Herr K., the principal focus of his masculine identification in the Dora case, was Hans Zellenka (Mahony 1996). The significance of the name may be overdetermined by its phallic associations. As Groddeck writes in letter 14 of *The Book of the It*: "don't you know that the name Hans is so beloved by young and old because it rhymes with *Schwanz* [tail, a slang word for the penis]?" (1923, 137; my translation).

4. The term "countertransference" first appears in "The Future Prospects of Psycho-Analytic Therapy" (1910b); "Oedipus complex" makes its debut in "A Special Type of Choice of Object Made by Men" (1910c).

tual development is usually told. For if, as I shall try to show, Freud's effort to prove the universality of his oedipal paradigm in the case of Little Hans rests upon a largely unconscious and unacknowledged identification with his young protagonist, this calls into doubt the soundness of his findings. The approach I am taking here specifically revises my own earlier meditation on these questions in *Freud and Oedipus* (1987, 64), where I highlighted the role played in Freud's self-analysis by a patient, "Herr E.," whom he treated from 1895 to 1900 and mentions frequently in his letters to Fliess.[5] I employed the concept of the hermeneutic circle to argue that when Freud was able to confirm the existence of incestuous and patricidal wishes both in himself and in Herr E., a representative Other, he concluded that his theory was universally true and sealed this claim by invoking the name of Oedipus.

The dynamics of Freud's relationship to Little Hans are, I think, much the same as those with Herr E., but I would now judge Freud's procedures as a scientist and a clinician more severely. Although no form of intellectual inquiry can take place without preconceptions of some sort—what hermeneutic philosophers would call a "horizon of expectation"—the crucial point is that the investigator must allow his or her hypotheses to be modified and even refuted by experience. However regrettable it may be, I do not think it can be denied that Freud was singularly impervious to empirical evidence that contradicted his theoretical claims. In a tragic paradox that may justly be termed oedipal, the same genius and driving force of personality that made Freud great also blinded him in that they prevented him, both in intellectual matters and in his personal relationships, from admitting that he was wrong and from seeing how he was forcing the data to fit the Procrustean bed of his *idées fixes*. Unless the "circle of understanding" that Heidegger defines as the structure of philosophical knowledge can be opened both by unforeseen results of one's own and by evidence brought forward by others, what we have is not a scientific procedure but a vicious circle, in which one constantly rediscovers what one already knows while never learning anything new.

This, I am afraid, is one lesson that I would now draw from Freud's strenuous exertions to demonstrate the universality of the Oedipus com-

---

5. For further discussion of the pivotal role played by this patient, identified by Peter Swales as Oscar Fellner, in Freud's psychic life and intellectual development during this five-year period, see Davis (1990).

plex in the case of Little Hans. A characteristic note of warning is sounded in "Epicrisis," the final section of the case history, in which Freud sums up the results of Hans's analysis with evident satisfaction:

> In his dealings with his father and mother Hans confirms in the most dazzling and palpable way [*aufs grellste und greifbarste*] everything that I have maintained in *The Interpretation of Dreams* and the *Theory of Sexuality* concerning the sexual relations of children to parents. He is really a little Oedipus who would like to have his father "away," gotten rid of, in order to be alone with the beautiful mother, to sleep with her.[6] (*G.W.*, 7:345; *S.E.*, 10:111)

Freud is not content to say that Hans corroborates *many* of his theoretical propositions; rather, Hans confirms "everything" that he has set forth in his two seminal works, and that in "the most dazzling and palpable way." The hyperbole in Freud's rhetoric—as in his peroration to the Oedipus complex in *Totem and Taboo* or his jubilant announcement that Jensen's *Gradiva* shows a "complete agreement" (1907a, 89) with the methods of *Studies on Hysteria*—should alert us that he is functioning here not as an impartial scientist but as a polemicist on behalf of a preconceived conviction.[7] The underside of this apparently boundless self-confidence, moreover, is an unacknowledged defensiveness on the emo-

6. With the exception of the phrase used in the title, where I have retained Strachey's rendering, all quotations from the case of Little Hans are my translation, with volume and page references to both the *Gesammelte Werke* and the *Standard Edition* included parenthetically in the text.

7. Freud's penchant for sweeping declarations is displayed as early as "Sexuality in the Aetiology of the Neuroses" (1898), in which he writes: "the most significant causes of every case of neurotic illness are to be found in factors arising from sexual life. . . . If we keep firmly to what we have inferred, we shall in the end conquer every resistance by emphasizing the unshakable nature of our convictions" (263, 269). As Breger remarks, "this statement shows how Freud collapsed the complex histories and life situations" of his patients "into a single, sweeping principle that cannot be contradicted" (2000, 117). After 1908, the Little Hans case functions as a magnet for such grandiose assertions. In his *Introductory Lectures*, Freud says that what he had inferred about the sexual life of children from previous analyses of adults had been "confirmed point by point by direct observations of children" (1916–17, 310); in *An Autobiographical Study*, he reiterates of his "surprising discoveries" that "it became possible to confirm them fully and in every detail by direct observations upon children" (1925a, 39); and in *The Question of Lay Analysis*, he proclaims that "afterwards, we undertook analyses on children themselves, and it was no small triumph when we were thus able to confirm in them everything we had been able to divine" (1926c, 214). In Freud's lexicon, to "observe" children means to psychoanalyze them.

tional plane as well as a disregard of the clear purport of much of the clinical data that he nonetheless furnishes with admirable honesty.

Freud's grandiose assertion about the significance of Hans's analysis occurs when he labels him a "little Oedipus." Although Oedipus is not explicitly named, a similar train of thought informs the passage from which I have taken the title of this chapter, which occurs when Hans, accompanied by his analyst-father, visits Freud for a single consultation. During their conversation, as Freud reports, he informed Hans that "he feared his father, precisely because he was so fond of his mother"; and "long before he was in the world, I had already known that there would come a little Hans, who would be so fond of his mother that he would have to be afraid of his father on that account, and had told this to his father." On the way home from Freud's office, the awestruck child asks his father: "'Does the Professor talk to God [*Spricht denn der Professor mit dem lieben Gott*], that he can know everything beforehand?'" To this Freud appends the comment, "I would have been extraordinarily proud of this acknowledgment from the mouth of a child, had I not provoked it myself by my joking boastfulness" (*G.W.*, 7:277–78; *S.E.*, 10:42–43).

Jocular though the tone may be, the underlying purport of this passage is wholly serious. Freud, possessed by his oedipal theory, depicts himself as the Delphic oracle who reveals to Hans the predestined riddle of his fate.[8] That Hans should wonder whether Freud is in communication with the Supreme Being accords with Freud's own fantasy of his omniscience. Despite his disclaimers, Freud is genuinely boastful and flattered by Hans's vindication of his bedrock beliefs. Earlier, ostensibly speaking in defense of Hans's mother, Freud asserts that "she plays a fated role and has a difficult lot" (*G.W.*, 7:263; *S.E.*, 10:28). That "fated role" is, of course, the one prescribed by the oedipal drama. Freud's confidence that he "knows everything beforehand" leads him to proclaim in the final paragraph, "I have, strictly speaking, learned nothing new from

---

8. In the course of his catastrophic meddling in the life of his patient Horace Frink, an American psychiatrist whom he encouraged to divorce his wife in order to marry the bank heiress Anjelika Bijur, who had been Frink's patient and was herself still married, Freud reported on September 12, 1921, to Frink about a cable ("No mistake, be kind and patients [*sic*]") that he had sent to Bijur exhorting her not to waver in her resolve: "I hope it was not oracular" (quoted in Edmunds 1988, 43). Freud, who hoped that Bijur's money would find its way into psychoanalytic coffers, is "oracular" not only in his obscurity but also in his certainty about what is best for other people. Freud's scheme backfired, however, when both of the abandoned spouses died and Frink fell into a major depression after the failure of his remarriage.

this analysis" (*G.W.*, 7:377; *S.E.*, 10:147). This may be true, but rather than lending credence to Freud's theories, it points to the closure of his hermeneutic circles.

Like his four textual companions—Dora, the Rat Man, Schreber, and the Wolf Man—Little Hans has elicited voluminous commentaries. Among the most eminent psychologists and psychoanalysts to reappraise the case are John Bowlby (1973, 283–87), Erich Fromm (1968), and Joseph Wolpe (Wolpe and Rachman 1960), the behavioral therapist and proponent of systematic desensitization as a technique for the treatment of phobias. (Although Wolpe denies any intrapsychic significance to Hans's phobia, which he explains exclusively in terms of a conditioned response to his fear at seeing a falling horse, his indictment of the fallacies in Freud's logic is trenchant.) The case has likewise attracted the attention of a host of object relations theorists, self psychologists, and family therapists, to say nothing of the classical analysts who have elaborated it from Freud's perspective.[9]

Although there is inevitably some divergence of emphasis, most contemporary analysts agree that Freud, who in 1909 remained wedded to the drive theory of the *Three Essays*, which explained anxiety as repressed libido, paid too little heed to the role of experience in the etiology of Hans's neurosis while placing inordinate weight on constitutional factors. Freud concludes that "the essence of the condition of illness remains completely tied to the nature of the drive components to be repulsed" (*G.W.*, 7:370; *S.E.*, 10:139). And when, many years later, Anna Freud wrote a foreword to her father's inaugural case of child analysis, she endorsed his theoretical stance: "The issue . . . is not the illness of a child who may be hereditarily tainted, or sexually overstimulated, or abnormally precocious, or otherwise individually predisposed; rather, it is a more or less typical occurrence" (1980, 280).

Notwithstanding the attempt of both Freuds to explain Hans's phobia as the efflorescence of "typical" drives, a consensus now exists that Hans's neurosis cannot be understood without paying much more attention than did Freud to the traumatic events that exerted a crippling impact on his emotional development. To name only the most obvious, these include threats of abandonment and castration by his mother, his

9. Two of the best essays are by Garrison (1978) and Lindon (1992). Jacobus (1995) offers an exegesis of the play of language in the text, which draws on earlier readings by Lacan and Kristeva. Most egregious is the paper by Robert Fliess (1956), which takes to an extreme Freud's belief in the impact of phylogenetic experience.

tonsillectomy, the use of enemas and laxatives by both parents in conjunction with overly rigorous toilet training measures, his father's handling of his penis to assist him in urination, and the purveying of false information about the female genital organs and childbirth. Despite these cumulative insults inflicted on Hans during his upbringing, Freud does not scruple to assure the reader that his parents, who were adherents of psychoanalysis, had resolved "to raise their first child with no more coercion than was absolutely necessary for the preservation of good morals" (*G.W.*, 7:244; *S.E.*, 10:8).

If one attempts to classify the distortions introduced by Freud into the case of Little Hans as a result of his theoretical biases, they fall under two rubrics: (1) his general neglect of environmental factors; and (2) his confusions specifically in the domain of gender, stemming from his assumption that children of both sexes are aware only of the penis and not of the vagina, a point I have documented in the previous chapter. These two weak spots can be correlated, respectively, with the indictments of Freud's position proffered by object relations theory and feminism. The former, along with Bowlby's attachment theory, counters Freud's drive theory by restoring a proper emphasis on the human need for affiliation; the latter attempts to undo the havoc wreaked by Freud's phallocentric models of sexuality and gender difference. These areas of vulnerability converge in the Oedipus complex, which is at once male-centered and views the human condition through the prism of sexual and aggressive drives.

All these points, although fundamental, should be familiar, and I recapitulate them here in order to provide a framework for the rereading of the Little Hans case to which I now turn. In keeping with my title, I propose to concentrate on two hitherto neglected factors: Freud's countertransferential identification with his patient and the role played by Jewish identity in the case. With respect to the latter, I shall be offering what is in effect an extended footnote to the pathbreaking work on Freud of Sander Gilman (1993a, 1993b). Both Freud's countertransference to Hans and the role of Jewish identity are repressed elements in the text; their excavation depends on the deployment of biographical information, which, once one has become aware of it, permanently alters our understanding of Freud's published work.[10] As we shall see, the

---

10. Analogously, the publication and preservation of Freud's letters to Fliess, which Freud never imagined would see the light of day, forever changes our reading of *The Interpretation of Dreams* and, indeed, the entirety of Freud's *oeuvre*.

theme of Jewish identity is bound up with Freud's quest to prove the universality of the Oedipus complex. To Freud's neglect of the role of the environment and his confusion in the domain of gender, accordingly, I shall add a critique of the Oedipus complex from the standpoint of race, since, as Gilman reminds us (1993b, 18), being Jewish was by the end of the nineteenth century as much a matter of race as of religion. Freud's countertransferential identification with Hans is the engine that propels him into all three of these theoretical dead-ends.

A crucial text on which I shall rely in my rereading of Little Hans is Max Graf's "Reminiscences of Professor Sigmund Freud," published in 1942 in *Psychoanalytic Quarterly*. Graf senior, the father of Little Hans (or Herbert, as he was actually named), was a Viennese musicologist who, after meeting Freud in 1900, joined his Wednesday evening circle. He presented papers on Beethoven, Wagner, and the psychology of creativity, and his monograph on *The Flying Dutchman* was included by Freud in his series on applied psychology.[11] In 1904, Freud gave Graf the manuscript of his first essay on literature, "Psychopathic Characters on the Stage," which remained unpublished at the time of his death in 1939; and it was as a preface to this essay that Graf wrote his memoir.

Graf's paper is historically important in many respects, not least for its portrait of Freud and account of his conflict with Adler that led to the schism in the Vienna Psychoanalytic Society. Notwithstanding his great admiration for Freud, Graf writes, "I was unable and unwilling to submit to Freud's 'do' or 'don't' . . . and nothing was left for me but to withdraw from his circle" (1942, 475).[12] For my purposes here, however, Graf's paper is invaluable for the light it sheds on the case of Little Hans. At the time of its publication, Max Graf's identity as Hans's father was a closely guarded secret. Thus, he makes disclosures under the cloak of anonymity that prove extremely revealing once their pertinence to

11. For a perceptive discussion of Graf's contributions to the Vienna Psychoanalytic Society, see Rose (1998, 46–48, 67–76). As Rose shows, Graf was aligned with Freud, and against Isador Sadger and Wilhelm Stekel, in arguing that artists could best be known through their works, rather than by a nearly exclusive focus on their personalities.

12. This statement almost certainly refers to Freud's ultimatum—for which an exception was made only for Lou Andreas-Salomé—that no one who attended the meetings of Adler's dissident group would be permitted to continue to attend the meetings of the Vienna Psychoanalytic Society. Compare Eugen Bleuler's declaration from the same period: "This 'who is not for us is against us,' this 'all or nothing' is in my opinion necessary for religious communities and useful for political parties. There I can understand the principle as such, but for science I consider it harmful" (quoted in Gay 1988, 215). I take up Graf's narrative of the history of the psychoanalytic movement again in chapter 8.

the case is recognized. Needless to say, commentators have long been aware of Graf's paper and mined some of its nuggets—for example, that his wife had been Freud's patient and introduced the two men. Surprisingly, however, there remain two details vital to our understanding of Little Hans, both of which have received only cursory attention from scholars.

The first of these is buried in Graf's testimonial that Freud took "the warmest part in all family events in my house," despite being an older and more eminent person. "On the occasion of my son's third birthday," Graf reports, "Freud brought him a rocking horse which he himself carried up the four flights of steps leading to my house" (1942, 474).[13] A rocking horse? For a child who (if Graf's chronology can be trusted) later developed a horse phobia? Surely there is reason here to prick up one's third ear and to go back to Freud's narrative armed with this piece of information.

At the very least, Graf reveals that Freud's emotional investment in Hans goes far beyond what might be gleaned from the case history, where Freud declares that he "intervened a single time in a conversation with the boy" (G.W., 7:243; S.E., 10:5), though he admits prior to his account of this consultation that "I knew the droll whipper-snapper already" (G.W., 7:276; S.E., 10:41). Even this avowal, however, does not suggest an involvement in the boy's life that would lead Freud to give him a birthday present, and a rocking horse at that. Given that Hans's phobia is one of horses, one cannot help wondering whether Freud's gift played a role in its etiology, though this is nowhere hinted at in the text. To employ a Lacanian formulation, if Hans's horse phobia is to be connected at least to some degree with his father, it can also be interpreted in relation to Freud as one occupying the position of the Name-of-the Father, who serves as a figure of paternal—indeed, quasi-divine—authority not only for Hans but for his biological father as well.

I intimated that there may be some doubt as to the reliability of Hans's father's dating of the rocking-horse episode. I did so on the strength of a second document, which remains unpublished and unknown to scholars, that bears directly on Hans's case. This is an interview given by Max Graf to Kurt Eissler in December 1952.[14] Among

13. Frankiel calls attention to this "fateful gift" (1992, 325), but without considering its etiological significance to the case.

14. I am indebted to Professor André E. Haynal of Geneva for furnishing me with a

other things, Graf reveals that two of his wife's brothers committed suicide, while one of her sisters made a suicide attempt, and that Hans's (that is, Herbert's) sister also committed suicide in America after the dissolution of an unhappy marriage. These tragic events place Hans's anxiety in a transgenerational context, supporting the view of family therapists that a child labeled as an "identified patient" is often the split-off carrier of a breakdown in the entire family system. In his 1922 postscript to the case, Freud informs the reader that Hans's parents had divorced and were remarried to other people, but the interview with Eissler affords a glimpse of just how hellish life had been in the Graf household.

Graf reveals that before proposing marriage to his wife, who was Freud's patient, he sought Freud's advice. As in Ferenczi's later imbroglio with the mother-daughter pair of Gizella and Elma Pálos or Horace Frink's adulterous entanglement with Anjelika Bijur, Freud played the double role of analyst and matchmaker. Freud's words, as Graf reports them, were: "'Go ahead and marry, you'll have your fun!'" (1952, 17). When the marriage foundered, Freud encouraged Graf to stick with it. Apparently as a result, Graf decided that having children might be a way to preserve the marriage, leading to the births of Hans and his sister; but though the marriage lasted eighteen and a half years, it was permanently unhappy.

In the interview, Graf characterizes his wife as "undoubtedly a hysteric" (1952, 17). As one might guess, their sex life was no bed of roses: "after every night of love there was an explosion in the morning" (39). Graf discloses that his wife "had inhibitions against going out among people" and hence remained housebound, a condition, as Eissler remarked, with "a certain resemblance to the symptom of the child" (35). Her introversion is comprehensible in light of her siblings' suicidal behavior, and the entire family history belies Anna Freud's claim that "the issue . . . is not the illness of a child who may be hereditarily tainted."

For the historical record, I cannot refrain from making public an amusing anecdote about Freud from Graf's interview with Eissler. Recalling the heady days of the gatherings in Freud's apartment, he continues:

> Now, it's interesting that one time we proposed to Professor Freud that we would like to psychoanalyze him, the entire circle. Well, we got Freud to speak

---

transcript of this interview, which was conducted in German. Page numbers will be to the typescript; all translations are my own.

according to all the rules of psychoanalysis that we had learned, and when he showed resistances, we helped him to get over them. But we came to grief on a single point, and that was very interesting. Freud had told us something or other about his mother and in connection with that about a black fur muff, which lay on the table. And when he said that, we all began to laugh, because of course we knew the solution and told it to Professor Freud. But he absolutely refused to accept the erotic symbolism that was completely transparent and belonged to the A-B-C of the Freudian technique, and we could not continue the treatment. (1952, 6)

The closest parallel to this episode is Jung's account of his 1909 voyage with Freud and Ferenczi to America, during which the three men interpreted each other's dreams until Freud called a halt to the experiment with the comment, "'But I cannot risk losing my authority!'" (Jung 1965, 158). In both instances, Freud refused to abide in the role of patient. Graf's anecdote illustrates Freud's resistance to analyzing the mother-son relationship, a tendency likewise evident in the case of Little Hans. Freud's association of his mother to the fur muff, moreover, will appeal to readers of Fielding's *Tom Jones*, in which Tom's sexual desire for Sophia Western is symbolized by her muff and the plot comically exorcises the fear that he has committed incest with his mother . . .

But I digress. To return to Hans's rocking horse, in his interview with Eissler, Graf again recalls Freud's gift, but this time says that the birthday present was given to the boy *after* he was cured of his horse phobia (1952, 14). Although there is no way to be certain, this dating seems to me more probable than that in the published paper. (Incidentally, Freud predicted to the father that the boy would one day want to enlist in the cavalry, a proof of his lack of prophetic powers, since Herbert Graf went on to a distinguished career in the music world that culminated as stage director of the Metropolitan Opera and general manager of the Grand Théâtre in Geneva.) If Graf's revised dating of the gift is correct, there is a close parallel between Freud's behavior with Hans and with Herr E., whom, as he wrote to Fliess on December 21, 1899, he rewarded for having assisted him in his self-analysis by presenting him with "the picture of Oedipus and the Sphinx" (Masson 1985, 392), presumably in the version of Ingres.[15]

15. According to Fritz Wittels, "At one time, when Freud had brought an analysis to a successful completion, he used to show the patient an engraving after a painting by Ingres, 'Oedipus solving the riddle of the Sphinx'" (1924, 114). This testimony confirms that

If Freud's gift of the rocking horse occurs after Hans's analysis, it cannot have influenced the formation of his symptom, but the episode remains indispensable to understanding Freud's relationship to Hans. For even if the gift is Freud's way of marking the completion of the analysis, it still proves that his involvement with Hans goes far beyond anything that he is prepared to acknowledge in the published record. And as in the case of Herr E., where the oedipal symbolism of Freud's gift is explicit, so Freud's gift of the rocking horse commemorates Hans's confirmation of the universality of the Oedipus complex. Both Herr E. and Hans, that is, are alter egos who permit Freud to trace a hermeneutic circle; but rather than guaranteeing the truth of his discovery, Freud's countertransference should alert us to the danger that he may be projecting his a priori ideas upon a patient to whom they do not necessarily apply.

Whatever the timing of Freud's gift, it indicates that he is being disingenuous concerning his personal involvement in the case and the extent of his identification with Little Hans. Once we are attuned to this concealed autobiographical dimension, many of the details in Freud's narrative take on new meaning. Near the end of the clinical section, for example, Freud transcribes a dialogue in which Hans accepts his father's interpretation that he wishes to marry his mother, but adds the proviso that his father is to become the grandfather of the children born from this fantasied incestuous union. Freud comments: "Everything comes out all right. The little Oedipus found a more fortunate solution than that prescribed by fate. Instead of shunting his father aside, he grants him the same happiness that he demands for himself; he promotes him to grandfather and marries him as well to his own mother" (G.W., 7:332; S.E., 10:97). As in the later passage where Freud adduces Hans as "the most dazzling and palpable" proof of "everything" in *The Interpretation of Dreams* and *Three Essays*, he uses the phrase "little Oedipus," which signals that powerful unconscious currents are swirling beneath the surface of the text.

The strength of these currents is confirmed by the resemblance between Hans's promotion of his father to the role of grandfather, so that he might possess his mother undisturbed, and the situation in Freud's own family of origin. As I have noted, Freud's father had two grown sons by a first marriage by the time he wed Freud's mother, a woman half his age. What is more, the elder of these two sons had a son and daughter of

---

Freud used the Ingres engraving, which hung on the wall over the foot of his couch, as a talisman of initiation into the oedipal mysteries of analysis.

his own about the time of Freud's birth. Thus, Freud's father was simultaneously a *grandfather* to children of Freud's own age. Freud's removal of his father to a more remote third-generational role was facilitated by the presence in the household of a Catholic Czech nanny, whom Freud invariably describes as "elderly," although she was in fact middle-aged, with whom it was logical to pair off his father, just as he fantasized that his half-brothers were the consorts of his mother.[16] Thus, when he calls Hans a "little Oedipus," Freud might just as easily have called him a "little Sigmund," since Hans's "more fortunate solution" to the threats of incest and patricide was precisely the same one that Freud had crafted in his own life. Once again, Freud's invocation of Oedipus signals a moment of heightened countertransferential pressure in the text, in which an apparently impersonal observation screens Freud's imperative to remake Hans in his own image.

In addition to this convergence between their "solutions" to the Oedipus complex, other aspects of Hans's history resonate with autobiographical significance for Freud. Like Freud, who shared his parents' bedroom for his first three years, Hans slept in his parents' bedroom until the birth of his sister when he was three and a half. Although unable to confirm his reconstruction, Freud surmises that "a reminiscence had been aroused in the child of a sexual intercourse [*Verkehr*] of the parents observed by him" (*G.W.*, 7:367; *S.E.*, 10:135–36). Whether or not this is true for Hans, the effects of Freud's exposure to the primal scene can be detected in many of his dreams and fantasies.[17]

What is more, the occurrence of the word "*Verkehr*," which in German means both "traffic" and "sexual intercourse," leads Freud to propose that Hans's phobia, which begins with horses but extends to carts and trains, operates under the "sign of traffic": "So a railway anxiety mingles itself in the course of time with every street phobia" (*G.W.*, 7:319; *S.E.*, 10:84). As is well known, Freud himself suffered from lifelong travel anxiety stemming from a train journey in his early childhood

16. In his interview with Eissler, Max Graf states that Herbert had "an old nursemaid, who taught him a few Viennese songs" (1952, 26).

17. Compare Mahony's remarks on Freud's "countertransferential complex" (1986, 96–97) in the case of the Rat Man, particularly the three exclamation points in his private process notes following the Rat Man's mention of the name of his beloved, Gisela Fluss, which was coincidentally also the name of Freud's adolescent flame. The issue of the primal scene, which Freud tentatively broaches in the case of Little Hans, becomes the linchpin in the case of the Wolf Man, where one can again observe Freud's efforts to remake his male patient in his own image.

when (according to a reconstruction in his letter to Fliess of October 3, 1897) he saw his mother naked (Masson 1985, 268). Thus, in positing an affinity between "street phobia" and "railway anxiety," Freud is again aligning Hans's symptomatology with his own.[18]

As a final example of the submerged parallels between Hans and Freud, it bears noting that the Graf family vacationed in Gmunden, a resort town in the mountainous Salzkammergut region. It was on a train journey to Gmunden that the three-year-old Hans noticed his mother's pregnancy with his sister and also in Gmunden (during his father's absence) that he wheedled his mother into taking him to bed with her. As it happens, Freud had his own connections to Gmunden. In the summer of 1883, the twenty-seven-year-old Freud was invited by his then-revered senior colleague Josef Breuer to accompany him to Gmunden, where Breuer's family had rented a house for the holidays. Freud's letters to his fiancée, Martha Bernays, interweave vivid descriptions of the Alpine scenery with an account of Flaubert's *Temptation of St. Anthony*, which, he rhapsodizes, "calls up not only the great problems of knowledge, but the real enigmas of life, all the conflicts of feelings and impulses, and it confirms the awareness of our perplexity in the mysteriousness that reigns everywhere" (quoted in Jones 1973, 279). While at the train station in Vienna, Breuer encountered a couple of his acquaintance, a woman of thirty-six and a man of twenty-six, who had married after a ten-year courtship. When asked by Breuer how he might explain this "curious relationship," Freud tells Martha, he replied that "an immature man is often attracted by a mature woman, and that such marriages are often successful. You must be wondering where I get such information from" (277). Where, indeed? More than a decade before his discovery of psychoanalysis, Freud's journey to Gmunden takes place under the aegis of the Oedipus complex; and it would surely not have es-

18. In writing to Fliess on December 21, 1899, Freud says that his analysis of Herr E. "has demonstrated the truth of my theories in my own person, for with a surprising turn he provided me with the solution of my own railway phobia (which I had overlooked). . . . My phobia, if you please, was a poverty, or rather a hunger phobia, arising out of infantile gluttony and called up by the circumstance that my wife had no dowry" (Masson 1985, 392). Beyond evincing a doubling of self and other prefiguring that in his identification with Hans, this passage links Freud's phobia to his conflicted relationship with his pre-oedipal mother. The presumed glimpse (or retrospective fantasy) of her pubic hair during their train journey together would help explain Freud's refusal to analyze his associations to the "black fur muff" before his Viennese colleagues.

caped his attention that for both himself and Little Hans Gmunden was a privileged site of forbidden knowledge.

Reinforcing these multiple analogies between the destinies of Freud and Hans is a rhetorical strategy whereby Freud depicts both himself and Hans as solvers of the Sphinx's riddle. When Freud hails Hans's fantasy of marrying his father off to his own mother as "a more fortunate solution [*eine glücklichere Lösung*] than that prescribed by fate," this is one in a series of repetitions of the words "riddle" and "solution," which Freud applies interchangeably to Hans's efforts to unravel the mysteries of birth and sexuality and to his own efforts to unravel the mystery of Hans's neurosis.[19] Near the end of the case, Freud states that the birth of his sister incited Hans to

> a labor of thought, which on the one hand could not be brought to a solution [*Lösung*], and on the other entangled him in conflicts of feelings. The great riddle [*Rätsel*] of where children come from presented itself to him, perhaps the first problem—of which the riddle [*Rätsel*] of the Theban Sphinx probably refracts only a distortion—whose solution [*Lösung*] puts a claim on the mental powers of the child. (*G.W.*, 7:364–65; *S.E.*, 10:133)

Once again, Hans is cast as a juvenile Oedipus who must come to terms not only with his incestuous and patricidal fantasies but also with his mother's pregnancy and the birth of a sibling rival—experiences that likewise exerted a formative impact on Freud's childhood.[20] Freud's en-

19. On the antithesis of "riddle" and "solution" in the case of the Rat Man, which, as in the case of Little Hans, is not always preserved in Strachey's translation, see Mahony (1986, 19–21). Mahony cites a passage from "The Sexual Enlightenment of Children," which concerns not the Rat Man but Little Hans, where Freud calls the origin of babies "the oldest and most burning question that confronts immature humanity" and connects it to "the riddle which the Theban Sphinx set to Oedipus" (1907b, 135).

20. Expressing his wish that the stork should return his baby sister, Hans adds that it should bring no more "from the big chest [*Kiste*] where the children are" (*G.W.*, 7:303; *S.E.*, 10:68–69). Later, just after the passage concerning the "Theban Sphinx," Freud explains that Hans rejected the fable of the stork because he had noticed his mother's enlarged body and that, after the birth of Hanna, "she got up slender [*schlank*]" (*G.W.*, 7:365; *S.E.*, 10:133). These references to pregnancy bristle with significance for Freud, who on several occasions refers to a childhood memory—conflating the birth of his sister Anna and the imprisonment of his nanny—in which his half-brother Philipp joked that the nanny had been "boxed up" (*eingekastelt*). Besides the play on the word "chest" (*Kasten*), Freud emphasizes satisfaction at his mother's being "beautiful and slim [*schlank*]" (1901, 49–52).

thusiasm for the image of Hans before the "Theban Sphinx" prompts him to employ the antithesis of "riddle" and "solution" not once but twice in successive sentences.

A page later, Freud reverts to the same metaphor to summarize Hans's struggles with sexual difference: "But although he was on the way, aided by the sensations in his penis, to postulating the existence of the vagina, he still could not solve the riddle [*das Rätsel nicht lösen*], because to his knowledge no such thing existed as his wiwimaker needed; much rather did the conviction that his Mama possessed a wiwimaker like his own stand in the way of the solution [*Lösung*]" (*G.W.*, 7:366; *S.E.*, 10:134–35). According to Freud, a child's discovery of the existence of the vagina is an achievement no less formidable than solving the Sphinx's riddle. Freud's identification with Hans as a paradigm of the Oedipus complex, that is, leads him to depict both himself and his double as heroes engaged on an oedipal quest.[21] The androcentric bias that warps Freud's theory of sexual difference, which, as I have argued in the preceding chapter, takes shape in the case of Little Hans, is thus not simply enshrined in a set of doctrines but enacted in the process by which Freud conducts his investigation.

Since both he and Hans are embarked on a quest for knowledge, Freud characterizes Hans, like himself, as a researcher. Stressing the inseparability of the "craving for knowledge [*Wißbegierde*] and sexual curiosity [*Neugierde*]," Freud remarks that Hans's curiosity "makes him also into a researcher [*Forscher*], permits him genuine conceptual recognitions" (*G.W.*, 7:246–47; *S.E.*, 10:9).[22] In thus linking sexual to intellec-

21. Again in the final section, Freud writes of himself as author-detective, "Now we no longer have many riddles [*Rätsel*] to await" (*G.W.*, 7:362; *S.E.*, 10:130); earlier he declares that the origin of Hans's horse phobia "is still a riddle [*Rätsel*] of the case, whose further development we must now pursue, in order to find the solution [*Lösung*]" (*G.W.*, 7:262; *S.E.*, 10:27). He rings the changes on "*Lösung*," which can refer to the answer of a riddle, a medicine in liquid form, or the cure of a disease, in a climactic passage: "But that which has thus remained not understood comes again; like an unredeemed [*unerlöster*] ghost, it does not rest until it has come to a solution [*Lösung*] and dissolution [*Erlösung*]" (*G.W.*, 7:355; *S.E.*, 10:122). A similar ambiguity subtends this word in the dream of "Irma's injection," where Freud reproaches his composite female patient "for not having accepted my 'solution' [*Lösung*] yet" (1900, 107). The belief that the correct interpretation of a symptom would cause it to vanish is, as I have noted in chapter 1, a hallmark of the therapeutic optimism of Freud's early period.

22. In a footnote concerning the female sexual anatomy, Freud wonders: "Why don't these young researchers [*Forscher*] grasp what they really see, namely, that no wiwimaker is present?" (*G.W.*, 7:249; *S.E.*, 10:12*n*3). At the end of the second section, he uses the first-person plural pronoun to elevate Hans to the status of a psychoanalyst: "our little re-

tual curiosity, Freud implicates himself as well as Little Hans. "From the childhood history of men later recognized as 'great,'" he writes, "one knows that . . . sexual precocity is a rarely misleading correlative of the intellectual, and is therefore to be found more frequently in talented children than one might expect." Earlier in the same paragraph Freud hails Hans as a youngster "in whom not only his own father can find joy [*Freude*]" (*G.W.*, 7:372–73; *S.E.*, 10:142). If, as I have suggested, Freud's birthday gift to Hans of the rocking horse—whatever its timing—places Freud in the position of the Name-of-the-Father, he here in effect adopts Hans as his son and bestows on him a version of his own name.

As I have stressed, Freud gives no indication in his case history of the extent of his identification with Hans, but seeks rather to portray himself as a dispassionate scientist, albeit one benevolently concerned with the child's welfare. Having documented Freud's unanalyzed counter-transference, I turn now to the second detail in Max Graf's "Reminiscences of Professor Sigmund Freud" that solicits our attention, and which brings the theme of Jewish identity to the fore. In addition to the bombshell concerning the gift of the rocking horse, Graf reveals that Freud was responsible for the decision to raise Hans as a Jew. To convey the "personal contact" that had arisen between Freud and his family, Graf writes:

> When my son was born, I wondered whether I should not remove him from the prevailing antisemitic hatred, which was at that time preached by a very popular man, Doctor Lueger. I was not certain whether it would not be better to have my son brought up in the Christian faith. Freud advised me not to do this. "If you do not let your son grow up as a Jew," he said, "you will deprive him of those sources of energy which cannot be replaced by anything else. He will have to struggle as a Jew, and you ought to develop in him all the energy he will need for that struggle. Do not deprive him of that advantage." (1942, 473)

Not only does Freud say nothing about his own role in shaping Hans's religious identity, but even that Hans is Jewish goes unmentioned in the case history. The question of Jewishness does, however, surface on a single occasion, albeit in an impersonal and marginalized form. To his

---

searcher [*Forscher*] has only made the discovery prematurely that all knowledge is piece-meal and that at every stage an unsolved remnant [*ungelöster Rest*] remains" (*G.W.*, 7:335; *S.E.*, 10:100).

exposition of the castration complex, Freud appends a footnote that shifts the focus from gender to race: "The castration complex is the deepest unconscious root of anti-Semitism, for already in the nursery the boy hears that the Jew has had something cut off from his penis—by which he understands a piece of the penis—and that gives him the right to despise the Jew. The sense of superiority to woman likewise has no stronger unconscious root." Freud invokes Otto Weininger, the self-hating Jewish author of *Sex and Character* whose suicide in 1903 at the age of twenty-two sealed his notoriety: "As a neurotic, Weininger stood wholly under the sway of infantile complexes. The relation to the castration complex is from that standpoint what the Jew and the woman have in common" (*G.W.*, 7:271; *S.E.*, 10:36).

Thanks to Graf's memoir, we know that Freud had a personal stake in Hans's Jewishness, which he fails to disclose to his readers. The effect of this awareness is to highlight Freud's omission of any reference to Hans's Jewishness—and his own—as a problem requiring explanation, whereas previously it might have seemed to be simply (and hence invisibly) the natural order of things. Like Sherlock Holmes's dog that didn't bark, the absence of the theme of Jewish identity from the body of the text becomes a positive piece of evidence from which the extreme sensitivity of the subject can be inferred. Freud's footnote on anti-Semitism, by extension, takes on the quality of a neurotic symptom in which the Jewish question returns in a distorted form. Like all symptoms, the footnote is a compromise formation. It represses the issue of Jewish identity by displacing it to the margins of the text and handling it in what appears to be a dispassionate fashion. But it confesses it in mentioning so threatening a topic at all. The ostensible impersonality of the footnote cannot be taken at face value, but is rather the result of a deadlock between Freud's conflicting impulses to self-concealment and self-revelation.

Once the subjective component of Freud's footnote on anti-Semitism is recognized, moreover, it can be used as an Archimedean point from which to reinterpret the concept of the Oedipus complex. As I have acknowledged, my argument here is indebted to the work of Gilman, who, though he has not commented in detail on the case of Little Hans, has provided the most comprehensive account of the impact of Freud's Jewish identity on psychoanalytic theory.[23] Because Jewishness was deemed

23. Among other observations, Gilman cites Freud's admonition to Max Graf to raise his son as a Jew, but without considering its bearing on Hans's circumcision (1993a, 88).

by fin-de-siècle Viennese culture to be a pathological condition, Gilman contends, and because Jewish identity was defined by the practice of circumcision, Freud was constrained to obliterate the traces of his racial difference in order to cultivate a stance of objectivity that would enable him to gain acceptance by the scientific establishment. In Gilman's words, "it was through the assumption of the neutrality of the definition of the (male) scientist that Freud was able in his scientific writing to efface his own anxiety (which he expressed in private) about the limitations ascribed to the mind and character of the Jewish male" (1993b, 37).

In the case of Little Hans, not only is Freud's elision of the theme of Jewishness a result of countertransference, but the bond of Jewish identity provides a motive for his identification with Hans in the first place. What is more, if Freud is responsible for Hans's rearing as a Jew, he is presumably indirectly the agent of his circumcision.[24] Thus, in Hans, Freud confronts a young Jewish male whose circumcised body is the mirror image of his own. Since, as Gilman insists, the Jewish physician is at once "the diseased patient, the source of the disease, and the healer" (1993a, 42), Freud's refusal to acknowledge his likeness to Hans constitutes an attempt to deny his own contamination as a "diseased pa-

24. The question of Herbert Graf's religious identity is vexed. In his introductory essay to a French translation of a four-part interview of Herbert Graf by Francis Rizzo, originally published in *Opera News* in 1972, François Dachet points out that Graf refers to Gustav Mahler as his "godfather," which might imply that Herbert Graf was baptised (1993, 9). Dachet cites an 1899 letter from Mahler to Max Graf in which Mahler expresses his appreciation for "the honor of standing godfather to one of your children," but cautions that this letter concerns not Herbert's birth, which occurred in 1903, but rather Graf's dedication of his book, *Wagner Problems*, to Mahler. Mahler, moreover, had converted from Judaism to Catholicism in 1896 in order to accede to the directorship of the Imperial Opera in Vienna. Whatever the sense in which Mahler was Herbert Graf's godfather, the equation of books and children seems fitting in light of the latter's immortalization as Little Hans in Freud's text. In his "Reminiscences of Professor Sigmund Freud," Max Graf makes an oddly abrupt transition from the incident concerning Freud's admonition to raise Graf's son as a Jew to refer to Freud's admiration for Mahler; this is followed by the business about the rocking horse (1942, 473–74). Dachet conjectures that the mention of Mahler may be due to his status as a "godfather" to Graf's books or children. These ironies are compounded by the fact that Freud apparently did not have his own sons circumcised (Gilman 1993b, 86; see also Geller 1999, 363). Vitz (1988) has argued that "Freud was tempted to convert—really, to assimilate—for reasons of ambition and self-interest" (81). If true, this would lend an additional layer of significance to Freud's identification with Hans and insistence that the boy be raised as a Jew. For Herbert Graf's reference to Mahler, see *Opera News*, February 5, 1972, p. 26. For Mahler's letter to Graf, see La Grange (1983, 475).

tient" in order to consolidate the authority of a "healer" in his scientific discourse.

Just as the case of Little Hans is a bench mark for Freud's views on female sexuality, so too is it for those on anti-Semitism. What femininity and anti-Semitism have in common, according to Freud, is their derivation from the castration complex. Freud's footnote on circumcision as the explanation for anti-Semitism in this case foreshadows his assertion in *Moses and Monotheism* that circumcision is the "symbolic substitute for the castration which the primal father once inflicted upon his sons in the plenitude of his absolute power" (1939, 122). Having been attuned to the dynamics of countertransference and to Jewish identity as a motive for Freud's concealment of his identification with Hans, however, one might be inclined to turn the tables and propose that the hypothesis of a primordial castration complex is rather a "symbolic substitute" for the circumcision inflicted in actuality on Freud.

Freud's occlusion of the theme of Jewish identity in the case of Little Hans exemplifies a characteristic pattern in his clinical narratives. As Gilman has observed (1993b, 138, 144), in the case histories of both the Rat Man and Schreber Freud suppresses Jewish themes, although references to anti-Semitism surface in the process notes to his treatment of the Rat Man and in Schreber's *Memoirs of My Nervous Illness*. In every instance, Freud eschews an account of his patients' pathology in terms of the sociology of race in favor of the universalizing paradigm of the Oedipus complex. From this standpoint, the Oedipus complex comes into focus as an elaborate defensive formation designed to ward off Freud's anxieties not only about his relationship to his preoedipal mother but also about his Jewish identity.[25]

25. Gilman goes so far as to contend that Freud's misogyny is a derivative of his anxiety about Jewishness: "My task will be to show . . . the construction of specific concepts of gender onto which the anxiety about the Jew's body and mind (and, directly, Freud's own body and mind) are displaced" (1993b, 11). Although Jewish identity obviously touched Freud directly in a way that femininity did not, I would argue that race and gender were for him reciprocally reinforcing categories rather than that gender was simply an epiphenomenon of race. Just as Freud's case histories leave aside Jewish issues, so too do they consistently minimize the role of the mother in favor of father-son dynamics. On Freud's attenuation in the Rat Man case of the emphasis given to his mother in the process notes, see Mahony (1986, 35-36). Still, when Freud writes a footnote to the Hans case that, "the little girl also possesses a little wiwimaker, which we call the clitoris, although it does not grow, but remains stunted" (*G.W.*, 7:249; *S.E.*, 10:12), it is doubtless relevant, as Gilman reminds us, that "the clitoris was known in the Viennese slang of the time simply as the 'Jew'" (1993b, 39). At least some of Freud's contempt for the clitoris seems to be due to its

I prefaced this rereading of Little Hans by suggesting that the Oedipus complex is liable to a critique from three converging angles—object relations theory, feminism, and race. Each of these critiques points up how Freud's normative construct causes him to turn a blind eye to issues and empirical data thrown into relief by alternative perspectives. Just as Jewish identity is conspicuous by its absence from the case of Little Hans, so too Freud's choice of a Greek hero as his paradigm of the human condition can be seen to be ideologically motivated. In a 1920 footnote to the *Three Essays on the Theory of Sexuality*, Freud avers that the Oedipus complex "has become the shibboleth that distinguishes the adherents of psycho-analysis from its opponents" (1905b, 226). Although meant to affirm the universality of the Oedipus complex, Freud's claim is ironically undermined by his use of the term "shibboleth." For his allusion to the story, recounted in chapter 12 of Judges, of how the men of Gilead exposed the deceit of the Ephramites by their inability to pronounce a Hebrew word reinscribes the repressed theme of Jewish difference. As Gilman has pointed out, "no Jew haunts the literature or culture of classical Greece" (1993a, 110). In his letter to Fliess of October 15, 1897, Freud called his insight into *Oedipus Rex* his "single idea of general value" (Masson 1985, 272). He thereby sought to persuade himself (and soon the world) that what had shaped his destiny was not the stigma of difference but the common lot of humanity. But if the Oedipus complex is a "shibboleth," it cannot efface the scar of circumcision that distinguishes the Jew from the Gentile.

Just as, with respect to race, the Oedipus complex provides a refuge from Jewishness, so too on the axis of gender it functions as a bulwark against the realm of the mothers. Thus, when Freud writes that "this early, pre-Oedipus phase in girls comes to us as a surprise, like the discovery, in another field, of the Minoan-Mycenean civilization behind the civilization of Greece" (1931, 226), his archeological metaphor defines early female sexuality not as classical but as archaic. Rather than between Hellenism and Hebraism, Freud's opposition here is between what is Greek and "Minoan-Mycenean," but in both instances the defensive function of his promulgation of the Oedipus complex is shown by its pairing with a culture that is not classically Greek.

Finally, object relations theory, which in its non-Kleinian form highlights the influence of external reality on the inner world, may remind us

---

functioning as a surrogate for that other "stunted" appendage, the circumcised Jewish penis.

of the homosexual rape committed by Laius on Chrysippus, the son of Pelops, prior to the birth of Oedipus. This sexual assault on a child belongs to the ancient storehouse of Theban legends, but goes unmentioned by Sophocles in *Oedipus Rex*, just as its implications are not addressed in Freud's formulation of the Oedipus complex in the wake of his abandonment of the theory of paternal seduction as the cause of neurosis (Balmary 1979). In *Freud and Oedipus*, I adduced this shared rejection of the notion of an inherited curse to argue that Freud, like Sophocles, reconceives the Oedipus myth "from the point of view of the son as a tragedy of self-knowledge" (1987, 255). Although I continue to think that the hermeneutic circles of both Freud and Sophocles have much to teach us, I would now want to stress that there is also a cost to Freud's neglect of race, gender, and cultural factors, as exemplified by his occlusion of familial dynamics in the case of Little Hans.

In his address to the B'nai B'rith—the name of which means "sons of the Covenant"—Freud declared that to be Jewish meant for him partaking of "many obscure emotional forces, which were the more powerful the less they could be expressed in words, as well as a clear consciousness of inner identity, the safe privacy of a common mental construction" (1926a, 274).[26] This passage retrospectively glosses his countertransference to Little Hans, which likewise depends on a "common mental construction" and is augmented by being relegated to a "safe privacy." In "The Future Prospects of Psycho-Analytic Therapy," Freud warns that "no psycho-analyst goes further than his own internal complexes and feelings permit" (1910b, 144–45); and in "Recommendations to Physicians Practising Psycho-Analysis," he adds that without the safeguard of personal analysis, one could "easily fall into the temptation of projecting outwards some of the peculiarities of his personality, which he has dimly perceived, into the field of science, as a theory having universal validity" (1912, 117). There could be no more telling indictments of his own failure in the case of Little Hans—a failure paradoxically born of Freud's con-

26. The final phrase reads in German: "*die Heimlichkeit der gleichen seelischen Identität*." The word "*Heimlichkeit*" evokes the theme of the uncanny. As Gilman remarks concerning the slang meaning of "the Jew" as the clitoris, "the essence of the Jewish body is too well known to be hidden and too well hidden to be known. It is 'canny' and 'uncanny' simultaneously" (1993b, 42). In "The Uncanny," Freud writes of the neurotic male's fear of the female genital organs: "This *unheimlich* place, however, is the entrance to the former *Heim* [home] of all human beings, to the place where everyone dwelt once upon a time and in the beginning" (1919b, 245). Once again, race and gender are intertwined in the discourse of the uncanny, and neither can be accorded primacy.

viction of his unqualified success. Despite his intellectual recognition of the dangers of countertransference, that is, Freud (who himself, of course, was never analyzed) in practice falls victim to them in exemplary fashion. If the consequence is to make the case of Little Hans not less but more enlightening and enthralling, it is because Freud's genius enables him to rise above the carpings of his detractors and even his own oedipal blindness.

4

The Incest Theme and the Oedipus Complex

I

The first three meetings of the Psychological Wednesday Society for which minutes are extant took place on October 10, 17, and 24, 1906. As early as 1902, Viennese physicians and other intellectuals interested in Freud's ideas had begun gathering for weekly discussions in his apartment at Berggasse 19. But not until 1906, with Otto Rank's appointment as salaried secretary to the group—an appointment that lasted until 1915, when World War I intervened—were the proceedings recorded in writing.

Rank's function at these October 1906 meetings was pivotal in two respects, for he not only transcribed them but also read the paper that was discussed. His three-part presentation, "The Incest Drama and Its Complications," outlined the ideas that he elaborated in his 1912 *magnum opus, The Incest Theme in Literature and Legend: Fundamentals of a Psychology of Literary Creation*, which appeared in English translation for the first time in 1992.[1]

1. Unfortunately, Gregory C. Richter's rendering of Rank's German text is often only approximate, and he was obliged to omit Rank's copious footnotes. In this chapter, all translations from *The Incest Theme* are my own, with page numbers of both the German and the English editions given parenthetically. Occasional references to Rank's re-

Beyond Rank's double function as speaker and reporter, there is a symbolic appropriateness in the fact that the minutes of the Psychological Wednesday Society should begin with a sketch of *The Incest Theme*. During the period 1906–1912, the psychoanalytic movement grew to maturity. In 1908 the group to which Rank delivered his ideas was renamed the Vienna Psychoanalytic Society; in 1910 its meetings ceased to take place in Freud's apartment. In the same year, in the aftermath of the Nuremberg Congress, the International Psychoanalytic Association was founded, with Jung as president. After the adjournment of the Nuremberg Congress, Freud wrote to Ferenczi on April 3, 1910: "The infancy of our movement has ended with the Nuremberg *Reichstag*; that is my impression. I hope that a rich and beautiful youth is now coming" (Brabant, Falzeder, Giampieri-Deutsch 1993, 156).

By virtue of its existence in preliminary and final form at either end of the 1906–1912 period, Rank's work frames the years in question. It thus recapitulates, as it were, the emergence of the Oedipus complex as the touchstone of psychoanalytic truth. As Rank summarizes his main thesis, "the incest fantasy is not simply the 'nuclear complex of neurosis,'" which "dominates the unconscious psychic life of the normal person and decisively determines his social and erotic orientation in life," it is also "of surpassing importance in the psychic life of the creative writer" (1912, 13; 1992, 12). Not surprisingly, Rank begins his opening chapter, "The Individual Roots of the Incest Fantasy," by appealing to Freud's revelations in *The Interpretation of Dreams* about the "regular impact of sexuality on the child's relationship to its parents," and then immediately invokes the case of Little Hans as having confirmed these hypotheses in "the most brilliant fashion" (1912, 25–26; 1992, 21–22).

In a valuable study, John Forrester (1980, 84–96) has documented how painstakingly Freud arrived at his conception of the Oedipus complex, which permitted him to integrate such assorted themes as infantile sexuality, generational conflicts, the family romance, Jung's idea of a "complex" derived from word association experiments, and the triangular relation between a child and its parents into a single comprehensive explanatory schema. As I have noted in the preceding chapter, moreover, the term did not appear in Freud's writings until "A Special Type of Choice of Object Made by Men" (1910c). Challenging received accounts of Freud's career, Forrester argues that he "did *not* discover the Oedipus

---

vised 1926 edition of the work are also my translation, with page references in parentheses.

complex *as such* during his self-analysis. . . . Rather, he discovered oedipal impulses. If we mean by the Oedipus complex the nucleus or core of a neurosis, then it seems clear that Freud did not establish this until the period 1908–10" (1980, 232–19).

Building on Forrester's work, John Kerr (1988, 25–30) has charted the evolution of Freud's belief in a "nuclear complex" (*Kernkomplex*) of the neuroses. As Kerr shows, it was again only gradually that the "nuclear complex" became synonymous with the Oedipus complex, so that Freud could declare in *Totem and Taboo*, "we have arrived at the point of regarding a child's relation to his parents, dominated as it is by incestuous longings, as the nuclear complex of neurosis" (1912–13, 17). Kerr points out that Freud's first reference to the "nuclear complex," in a letter to Jung of December 11, 1908, occurs in connection not with Oedipus but with the altogether different notion of a "poisoning complex": "I am so obsessed by the idea of a nuclear complex in neuroses such as is at the heart of the case of Little Herbert [Hans] that I cannot make any headway. A recent observation tempted me to trace the poisoning complex, when it is present, back to the infant's interpretation of the mother's morning sickness" (McGuire 1974, 186). Kerr links Freud's interest in the poisoning complex—a bewildered child's inference that sexual intercourse has made his pregnant mother sick—to Freud's tenaciously held belief that libido would prove to be a toxic chemical process located in the brain.

The historical inquiries of Forrester and Kerr complicate the traditional narratives of Freud's career—such as my own in *Freud and Oedipus* (1987)—which stress his abandonment of the seduction theory in September 1897 as a pivotal moment in his intellectual development, but they do not seriously undermine them. (As I argued in my readings of the Little Hans case, the Oedipus complex can be seen in contemporary terms as a defensive formation, but that issue is not at stake here.) In *An Autobiographical Study*, Freud stated that "the ubiquity of [the Oedipus complex] gradually dawned on me" (1925a, 63), and the labors of the revisionist historians simply corroborate this retrospective realization.

Although the Oedipus complex did not spring fully armed from Freud's head, a chain of references in his writings beginning with the section on "Typical Dreams" in *The Interpretation of Dreams*—itself a public reformulation of remarks in his letter to Fliess of October 15, 1897—attests that Freud associated the incest theme with Oedipus from the time of his self-analysis. In *Three Essays on the Theory of Sexuality*, he affirms: "Among these [infantile] tendencies the first place is taken with uniform frequency by the child's sexual impulses towards his parents, which are as a rule already differentiated owing to the attraction of the opposite sex—the son being drawn towards his mother and the daughter towards her father." A footnote directs the reader "to my remarks in *The Interpretation of Dreams* on the inevitability of fate in the fable of Oedipus" (1905b, 227). Similarly, Freud alludes to both *The Interpretation of Dreams* and the *Three Essays* in the Dora case:

> I have shown at length elsewhere at what an early age sexual attraction makes itself felt between parents and children, and I have explained that the myth of Oedipus is probably to be regarded as a poetical rendering of what is typical in these relations. Distinct traces are probably to be found in most people of early partiality of this kind—on the part of a daughter for her father, or on the part of a son for his mother; but it must be assumed to be more intense from the very first in the case of those children whose constitution marks them down for a neurosis, who develop prematurely and have a strong craving for love. (1905a, 56)

In the case of Little Hans, as we saw in the previous chapter, Freud again looks back to his two seminal works in a recasting of the foregoing passage from the Dora case: "In his attitude toward his father and his mother Hans confirms in the most concrete and uncompromising manner what I have said in my *Interpretation of Dreams* and my *Three Essays* with regard to the sexual relations of a child to his parents. Hans really was a little Oedipus who wanted to have his father 'out of the way,' to get rid of him, so that he might be alone with his beautiful mother and sleep with her" (1909a, 111). And though he does not mention Oedipus by name in the case of the Rat Man, Freud defines "*the nuclear complex of the neuroses*" as "the complex which comprises the child's earliest impulses, alike tender and hostile, towards its parents and brothers and sisters" (1909b, 208). He remarks of his obsessive patient: "There can be no question that there was something in the sphere of sexuality that stood between the father and the son, and that the father had come into some sort of opposition to the son's prematurely developed erotic life. Several years after his father's death, the first time he experienced the pleasurable sensations of copulation, an idea sprang into his mind: 'This is glorious! One might murder one's father for this!'" (201).

When one reads these excerpts from Freud's writings published between 1905 and 1909, it becomes clear that the Oedipus myth never had a serious rival as an explanatory paradigm. The passages from the two later case histories directly refute Forrester's contention that in 1909 "Freud and his co-workers were not particularly concerned with the triadic relation of father, mother, and child" (1980, 89). With commendable honesty, Kerr concedes that the poisoning complex "was not destined for great things in the evolution of psychoanalysis" and that it was "one of the few ideas that Freud seems simply to have discarded altogether" (1988, 28–29).[2]

Thus, Oedipus inheres in the very origins of psychoanalysis. The words of Freud's famous letter to Fliess of October 15, 1897, are characteristically hyperbolical: "A single idea of general value dawned on me. I have found, in my own case too, being in love with my mother and jealousy of my father, and I now consider it a universal event in early childhood. . . . If this is so, we can understand the gripping power of *Oedipus Rex*" (Masson 1985, 272). He omits the first person in *The Interpretation of Dreams*, but his rhetoric is no less sweeping: "It is the fate of all of us, perhaps, to direct our first sexual impulse towards our mother and our first hatred and our first murderous wish against our father. Our dreams convince us that this is so" (1900, 262). Since Freud in 1897 had already postulated the oedipal paradigm to be his "single idea of general value" and a "universal event," when in 1910 he coined the term "Oedipus complex" and two years later proclaimed it to be the "nuclear complex," he was simply raising the stakes on the theoretical wager he had made in the wake of his abandonment of the seduction theory. In psychoanalytic terms, Freud's progression from the letter to Fliess to *Totem and Taboo* exemplifies the principle of deferred action, according to which later events retroactively complete the meanings of earlier ones, but the two cannot be understood independently of one another.

Freud's preoccupation with the Oedipus myth forms the backdrop to Rank's achievement in *The Incest Theme*. Rank's trajectory from his 1906 presentations to the Vienna Psychoanalytic Society to his 1912 publication of the completed work parallels Freud's odyssey and forms an integral subplot to the history of psychoanalysis during this period. In his comments on Rank's first talk, Freud criticized the lack of clarity in the

2. Although set aside without ever having been put into print by Freud, the idea was independently rehabilitated by Groddeck, who argued that the vomiting of pregnant women expresses "a desire on the part of the It to get rid of something inside it, something poisonous," and that "conception is often seen as a poisoning and treated as such by the unconscious" (1920, 148).

organization and proposed: "Oedipus should be presented as the core [*Kern*] and model; then the one tried and tested method of presentation would be on the one hand to group the material around this core, and on the other, by developing a series, to follow the theme from its core to its further ramifications" (Nunberg and Federn 1962, 10). In the earliest recorded meeting of the Vienna Psychoanalytic Society, Freud heralds his search for a nuclear complex, and does so in connection with Oedipus.[3] That Rank took Freud's strictures to heart is clear from *The Incest Theme*, not only in the introductory passage I have already quoted but also in the conclusion, where he reaffirms that "the incest complex with all its manifold aspects, hidden sides, and derivatives represents the nuclear complex of neuroses as well as of the literary creative compulsion" (1912, 681–82; 1992, 570).

Rank's relationship to Freud is triangulated by Jung, who in 1912 published *Wandlungen und Symbole der Libido* (*Transformations and Symbols of the Libido*), translated into English in 1916 as *Psychology of the Unconscious*. Not only were *Transformations and Symbols* and *The Incest Theme* published in the same year, but the two works mirror each other in that they approach the problems of incest and libido from antithetical vantage points. Jung's work announces his dissatisfaction with Freud's system; Rank's champions Freudian orthodoxy. As Jung wrote to Freud on August 2, 1912, upon receiving Rank's book: "It is a very distinguished piece of work and will make a big impression. But, as you know, I am not in agreement with his theoretical position on the incest problem. The salient fact is simply the regressive movement of the libido and not the mother" (McGuire 1974, 512).

This doubling between Jung and Rank is redoubled, since each published a revised edition of his landmark book. The second edition of *The Incest Theme* appeared in 1926; Jung reissued his treatise, under the title *Symbols of Transformation*, in 1952. Both later editions reflect the changes in their authors' relationship to Freud.[4] A distillation of Jung's mature

3. The English edition of the *Minutes* ascribes to Eduard Hitschmann the comment that Rank's paper is "no more than a rather superfluous extension of Freud's discovery of the Oedipus complex" (Nunberg and Federn 1962, 9). But this is an anachronistic mistranslation, since Freud did not begin using the term "Oedipus complex" until several years later. In the original German, Hitschmann refers simply to "*der von Freud aufgedeckten Tatsache (Ödipus)*," that is, "the fact uncovered by Freud (Oedipus)" (Nunberg and Federn 1976, 9).

4. In addition to the 1926 edition of *The Incest Theme*, a further revised French translation of the work appeared in 1934. The Otto Rank collection in Columbia University's

thought, *Symbols of Transformation* is implacably anti-psychoanalytic. By contrast, the second edition of *The Incest Theme* stems from the period between 1924 and 1927, after Rank had broken with Freud over the crisis precipitated by *The Trauma of Birth* (1924e) but still continued to regard himself as a psychoanalyst. Thus, whereas in Jung's case the first edition is transitional and the second definitive, for Rank the reverse is true. Still, the existence of revised editions testifies to the importance attached by both authors to the works in question, and a comprehensive comparative reading would require a scrutiny of the disparities between the two versions of each.

I cannot pause to consider Jung's modifications here, and even Rank's can be only cursorily assessed. But it surely bears mentioning that both occurrences of the phrase "nuclear complex" I have cited from the 1912 edition of *The Incest Theme* (1912, 13, 681–82; 1992, 12, 570) are eliminated in the 1926 edition (19, 623). In *The Trauma of Birth*, by contrast, Rank refers to the disturbance of the "blessed peace" enjoyed by the fetus in its mother's womb by the penis during intercourse as the "nuclear complex of the neuroses," of which the later Oedipus complex is merely the "psychosexual elaboration" (1924e, 194). He thereby displaces Freud's oedipal paradigm from its position of primacy in favor of the primordial mother-child relationship. The recently elaborated notion of the birth trauma, however, receives only two passing glances in the 1926 *Incest Theme*. First, Rank claims that the child's "original bodily relationship to the mother" is the "deepest biological source" of its love for its parents (1926a, 35; cf. 1912, 27; 1992, 23). Second, he writes of Cronus's castration of his father Uranus during intercourse that "besides the sexual rivalry over the mother, we must discern as well its previous infantile stage, namely separation, or, if one may so call it, 'castration' from the mother, whose root I have shown to be the actual separation from the mother in birth" (1926a, 277–78; cf. 1912, 287; 1992, 231–32). Although he does not succeed in fully integrating the birth trauma into the revised *Incest Theme*, by depicting castration as a form of separation, Rank signals the shift in focus from oedipal to preoedipal issues that characterizes his 1924–1927 period.

The intertwining of the fates of Rank and Jung culminates in their roles as psychoanalytic apostates. In the *New Introductory Lectures* Freud

---

Butler Library contains a final shorter manuscript version, as well as an English translation by George Wilbur entitled *The Incest-Motif in Poetry and Saga: An Anthropological Study of Literature*.

contemplates the schisms that have taken place in psychoanalysis: "Suppose, for instance, that an analyst attaches little value to the influence of the patient's personal past and looks for the causation of neuroses exclusively in present-day motives and in expectations of the future. . . . We for our part will then say: 'This may be a school of wisdom; but it is no longer analysis.' Or someone else may arrive at the view that the experience of anxiety at birth sows the seed of all later neurotic disturbances" (1933a, 143). These unnamed heretics are readily identifiable as Jung and Rank, since the former slights "the influence of the patient's personal past" by his doctrine of the collective unconscious, while the latter is synonymous with the birth trauma. Although they "start from diametrically opposed premisses," Freud adds, they share the characteristic that "each of them takes hold of one fragment out of the wealth of themes in psychoanalysis and makes itself independent on the basis of this seizure" (143–44).

Characteristically, Freud seeks to exonerate himself of any responsibility for the ruptures in the psychoanalytic movement by claiming that they were simply a series of partings that became inevitable when theoretical differences became intolerable. To the extent that "strong emotional factors" were involved, he imputes them not to himself but to his opponents, who (with the exception of Wilhelm Stekel) "excluded themselves" because they found it difficult "to fit themselves in with others or to subordinate themselves" (143–44). Freud's polemic is a tour de force, but it serves a defensive function, and his portraits of Jung and Rank show for whom he reserved his greatest scorn.

Freud's assimilation of Jung and Rank as dissidents was taken over by Jones in his biography of Freud. Indeed, Jones maintains that this parallel is in one important respect unfair to Jung: "The outstanding difference between the two cases is of course that Jung was not afflicted by any of the mental trouble that wrecked Rank and so was able to pursue an unusually productive and fruitful life" (1957, 77). Jones's depiction of Rank (as well as Ferenczi) is prejudiced in the extreme, for though Rank did exhibit manic-depressive tendencies, particularly at the time of his conflict with Freud and in his relationship with Anaïs Nin, he was never "wrecked" and he retained the productivity of genius until his death in 1939 at age fifty-five.[5]

5. The distortion in Jones's portrait of Rank has been trenchantly exposed by Lieberman (1985, xxxi–xxxiii, 400–401). I return to the question of Rank's possible mental illness in the next chapter.

Despite Jones's personal animus, however, his assimilation of Rank to Jung remains valid in the intellectual sphere. As I have contended in *The Psychoanalytic Vocation*, although Rank's early thought was antithetical to Jung's, by the end of his career his espousal of "will therapy" did not prevent him from embracing many Jungian views (1991, 48–50).[6] As late as *The Trauma of Birth*, Rank attacked Jung for slighting sexuality (1924e, 27), instancing the passage in *Transformations and Symbols* where Jung asserts of the longing to return to the mother's womb: "It is not incestuous cohabitation which is desired, but the rebirth. . . . Thus the libido becomes *spiritualized in an imperceptible manner*" (1912, 251). Six years later, however, Rank reverses himself and affirms in *Psychology and the Soul*: "Symbolic and anxiety dreams . . . can be understood only in relation to that 'unconscious' which never becomes conscious, and which Jung has properly called 'collective' because of its identity with the spiritual. The typical sexual symbols of serpent, mouse, and bird originally had spiritual meanings" (1930a, 126). Confirming his conversion to the doctrine of a "collective" unconscious replete with "spiritual" meanings, Rank in *Art and Artist* takes aim at Freud's "concrete" view of the mother and the birth trauma, which he now disdains "only as typical and ideological," and approvingly quotes *Transformations and Symbols* on "the symbolic significance of the mother" (1932, 378). Thus, in his final phase, Rank repudiates psychoanalysis and his own earlier work in *The Incest Theme* while endorsing Jung's critique that "the salient fact is simply the regressive movement of the libido and not the mother."

Like Jung, Adler served as a mediator between Rank and Freud. Unlike Jung, however, who lived in Zurich, both Adler and Rank belonged to Freud's circle in Vienna. In an excellent study, Paul Stepansky has warned against reading Adler's place in the early history of psychoanalysis from the anachronistic standpoint of his 1911 break with Freud. From 1906 to 1910, Adler was a leading member of the Vienna Psychoanalytic Society whose "emphasis on the psychological repercussions of organ inferiority was neither exceptional nor controversial" and whose contri-

6. Robert Kramer (Rank 1996, 225*n*5) has objected to my comparison of Rank's later views with Jung's, but Rank himself was the first to draw this analogy. That Rank, despite being a prolific author, can in his later years justly be termed anti-intellectual is borne out by the very passage Kramer adduces from *Will Therapy* to argue the opposite, since in it Rank states that intellect must be placed "at the service of the will" (1929–31, 177). As he told Anaïs Nin, "'You will be able to make a better synthesis of my philosophy than anyone, because you do not intellectualize'" (Nin 1992, 344).

butions "were generally welcomed for the clarifying connections they provided between clinical medicine and psychoanalysis" (1983, 104). Since Adler's views remained largely unchanged during the years of his association with Freud, Stepansky persuasively suggests that the reasons for his ouster in 1911 were not intellectual but political. After the Nuremberg Congress and the founding of the International Psychoanalytic Association, Freud's heightened emphasis on ideological purity in the psychoanalytic movement and confidence that its future rested with Jung caused him to become intolerant of diversity among his Viennese followers and to "reinterpret the status of his own prior reservations about Adler's theories with a view to ending Adler's active collaboration" (136).

Stepansky (91–92) adduces as the best example of Adler's respected position during the earlier, open-ended years of the Vienna Psychoanalytic Society Rank's attempt on March 4, 1908, to prove that "the inferiority of Schiller's eyes" was "one of the roots of his Tell figure by referring to the myth of the blind archer and to some characteristic passages in the Wilhelm Tell drama" (Nunberg and Federn 1962, 341). Ironically, several members of the group who subsequently sided with Adler against Freud found greatest fault with Rank's presentation. Stekel complained that "the continuous recourse to the doctrine of inferiority has by now become painful"; Eduard Hitschmann agreed that Rank's explanation was "paradoxical and forced," with inferiority "dragged in by the hair." Freud, in contrast, came to Rank's defense and pronounced his exegesis "a particularly beautiful mythological confirmation of Adler's principle and secure as are few interpretations" (341–43).

Like Rank's three-part 1906 paper, his 1908 presentation shows *The Incest Theme* in the making. His Adlerian reading of *Wilhelm Tell* was incorporated into the published text (1912, 115–18; 1992, 88–91). Rank argues that the theme of blindness is displaced from the shooter Tell to his son Walter, who refuses to be blindfolded, although Tell's own eyes are overcome with dizziness at the moment of shooting. He interweaves biographical evidence of defects in Schiller's eyesight with the etymological detail that the name Schiller, given to the poet's ancestors, is derived from the verb "*schielen*" (to squint). Here Rank's 1912 edition reflects the ecumenical spirit that prevailed through 1910 in the Vienna Psychoanalytic Society. Elsewhere, however, Rank flies his Freudian colors by discounting an Adlerian explanation of sibling love in Shelley and Byron in terms of "masculine protest" (1912, 542; 1992, 447). This polemic was deleted from the 1926 edition of *The Incest*

Theme (514), when Rank no longer sought to cast himself as Freud's disciple.

Stepansky's analysis reveals that the politics of the international psychoanalytic movement "provided a structural foundation for the crystallization of rival 'Freudian' and 'Adlerian' conflict groups within the Viennese psychoanalytic community" and that Adler's ensuing departure from the group "was the product of a premeditated assault engineered entirely by Freud" (1983, 144, 146). Its upshot is to expose as disingenuous Freud's intertwined claims in the *New Introductory Lectures* that the rifts in the psychoanalytic movement were intellectual in origin, that his opponents' decisions to depart were voluntary, and that he himself was without responsibility for what occurred. On the contrary, as Stepansky points out, the pattern detectable in Freud's dealings with Adler emerges even more distinctly in his relationship with Jung. From his initial letters, Jung acknowledged his reservations about Freud's theory of sexuality. Freud, keen first to secure Jung as a convert and then to anoint him as his heir apparent, did not accept these qualms at face value, but "resorted to the wish-fulfilling prophecy that Jung's theoretical timidity would inevitably yield to the input of additional clinical experience" (177). Only after the rift between the two men became irrevocable did Jung's expanded definition of libido as general psychic energy, which followed consistently from his original premises and drew upon Freud's own analysis of paranoia in the Schreber case, retroactively receive its "deviant" stamp (177–78).

The same pattern of emotional reversal surfaces for a final time in Freud's rupture with Rank. To grasp the crisis surrounding *The Trauma of Birth* it is necessary to realize that Rank, like Jung a decade earlier, had reason to regard himself as Freud's probable heir. In a letter of August 4, 1922, Freud regrets that he had not encouraged Rank to study medicine, for he then would not "be in doubt as to whom I would leave the leading role in the psychoanalytic movement. As it now stands I cannot help but wish that Abraham's clarity and accuracy could be merged with Ferenczi's endowments and to it be given Jones's untiring pen" (quoted in Taft 1958, 77–78). Although Freud's tone is rueful, such praise sparked Rank's ambition, which burst into flame at the news of Freud's cancer in the spring of 1923.[7] Rank initially envisioned *The Trauma of Birth* as a capstone to the

---

7. According to Breger, "there was never any evidence to support" the allegation that Rank's revolt was "motivated by his unconscious reaction to Freud's cancer" (2000, 323),

psychoanalytic edifice with which he would simultaneously consummate Freud's ideas and stake his own claim to the throne. Only when Freud, heeding the warnings of Abraham and Jones, the conservative members of his inner circle, refused to bestow unqualified approbation did Rank manifest the negative side of his ambivalence and redefine his innovation as a birth trauma heralding his own intellectual independence.

Like his predecessors in Freud's disfavor, Rank had his quota of personal failings and must be apportioned some of the blame for the painful quarrels that took place. As in the cases of Adler and Jung, moreover, Rank's secession from Freud was in part a political drama in which events spun out of Freud's control. But the litany of broken friendships—including those with Breuer and Fliess in the 1890s—mandates the conclusion that their ultimate cause lies in Freud's early experiences and their effects on his unconscious mind. Hence, Peter Gay's contention that Freud "was not the victim of some obscure repetition compulsion" (1988, 242) must be dismissed as an idealization, and no more convincing than Freud's own apologia in the *New Introductory Lectures*. The triumph of psychoanalysis was also its tragedy.

2

In *On the History of the Psycho-Analytic Movement*, Freud wrote that "among the strictly scientific applications of analysis to literature Rank's exhaustive work on the theme of incest easily takes the first place" (1914a, 37). This verdict remains true today. In its encyclopedic erudition, interpretative brilliance, and theoretical cogency *The Incest Theme*

---

but I think that my case for this view (1991, 31–45) is compelling. Like Freud himself as a younger man, Rank combined an outward modesty—exemplified by his dedication of *The Trauma of Birth* to Freud, as a *birthday* present, no less—with overweening ambition. Even at the time, Freud was convinced that his cancer served as a catalyst for the conflict with Rank. As he wrote to Ferenczi on August 29, 1924, "under the influence of the analytic welling up of his material success and my threatening illness, a hitherto latent neurosis has gained mastery over him" (Falzeder and Brabant 2000, 167). He added on September 13: "I can only imagine that my apparently imminent demise uprooted him so, and that my recovery upset his calculations" (178). See also chapter 8, note 58 below, for Groddeck's (1926h) contemporaneous, albeit characteristically exaggerated, linking of Rank's challenge to the Oedipus complex as early as *The Trauma of Birth* to his learning of Freud's illness. Strikingly, Groddeck attributes Freud's recovery to the tonic effect of Rank's book.

in Literature and Legend is the greatest and most important single work of psychoanalytic literary criticism.

Rank's book belongs to the first dazzling efflorescence of psychoanalytic theory, before the turn toward analysis of the ego initiated by Freud in "On Narcissism" (1914b). It thus culminates the already substantial body of psychoanalytic writings on art and literature that had appeared by 1912. These include Freud's *Delusions and Dreams in Jensen's "Gradiva"* (1907a), "Creative Writers and Day-Dreaming" (1908a), and *Leonardo da Vinci and a Memory of His Childhood* (1910a), as well as Rank's own earlier publications—*The Artist* (1907), *The Myth of the Birth of the Hero* (1909), and *The Lohengrin Legend* (1911).[8] Other major works of applied analysis cited by Rank in *The Incest Theme* are Abraham's *Dreams and Myths* (1909), Jones's *The Problem of Hamlet and the Oedipus Complex* (1911), and the "pathographies" by Isidor Sadger.[9] Although Rank affirms in his preface that the "essential content" (1912, v; 1992, 1) of *The Incest Theme* was extant by the time of his presentations to the Vienna Psychoanalytic Society in 1906, the numerous references to later sources make clear that he must have been revising the book up to the last minute and that much of it was in fact written after that date.

Both psychoanalysis and literary criticism have undergone profound evolutions in the nine decades since Rank published his work. Object relations, Lacanianism, reader-response criticism, feminism, and deconstruction are among the movements that have changed the face of psychoanalytic and literary studies in the intervening years. But if these later developments point up limitations in Rank's perspective, or at least raise questions different from the ones he addressed, his work remains a classic, because it articulates with superlative rigor and consistency a theoretical position that will always have to be taken into account when literary issues are debated.

Rank's guiding premise is that since literary works are "the completely

8. *The Artist* was the manuscript that, in 1905, prompted Adler to introduce Rank to Freud; *The Lohengrin Legend* was Rank's Ph.D. dissertation at the University of Vienna. As Rose has documented (1998, 195n64), Rank's thesis was not the first but the second to employ a psychoanalytic methodology. Theodore Reik's study of Flaubert's *Temptation of St. Anthony* was submitted on July 10, 1911, and accepted on October 7, 1911. Rank's work on Lohengrin was submitted on June 3, 1912, and accepted on June 13, 1912.

9. Sadger's *From the Love-life of Nicholas Lenau* (1909), the monographs by Jones and Abraham, Freud's studies of Jensen and Leonardo, and Rank's *Myth of the Birth of the Hero* all originally appeared in Freud's series, *Schriften zur angewandten Seelenkunde* (*Papers on Applied Psychology*). Sadger also wrote pathographies of Conrad Ferdinand Meyer (1908) and Heinrich von Kleist (1910).

personal, individually determined achievements of a unique psychic life" (1912, 1; 1992, 3), it is legitimate to approach literature in biographical terms. Rank's focus is less on literary history than on the psychology of creativity, although he hopes to afford insight into the works he discusses. In framing the problem as he does, Rank adopts a position complementary to that of René Wellek and Austin Warren, who, despite their new critical preference for a purely "intrinsic" mode of literary analysis, concede that "there is use in biographical study" if it is borne in mind that "a work of art may rather embody the 'dream' of an author than his actual life, or it may be the 'mask,' the 'anti-self' behind which his real person is hiding, or it may be a picture of the life from which the author wants to escape" (1942, 78–79). By stressing the elements of fantasy, disguise, and frustration embodied in the work of art, moreover, Wellek and Warren actually vindicate the psychoanalytic tenets put forward by Freud in "Creative Writers and Day-Dreaming" that were expanded by Rank.

In his introduction, Rank situates Freud's understanding of literature in a historical context. He aligns Freud with Aristotle through the idea of catharsis (1912, 3–4; 1992, 5–6), citing Jacob Bernays's medical interpretation of the *Poetics* and an 1897 paper by Baron Alfred von Berger comparing Breuer and Freud's "cathartic method" of therapy in *Studies on Hysteria* (1895) to the cathartic effects of drama.[10] From the ancient distinction between imitation and inspiration, Rank moves to Nietzsche's opposition between the Apollonian and Dionysian elements in tragedy and to the psychology of literary creation advanced in 1887 by Wilhelm Dilthey. Rank lauds Dilthey as having been the first "to derive for the present an appropriately serviceable poetics, not through abstraction from exemplary works but rather from the continually validated laws of literary creativity" (1912, 5; 1992, 7). He sees Dilthey's project as brought to completion by his own investigation, which is able to delineate, "based on our deepened knowledge of unconscious psychic life, both the original content of creative fantasies, or at least of a group of them, as well as the mechanism of their inception and artistic transformation" (1912, 7; 1992, 8). Since Dilthey is the founder of modern hermeneutics, Rank's sketch of the intellectual antecedents of psycho-

---

10. Although Rank does not mention it, Jacob Bernays was the uncle of Freud's wife Martha. His medical exegesis of catharsis in the *Poetics* contested Lessing's moral interpretation (Worbs 1983, 320–33). In addition to Berger, the comparison between Aristotle and Freud was drawn by Hermann Bahr in *Dialogue on the Tragic* (1904).

analysis brings these two discourses of self-reflective inquiry into direct conjunction.

Rank's is primarily a psychology of literary creation, not literary effect. Unlike some fanciful contemporary reader-response critics, he does not suppose that the work is an invention of the reader nor does he substitute his own private associations for an analysis of the text. The role of the author is not symmetrical with that of the reader since he (Rank's examples are almost exclusively male), as the maker of the text, stands in a privileged relation to it. Still, Rank recognizes that Aristotle's doctrine of catharsis focuses on audience response, and he does not neglect issues of reception. Rank contends that the literary work arouses in its reader or spectator a milder version of the same emotions that animated its creator:

> The satisfied recipient of the work of art, who thus "likes" the work, experiences the same psychic impulses that drove the artist to create, and so also an analogous satisfaction. The only difference is that the artist must accomplish for himself the psychic work that makes possible the expression of these impulses, while he who enjoys the work of art, in whom these impulses are, by the way, counteracted by stronger (normal) inhibitions, permits the artist to accomplish this psychic expenditure also on his own behalf. (1912, 151; 1992, 119–20)

Accordingly, from "the freely inventing, self-creating writer to the unproductive spectator," there is an unbroken chain "of the same unconscious impulses and their satisfaction in the work of art" (1912, 152; 1992, 120). The continuity between the dynamics of creation and response is exemplified for Rank by translations and adaptations, in which the author, himself a reader, is drawn to his material out of psychological motives and then reshapes it in a subjectively determined way.

In common with Freud's other early followers, Rank takes for granted the universality of the findings of psychoanalysis. The creative works of diverse periods and cultures exhibit the same patterns because the psychic complexes that give rise to them "belong in principle to the uniform development of all humanity" (1912, 15; 1992, 14). What Rank says of Schiller's *Don Carlos* therefore holds true for all literary works: "the characters who make their appearance can from such a psychological standpoint be reduced in the first instance to only three—the writer-hero and his parents in their various attitudes and manifold relationships to the son" (1912, 60–61; 1992, 49). A corollary is that "the political drama has uninterruptedly been put forward as a façade for that of incest" (1912, 80; 1992, 63). Rank's belief in an essential human nature and the priority of psychological over political meanings may be unpopular in many quarters today, but it is far from having been discredited. Jung, too, emphasizes that "the human mind possesses general and typical modes of functioning" that "can easily produce in the most widely differing individuals ideas or combinations of ideas that are practically identical" (1952b, 313). But whereas Jung explains this uniformity by a theory of innate archetypes, Rank appeals to conditions of infancy and parent-child relationships grounded in lived experience.

Despite his concentration on typically recurring patterns, Rank possesses a model of historical change. In *The Interpretation of Dreams* Freud had famously contrasted *Oedipus Rex*, where "the child's wishful phantasy that underlies it is brought out into the open," with *Hamlet*, where "it remains repressed" and "we only learn of its existence from its inhibiting consequences," and accounted for this difference by "the secular advance of repression in the emotional life of mankind" (1900, 264). Rank endorses this theory of advancing repression in chapter 2 of *The Incest Theme*, where he nominates *Don Carlos*, in which the stepmother replaces the mother as the object of the son's desire and the father remains alive to bar their union, as a third in the series begun by *Oedipus Rex* and *Hamlet*.[11] Rank compares the continuous heightening of repression in culture as a whole to that in an individual writer, in whose composition of a given work, "from the first sketch to the final version, a gradual weakening and disguising of certain sexual themes can be discerned, such as we were able to detect in the general psychic developmental process" (1912, 68; 1992, 54).

As a theory of history, this model of progressive attenuation of an originally unrepressed incest fantasy leaves much to be desired. When, in discussing the three-generational sequence of filial rebellion by the Greek gods recounted in Hesiod's *Theogony*, Rank asserts that "the progress of sexual repression . . . can be fully equated with general cultural progress" (1912, 286; 1992, 230), it is not necessary to be a Marxist to agree that too many important social and economic factors are being

11. From the standpoint of what Freud would later call the negative Oedipus complex—the son's love for the father and hostility toward the mother—Rank sees in the matricide of Orestes "a more complete Hamlet-tragedy," with again the difference that Aeschylus's hero is able to "carry out what Hamlet . . . cannot without profound upheavals even dare to contemplate" (1912, 330; 1992, 266).

ignored. Moreover, Freud's assumption that *Oedipus Rex* depicts the fantasies of incest and patricide in unrepressed form is suspect, since Oedipus commits these deeds unwittingly. As Rank points out, "the first coherent mythological forms must already carry the stamp of repression," and such a "preliminary stage" can be said to have merely a "psychological" existence (1912, 165; 1992, 132–33).[12] Despite its conceptual limitations, however, Rank's schema proves to be of considerable heuristic value when applied to literature.

Rank devises brilliant classificatory typologies throughout *The Incest Theme*. He juxtaposes the "Carlos schema," in which the son passionately but hopelessly loves his stepmother, with the "Phaedra schema," in which the stepmother is spurned by the son whom she desires (1912, 120; 1992, 93). (A subcategory of the Phaedra schema is the Potiphar theme— the false accusation of the son by the father's wife—which "seeks on the one hand to realize the son's incest fantasy without reproach, while on the other it gives expression to the fear that the father's suspicion may have been aroused" [1912, 159; 1992, 127].) Schiller's play thus culminates the progression both from *Oedipus* to *Hamlet* and from Euripides's *Hippolytus* to Racine's *Phaedra*, since Carlos, like Hippolytus, dies through his father's wish and there is likewise an advance in repression from Euripides to Racine (1912, 156; 1992, 124). Schiller, moreover, translated *Phaedra* into German (1912, 150–51; 1992, 119). The thematic connection between Sophocles and Shakespeare had been canonized by Freud and Jones, but Rank is the first to integrate that between Euripides and Racine, which entails direct literary influence, into a psychoanalytic framework.

Rank's original presentations to the Psychological Wednesday Society treated the incestuous relationship between siblings separately from that

12. Freud's belief that the Oedipus myth depicts its underlying fantasies in undisguised form explains why he placed his discussion of it in the chapter on "Typical Dreams" in *The Interpretation of Dreams*, but it created a stumbling block for his expositors. To the question why dreams of incest and patricide should be exempted from the distortions of censorship, Abraham unconvincingly answers that since "we believe ourselves to be further removed from such wishes than from all others," the censorship is "unprepared for such enormities," and bewilderingly adds that the Oedipus legend is "very poor in symbolic means of expression" (1909, 161). Rank grants that patricidal wishes are disguised both in dream and myth, but claims that incest dreams are frequently undisguised because they are orgasmic, and hence "the tension of the present-day libido ruthlessly clears away the defenses" (1912, 258; 1992, 210). This, too, raises more questions than it answers. Are all incestuous dreams orgasmic? Are all orgasmic dreams incestuous? Are all orgasmic dreams undistorted?

between parents and children, and this organizational principle is preserved in the book. Its model lies in *The Interpretation of Dreams* where, in his elucidation of typical dreams, Freud first takes up "the child's death-wishes against his brothers and sisters" before turning to "dreams of the death of parents" (1900, 255–56). In 1912, Rank assumes that the sibling complex belongs "to a later stage and falls victim to a later thrust of repression" than the parental complex, and can be classified as a "subcategory" of the latter (1912, 444–45; 1992, 365). By 1926, however, Rank regards sibling relationships as belonging to a "pre-Oedipus situation"—a term of his own devising—in which an elder child's newly arrived brother or sister plays the role of the "disturbing third" in competition for the mother's attentions even before the father gains this significance (1926a, 407). Rank's comments on Eteokles and Polyneikes, the reciprocally fratricidal sons of Oedipus, exemplify the evolution of his views from 1912 to 1926. Whereas in 1912 Rank wrote that it was inevitable that one should find this "second level of the incest complex" in the Oedipus legend (1912, 586; 1992, 487), in 1926 he changed "second level" to "prior stage" (1926a, 460).

One of Rank's classifications for sibling incest is the "Ancestress schema," in which the protagonist combines hatred toward his father with love for his sister, although the identity of these characters is initially unknown (1912, 494; 1992, 405). Rank names this configuration after *The Ancestress*, the first play by the nineteenth-century Austrian dramatist, Franz Grillparzer. Rank's biographical analysis turns on the thesis that Grillparzer, who had no sister, defended himself against his incestuous desire for his mother by reversing his actual situation and creating a drama in which there is a real sister but an imaginary mother (the specter of the ancestress), although the images of the two women are confounded by the characters in the play as in Grillparzer's own fantasy (1912, 470; 1992, 385). In thus granting priority to fantasy over fact, Rank anticipates Wellek and Warren's recognition that "a work of art may rather embody the 'dream' of an author than his actual life."

Rank's discussion of Grillparzer has extensive ramifications for the history of psychoanalysis. Both in his letter to Fliess of October 15, 1897, and again in *The Interpretation of Dreams*, Freud adduces Grillparzer's *Ancestress* as an example of the modern "tragedy of fate" that fails to move its audience in the way that *Oedipus Rex* and *Hamlet* continue to do. *The Ancestress* was thus for Freud a defective counterpart to what *Don Carlos* became for Rank—a work to be set beside those of Sophocles and Shakespeare. Rank does not allude to Freud's low opinion of *The Ances-*

tress, but he would of course have been aware of it. (He notes that Grill-parzer always objected to the appellation "tragedian of fate" [1912, 474; 1992, 388].) Since Rank is at pains to show in chapter 22 that tragedies of fate—not merely Grillparzer's play, but the entire nineteenth-century genre—are structured by incestuous fantasies and defenses, his analysis of *The Ancestress* in *The Incest Theme* is implicitly an exercise in rehabilitation that mitigates Freud's disparagement.

Rank's chapter on Grillparzer concludes with an excursus concerning the playwright's insane younger brother Karl, who pled guilty in a Vienna court to a murder that he did not commit (1912, 485–93; 1992, 397–404). Franz Grillparzer wrote an official report that clarified his own role in his brother's behavior. In Rank's psychoanalytic interpretation, Karl's chief symptom—the fear that Franz would meet with an accident—concealed his repressed wishes for Franz's death and led him, out of unconscious feelings of self-reproach, to confess to murdering a journeyman who reminded him of his brother. The case of Karl Grill-parzer strikingly parallels that recounted by Freud in The *Interpretation of Dreams* of a young obsessional neurotic who was unable to leave his room out of a fear that he would kill everyone he met (1900, 260). As I have argued in *Freud and Oedipus* (1987, 65–75), this patient is one of two with whom Freud identified in the course of his discovery of the oedipal structure. That Freud was impressed by Rank's analysis of Karl Grill-parzer, which highlights the connection between insanity and artistic creativity in a single family, is evident from the minutes of the Vienna Psychoanalytic Society, where Freud singled it out for "special praise" (Nunberg and Federn 1962, 19).[13]

In plots structured by parental as well as by sibling incest, Rank distinguishes between *rivalry*, in which two men compete over one woman, and *double love*, in which one man is torn between two women (1912, 108, 507–8; 1992, 83, 418). (The same alternatives could also be contemplated from the female point of view.) Invoking Aristotle on the power of recognition scenes among family members in tragedy, Rank further contrasts those plots, like that of *Oedipus*, in which incest is committed by family members who are unaware of their relationship (or who discover their kinship in time to avoid consummation), with others in which the presumed blood relationship proves false, thus allowing the lovers to seal their heretofore forbidden union. Rank observes that the

---

13. The editors mistakenly assume that Freud commends Rank's analysis of Franz Grillparzer, and not of his insane brother Karl.

latter type of plot exhibits "a more complete, so to speak less guilt-ridden wish-fulfillment" than the former, since "the mechanism of the discovery of kinship, which originally served for defense, is here used in a more refined fashion to further a disguised accomplishment of incest" (1912, 519; 1992, 427).

All these typologies corroborate Rank's overarching hypothesis that the universal impulses of mental life generate "distinctive compromise formations whose brilliant two-sidedness is exhausted in a few stereotypical forms" (1912, 588; 1992, 489). Although Rank duly notes the presence of conscious influence whenever it occurs, he reverses the emphasis of most literary historians, who seek to explain a writer's use of a given motif by tracing its antecedents or its conventionality. For Rank, the subjective motives for this choice are rather the issue, since the writer "does not come to treat given material externally through borrowing or assimilation, but rather from a deep psychic need" (1912, 683; 1992, 571). Among the "stereotypical forms" to which Rank draws attention are those of lovers who die together, which is "a symbolic expression of sexual union influenced by defensive, guilt-conscious impulses" (1912, 130; 1992, 102); and reciprocal murder—such as that between Eteokles and Polyneikes—where again "besides the fulfillment of the wish for the brother's murder, the defense against it is simultaneously expressed in the form of the same punishment" (1912, 586; 1992, 487).

Rank's typology of literary motifs is empirically grounded, and even a skeptical reader can profit from it. But his theory constitutes a coherent whole and gains much of its power from the inferences and extrapolations that psychoanalytic principles permit him to make. For example, whenever an episode in a myth appears to be weakly motivated, Rank suggests that repressed meaning must be sought elsewhere in the narrative (1912, 320–21; 1992, 257). Yet another methodological principle—allied to his dubious notion of advancing repression in human culture, but not dependent on it—is that fragments and first drafts are more revealing psychologically than final versions, since they express the artist's underlying fantasy "in a much more undisguised, more complete manner" (1912, 579; 1992, 481). Above all, by presenting the Oedipus paradigm as the "core and model," as Freud had recommended, Rank is able to map the panorama of world literature with reference to its coordinates. This capacity for logical subordination forms a decisive contrast between Rank's psychoanalytic perspective and Jung's analytical psychology, which, in addition to ignoring individual determinants, discerns analogies between various archetypes, but has no means of deriving one manifestation from any other.

Rank's range of reference in *The Incest Theme* is so vast as to defy summation. It extends from crimes reported in the popular press to folktales to canonical works of European literature, though his major emphasis falls on classical mythology, the Bible, Shakespeare, Schiller, Goethe, Grillparzer, and Byron. An excellent specimen of Rank's interpretative technique is furnished by his exegesis of the story of Jacob in Genesis (1912, 297–302; 1992, 239–43). Focusing on Jacob's dream of wrestling with a mysterious stranger who blesses him and tells him his name is Israel, Rank notes elements in the dream that refer to Jacob's relationship with his brother Esau, with whom he had struggled even in the womb, and with his father Isaac, who had blessed him and asked his name, and argues that "the dream image unites brother, father, and God, all of whom are supposed to forgive Jacob and sanction his deed" (1912, 301; 1992, 242).

Although incest themes proliferate in both the Judeo-Christian and the classical traditions, Rank holds that the heightened degree of instinctual repression in Christianity "could be maintained only at the cost of a most luxuriously developed activity of fantasy" (1912, 336; 1992, 271). Hence the medieval fables of saints and martyrs reveal an admixture of sadistic and masochistic elements largely absent in antiquity. Like pagan gods, who are permitted to gratify the desires that individuals must renounce (1912, 277–78; 1992, 223–24), Christian heroes and heroines show the forbidden impulses of the populace in projected form, but with an exaggerated emphasis on "punishment and expiation" that allows the repentant sinner "to receive a correspondingly more profound divine grace" (1912, 337; 1992, 272). Rank interprets the Griselda legend, best known to English readers from Chaucer's "Clerk's Tale," as expressing the fantasy of "the father's second marriage with his own daughter, which, to be sure, in the traditions has already become a pseudo-marriage with the rationalized motivation of testing the fidelity of the wife, who is then herself, as it were in the daughter's place, married for a second time" (1912, 377–78; 1992, 308).

The Griselda legend, like that of Apollonius of Tyre used by Shakespeare in *Pericles*, turns on father-daughter incest. By contemporary feminist standards, Rank's attitude toward this second great constellation of cross-generational incest themes is at once benighted and enlightened. He observes that "as the fantasy formations of the mother complex stem from the jealous son . . . , so the fantasied substitute formations of the father-daughter complex do not emanate from the perspective of the young child, the daughter, as one would expect by analogy, but appear for the most part to be elaborated from the standpoint of the father." Deplorably, Rank seems to take this disparity for granted and therefore to portray it as inevitable: "Just as the man is the active one in wooing and procreation, so too mythic formations, religious creations, and artistic activity turn on the satisfaction and justification of male sexual fantasies" (1912, 368; 1992, 300).

If, however, Rank's diagnosis is regarded as descriptive rather than prescriptive, his male-centered perspective can be credited with drawing attention to an undeniable imbalance in the relations between the sexes.[14] A far greater proportion of Western literature has been written by men, and hence reflects masculine fantasies, than one might expect, given that girls and boys lead comparably active imaginative lives. Rank's most chauvinistic sentence, which refers to women as "less favored by nature and life" than men (1912, 368; 1992, 300), is deleted in the 1926 version (1926a, 337). Despite his attention to fantasy, Rank does not turn a blind eye to the tragic realities of sexual abuse and rape, pointing out that "incestuous relations between father and daughter (often stepdaughter), especially rape of the daughter, are numbered among the most frequent sexual crimes" (1912, 369; 1992, 301).

As in his discussion of mother-son incest, Rank discerns "a steadily increasing repression of the attraction between father and daughter, which expresses itself in the heightened obscurity and delicacy with which this incestuous relationship is represented" (1912, 405–6; 1992, 330). As his father-daughter equivalent to *Don Carlos*—a work in which the core fantasy has been thoroughly disguised—Rank (1912, 404–6; 1992, 329–30) selects Ibsen's *Rosmersholm*, the analysis of the incest theme in that modern tragedy being taken over, with due acknowledgment, by Freud in "Some Character Types Met with in Psycho-Analytic Work" (1916).

In assessing *The Incest Theme* from a feminist standpoint, it cannot be overlooked that virtually all the authors discussed by Rank are male. The travails of Schiller's sister, Christophine, are examined at some length (1912, 573–79; 1992, 476–81), but the only female writer to rate even a

14. For a feminist analysis of sex differences in the observance of the incest taboo, see Herman (1981). As Herman argues, "it is the operation of the incest barrier through the institutions of male dominance and the sexual division of labor . . . which determines the relative weakness of the barrier against father-daughter matings" (53).

perfunctory mention is the playwright Karoline von Günderode, who died in 1806 at the age of twenty-six (1912, 638–39; 1992, 532–33). Were *The Incest Theme* to be rewritten today, it would surely be necessary to expand Rank's canon to include female authors and to employ a psycho-analytic psychology that does not presuppose masculine criteria. But though Rank's work can be criticized for its androcentric bias, it would be a churlish feminism indeed that refused to profit from his dissection of the Western patriarchal tradition or assumed that women are ex-empted from incestuous fantasies because Oedipus is a male hero.

The Incest Theme contains a number of internal tensions or contradic-tions in its argument. In the first place, Rank affirms that, "as with the neurotic, the experiences of the creative writer must be considered in the interpretation" of his works (1912, 90; 1992, 70). However, as we have seen, he qualifies this assertion by remarking that "it is psychologically misguided to want to look for the corresponding real experience of every creative thematic formation, since it is a matter of the products of fantasy, to which experiences serve only as raw material subjected to the most extreme modifications" (1912, 121; 1992, 94).

Rank's juxtaposition of the artist and the neurotic points to a second, more profound contradiction than that concerning fantasy and experi-ence. On the one hand, he rejects Stekel's equation of art and neurosis: "rather, we should endeavor to keep hold of the one certain thing that we can say about this relation—namely, that the artist's achievement, which has a liberating effect for him while being highly valued by soci-ety, will always distinguish him from the neurotic's incapacity for achievement so sharply that even the innermost affinity of their precon-ditions can never efface this clearly visible boundary" (1912, 479; 1992, 393). On the other hand, Rank elsewhere blurs the distinction on which he here insists categorically: "the artist's symptomatology in the incest dramas indeed reveals that he has been unable to deal successfully, once and for all, with his incestuous impulses; and in life, he almost always loves 'unhappily'" (1912, 615; 1992, 513). Far from epitomizing psychic health, the writer "brings to representation all the possibilities of his own being, lying within him, through a sort of neurotic turning away from life" (1912, 682; 1992, 571).

Rank's third internal tension concerns his model of advancing sexual repression. Although his theory would predict the opposite, Rank ad-mits that "modern literature in fact is inclined to a far-reaching extent to the undisguised depiction of sexual, especially incestuous themes" (1912,

659; 1992, 549). His explanation is at best slippery. Because consciousness has advanced along with repression, he surmises, the impulses now being exhibited in art are under its control and hence continue to be suppressed, although they are no longer disguised.

These three examples of inconsistency are of qualitatively different orders. That concerning fantasy and experience is the least unsettling, since a psychoanalytic awareness of fantasy does not preclude an attentiveness to actual experiences; the influence of a writer's inner and outer worlds on the creative process is not called into doubt. That concerning art and neurosis is the least resolvable. Rank here addresses a conundrum that has been pondered from Plato and Aristotle to Edmund Wilson and Lionel Trilling, and to which no definitive solution can ever be found. Art is at once a sign of mental health and yet as inseparable from suffering as Milton's epic is from his blindness or the bow of Philoctetes is from his festering wound. Rank's self-contradiction on this point reflects his complexity as a thinker. The inconsistency concerning modern literature is the most debilitating. As already noted, Freud and Rank's theory of cultural progress is subverted by the presence of repression in *Oedipus Rex*, the paradigmatic ancient text, and Rank's confusion in trying to explain how sexual explicitness can coexist with heightened consciousness delivers the death blow to all but the most allegorical uses of this schema.

Rank's theory of history reflects the underlying ambivalence in his attitude toward art. In coming to praise creativity, Rank ends by burying it. He concludes *The Incest Theme*, as he did *The Artist*, by exhorting that "the artist, with his increased need for repression, must learn to overcome himself *consciously*, and thereby teach us to overcome him" (1912, 685; 1992, 573). The artist, in short—like Rank himself—must become a psychoanalyst. When this happens, contemporary literature, which "clings with astonishing conservatism to the tragic conflicts and solutions of Sophoclean Athens, will free itself from these primitive complexes as soon as the requisite spheres of consciousness are attained."

The fallacy in Rank's assumption that creativity could ever be rendered obsolete by advancing consciousness was pinpointed by Adolf Häutler in the discussion following the last of his three presentations in 1906 to the Psychological Wednesday Society. As Häutler objected: "So much will never become conscious as to impair a normal individual's power of imagination. Much will always remain obscure in the human mind, hence one of the driving forces of creative writing will never cease to exist; such an end could only come if all sexual energies were obliterated" (Nunberg and Federn 1962, 23). Rank's prediction of the end of art is thus a utopian (or dystopian) fantasy undercut by the logic of his own psychoanalytic position. Despite the allowances that must be made for cultural diversity, it can be safely assumed that human beings will not overcome their "primitive complexes," and the "tragic conflicts and solutions of Sophoclean Athens" continue to resonate even in our postmodern era.

In insisting that art is not a "psychic luxury," but rather "arises from the tormented compulsion of psychic self-preservation, which can be sustained only with the aid of the colossal compensations of fantasy" (1912, 647; 1992, 540), Rank is a scion of the Romantic tradition. Although he grants "how much more the 'how'—technique and design—is valued in art than the 'what'—the material" (1912, 649; 1992, 541), Rank's allegiance to Freudianism reduces creativity to an overly exuberant fantasy life stimulated by premature sexual arousal: "What the creative writer, at bottom, has in common with the neurotic is an inordinately strong sexual drive, precociously striving after activation and fantasy formation, as well as the powerful inhibitions required to dam it up, and which constitute the feeling of guilt" (1912, 485; 1992, 397).[15] (This passage was deleted from the 1926 edition [1926a, 543].) Despite his earlier protestations, Rank ultimately gives priority to content over form: "if one hears time and again that even such powerful repressed complexes do not make an artist in the absence of technical talent, there is even more truth in the reverse of this statement—namely, that an individual endowed with a talent for form, however complete it may be, remains nothing but a good craftsman unless he has psychic struggles and sorrows to depict and overcome with the help of his technique" (1912, 682; 1992, 570).

How much of Rank's psychoanalytic theory of art continues to speak to us today? To all but the most doctrinaire formalists or postmodernists, his guiding assumption that an artist's creative work has biographical roots should be self-evident. In my view, psychoanalytic crit-

15. Rank's comparison between artists and neurotics foreshadows his classificatory schema of normal, neurotic, and artistic types in *Art and Artist* (1932) and other post-psychoanalytic works. This adumbration is clearest in the last sentence of *The Incest Theme*, where Rank writes of unconscious infantile complexes: "the normal person is able to get them under control with relative smoothness, whereas the neurotic comes to grief over them, though he can under favorable circumstances learn to master them consciously with the help of psychoanalysis, just as the artist—again under favorable circumstances—unconsciously abreacts them" (1912, 685; 1992, 573).

icism must always be mindful of the subjective aspects of creativity, although it is possible to interpret works of art psychoanalytically (or to study the dynamics of aesthetic response) without reference to the author's life, just as one can have a biographical criticism that is not psychoanalytic.[16] Rank's further claim that "in comparison with childhood experiences and impressions and their unconscious memory traces and affects, to which no one has previously paid heed, all subsequent experiences come into consideration only as awakeners and revivers of those infantile experiences" (1912, 135; 1992, 106), although far more controversial, in my judgment still rings true. That experiences of early childhood exert a lasting influence on later life remains an indispensable cornerstone of psychoanalytic theory. The research of subsequent developmental psychologists, however, has extended the critical period well beyond Freud's "prehistoric" epoch before the age of three. As Bowlby writes, the hypothesis that "various forms of cognitive disturbance seen in children and also in later life are to be traced to influences acting initially during the pre-adolescent years is compatible with indications that during these years children's minds are especially sensitive to outside influences. . . . After a child has reached adolescence, clearly his vulnerability to such threats diminishes" (1985, 109).

No less incontestable scientifically is Rank's claim, also forcefully articulated in *The Myth of the Birth of the Hero*, that myths are *projective* phenomena, whose meanings must be sought not in the heavens but in the human psyche. Rank dryly observes: "If, for instance, one conceives of Oedipus as a sun-hero who murders the father who begat him, the darkness, and who shares his bed with his mother, the dawn, from whose womb he sprang forth, this explanation will perhaps suffice if one has modest expectations." However, he continues, "these ideas of incest with the mother and the slaying of the father arose from human life," and "the myth could never have been read off from the heavens in this human garb without there being a corresponding psychic idea . . . that may indeed already have been unconscious at the time the myth was formed" (1912, 278; 1992, 224). Although not written with Jung in mind, Rank's critique of those who accept the astral explanations of myth at face value attacks a stronghold of the latter's position in *Transformations*

16. For a systematic review and critique of psychoanalytic approaches to art, see Spitz (1985). In a later essay, Spitz (1989) points out that in *Art and Artist* Rank repudiates his own earlier position and assails any attempt to explain an artist's work biographically.

and Symbols. That Rank himself later came to share Jung's point of view is an irony that does not diminish the cogency of his argument or its value as an exemplary formulation of the psychoanalytic case.

Rank's outlook requires modification in light of contemporary psychoanalysis above all in his exclusive emphasis on the sexual wellsprings of artistic creativity. For Rank, as for Freud in "Creative Writers and Day-Dreaming," the artist seeks to reenact the ideal circumstances of his infantile erotic constellation, but the inevitable insufficiency of all later approximations causes him "to turn away disappointed from this experience and from reality in general." He then resorts to fantasy and "creates in his works the possibilities that reality has denied him and that, in a deeper sense, it can never grant him" (1912, 91; 1992, 71). The paradigm for art, even anterior to the daydream, is thus *masturbation*: "From these masturbation fantasies with their forbidden objects and severe self-reproaches and self-punishments, a broad path leads to artistic fantasy activity" (1912, 293; 1992, 236). As would have been true of any psychoanalytic work written during this period, Rank's model of the mind in *The Incest Theme* relies upon Freud's theory of the drives. From this standpoint, he maintains of the artist that "the tragic conflicts that he continually attempts in this fashion to resolve in his works simply correspond to his raging inner antagonism between repressed wishes and cultural demands, unconscious inclinations and their conscious adversary, in brief, the conflict between drive and repression, which Freud has formulated as the disharmony between the ego and sexuality" (1912, 683; 1992, 571).

Among theorists and practitioners of psychoanalysis today, however—at least those whose thought is informed by empirical research—a consensus has emerged that Freud's solipsistic drive theory must be rejected in favor of one that recognizes that the overriding need of human beings is not for sex but for *attachments*. The consequences of placing object-seeking in the forefront for the understanding of art are spelled out by Winnicott in *Playing and Reality* (1971b). The nub of the matter is that the prototype for aesthetic experience is no longer masturbation but *play*. This play takes place in what Winnicott terms a *potential space* between child and mother that is neither purely internal nor external and becomes filled with *transitional objects* that are paradoxically symbols of both separation and union. Play differs from masturbation in that it suspends somatic urges, which terminate the activity if they become too insistent. Winnicott's achievement, by contrast with Freud and Klein, is to have articulated a psychoanalytic account of art that respects its integrity as an autonomous human activity and does not reduce it to a sublimation of either sexual or aggressive drives.[17]

There are then two rival mainstream psychoanalytic paradigms for art—masturbation in drive theory, and play in object relations theory. Proponents of both traditions concur that the origins of art lie in childhood experience. Although relational theorists have dislodged the Oedipus complex from the center of the conceptual universe, incest is still, as John Forrester has observed, "the psychoanalytic theme par excellence" (1997, 83). Thus, the degree to which classical and contemporary outlooks are ultimately compatible remains an open question. On this score, as on others, to read *The Incest Theme in Literature and Legend* is to embark on a voyage of discovery.

17. For a more detailed exposition of Winnicott's aesthetics, see my introduction (1993a) to *Transitional Objects and Potential Spaces: Literary Uses of D. W. Winnicott*, as well as the essays by analysts and literary scholars gathered in that volume.

5

Rereading Rank

Unlike those who consider themselves Rankians, I have never been able to muster much enthusiasm for the writings of Rank's final period. If the prodigious labors during his first two decades in Freud's circle are limited by what can now be seen to be excessive orthodoxy, those of his final twelve years are, in my view, even more limited by his repudiation of the entire Freudian tradition. In particular, I regret that after 1927, when he began to espouse "will therapy," until his premature death in 1939, Rank cast aside both the concepts of the unconscious and of genetic explanation, two pillars of the psychoanalytic edifice that remain standing even after Freud's libido theory and his phallocentric construction of sexual difference have been shattered by the critiques of object relations theory and feminism, respectively.[1]

Thus, in proposing to reread Rank's work from the standpoint of contemporary psychoanalysis, I shall again concentrate, as I did in *The Psychoanalytic Vocation* (1991), on the brief interlude from 1924 to 1927—the *anni mirabiles* during which he became the first object relations

1. In *Will Therapy*, Rank categorically avers that "there is no use in searching out past events and experiences for the understanding of the present" (1929–31, 31); he alleges in *Truth and Reality* that "the whole of psychology becomes of necessity a psychology of consciousness" (1929, 25). The latter passage contradicts Kramer's (Rank 1996, 225n5) contention that Rank did not abandon the concept of the unconscious in his final period.

psychoanalyst.[2] During this transitional period after the schism precip-itated by *The Trauma of Birth*, Rank had freed himself of personal loy-alty to Freud but still conceived of his theoretical project as a revision rather than a renunciation of psychoanalysis. With this attitude, Rank achieved a delicate balance that he soon lost, and his example exerted no lasting influence; but it serves as a beacon for subsequent relational analysts.

Despite having initially made his reputation as a master of the appli-cations of psychoanalysis to literature and myth, when Rank returned to Vienna from Kraków as a married man at the close of World War I, he plunged into the practice of analytic therapy for the first time. This in turn led him to shift his attention to issues of theory and technique, a reorientation integral to his emergence as an original thinker. Simply to enumerate his publications from 1924 to 1927 conveys the magni-tude of his achievement during this span: *An Analysis of a Neurosis in Dreams* (1924b); *The Trauma of Birth* (1924e); *Sexuality and the Sense of Guilt* (1926b), consisting of five papers written from 1912 to 1923; the first volumes of both *Technique of Psychoanalysis* (1926c) and *Fundamen-tals of a Genetic Psychology* (1927a); and the many papers extant in Eng-lish edited by Robert Kramer under the title *A Psychology of Difference* (1996).[3]

In looking back at Rank from a contemporary perspective, I shall in-evitably be evaluating his work anachronistically. To the extent that my judgments will be critical, it might be objected that this is an unfair pro-cedure, since Rank cannot be expected to have foreseen all the paths taken by psychoanalysis in the more than six decades since his death. But if we are prepared to give Rank credit for the brilliance that made him in many respects ahead of his time, it is also legitimate to take him to task when he seems obtuse and wrongheaded. As is true of Freud or indeed any historical figure, the same hindsight that allows posterity to admire Rank's greatness also throws his defects into relief; and I mean it as a

2. My conception of Rank as an unacknowledged precursor of object relations theory, and of the years from 1924 and 1927 as his most important period, has received useful cor-roboration from Leitner (1997). Fogel (1993) has characterized Ferenczi and Rank's *The Development of Psychoanalysis* (1923) as marking a "transitional phase" between classical and contemporary conceptualizations of the psychoanalytic process, but he passes over Rank's contribution to this joint work.

3. Many of the papers in Kramer's collection are chapters in volume 1 of the *Genetic Psychology*. Unless otherwise noted, or no German original of the paper in question is ex-tant, all English translations of Rank's works in this chapter are my own.

sign of my respect for Rank that I subject his work to a scrutiny no less rigorous than that routinely given to Freud.

In rereading Rank, however, a problem arises that does not occur in the case of Freud, whose work falls readily into early, middle, and late phases, but nonetheless coheres as an organic whole. As I argued in *The Psychoanalytic Vocation* (1991, 46–47), Rank exhibits a self-imposed "devaluation" of his past following his break with Freud. In "The Psychology of the Poet," the final chapter of *The Don Juan Legend* (originally published as a paper in 1922), Rank writes: "whenever we find distinct periods in the work of a poet . . . a process of devaluation of the poet's previous ego ideal formation is at work" (1924a, 123). Rank reprinted this passage in the foreword to the 1925 edition of *The Artist*, where it becomes a self-conscious comment on his own development. Because Rank repudiated psychoanalysis, his later views are diametrically opposed to those of his Freudian period, and he can be quoted on both sides of any question. Although dyed-in-the-wool Rankians like to imagine that only the works of his final period express his true beliefs, this assumes that what comes later must supersede what precedes it, an unwarranted teleological bias. Given the impossibility of reconciling his pro-Freudian and anti-Freudian periods, it becomes less urgent to try to decide which of these is the "real" Rank than to recognize that his oscillation from one extreme to the other is itself a phenomenon demanding explanation.

The humpbacked shape of Rank's career raises the question of whether he might have been afflicted with manic-depressive illness. This thesis was first advanced publicly by Jones in his biography of Freud, where he alleged that both Rank and Ferenczi exhibited "psychotic manifestations" that "revealed themselves in, among other ways, a turning away from Freud and his doctrines" (1957, 45, 47). The notion that disagreement with Freud constitutes a symptom of psychosis is, of course, absurd if not itself delusional; and, with good reason, Rank's biographer, E. James Lieberman, has denounced Jones's tendency to use a diagnosis of mental illness as a stick with which to beat his opponents as a "libel" (1985, xxxi–xxxiii, 400–401).

But though Jones deserves to be reprehended for his *ad hominem* attacks, it would be a mistake to assume that his diagnosis of Rank is wholly unfounded. What chiefly lends credence to his assessment of Rank's "cyclothymia" is that it did not originate posthumously, but can rather be traced to contemporaneous observations by his closest colleagues. Perhaps the most telling document is Freud's letter to Ferenczi of March 15, 1920, in which he writes that "Rank, who is as well behaved as ever, does seem to me to be depressed and not properly capable of accomplishment. He is very probably a periodic" (Falzeder and Brabant 2000, 13). At this time, Freud was on the closest possible terms with Rank and thus had no motive to depict him in an unfavorable light. Similarly, Ferenczi wrote to Groddeck on April 18, 1925: "Rank is in a deep depression. Berlin [the center of his opponents] is *en vogue* [with Freud]" (Ferenczi and Groddeck 1982, 65). This was during the upheaval following *The Trauma of Birth*, but Ferenczi too had nothing to gain from slanting the truth in a private communication to his friend.[4]

In an effort to rebut Jones's account, Louis Breger has asserted that neither Jones nor Freud "had any contact with Rank after the final break, and those who did saw no signs of depression or mania" (2000, 323). But the second part of this statement is incorrect. Anaïs Nin, who was Rank's patient and lover during his years in Paris and New York, wrote in her journal on May 2, 1935, that a "black pall" had descended over Rank: "His depressions are terrible and like an animal's. He lies there sighing, collapsed, with an earth-colored face, with a breath like death" (1995, 79). What is more, before Rank's rupture with Freud, in a letter to Freud on September 29, 1924, Jones alludes to Rank's "manifest neurosis of 1913, which disappeared in the war" (Paskauskas 1993, 555). Jones goes on to refer to the return of Rank's "neurotic character" in the form of a "denial of the Oedipus complex." This can be dismissed as polemics; but the mention of Rank's prewar troubles—at which time, as Andrew Paskauskas informs us, he "appears to have been in the throes of

4. There is further testimony from less reliable sources. On September 8, 1925, Abraham wrote to Freud that Rank's behavior at the Bad Homburg Congress showed that he was "really ill" and in a "manic phase" (Freud and Abraham 1965, 393–94). On November 28, 1924, Freud informed Ferenczi that Rank had suddenly returned from Paris, "supposedly because it had occurred to him that he hadn't said good-bye to his wife tenderly enough, in reality because he is in a deep depression" (Falzeder and Brabant 2000, 189). And in an abject January 1925 *Rundbrief*, Rank himself explained that it had been impossible for him "to leave the Professor that way—to leave him in the lurch—as I was capable of it the first time in my manic condition, which, as a direct response to his illness, was supposed to spare me the grief over his loss" (200n4). Despite the animus of Abraham and Freud, as well as the collective pressure placed on Rank to bow to the diagnosis of his conduct as pathological, these imputations of Rank's manic-depressive illness are too numerous and too consistent to have had no basis in reality.

a deep depression . . . and was in fact considering a personal analysis with Jones" (556n4)—has the ring of truth.

To suggest that Rank suffered from manic-depressive illness is not to cast aspersions on his character. Both major depression and manic-depressive disorder are now thought to be organic conditions, and manic depression afflicts many highly creative people (Jamison 1993). Jones writes of the character of Hamlet that "the likeness to manic-depressive insanity, of which melancholia is now known to be but a part, is completed by the occurrence of attacks of great excitement that would nowadays be called 'hypomanic'" (1949, 75). Although it is only a conjecture, I suspect that Jones may have had Rank in mind when he drew his clinical picture of Shakespeare's hero, which would hardly be to Rank's discredit.

If Rank was indeed touched by the fire of manic depression, he must have known it better than anyone else. Any allusions to this condition in his writing thus take on covert autobiographical meaning. In *The Trauma of Birth*, Rank says that cyclothymia, "with its sudden changes from melancholy to mania, goes back entirely without mediation to the reproduction of sensations before and after the birth trauma in that the primal mechanism of the transformation from pleasure to pain at the loss of the first libido object, the separation from the mother's womb, is experienced anew" (1924e, 77). It is not necessary to agree with Rank that manic-depressive illness originates in the birth trauma to think that he here offers a veiled self-diagnosis. Similarly, in volume 1 of the *Genetic Psychology* he calls manic-depressive individuals "conspicuously egotistical types" who have "as a rule an extremely good memory, that is, in other words, they recall all painful experiences, instead of repressing the memory of them" (1927a, 158). Read in its historical context, I take this to be Rank's confession of his own egotism and inability to repress the "painful experience" of his rupture from Freud.

Beginning with Freud, psychoanalytic theorists have often written most perceptively when they were exploring their own pathologies, albeit in disguised form. Rank's reference to manic-depressive people as "conspicuously egotistical types" is no exception, though he gives no indication that he is being self-analytic. His belief that, after the departure of Jung, no one stood in the way of his becoming Freud's successor subtends a passage from the last chapter of *The Don Juan Legend*, which Rank reprinted in the 1925 foreword to *The Artist*:

Dissatisfied with the ideal of the group, [the poet] forms his own individual ideal in order to proffer it to the group, without whose recognition his creation remains very unsatisfactory. The impulse to his formation of an individual ideal obviously comes from a very strong narcissism, which prevents him from accepting the common ideal and makes it necessary for him to create an individual one. . . . In a psychological sense the poet thereby recreates the primal crime, for the new ideal which he has created is his own—it is himself in identification with the primal father. (1924a, 121)

Rank's account of the rebellious poet's "very strong narcissism" is another unsigned self-portrait. In *The Don Juan Legend*, moreover, Rank prophetically accounts for his offer of the "new ideal" of the birth trauma to the psychoanalytic horde as an "identification with the primal father" and an attempt to reenact Freud's "primal crime" by slaying his "common ideal" of the Oedipus complex.

That Rank perceived himself as a hero-poet is further attested by *The Trauma of Birth*, where he endorses Freud's hypothesis of the slaying of the primal father in *Totem and Taboo*, with the proviso that there is "always only one who can accomplish the primal deed, namely, the *youngest*, who had no successor with the mother" (1924e, 103). Rank was the youngest sibling not only in his family of origin, where he had a favored older brother (as well as a middle sister who died before his birth), but also in the psychoanalytic movement, where he was the youngest member of Freud's inner circle. (Freud was born in 1856; Groddeck in 1866; Ferenczi in 1873; and Rank in 1884.) Rank's insistence that the last-born child is the mother's favorite rectifies his disadvantaged position in both his natural and his adoptive families, promoting a hidden subjective agenda.

Frank Sulloway's research on birth order sheds further light on Rank's stratagems. As Sulloway convincingly shows with the aid of statistics, later-borns have a greater propensity to rebellion than do their elder siblings. In words that recall Rank's own in *The Trauma of Birth*, he concludes: "Last-borns fare better [than middle children] because they are the only member of the family to receive parental investment undiluted by the needs of a younger rival" (1996, 305). In contrast to Rank, Freud was his mother's first-born child; and Sulloway captures a crucial dynamic of their struggle when he generalizes: "The most tough-minded individuals are first-borns. Last-borns are militant, too, but for different reasons. Their militancy arises because they are daring, zealous, and liberal, not because they are particularly dominant or punitive (first-born traits)" (302).

The Trauma of Birth is a work in the great tradition of psychoanalytic speculation that includes *Totem and Taboo* and Ferenczi's *Thalassa*. Not only is *The Trauma of Birth* the book in which Rank's personal stakes were highest, it is also the one where both the strengths and the limitations of his thought are most conspicuous. Although its central thesis is farfetched, the book is by no means, as Marina Leitner has complained, "confusing and difficult to read" (1997, 44). On the contrary, Rank expounds his vision of the cosmic consequences of the birth trauma with clarity and tenacity in a series of concentrically expanding chapters.[5] Like Freud, Rank frequently manages to be at once profound and preposterous; and in this respect, as in others, *The Trauma of Birth* is quintessentially Rankian.

Coming now to the question of what is living and what is dead in Rank's psychoanalytic legacy, I cannot gainsay my conclusion that comparatively little has stood the test of time.[6] Although Rank's historical importance is incontestable and he deserves to be regarded as the first object relations psychoanalyst, Ferenczi has had a far greater impact on contemporary clinicians. Groddeck, if anything, has been even more neglected than Rank; but as I shall try to show in chapter 8, he, like Ferenczi, speaks to present concerns in a way that Rank does not.

To begin on the positive side of the ledger, Rank's enduring achievement seems to me to be twofold. First, in the domains of both theory and technique, he led the way in shifting the vector of psychoanalytic inquiry from the oedipal to the preoedipal realm and he rectified Freud's disproportionate stress on the father-child—indeed, father-son—relationship by foregrounding the mother-child bond. Second, in purely

5. In the original German text, all the chapter titles (after the introduction) have the three-word form of article, adjective, and feminine noun (e.g., "Die analytische Situation," "Die infantile Angst," etc.). This repetition drives home Rank's conviction of the proliferating ramifications of the birth trauma.

6. For an appreciation of Rank and Ferenczi as spokesmen for the "two complementary postulates of autonomy and mutuality," which together "represent the nucleus of relational theory," see Aron (1996, 159–87). Aron's treatment of Rank, however, is both more cursory and less critical than his treatment of Ferenczi. For the reasons set forth in this chapter, I believe Rank's view of human development, which Aron compares to that of Margaret Mahler, "from merger toward separation and individuation . . . culminating in the independence of self" (183), to be misguided in important respects. In an interview with me (2000, 49), Mary Salter Ainsworth offers a critique of Mahler's outlook from the standpoint of attachment theory.

human terms, more than anyone after Jung, Rank had the courage to risk opprobrium by defying Freud and taking him to task at once on intellectual and personal grounds. In his Introduction to volume 1 of the *Genetic Psychology*, he remarks that Freud's *Inhibitions, Symptoms and Anxiety* is "full of contradictions that go back primarily to his resistances against drawing the consequences of the way I have posed the problem," namely, "the enigmatic mechanism of the conversion of libido into anxiety" that underpins the libido theory (1927a, 32).[7] Sharpening the barb, he adds that if Freud finds himself in a quandary, "then his resistance against accepting the ideas of others, including his coworkers, is partly to blame" (33). In yet another incisive passage, Rank links Freud's occlusion of the role of the preoedipal mother to the misogyny in his account of sexual difference: "He has never seen the 'bad mother,' but rather only the later displacement onto the father, who consequently plays such a predominant role in his theory. The image of the bad mother has, however, been preserved in his estimation of woman, who was for him exclusively a passive object and 'castrated,' that is to say, inferior" (44).

Rank's public excoriation of Freud's defects contrasts with the inhibition that led Ferenczi to confine his recriminations to the pages of his *Clinical Diary*. Nonetheless, even Rank's writings from 1924 to 1927 are ultimately a disappointment. This is true above all because of his attitude toward the analytic situation. As Lewis Aron has contended, the paradigm shift brought about by relational theory owes less to its abandonment of the drive model and its uncovering of the preoedipal realm than to its "emphasis on the mutuality between patient and analyst in the psychoanalytic process" (1985, 123). Like Ferenczi and Groddeck, Rank achieved a breakthrough on the level of theory, but he remained dogmatic and inflexible in his clinical practice.[8]

In his papers on technique, written between 1912 and 1915, Freud notoriously likened the analyst to a surgeon. A principal function of this similitude was to deny the emotional bond between analyst and patient. In his definitive study of the vicissitudes of this metaphor in Freud's work, Paul Stepansky has demonstrated that, though he never renounced the comparison, Freud distanced himself from it following his

7. Rank's appraisal of *Inhibitions, Symptoms and Anxiety* appeared separately as a book review in *Mental Hygiene* (1927b). I discuss this text in greater detail in *The Psychoanalytic Vocation* (1991, 55–58).

8. In the works of his final period, Rank adopted a far more empathic and flexible stance; but his rejection of the unconscious and genetic explanation—as well as of a scientific outlook—limits their usefulness for other reasons.

own "surgical *annus horribilis*" of 1923 (1999, 148). As Stepansky notes, the "only bona fide transformation of Freud's surgical metaphor" (89) was accomplished by Ferenczi, who as early as 1919 urged the analyst to emulate the empathic obstetrician. In Ferenczi's words:

> The doctor's position in psychoanalytic treatment recalls in many ways that of the obstetrician, who also has to conduct himself as passively as possible, to content himself with the post of onlooker at a natural proceeding, but who must be at hand at the critical moment with the forceps in order to complete the act of parturition that is not progressing spontaneously. (1919, 182–83)

Ferenczi transmutes the surgical metaphor, countenancing the use of "forceps" or active intervention as a last resort, but for the most part exhorting the analyst to adopt a stance of wise passiveness.

Given Ferenczi's innovative thinking, it is disturbing to find Rank in the mid-1920s continuing to insist that the analyst should emulate the detached surgeon. Despite superficial similarities to Ferenczi's analogy to obstetrics, Rank's conviction that analysis entails a reenactment of the birth trauma retains the coldness and impersonality of Freud's surgical metaphor.[9] In Rank's view, the analyst's duty is to prepare the patient for "the surgical cutting of this psychological umbilical cord, with which the patient has hitherto always been burdened" (1924d, 74). Relying on Freud's precedent in the Wolf Man case, he seeks to achieve this goal by imposing a termination date for the treatment and then turning a deaf ear to the patient's cries of protest. In the *Technique of Psychoanalysis*, he proclaims it to be "the essential advantage of my conception that it gives the therapeutic intervention of the analyst a definite meaning and content, which can best be compared with the exactness of a surgical operation on a precisely specified location, namely, the pathologically altered" (1926c, 21). He elaborates: "Analysis is after all to be compared much less to a process of healing or restitution than to an operative procedure, which is to be accomplished as quickly as possible" (23).

9. Aron has contrasted Rank's view of the psychoanalytic process as one "in which patients create themselves anew with the help of the analyst, who serves as a midwife," with Freud's "portrayal of the analyst as a (presumably male) surgeon" (1996, 181). Although Rank compares the analyst to a midwife in *The Trauma of Birth*, he does so simply in order to argue that the analyst's intervention should be "not less active than that of the surgeon and have as its goal the dextrous freeing of the primal libido from its fixation" (1924e, 208). For Rank, the midwife's task is conceived entirely as one of cutting or severing, and is thus paradoxically identical to that of the surgeon.

Even when every allowance has made for hindsight, Rank's view of analysis as a surgical procedure to be dispatched at top speed must be rejected as misguided. It is fundamental to both object relations theory and Bowlby's attachment theory that, just as the tie between a child and its caretaker provides a foundation for emotional growth throughout the life cycle, so too the therapeutic relationship should aim to furnish the patient with a secure base for coping with life's tribulations. Because he takes the birth trauma as his paradigm, Rank exhorts the analyst to inflict a violent "cutting of this psychological umbilical cord" on the patient; but this defines development in terms of separations rather than attachments and risks harming the vulnerable person whom one is seeking to help.

Rank's use of the surgical metaphor follows ineluctably from his conception of the therapeutic process. Once the analyst has grasped the skeleton key of the birth trauma, he contends, "the whole analytic procedure for the first time has a definite, sharply outlined content. In other words, the analyst knows exactly what he has to do and what he has to expect" (1924g, 80). Lest there be any doubt, in the *Technique of Psychoanalysis* Rank reiterates that the analyst "knows his goal and his assignment and is also in the position in every moment of the analysis to be able to orient himself with certainty about the state of the cure" (1926c, 20).

As opposed to Groddeck, Ferenczi, and Winnicott, all of whom stress the need for humility on the part of the analyst and the capacity to tolerate *not* understanding the patient's communications, Rank assumes that the analyst can at all times "orient himself with certainty" and "knows exactly what he has to do and what he has to expect." This outdoes in arrogance anything found in Freud, who cautioned other analysts against assuming an omniscient attitude, though he himself did not always refrain from doing so in practice. Indeed, Rank goes so far as to say that the analyst, "entirely conscious of his goal and certain of his purpose, must much rather keep his assignment before his eyes often even despite the associations and intentions of the patient" and "have the confidence in this manner entirely to remove the conduct of the analysis from the patient" (20).

These passages show why Rank, despite his theoretical advances over Freud, has relatively little to offer contemporary analysts. In contrast, Groddeck warns that "in the treatment itself it is not the doctor who is the essentially active partner, but the patient. The doctor's chief enemy is Hubris" (1926b, 126). Reinforcing his dogmatic conception of the analytic relationship, Rank asserts that "we do not by any means always need to ask the patient about his associations" in order to interpret his dreams (1926c, 59) and that "knowledge of all these unconscious complexes makes it superfluous for the analyst today to take the same difficult route in every case" (1924c, 55). Because he believes his discovery of the birth trauma provides a shortcut to the unconscious, Rank holds it to be no longer necessary to begin anew in a state of uncertainty before each patient. "In order to prevent the patient from unconsciously reproducing the birth trauma at the *end* of the analysis," he avers, "I proceed in every case, regardless of sex, to reveal right at the beginning this regular strong manifestation of the mother libido in the transference situation" (1924e, 80). Like his wielding of the surgeon's scalpel, Rank's reliance on the same facile stratagem "in every case" and his confidence that merely by disclosing the birth trauma he can prevent its repetition by the patient epitomize his superficial and authoritarian approach to the therapeutic process.

The problems in Rank's formulations about analytic technique reach their apogee in *An Analysis of a Neurosis in Dreams*, a work that reflects Rank's longstanding interest in dreams.[10] Although untranslated and virtually unread today—the text goes unmentioned in Lieberman's biography—*An Analysis of a Neurosis in Dreams* is the longest and most ambitious case history in the psychoanalytic literature between Freud's Wolf Man (1918) and Klein's *Narrative of a Child Analysis* (1961). One therefore approaches it with high hopes, but these are soon dashed because the patient never comes alive for the reader, nor does Rank himself play a dynamic role in his narrative. Instead he plods monotonously through the sequence "Dream—Associations—Interpretation," in which the associative thread is furnished not by the patient but by his own theoretical agenda. Throughout, Rank stipulates what something "means" (1924b, 29), "explains" to the patient what is going on (106, 186, 189), and interprets sexual symbolism in an arbitrary manner: a flat landscape, for example, corresponds to "a full, unconscious acceptance of the female role, the renunciation of the neurotic penis wish, and the accept-

10. Rank carved out a niche as an expert on dreams as early as "A Dream That Interprets Itself" (1910), an extended exegesis of the dream of an anonymous female friend. Freud included Rank's "Dream and Literature" and "Dream and Myth" from the fourth (1914) through the seventh (1917) editions of *The Interpretation of Dreams*. In volume 1 of the *Technique of Psychoanalysis*, subtitled *Illustrated through the Technique of Dream-Interpretation*, Rank draws upon materials he had complied for "the "necessary practical counterpart to Freud's *Interpretation of Dreams*" (1926c, v).

ance of the separation (weaning) from the mother" (201). Inadvertently caricaturing the neutrality of the "surgical" analyst, Rank reveals that "'good day' is the only thing that I say to the patient outside the analysis" (199).

Although *An Analysis of a Neurosis in Dreams* exploits Rank's innovative emphasis on the maternal transference (even onto a male analyst) and his model of the analytic process as a reenactment of the birth trauma, the work remains hobbled by the masculine bias and a priori thinking of orthodox Freudianism.[11] Like *The Trauma of Birth*, to which it forms a pendant, *An Analysis of a Neurosis in Dreams* is animated by the longing to be Freud's son and heir. Rank seeks to ingratiate himself with Freud by extending the bounds of his empire without challenging any of its fundamental laws. What is more, the static quality of Rank's narrative disqualifies it from comparison to Freud's case histories or *The Interpretation of Dreams*, where each of Freud's dreams remains unique and memorable because its associations are embedded in the fabric of his life.

On September 21, 1924, while Rank was in America and Freud's attitude toward his disciple's innovations was beginning to harden, Lou Andreas-Salomé wrote a letter to Freud in which she shared her reactions not only to *The Trauma of Birth* but also to *An Analysis of a Neurosis in Dreams*.[12] Andreas-Salomé's loyalties are entirely with Freud, but her critique of Rank's case history is withering:

> the only difference between Rank's interpretations and those of others is that they are more isolated from the context—by which I mean that I have no clear picture of the dreamer. She never becomes a truly living person; I only hear what she says and how I am supposed to understand it. . . . One envies him the speedy (and no doubt actual) cure, but one does not see or experience anything (some short passages excepted). (Freud and Andreas-Salomé 1966, 139)

11. Rank attributes the patient's neurosis to her "masculinity wish," which gives way in the course of the analysis to "the normal wish for the penis (of the man)." One portion of a dream is said to be "a graphic illustration of this transformation of clitoral sexuality into vaginal" (102).

12. Ernst Pfeiffer glosses Andreas-Salomé's reference to Rank's "earlier book" as an allusion to *The Incest Theme in Literature and Legend*, but this appears to be erroneous. Her mention of Freud's "anxiety about Rank" makes sense only if it pertains to *The Trauma of Birth* (Freud and Andreas-Salomé 1966, 139, 234n170). Writing to Ferenczi on September 4, 1924, Freud reports that *An Analysis of a Neurosis in Dreams* "made the same impression on everyone; it is opaque and unconvincing; actually the book is totally unreadable" (Falzeder and Brabant 2000, 174).

The tediousness of *An Analysis of a Neurosis in Dreams* can in part be attributed to Rank's determination to exclude environmental factors from his case history. This absence is no less conspicuous with respect to the patient's life than it is to Rank's narrative of the actual course of the analysis. He asserts elsewhere that the "emotional attitude in the transference is quite independent of the personal qualities of the doctor" (1924d, 69). He refuses to consider that the analyst is likely to be at fault in some way if the patient evinces a lack of trust or there is a breakdown in the therapeutic process. Rank writes in the *Genetic Psychology* that "independently of the parents' real attitude, their character type, and educational influence, we nonetheless regularly find in analysis that the image of the bad, strict mother arises based on the biological renunciations emanating from her" (1927a, 113). In keeping with his denial of the influence of "the personal qualities of the doctor" on the transference, Rank contends that children's imagos of their parents are formed "independently of the parents' real attitude." Although Rank realizes that the analytic situation recreates the bond between mother and child, he fails to grasp the implication that patients are therefore exquisitely vulnerable to the attitudes and behavior of their analysts.

If Rank's dogmatic conception of the analytic relationship and one-sided tilt toward fantasy distinguish him from Ferenczi and Groddeck, they underscore by contrast his resemblance to Melanie Klein. In noting Rank's affinities with Klein, I shall not try to document any direct influence one way or the other, though there was undoubtedly some cross-fertilization until the mid-1920s, when Rank became a *persona non grata* due to the controversies over *The Trauma of Birth* and Klein took precautions to avoid being associated with his ideas (Grosskurth 1986, 127). But whereas Ferenczi and Groddeck are progenitors of the Independent tradition of object relations theory (associated notably with Winnicott and Balint) as well as of attachment theory, Rank between 1924 and 1927 was in effect a Kleinian analyst; and this, in my judgment, sums up what was wrong with him.[13]

To be sure, the Kleinian orientation has its good points, and these are exemplified in Rank's work. One such positive feature is his attention to the dynamics of intrapsychic processes, especially introjection and projection. "The Genesis of the Object Relation" presents an evocative account of how the ego is formed through the incorporation of lost objects

13. I have previously discussed the affinities between Rank and Klein in *The Psychoanalytic Vocation* (1991, 57–62).

and subsequent objects are invested in turn with narcissistic attributes. As Rank explains: "upon the withdrawal of the object, a substitute for it is sought not only in one's own ego, but every object relation for its part also contains distinct ego elements, that is, the ego seeks once again to find either itself or parts of its beloved self in the object" (1927a, 110). Rank, like Klein, also recognized at an early date both the ambivalence of the mother-child relationship and the asymmetries between the developmental processes of boys and girls in childhood.

Nonetheless, although both Rank and Klein pay lip service to the environment, neither truly integrates it into either theory or practice. In one passage, Rank acknowledges that social factors influence a child's upbringing: "Naturally, in these developmental processes the character and behavior of the parents, like the entire familial milieu altogether, play a decisive role, and it is no accident that in most cases of later faulty adaptation one finds disturbances of a traumatic kind in the family life; whether it be the premature death of a parent or a sibling, the divorce of the parents, step-parents, etc." (1927a, 43). But this statement is contradicted by his repeated denials that the child's imago of the bad mother has anything to do with her actual behavior. Similarly, in "The Importance of Symbol-Formation in the Development of the Ego" (1930), Klein does mention that her patient Dick, an autistic child, "nearly died of starvation" and "no real love was lavished on him," but then discounts the etiological force of these traumas by her insistence that "the sadistic phantasies directed against the inside of [the mother's] body constitute the first and basic relation to the outside world and to reality," and "the child's earliest reality is wholly phantastic" (221–23). Like Klein, Rank postulates that the child's oral-sadistic libido is the motor of psychosexual development.[14] Employing enlarged type for fanfare, he trumpets that "the entire social arrangement of human beings, including sexual upbringing, corresponds in its essentials to a mitigating, damming up, and distributing of sadism" (1927a, 50–51).

Beyond adhering to Klein's now discredited view of the neonate as a sadistic creature, Rank's thinking suffers from intractable literal-mindedness. Despite asserting in the *Genetic Psychology* that his "decisive step" beyond Freud in *The Trauma of Birth* was "the connecting of physiological birth-anxiety, which was all that Freud had kept in view, with separa-

14. In the margins to his copy of volume 1 of *Grundzüge einer genetischen Psychologie*, now in my possession, Abram Kardiner has written in exasperation: "What the hell is sadistic libido?" (83).

tion from the mother as a trauma of eminent *psychological* significance" (1927a, 24), Rank continues to regard life as governed by a biological desire to return to the womb: "the libido ultimately is nothing else than desire to return to a happy primal condition, which the ego once experienced and which individually can be nothing other than the prenatal state" (1924c, 60). By emphasizing the libidinal desire to restore the "prenatal state" instead of the emotional need to maintain a secure attachment with caregivers, Rank remains within the parameters of drive theory and fails to deliver on his promise to redefine the mother-child relationship in psychological terms.

Throughout the 1924–1927 period, Rank presupposes that ego development starts with the "biological mother-relation," whereas the father "represents social restrictions" (1927a, 45). But this premise is untenable, since, as Abram Kardiner has observed, "social demands make themselves felt long before the father appears as a rival" in the child's life.[15] Rank's assumption that the infant is under the sway of oral sadism, combined with his disregard of the social dimension of the mother-child relationship, explains his insistence that the infant's internalized image of the bad mother arises independently of her actual behavior. Both these assertions are byproducts of Rank's attempt to construct an object relations theory that ignores the environment—that is, of anticipating Klein rather than Winnicott and Bowlby, both of whom were at one time influenced by Klein but ended up espousing a radically different and more humane conception of psychoanalysis.

Rank during these years continued to practice the "active technique," the most notable feature of which was the setting of a termination date by the analyst but also entailed issuing commands and prohibitions concerning the patient's extra-analytic behavior. He writes: "The analyst must at all costs be careful not to spoil the patient in any way; because just the fact of being spoiled—namely, the habit of not being able to give up desires—has made the patient neurotic" (1924e, 75). Rank's severity contrasts with Ferenczi, who inaugurated his final period in "Contra-Indications to the 'Active' Psycho-Analytical Technique" (1925) by advocating indulgence and "spoiling" to facilitate the regressions of highly disturbed patients. Again, it is Ferenczi rather than Rank who opens up the productive paths followed by Winnicott and Bowlby. Bowlby cites

15. I quote again from Kardiner's marginalia to this passage in my copy of *Grundzüge einer genetischen Psychologie*.

observational studies showing that "by the end of the first year mothers who had attended promptly to their crying babies had babies who cried much less than did the babies of mothers who had left them to cry" (1979, 49). Contrary to Rank's premise that spoiling reinforces neurotic tendencies, an analyst who meets the emotional needs of his or her patient, like the mother who picks up and cuddles her crying baby, is likely to fare better than one who seeks to control the patient with edicts and deadlines.

The dispute between Ferenczi and Rank over whether to treat patients with indulgence or severity is replayed between Ferenczi and Freud. In a letter to Izette de Forest describing his final encounter with Freud in Vienna in 1932, Ferenczi reported that after he had read aloud his sublime valedictory paper, "Confusion of Tongues between Adults and the Child" (1933a), Freud warned him that he "was departing fundamentally from the traditional customs and techniques of psychoanalysis" because "such yielding to the patient's longing and desires—no matter how genuine—would increase his dependence on the analyst. Such dependence can only be destroyed by the emotional withdrawal of the analyst" (quoted in Falzeder and Brabant 2000, 443n1). When Ferenczi extended his hand "in affectionate adieu," Freud "turned his back on me and walked out of the room." As Ferenczi understood but Freud and Rank did not, a patient's emotional dependence is exacerbated rather than "destroyed" by "emotional withdrawal" on the part of the analyst.

Although a theory of the birth trauma would seem to entail an emphasis on the beginning of life, as Rank emancipated himself from Freud's influence he became increasingly convinced that exhuming a patient's past was of no use in therapy. "The chief accent of the entire psychoanalytic outlook lay in the overestimation of the infantile" (1927a, 47), he affirms in the introduction to the *Genetic Psychology*. Much of the indignation aroused in orthodox circles by the *Technique of Psychoanalysis* was due to the fact that Rank challenged Freud's interpretation of the pivotal dream of the Wolf Man as a memory of an infantile primal scene, ascribing it instead to observations that the Wolf Man had made from the couch in Freud's consulting room. Since the case of the Wolf Man represented Freud's effort to refute clinically the revisionist views of Adler and Jung, Rank's interrogation of Freud's conclusions revived the passions associated with these earlier schisms and endangered the heart of the Freudian enterprise. At the foot of the couch there was a window through which the Wolf Man could see a chestnut tree, just as had figured in his dream. On a wall column, moreover, he beheld photographs of "six or seven wolves"—that is, according to Rank, Freud's closest adherents—"who stare unmovingly at him, as it were, the family tree of psychoanalysis," as well as photographs of Freud and his sons (1926c, 152–53).[16]

Rank interprets the spontaneous opening of the window in the Wolf Man's dream as an allusion to birth, and the pair of white wolves sitting in the tree as the patient's elder sister and father, who possessed the mother before he was born (156). Rank's contention that the setting influences how the past is remembered in analysis prefigures the contemporary emphasis on the inherently intersubjective and constructed nature of therapeutic work. Rank, however, exaggerates what might have been a useful corrective to an unproblematic belief in the accuracy of memory to the point where he becomes no less reductive than his opponents. Thus, he avers in the *Technique of Psychoanalysis* that it "does not help the patient at all if he knows why and how things got to be the way they are, just as little as it cures my cold if I know where I came down with the infection" (203). This passage not only rejects the principle of genetic explanation but goes so far as to strip mental illness of meaning altogether.

In keeping with his manic-depressive temperament, Rank's odyssey from *The Trauma of Birth* to the *Technique of Psychoanalysis* veers from one extreme to the other. Whereas he asserts in the former work that his discovery of the birth trauma "signifies a first attempt to form psychoanalytic therapy into a quite definite procedure having but one meaning— namely, freeing from mother fixation and transformation of the libido thus gained into a new well-adjusted *ideal* formation based on father identification" (1924e, 81), by the latter he is convinced that all memories of the past produced by a patient in therapy stem from "a misunderstanding of the analytic situation." But whether Rank is under the spell of the archaic birth trauma or the current analytic setting, what he sees has only "one meaning," a tendency which fatally narrows his compre-

16. In letters to Ferenczi on June 6 and June 8, 1924, Freud vents his anger toward Rank. He insists that the Wolf Man reported his dream at the beginning of his analysis, in 1911, when the wall "could only have had two or three pictures, of Rank, Jones, and you. . . . So what remains of the source for the five to seven wolves?" (Falzeder and Brabant 2000, 261). In a footnote, Rank surmises that the Wolf Man knew that Freud had six children, which would make him the seventh, who, as in the fairy tale of "The Wolf and the Seven Little Kids," hid in the clock-case representing the body of the mother.

hension of the infinitely complex and variegated phenomena visible through a psychoanalytic lens.[17]

In the preface to *The Trauma of Birth*, Rank states that his concept permits one to discern "the ultimate biologically tangible substrate of the psychical" (1924e, 22). In this case, Rank's all-encompassing explanation reduces psychology to biology. He goes on to propose in chapter 1, "The Analytic Situation," that termination of analysis constitutes for the patient a reenactment of the birth trauma. Arguing that this process "permits the patient to repeat with better success in the analysis the separation from the mother that was incompletely accomplished at the time," Rank insists that his analogy is "by no means to be taken in any way metaphorically—not even in the psychological sense" (26).

Despite the profundity of Rank's comparison between the end of analysis and separation from the mother, his collapse of psychology into biology ensnares his argument in contradiction. His difficulty is compounded in the second half of the previously quoted sentence, which continues: "rather, the patient biologically repeats, so to speak, the period of pregnancy in the analytic situation; and at the conclusion of the analysis, with its renewed separation from the substitute object, he repeats the act of birth, for the most part faithfully in all its details" (26). Immediately after he insists that his comparison between analysis and pregnancy and between termination and separation from the mother's body is "by no means to be taken in any way metaphorically," Rank uses the phrase "so to speak" (*sozusagen*) to qualify his assertion. At the very moment in which he denies that he is speaking metaphorically, that is, Rank's rhetorical gesture exposes the figurative basis of his explanatory model. My objection is not that the birth trauma is a metaphorical concept. It is that Rank fails to recognize this to be the case and instead undercuts his valuable contribution to the theory of transference by asking that it be taken literally.

The same incapacity for dialectical thinking vitiates Rank's handling of the antinomy between reality and fantasy. Reflecting on the crucial moment in 1897 when Freud abandoned his seduction theory in favor of a belief in infantile sexuality, Rank writes: "If one had overestimated reality in the original trauma theory, so the next and essential phase of analytic development represents a clear overestimation of fantasy life,

---

17. As we saw in the previous chapter, Rank's orthodox Freudian phase was marked by a no less absolute faith in the Oedipus complex as the key to all mythologies.

which is designated by the concept 'psychical reality'" (1927a, 23). He adds that "the not yet fully appreciated significance of my conception advanced in *The Trauma of Birth* also lay, among other things, in the fact that it attempted to substitute so-called primal fantasies with real, individual experiences."

In endeavoring to rehabilitate Freud's pre-1897 trauma theory, Rank anticipates Ferenczi's luminous final papers. Although his attempt to redress an imbalance in Freud's thought is commendable and his indictment of Freud's tendency to resort prematurely to phylogenetic explanations astute, Rank remains hobbled by a one-dimensional understanding of what is "real." He alleges that his concept of the birth trauma "provides for the first time a real substrate for the psychophysiological connections and relations" (1924e, 70); the effectiveness of analysis in turn depends on the tendency of the unconscious "to reproduce 'the real'— namely, the primal situation" (29). He subsequently defends his work by reiterating that he had set himself the task of giving "the purely psychological state of affairs that analysis had uncovered in psychic life (fantasy) an actually experienced biological correlative, instead of contenting myself with a projection backward of psychic realities into historic or prehistoric pasts" (1927a, 24).

Contrary to Rank's assertion, the "real" cannot be equated with the "primal." Whatever the "real substratum" of "psychic realities" may be, its excavation in analysis takes place only through a process of "projection backwards" in which fantasy is involved. Without recognizing that this subverts his theoretical enterprise, Rank himself admits that "the 'primal scene' can indeed never be remembered, because the most painful of all 'memories,' the trauma of birth, is linked to it 'associatively'" (29). Rank seeks "to replace . . . primal fantasies with real, individual experiences," but this endeavor is doomed because reality and fantasy are never discrete realms, but rather inextricably fused dimensions of human experience.

According to Rank, "science has been a complete failure in the field of psychology" (1930b, 222). A corollary to this disdain of science, which intensified during Rank's final anti-psychoanalytic period, is his conviction that all theories are inadequate because they remain "purely descriptive and static, whereas the phenomena themselves are dynamic" (1927a, 59). As I shall argue in the last chapter, however, although natural science alone is insufficient to ground psychoanalytic practice, which involves the interpretation of meanings through intersubjective dialogue, a commitment to the scientific method remains indispensable in order to differentiate valid from invalid theoretical claims. Bowlby (1982, 37) quotes the aphorism of the social psychologist Kurt Lewin: "'There is nothing so practical as a good theory,' and, of course, nothing so handicapping as a poor one." If a sound theory is desirable in any sphere of intellectual endeavor, it is crucial to psychotherapists, because how they treat (or mistreat) their patients will depend on their understanding of psychic life and the principles of emotional development.

Citing Rank's recognition of the importance of the mother-child relationship, Lieberman has claimed that he is "the first feminist in Freud's inner circle" (1993, xii). Unfortunately, a careful scrutiny of Rank's pronouncements on women fails to sustain his claim to these laurels. Although Rank concedes that the point of view of men has historically dominated that of women, he rejects Adler's social explanation of this inequality, instead attributing it entirely to woman's "original connection with the birth trauma" (1924e, 55).[18] Rank's neglect of cultural factors precludes him from saying anything illuminating on gender relations. What is more, just as his attention to preoedipal dynamics in *An Analysis of a Neurosis in Dreams* is not accompanied by an emancipation from Freud's phallocentrism, so too in *The Trauma of Birth* he credits "clitoris libido" with enabling women through masturbation "to partake at least in this way in the inestimable advantage that man has over woman" (55), namely, the possession of a penis that allows him symbolically to regress to the maternal womb.[19]

Rank's pronouncements on gender become still more reactionary in

18. As Breger points out, Adler's "psychology of the ego" is an unjustly neglected forerunner of "contemporary approaches that stress attachment and a primary need to relate to others" (2000, 199, 414n203). Building on his notion of organic and psychological "inferiority," Adler very early recognized the "need for affection" as a basic drive. In Adler's words, "Children want to be fondled, loved, and praised. They have a tendency to cuddle up, always to remain close to loved persons, and to want to be taken into bed with them. Later this desire aims at loving relationships from which originate love of relatives, social feelings, and love" (1908, 40). What is more, Breger astutely remarks, Adler's "concept of masculine protest—that one exaggerates certain culturally defined masculine traits to repudiate threatening feelings of weakness and helplessness that are seen as feminine—fit Freud only too closely." Compounding the threat that Adler posed to Freud's "need to dominate and control psychoanalysis," the fact that his ideas "struck close to the core of Freud's persona" is thus a second source of "Freud's hatred of Adler" (2000, 204).

19. Rank's argument about the "advantage" of the penis is indebted to Ferenczi's *Thalassa*. But as I shall show in chapter 6, Ferenczi repudiated the androcentric perspective of *Thalassa* in his *Clinical Diary*. Ferenczi wrote to Freud on May 22, 1932: "It will interest you to know that in our group lively debates are going on about the female castration complex and penis envy. I must admit that in my practice these don't play the great role

his later post-psychoanalytic period. In volume 2 of the *Genetic Psychology*, he dismisses "the whole movement of feminism" as "the so-called endeavors of woman to become masculine," adding that women's rights "are actually psychical not social" (1927c, 186).[20] Rank is no less obtuse when it comes to homosexuality, imputing its recent efflorescence to the way that "man and woman have become psychologically too much alike, so that they no longer complement but inhibit one another biologically." The conflicts in same-sex relationships are set down to "biological dissatisfaction, whereas conflicts in heterosexual relationships are more apt to be caused by emotional frustration" (187). With this track record on gender and sexual orientation, it comes as no surprise that Rank believes that class conflict can be reduced to a battle of wills between the "leader" and the "average person," and "class war is as hopeless as vain, because it takes into consideration only the physical and mechanical labor on the one hand and the leader's material profit on the other" (1927d, 197). In other words, class conflict has in his opinion nothing to do with economics, but is simply a byproduct of a clash between personality types.

Although Rank broke away from Freud and began to evolve a new psychoanalytic paradigm from 1924 to 1927, he ironically remained too much like his erstwhile master in both his intellectual style and his conception of the therapeutic process. Now that most scholars and clinicians of psychoanalysis have finally moved beyond the equally sterile alternatives of Freudolatry and Freud-bashing, it would be regrettable indeed were the small band of Rankians to perpetuate the same baleful dichotomy with respect to their progenitor. If I take Rank to task for his missteps, it is because I take him seriously; and there has never been a hero who did not walk with a limp.

---

that one had expected theoretically" (Falzeder and Brabant 2000, 436). A remark such as this, of which Rank was incapable, attests that Ferenczi has a far stronger right to the honor of being hailed as the "first feminist in Freud's inner circle."

20. My quotations from volume 2 of *Genetic Psychology* are taken from the English translations in Kramer (Rank 1996).

6

Ferenczi's Turn in Psychoanalysis

To those who have come under its spell, the history of psychoanalysis is a subject of inexhaustible fascination. The appeal of psychoanalysis as a guide to living stems ultimately from the way that it enables its adepts to think theoretically about their own experiences. It thus functions, as it were, on a *meta*-level, not removing one from life, but immersing one in it more deeply by adding a dimension of self-conscious reflection to the fluctuating compounds of love and loss, repetition and regeneration, that are the staples of the human lot.[1] In turning to the history of psy-

1. As Louis Sass has remarked, the paradoxical concept of human subjectivity as "both a knowing subject and a primary object of knowing" was decisively introduced by Kant, whose self-reflexive focus "had the effect of turning subjectivity into a prime object of study, an empirical entity that would itself be investigated by newly developing human sciences that aspired to specify the nature or explain the sources of these very categories or cultural forms" (1994, 80–81). But if psychoanalysis has philosophical roots in the Kantian tradition, it must likewise acknowledge its kinship to schizophrenia, which represents the hypertrophy of consciousness in its diseased form. Freud's 1911 monograph on Schreber, which forms the backdrop to the "Palermo incident" with Ferenczi (discussed in note 13 below) and harks back to the themes of paranoia and homosexuality in his relationship with Fliess, provides a textual bridge between psychoanalysis and schizophrenia. Although self-consciousness is potentially paralyzing, it can also lead to health, much like Wittgenstein's philosophy, which, as Sass shows, seeks to tread the tightrope of thought in order to restore human beings to the ground of ordinary experience. This continuity

choanalysis, then, which inevitably comes down to posterity mainly in the form of written texts, and where we can witness how the personal and professional lives of those who have preceded us are intimately intertwined, we have an opportunity to observe this *meta*-quality of psychoanalysis in a concentrated form.

By any standard, the longest shadow in the history of psychoanalysis continues to be cast by Freud. However much one may disagree with Freud on matters of theory—his views on the drives and female sexuality being notable areas of controversy—and whatever criticisms one may make of his character, it cannot be disputed that psychoanalysis originated with Freud and that he is the leading actor in the drama of its development, which spans the twentieth century and constitutes one of the guiding threads to its intellectual history. On those who knew Freud personally, of course, his impact was overwhelming; and even now, over sixty years after his death, he remains an inescapable presence not only for those who wish to become psychoanalysts or scholars who employ psychoanalytic tools in their research, but for the culture at large, as witnessed by the ongoing "Freud wars" and concurrent skirmishes on the epistemological status of psychoanalysis. For both individuals and the myriad of interested professional groups, moreover, the ideological, economic, and sheerly narcissistic stakes in these disputes are high; and the self-blinding passion with which they are too often conducted is the unfortunate counterpart to the rewards to be derived from a theory that raises experience of all kinds to a higher power of intensity and self-consciousness.

Although Freud stands enduringly at the crossroads, one of the most remarkable features of the history of psychoanalysis from its inception is the exceptional caliber of the men and women whom he attracted to him as followers. And just as Freud's image is contested within and outside of psychoanalysis, so too the other gifted individuals who have left their mark on the movement—each of whom deserves to be seen as a unique being in his or her own right with a destiny and story to tell—become objects of positive or negative transference by their contemporaries and successors, and thereby also major or minor pieces in the incessant game of writing and rewriting the past.

In singling out any of the planets around Freud's sun for particular attention, there is a natural tendency to want to make the strongest pos-

___

between the philosophies of Kant and Wittgenstein is a variation on the Romantic topos of an "odyssey of consciousness" that, as I argued in *Freud and Oedipus* (1987), underlies the psychoanalytic enterprise.

sible case for that body's eminence. It is because something in the precursor's life and work speaks to our own condition that we initially gravitate to him or her, and in championing that thinker's point of view we are simultaneously advancing our own ideological agendas. In the best examples of psychoanalytic scholarship, however, a healthy idealization of a beloved ancestor's (or contemporary's) achievement is balanced by a recognition of limitations and frailties; conversely, criticisms that are directed against those who are cast as opponents should be tempered by generous doses of respect and empathy.

Sándor Ferenczi, the Hungarian disciple of whom Freud wrote in *On the History of the Psycho-Analytic Movement* that he "outweighs an entire society" (1914a, 33), and whom he lauded in his obituary as one who had "made all analysts into his pupils" (1933b, 228), is unquestionably one of the most brilliant orbs in the psychoanalytic firmament.[2] Apart from Freud, he is the first-generation pioneer who continues to be studied most closely by contemporary analysts; and, for those in the relational tradition, he has come to embody not simply a complement but a powerful alternative to Freud as well. The resurgence of interest in Ferenczi has much to do with his position in the early history of the psychoanalytic movement. Of the four leading members of the Committee that formed around Freud in 1912 to counter the incipient defection of Jung, there is a fundamental dichotomy between the two conservatives, Karl Abraham in Berlin and Ernest Jones in London, and the two innovators, Otto Rank in Vienna and Ferenczi in Budapest. Because psychoanalysis has, by common consent, undergone a shift from a drive (or "one-person") to a relational (or "two-person") paradigm, the reputation of Ferenczi and even Rank—who, in 1923, jointly authored *The Development of Psychoanalysis*—has largely eclipsed that of Abraham and Jones.[3]

Abraham is best remembered for his refinements of Freud's libido theory; Jones, the only one of the four to outlive Freud, for his biography of Freud. Completed in 1957, one year before Jones's own death, this three-volume work simultaneously settled old scores with his rivals (especially Ferenczi, who had been his analyst, and Rank) and gave definitive shape

2. For studies of Ferenczi in English, see Haynal (1988), Stanton (1991), and the essays collected in Aron and Harris (1993) and in my volume coedited with Antal Bókay and Patrizia Giampieri-Deutsch (1996). Notable works in other languages include Sabourin (1985), Harmat (1988), and Bertrand et al. (1994).

3. For an authoritative summary of this paradigm shift in the "new American psychoanalysis," see Wallerstein (1998b). A comprehensive collection of papers in the relational tradition has been compiled by Mitchell and Aron (1999).

to the Freud legend. Abraham's intellectual gifts were matched by Jones's as an administrator, but both remained unswervingly loyal to Freud and thus could not mount a challenge to his authority that might provide a point of departure for subsequent revisionist thinking.

Rank stands at the antipodes from Jones and Abraham since he broke away from Freud after the publication of *The Trauma of Birth* (1924e) and, like Jung, became a dissident. As such, however, his influence waned, and his post-1927 writings on will therapy and creativity found an audience chiefly among artists, social workers, and cultural critics. Only in recent years has his innovative work of the 1924–1927 period received renewed attention. By contrast, Ferenczi's decision to remain within the psychoanalytic fold has contributed decisively to his revival. Although, in Michael Balint's words, "the disagreement between Freud and Ferenczi acted as a trauma on the analytical world" (1968, 152), it was impossible for Jones and other detractors to deny the intimacy of Ferenczi's relationship to Freud or to excommunicate him completely from the psychoanalytic movement. Through Balint, there was a direct link between Ferenczi and the Independent tradition of British object relations theory, just as there was through Clara Thompson between Ferenczi and the American interpersonalists. Thus, as relational psychoanalysis has consolidated its paradigm shift in recent decades, Ferenczi has taken on increasing importance not only because of his theoretical ideas and technical experiments, but because he serves to exemplify how one can have a psychoanalytic identity without being a Freudian.[4]

Scholarly understanding of Ferenczi's relationship to Freud has been transformed by access to long-suppressed documents. Above all, the *Clinical Diary*, the private journal Ferenczi kept in 1932, the year before his death, was published in 1985; and the Freud-Ferenczi correspondence—its 1,246 letters make it Freud's longest with a colleague—has now likewise been published in its entirety. Commentators will inevitably diverge in their interpretations, but the outcome of this rela-

4. In his interview with me, Stephen Mitchell agreed that his lineage is one that, "through Clara Thompson and Frieda Fromm-Reichmann," goes back to Ferenczi, "who never became a 'dissident' but who sponsored a view of psychoanalysis alternative to the classical Freudian one" (Rudnytsky 2000, 112). Mitchell and I went on to discuss the Freud-Ferenczi relationship in the context of the political history of psychoanalysis, drawing an analogy between Freud and the formerly restrictive institutes of the American Psychoanalytic Association, on one hand, and Ferenczi and the Local Chapters movement connected with Division 39 of the American Psychological Association, on the other (114).

tionship in my view is a tragedy stemming ultimately from the conjunction between Freud's tendency to impose a choice between submission or rebellion on his disciples and Ferenczi's docility and need for approval by authority figures.

Throughout most of their lengthy association, Ferenczi strove to gain satisfaction from playing the role of Freud's beloved son and resolutely suppressed all murmurs of discontent. Indeed, after the schisms of both Jung and Rank, Ferenczi affirmed his loyalty to the master in the strongest possible terms. Unwittingly condemning his own much-maligned later technical innovation, he denounced Jung to Freud in a letter on December 26, 1912: "*Mutual analysis* is nonsense, also an impossibility. . . . I, too, went through a period of rebellion against your 'treatment.' Now I have become insightful and find that you were right in everything" (Brabant, Falzeder, and Giampieri-Deutsch 1993, 449). Similarly, after Rank became an outcast, Ferenczi in 1927 published a scathing review of *Technique of Psychoanalysis* in which he atoned for their former collaboration. He again flattered Freud on May 30, 1926, "I am happy that through this . . . I can finally free myself from him, since his character traits also downright force me to tear up *coram publico* [in public view] the all too brotherly commonality that we manifested publicly for a time" (Falzeder and Brabant 2000, 258).

Just as Ferenczi's chastisement of Jung's desire for "mutual analysis"—presumably, a reference to their 1909 voyage to America, when the three men interpreted one another's dreams—proved ironically prophetic, so, too, when, in 1926, Ferenczi accidentally ran into Rank in New York's Pennsylvania Station, he refused to speak to him. This snub received its deferred comeuppance in Ferenczi's final encounter with Freud in Vienna in 1932 at the conclusion of which, as I noted in the previous chapter, Freud turned his back and refused his comrade's proffered handshake.[5] The anguish inflicted on Jung, Rank, and the others whom Freud had ostracized with Ferenczi's collaboration was in the end visited

5. Ferenczi's snubbing of Rank is documented by Taft (1958, xvi). Freud's literal turning of his back on Ferenczi is characteristic of his behavior with discarded colleagues. Breuer's daughter-in-law, Hanna, reports "a significant little incident that happened when [Breuer] was already an old man: he walked in the street in Vienna when, suddenly, he saw Freud coming head on towards him. Instinctively, he opened his arms. Freud passed professing not to see him" (quoted in Breger 2000, 125). Like Breuer, Stekel "lived on for many years in Vienna and never returned the hatred Freud directed at him," writing him letters when he learned of Freud's cancer, on Freud's seventy-fifth birthday, and when the Freuds arrived in London; but "all of these friendly overtures were angrily rebuffed by Freud" (207).

also on Ferenczi. In his last entry in the *Clinical Diary*—written on October 2, 1932, less than a week after parting from Freud—Ferenczi tried to set down what it meant to "feel abandoned by colleagues (Radó etc.) who are all too afraid of Freud to behave objectively or even sympathetically toward me" (1985, 212).

As Louis Breger has commented, "in his son role, [Ferenczi] could sound like the doctrinaire Karl Abraham or follow Freud into the deep waters of theoretical speculation" (2000, 347). Despite Ferenczi's efforts at dutiful obedience, however, there was always a side of him that was aware of his dissatisfaction and longings for independence. Above all, because of his passionate nature and the intensity of his relationship with Freud, he, more than any other disciple, was able to take Freud to task when he failed to live up to his own psychoanalytic ideals. These for Ferenczi centered on the need for truth and honesty between partners in an intimate dyad, whether that dyad happened to be romantic or therapeutic. It took decades for Ferenczi to realize that his demand for honesty was more than Freud could bear; but when he did so, and went into internal exile as a result, it freed him to blaze the trails down which succeeding generations have traveled.

One consequence of reading the *Clinical Diary* and the Freud-Ferenczi correspondence is that it exposes the tendentiousness of Freud's narratives of their relationship, about which he wrote on three occasions. In the first, a testimonial on the occasion of Ferenczi's fiftieth birthday, when the latter was—at least outwardly—still very much a loyal disciple, Freud affirmed that he and Ferenczi had enjoyed "a long, intimate and hitherto untroubled friendship," and praised him as "a master and teacher of psycho-analysis" (1923a, 267). On the psychological side, Freud limited himself to the observation that Ferenczi, "who, as a middle child in a large family, had to struggle with a powerful brother complex, had, under the influence of analysis, become an irreproachable elder brother, a kindly teacher and promoter of young talent" (268). He likewise noted in conclusion that "Ferenczi has held back even more than he has made up his mind to communicate" (269), a reference to his long delay in the publication of *Thalassa*, which came out the following year and proved to be Ferenczi's only book-length work.

There is no doubt that sibling rivalry was an important issue in Ferenczi's life. He was the eighth of twelve children, one of whom, a sister four years his junior named Vilma, died at the age of one.[6] But Freud

6. A complete list of Ferenczi's siblings, with their dates of birth, is provided by Judith Dupont in her introduction (1982, 19) to the Ferenczi-Groddeck correspondence. As I observed in chapter 5 that Sulloway's generalizations about first-borns and last-borns apply neatly to Freud and Rank, so too his profile of the typical middle child fits Ferenczi

does not consider its possible ramifications for Ferenczi's attachment to his mother, just as he was unable to probe beneath his own sibling conflicts to analyze the cumulative impact of, in Breger's words, "the loss of [his mother] to new babies, her later absences due to illness, and his frustrated longing for her care" (2000, 20). By Ferenczi's "brother complex," Freud means Ferenczi's competition with other leading disciples for Freud's favor, a recurrent theme in the first volume of their correspondence. As Ferenczi wrote on April 5, 1910: "you are right in your supposition that brother envy has not yet been overcome within me. As an antidote to this it will also be good to take younger brothers under my tutelage; the teacher (father) role will satisfy my ambition, and I will be able to walk up to my elder brothers (Jung, Adler) *sine ira et studio* [without anger and partiality]" (Brabant, Falzeder, and Giampieri-Deutsch 1993, 157). Thus, by an "irreproachable elder brother" Freud means that Ferenczi became the leader of the small psychoanalytic society in Budapest, the "young talent" that he was able to recruit while accepting his own modest place at the table around Freud.

That Freud should have passed over the maternal dimension of Ferenczi's "brother's complex" (in what was, after all, intended as a public tribute) is not difficult to understand, given that he did not have access to this stratum of his own psyche. What is perhaps more surprising is that Freud also fails to mention Ferenczi's father, who died when Ferenczi was fifteen. By calling Ferenczi an "elder brother," Freud implies that, "under the influence of analysis," he has been able to move up in the hierarchy of siblings; but he omits any reference to Ferenczi's Oedipus complex, which would inevitably mean that he had had conflicts not only with his biological father but also with himself, as Ferenczi's analyst. This elision of any hint of discord is reinforced by Freud's claim that his friendship with Ferenczi had been "long, intimate and hitherto untroubled," though the word "hitherto" paradoxically conjures up the very specter of loss that he has otherwise banished from the text.

Freud's second, equally brief appraisal of Ferenczi is his obituary, published in 1933. In the preceding decade, Freud and Ferenczi had undergone the estrangement chronicled in the third volume of their correspondence, though their ties were not totally severed even after their

---

to a tee: "Compared with other siblings, middle children are more flexible and favor compromise. When they rebel, they do so largely out of frustration, or compassion for others, rather than from hatred or ideological fanaticism. Middle children make the most 'romantic' revolutionaries" (1996, 302–3).

last meeting in Vienna in 1932. Freud's true feelings about Ferenczi emerge in his letters to Jones and Eitingon, while Ferenczi's are preserved in the *Clinical Diary*. In the obituary, Freud praised *Thalassa* as Ferenczi's "most brilliant and most fertile achievement" and "perhaps the boldest application of psycho-analysis that was ever attempted" (1933b, 228). Although not published until 1924, Ferenczi had begun *Thalassa* during World War I in cooperation with Freud, and its synthesis of Lamarckian principles and Haeckel's so-called biogenetic law that "ontogeny recapitulates phylogeny" was close to Freud's heart. Freud's enthusiasm is thus understandable. But *Thalassa*, like Freud's contemporaneous *Phylogenetic Fantasy* (1985)—long one of his seven lost metapsychological papers, but which was published after having been discovered in London in a trunk of papers bequeathed by Ferenczi to Balint—is a flight of evolutionary whimsy that, for all its antiquarian interest, is a scientific dead end with no discernible relevance to contemporary psychoanalysis.[7] Of the three masterpieces published within a year by Ferenczi, Rank, and Groddeck—*Thalassa*, *The Trauma of Birth*, and *The Book of the It*—*Thalassa* has least successfully stood the test of time.

With the benefit of hindsight, we can conclude that Freud missed the mark in his estimation of *Thalassa*. It is noteworthy that Ferenczi did not. Writing to Freud on September 21, 1930, after Freud had equivocally praised his attempt to resurrect the pre-1897 trauma theory (outlined in an earlier letter) as "very ingenious" and analogous to *Thalassa*, Ferenczi responded by sharply distinguishing his most recent from his earlier work: "The 'theory of genitality' was the product of pure speculation at a time when, far removed from any practice, I gave way to contemplation (military service). The newer views, only fleetingly alluded to, originate from the practice itself, were brought to the surface by it, extended and modified daily; they proved to be not only theoretically but also practically valuable, that is to say, useful" (Falzeder and Brabant 2000, 400). No longer confined to the "son role," Ferenczi is able to see his cruise into the "deep waters of theoretical speculation" (to echo Breger's phrase) in *Thalassa* as arid and unprofitable by comparison with

---

7. The English titles of both these texts embellish the German originals. *Thalassa* is properly *Versuch einer Genitaltheorie* (*Attempt at a Genital Theory*), while *A Phylogenetic Fantasy* is *Übersicht der Übertragungsneurosen* (*Overview of the Transference Neuroses*). Given the unscientific nature of these works, however, the imaginative titles bestowed by their translators seem quite fitting.

his inquiry into the effects of trauma forged in the crucible of his clinical work with Elizabeth Severn and other severely disturbed patients.

Among its other liabilities, *Thalassa* accentuates Freud's phallocentric perspective. In it, Ferenczi contends that, with the loss of an aquatic mode of life and the need to adapt to existence on land, both sexes "developed the male sexual organ, and there came about, perhaps, a tremendous struggle, the outcome of which was to decide upon which sex should fall the pains and endurance of motherhood and the passive endurance of genitality" (1924, 103). Ferenczi elevates Freud's fantasy, first expounded in the case of Little Hans, that there is primordially only one genital organ to the status of a literal truth. But the misogyny that skews this view of sexuality became no less apparent to Ferenczi by the time he penned the *Clinical Diary* than it is to modern readers. Taking both himself and Freud to task, he recants his earlier view:

> The ease with which Fr[eud] sacrifices the interests of women in favor of male patients is striking. This is consistent with his unilaterally androphile orientation of his theory of sexuality. In this he was followed by nearly all his pupils, myself not excluded. My theory of genitality may have many good points, yet in its mode of presentation and its historical reconstruction it clings too closely to the words of the master; a new edition would mean a complete rewriting. (1985, 187)

In skewering the "unilaterally androphile orientation" of Freud's theory and the way he "sacrifices the interests of women," Ferenczi formulates a feminist critique of "the master" no less radical than that of Horney in her early essays.

The corollary of Freud's overestimation of *Thalassa* is his depreciation of the work of Ferenczi's final period, which he characterizes in the obituary as one of decline after the "summit of achievement" (1933b, 229) reached in the former work. Even more disturbingly, Freud concludes by imputing Ferenczi's preoccupation with "the need to cure and to help" to his personal pathology: "From unexhausted springs of emotion the conviction was borne in upon him that one could effect far more with one's patients if one gave them enough of the love which they longed for as children." The problem here is not that Freud's diagnosis is inaccurate. The deprivations Ferenczi suffered as a child may well have left him with unmet needs that stoked his passion for therapy.[8] What is troubling about what Breger calls Freud's "subtle yet insidious" propaganda (2000, 350) is that it mocks such efforts as both doomed and infantile. Freud's reference to giving patients love is a dig about the alleged improprieties of Ferenczi's "kissing technique." At the close of his obituary, Freud states that "signs were slowly revealed in [Ferenczi] of a grave organic destructive process which had probably overshadowed his life for many years already" (1933b, 229). Since, as Breger notes, "Freud knew that Ferenczi's anemia only appeared in his last year," this comment is a "deliberate distortion" (2000, 350); it self-servingly interprets the conflicts that had severely strained their relationship "for many years already" as the consequence of an "organic destructive process" solely afflicting Ferenczi. In placing the blame on the other person, Freud strategically omits the "organic destructive process" by which his own life had been "overshadowed" since 1923.

Freud's 1923 tribute and the 1933 obituary are landmarks in his assessment of Ferenczi's career, but it is the unacknowledged yet transparent "case history" of Ferenczi in "Analysis Terminable and Interminable" (1937) that most clearly shows the defensiveness and unreliability of Freud's version of events. In the course of discussing "the obstacles that stand in the way of . . . a cure" (221), Freud seeks to rebut Ferenczi's criticism (never expressed publicly) that his analysis, which occurred in 1914 and 1916 in three periods each of which lasted for only a few weeks, had been inadequate because Freud did not analyze his negative transference. As Freud tells the story, his anonymous patient's analysis had "a completely successful result" because "he married the woman he loved and turned into a friend and teacher of his supposed rivals." What is more, the patient's relations with his former analyst—that is, Ferenczi's relations with Freud—"remained unclouded" for "many years" until, "for no assignable external reason, trouble arose," and "the man who had been analyzed became antagonistic to the analyst and reproached him for having failed to give him a complete analysis."

Freud's narrative in "Analysis Terminable and Interminable" is a continuation of his two earlier accounts of Ferenczi, but gives the screw sev-

8. For an outline of how Ferenczi's mother may have transmitted a "primary depression" that Ferenczi reenacted as a "transference depression" in his relationships both with his patients and with Freud, see Bokanowski (1994). Bokanowski, however, does not consider the full range of childhood traumas inflicted on Ferenczi or the possibility that Freud's perspective may have been distorted in any way by traumatic experiences of his own that he was less able to confront than Ferenczi.

eral additional turns. The description of Ferenczi as "a friend and teacher of his supposed rivals" is a variation on the theme of how he had become an "irreproachable elder brother" thanks to his analysis. But Freud now adds as a further proof of the "completely successful result" of his treatment that Ferenczi "married the woman he loved." In saying this, Freud leaves out the by now notorious fact that Ferenczi had been in love with not one but *two* women—Gizella Pálos, a married woman seven years his senior who became his lover in 1900, and the elder of her two daughters, Elma, born when Gizella was twenty-one and thus fourteen years younger than Ferenczi, whom he took into analysis in 1911.[9] Ferenczi finally married Gizella in 1919—her ex-husband, Géza, died on the day of the wedding—and though the marriage was emotionally nurturing to Ferenczi, it also proved a source of frustration and resentment. As well as being uninspiring to him sexually, Gizella was no longer able to have children,, and Ferenczi harbored fantasies (on which he occasionally acted) about other women.[10]

Throughout Ferenczi's prolonged period of vacillation between Gizella and Elma, Freud made clear his preference for the mother over the daughter. When Ferenczi decided to propose to Gizella, he did so by asking Freud to write her a letter, which he did on March 25, 1917. Freud rose to the occasion: "Our friend writes to me that his previous neurotic uncertainty is at an end, . . . and is asking you through me to give your consent and put aside your consideration for your daughter" (Falzeder and Brabant 1996, 191–92). That Ferenczi could bring himself to take the plunge with Gizella only through Freud's mediation is sufficient proof of his ambivalence. Freud's desire that Ferenczi marry Gizella may have been unequivocal, but Ferenczi's own desire clearly was not. Notwithstanding Freud's protestations—or his own—Ferenczi's "neurotic uncertainty" was not "at an end," nor would it be as long as he drew breath.

Freud's misrepresentation of Ferenczi's marriage is of a piece with his

9. For an illuminating discussion of Ferenczi's romantic triangle against the backdrop of his relationship to Freud, see Forrester (1997, 44–106). Ferenczi's love for Elma was never consummated, but it was a grand passion.

10. On November 18, 1917, Ferenczi wrote to Freud about his "infrequent intimate encounters" with Gizella: "I often became unpleasantly aware of the duty-like character of the execution of this love." He complains about "the undeniable signs of age on Gizella's form and features" and "the hopelessness of marriage without children" (Falzeder and Brabant 1996, 246). Ferenczi's infidelities—chiefly with prostitutes and servants, but including one occasion in 1916 when "I couldn't resist having my way . . . at least manually" with Gizella's sister Saroltà (Falzeder and Brabant 1996, 155)—are documented in his letters to Freud and Groddeck.

portrayal of their relationship. Since Ferenczi's marriage was an outcome of his analysis with Freud, and Ferenczi, while superficially reconciled to his fate, was dissatisfied with Gizella, he had ample reason to be "antagonistic" to Freud. But Freud refused to recognize Ferenczi's ambivalence toward Gizella, claiming that Ferenczi's analysis had had "a completely successful result." He thus could also give it out that when "trouble arose" between himself and Ferenczi, it was for "no assignable external reason"—that is, not based on reality or anything for which he himself might have been responsible—but was rather simply the delayed effect of an unfathomable perversity on Ferenczi's part.

There is a close connection between Freud's distortions of the truth on a personal level and his theoretical convictions. From a contemporary standpoint, the problems I have outlined with Freud's narrative of Ferenczi's analysis can be summed up by saying that it relies entirely on a "one-person" model and does not allow for the impact of the analyst's subjectivity or countertransference on what is inherently an interactive process. "Analysis Terminable and Interminable" is, of course, the paper in which the therapeutic pessimism of Freud's final period finds its fullest expression. In seeking to explain why so many analyses turn out badly—either at the time or, as in Ferenczi's case, many years later—Freud takes it for granted that the "obstacles" to a cure are largely due to "a constitutional strength of instinct" (1937, 220). As he goes on to argue, the instinct in question is ultimately the death instinct. Compounding his missteps, Freud in the last section reasserts his "unilaterally androphile orientation" toward sexuality by insisting that the two most intractable sources of resistance to analysis are, "in the female, an *envy for the penis*—a positive striving to possess a male genital—and, in the male, a struggle against his passive or feminine attitude to another male" (1937, 250).

In general terms, Freud's purpose in "Analysis Terminable and Interminable" is to minimize the importance of external factors in the formation of neurosis, just as he holds the transference to be a phenomenon arising spontaneously in the patient independently of the analyst's conduct. As Freud writes, "there is no doubt that an aetiology of the traumatic sort offers by far the more favorable field for analysis" (220); but since the thrust of the paper is to demonstrate the difficulty of effecting a lasting cure, traumas can be nothing more than inconsequential "accidental" variables.[11] In addition to avenging himself on Ferenczi through

11. The same problem vitiates Freud's theory of war neuroses. In his paper on the topic, written in the aftermath of World War I, Freud opined that, "when war conditions

a presentation of his case history, therefore, Freud implicitly rebukes Ferenczi's rehabilitation of the pre-1897 traumatic theory of neurosis in his final papers.

This reading of "Analysis Terminable and Interminable" gains further credence from the fact that, immediately after his vignette of Ferenczi, Freud turns to a second case history—that of a woman from "the earliest years of my work as an analyst" (1937, 222) who turns out to be none other than Emma Eckstein, on whom Fliess performed his infamous nasal operation in 1895.[12] As in the case of Ferenczi, Freud misleadingly asserts that analysis had "removed the trouble" that led Eckstein to seek treatment with him—a paralysis which "was obviously of a hysterical nature"—although he adds that more than a decade later she suffered a relapse owing to "profuse haemorrhages" for which she underwent a hysterectomy.

As Ferenczi revived Freud's seduction theory, so Eckstein was the patient who had figured centrally in his abandonment of it in the first place. On April 26, 1896, more than a year after the bungled operation, Freud exultantly informed Fliess that, as his analysis had disclosed, Fliess was not responsible for what had happened: "her episodes of bleeding were hysterical" (Masson 1985, 183). Thus, when in "Analysis Terminable and Interminable" Freud alleges that his unidentified former patient's symptoms were "of a hysterical nature," he is echoing his letter written more than four decades earlier. With both Eckstein and Ferenczi, Freud compounds an initial injury—the disastrous operation, the pressure to marry Gizella—by denying his own culpability and ascribing his victims' reactions—Eckstein's bleeding, Ferenczi's antagonism—to fantasy. Because the return to the trauma theory in Ferenczi's final papers is precisely a critique of the overestimation of fantasy in

---

ceased to operate, the greater number of the neurotic diseases brought about by the war simultaneously vanished" (1919a, 207). As Breger observes, this wholly mistaken idea "was based on the conviction that all neuroses originated in early childhood, so that adult trauma could not, by definition, have long-lasting effects" (2000, 261).

12. Eckstein was identified as the patient in question by Masson (1984, 241–58). Freud's preoccupation in "Analysis Terminable and Interminable" with not only Ferenczi and Eckstein but also Rank and the Wolf Man, who collectively represented "old wounds that refused to heal," is pointed out by Breger (2000, 367). Mahony (1989, 60–62) appositely notes that Freud began writing this paper in January 1937, less than a month after he learned from Marie Bonaparte of the preservation of the Fliess correspondence, as well as in the immediate aftermath of the first recurrence of the cancer in his jaw since the massive operations of 1923. The resurfacing of his letters to Fliess, with the attendant threat of exposure of the secrets of his self-analysis, helps to explain why the Eckstein episode would have been on his mind at this time.

Freud's work, as well as of the way that an analyst who lacks compassion can retraumatize the vulnerable patient, Freud felt impelled to mount a counterattack in "Analysis Terminable and Interminable," the third and last reckoning with his most gifted disciple.

An indispensable window on the Freud-Ferenczi relationship is furnished by Ferenczi's correspondence with Groddeck. Groddeck's first letter to Freud came in 1917, lifting his spirits during the gloom of the world war, and he met the psychoanalytic world in 1920 at the congress in The Hague. Ferenczi then visited Groddeck at his sanatorium in Baden-Baden in September 1921—three months after the death of Ferenczi's mother—and he returned, usually accompanied by his wife and patients, almost every summer thereafter until 1932 (Will 1994, 723).

A parallel reading of the Ferenczi-Groddeck and Freud-Ferenczi correspondences shows just how profound an impact the 1921 visit to Groddeck had on Ferenczi. In its wake, Ferenczi's letters to Freud become markedly less frequent and less passionate. As he observed on May 15, 1922, "I must wonder myself about the fact that I don't give in more to the impulse to write to you." Ferenczi went on to depict his heightened "intellectual self-reliance" as both a gain and a loss: "This matter-of-factness comes to the advantage of the sobriety of my views. But I admit that I think not without sadness about the time when I was that much more stormy, happy-unhappier" (Falzeder and Brabant 2000, 80).

In stark contrast, Ferenczi on Christmas Day 1921 wrote a letter to Groddeck in which he bared the secrets of his soul, the most prominent of which concerned his resentment of Freud, going back to their 1910 trip to Sicily, as well as his frustration in his marriage and continued longing for Elma Pálos.[13] These are, of course, the two topics about which Freud wrote so disingenuously in "Analysis Terminable and Interminable" when he gave his readers the impression that Ferenczi had "married the woman he loved" and that his analysis had been "com-

---

13. This letter contains the only extant account of the "Palermo incident" that marked the first crisis in Ferenczi's relationship to Freud. As Ferenczi recounted to Groddeck, when he and Freud began to work on the Schreber case, Freud sought to dictate to him, as to an amanuensis; he then protested that this was no way to collaborate. Freud replied, "Obviously you want the whole thing for yourself?" and thereafter worked alone, relegating Ferenczi to the ancillary role of copyeditor, which knotted his throat with bitterness (Ferenczi and Groddeck 1982, 37). In his subservient filial mode, Ferenczi on March 8, 1912, wrote contritely to Freud: "You were right when, on my first trip to Vienna where I revealed my intention to marry [Elma], you called attention to the fact that you noticed the same defiant expression I had on my face when I refused to work with you in Palermo" (Brabant, Falzeder, and Giampieri-Deutsch 1993, 353).

pletely successful." Ferenczi ties these topics together by informing Groddeck of how he had again recently spoken to Gizella "of my dissatisfaction, of my suppressed love for her daughter (who should have been my bride. And she was, until a dismissive utterance by Freud compelled me desperately to subdue this love, formally to reject the girl)" (Ferenczi and Groddeck 1982, 37). That Ferenczi characterizes Freud's language as "dismissive" (*abfällige*) is significant because, two paragraphs earlier, he recalled how as a young man he had felt wounded by his mother's "dismissive [*abfällige*] judgment" on his literary productions. In the course of his self-analytic letter, Ferenczi discloses that as a child he received "too little love and too much severity" from his mother (36), and complains of a panoply of psychosomatic symptoms—writer's block, arthritis of the right wrist, insomnia, loss of breath, cardiac pains, etc.—all connected to his long-suppressed anger toward Freud.

Ferenczi continues in the same vein in his ensuing letter to Groddeck, dated February 27, 1922, more than a month after he had paid a visit to Freud in Vienna. As Ferenczi reports, Freud in conversation had "stuck to his earlier opinion that the main thing in my case was the hate against *him*, who (just as the father had formerly done) blocked my marriage to the younger bride (now step-daughter)." "I must confess," Ferenczi added, "it did me good to be able to speak with the beloved father for once about these feelings of hate" (Ferenczi-Groddeck 1982, 41). Whatever the defects of "Analysis Terminable and Interminable," if Freud avowed Ferenczi's "hate" for him, this would appear to refute Ferenczi's claim, spelled out in a letter of January 17, 1930, that Freud had failed to analyze his negative transference. Ferenczi, however, seems to be distinguishing between what took place in his analysis proper (in 1914 and 1916) and extra-analytic talks such as this one in 1922 that he acknowledged to be very helpful.[14] Both Freud, in conversation with Ferenczi, and Ferenczi, in writing to Groddeck, focus exclusively on the paternal dimension of Ferenczi's transference; but, as is clear from the repetition of "dismissive" in his Christmas 1921 letter, the "too little love and too much severity" that he received from Freud evoked even more fundamentally his treatment at the hands of his mother.

After Ferenczi's visit to Groddeck in 1921, then, there was a decisive shift in his relationship to Freud, though it took almost a decade before

14. Bokanowski accounts for the apparent discrepancy by suggesting that "what Freud and Ferenczi meant by the negative transference is of a qualitatively different order" (1994, 125), but this strikes me as unconvincing.

his increased inner freedom began to bear fruit in his work. In Grod-deck, Ferenczi found the unconditional acceptance that he never got from Freud. Groddeck's personal warmth as well as his idiosyncratic combination of massage with psychotherapy contrasted starkly with Freud's unbending aloofness and recommendation of a technique of sur-gical abstinence. In 1923, moreover, after the dissolution of his first mar-riage, Groddeck married Emmy von Voigt, a younger woman who had been his patient before becoming his assistant at the sanatorium in Baden-Baden. As Bernard This (1982, 25) has pointed out, Groddeck thereby fulfilled Ferenczi's fantasy, since he lived out the "family ro-mance" that Ferenczi had under duress renounced with Elma Pálos.[15]

To find a document comparable to Ferenczi's Christmas 1921 letter to Groddeck it is necessary to go back almost exactly nine years, to his let-ter to Freud of December 26, 1912, to which I have already alluded be-cause of its ironic denunciation of Jung's desire for *"mutual analysis"* as "nonsense." Taken in conjunction with the *Clinical Diary*, this letter— perhaps the most extraordinary piece of self-analysis in the history of psychoanalysis—reveals that Ferenczi in early childhood was subjected to severe emotional and sexual traumas inflicted chiefly by his mother and other female caretakers. These traumas help to explain the somatic symptoms—the breathing disturbances, insomnia, and the rest—that tormented Ferenczi throughout his life.

In the course of analyzing a dream of his about a black cat, Ferenczi tells Freud of how he had been caught by a cook at the age of three (or earlier) in mutual genital touching with his sister Gisela, one year his elder. After reporting the boy to his mother, the cook threatened to cas-trate him with a kitchen knife. The name of his sister links her to Gizella Pálos, and Ferenczi reluctantly admits that he now wants "to treat Frau *Gisela* in a similarly bad way as I once did my sister" (Falzeder, Brabant, and Giampieri-Deutsch 1993, 452). But if Gizella Pálos, as his adulterous lover, is a transferential replacement for Ferenczi's sister, she is likewise a surrogate for the cook and his mother in that she stands in the way of his desire for the still more forbidden Elma: "Now, possibly, I ucs. hate Frau G. because she (as earlier the cook and my mother) prevented mar-

15. As Ferenczi ruefully wrote to Freud on January 20, 1912, after the latter had agreed to take Elma into analysis, the tacit purpose of which was to pry her loose from Ferenczi: "I threw myself with youthful bravado into this adventure, the last thing that brought me close to the realization of the family romance. Now I have become a modest man" (Bra-bant, Falzeder, and Giampieri-Deutsch 1993, 326).

riage with Elma (earlier touching my sister). I can also impute to her the threat of cutting off my penis" (453). At the conclusion of his letter, Ferenczi connects Gizella Pálos and Freud in their capacity as impediments to his marriage with Elma: "My ucs. placed the responsibility for it in your and Frau G.'s hands" (454).[16]

Gizella Pálos is therefore at once the object of Ferenczi's desire and the obstacle to his desire for Elma. The same holds true of Freud, though Freud understands Ferenczi's ambivalence exclusively in oedipal terms. As we have seen, he insisted that "the main thing" was Ferenczi's hatred of him because, "as the father had formerly done," he "blocked [Ferenczi's] marriage to the younger bride"; Freud likewise performed a classically paternal function in mediating Ferenczi's marriage proposal to Gizella. On the other hand, in his letter of December 26, 1912, Ferenczi wrote: "As a small boy I had a colossal un. . . . . rage against my mother, who was too strict with me; the fantasy of murder (which I don't remember with certainty) was immediately turned toward my own person" (452). The dots after "un-" represent Ferenczi's inability (despite his fluency in the language) to remember the German equivalent of the Hungarian word *tehetetlen*, meaning "inhibited" or "impotent." His lapse is therefore an enactment of the "impotent rage" he not only felt in the past toward his mother but also feels transferentially in the present toward Freud, whom he had servilely praised at the outset of his letter as "right in everything." Like the psychosomatic symptoms catalogued in his Christmas 1921 letter to Groddeck—which include arthritis of the wrist and writer's block, and where Ferenczi again lamented having received "too little love and too much severity" from his mother—the "fantasy of murder" to which Ferenczi confesses in this letter nine years earlier is aimed against Freud not primarily as a father but as a mother.

At least to some extent, Ferenczi presciently recognized the theoretical implications of his maternal transference. Just at the period when Freud in *Totem and Taboo* was pronouncing the Oedipus complex to be

16. Ferenczi interprets his dream of the black cat as a "defiant apology" that wards off castration fears arising from his illicit desires for Elma: "I satisfy my forbidden sexual desires; they won't cut off my penis after all, since 'adults' are just as 'bad' as 'children'" (453). In the course of his associations, he moves from a childhood incident in which "my father, unsuspecting of my presence, told my mother that so-and-so had married a whore," to the fact that Freud "once took a trip to Italy with your sister-in-law (*voyage de lit-à-lit*)." Although Ferenczi dismisses this last as "only an infantile thought," it provides corroboration for the theory, espoused preeminently by Swales (1982), that Freud had an affair in 1900 with Minna Bernays.

"the nuclear complex of neurosis" (1912–13, 17), and Rank was copiously vindicating his thesis in *The Incest Theme in Literature and Legend*, Ferenczi through his self-analysis grasped its limitations as a universal truth. Anticipating Freud's later attempt to preserve his "shibboleth" by introducing the notion of a "negative Oedipus complex," he adds in his letter: "my mother's strict treatment (and my father's mildness) had the result in me of a displacement of the Oedipus complex [mother's death, father's love]" (Brabant, Falzeder, Giampieri-Deutsch 1993, 452; brackets in original).

Reformulated in contemporary terms, Ferenczi's "displacement" of the Oedipus complex means that his conflicts—like those of the fictional Norbert Hanold in Jensen's *Gradiva*—rest on a preoedipal foundation. The plot of his marriage follows a classic oedipal script—he married his surrogate mother, and his surrogate father dropped dead on the day of the wedding—but in addition to viewing his father as a rival, Ferenczi turned to him for the affection of which he was deprived by his abusive mother. The "strict" Freud is then in the position not only of Ferenczi's father but also of his mother, while Gizella's "mildness" makes her the heir not only of his mother but also of his father. To give this unconscious logic its most paradoxical formulation, in Gizella Ferenczi symbolically married his *father*, who was simultaneously a double for Freud.

As Freud did with Fliess in the aftermath of the latter's bungled operation on Emma Eckstein in 1895, Ferenczi responded to the first trauma in his relationship with Freud by heightening his idealization and repressing his stirrings of criticism and revolt. On October 3, 1910, one month after the Palermo incident, in a letter that he described as "the confession of a man who exists in psychoanalytic ferment," Ferenczi drew his most poignant analogy between Freud and his future wife: "Just as in my relationship with Frau G. I strive for *absolute* mutual openness, in the same manner—and with even more justification—I believed that this, apparently cruel but in the end only useful, clear-as-day openness, which conceals nothing, could be possible between two ψα [psychoanalytically]-minded people" (218, 220). In the course of their twenty-five-year relationship, Ferenczi underwent every vicissitude of emotion toward Freud, but his importance today stems above all from his willingness to challenge Freud to live up to the truths he taught and to "contradict [him] on some essential points" (217), even as he pays unstinting homage to his genius.

In his letter, Ferenczi imparts a dream "in which I saw you standing naked before me" (218). Not discounting his homosexual impulses, Ferenczi interprets the dream as expressing his desire for "absolute mutual openness" with the man he loved. Asking how he could come "to demand still more—indeed everything" from one who had given him so much, Ferenczi continues with a passage that speaks for all of us who have placed Freud at the center of our lives and work and at times felt daunted when measuring ourselves against his achievement:

> But don't forget that for years I have been occupied with nothing but the products of your intellect, and I have also always felt the man behind every sentence of your works and made him my confidant. Whether you want to be or not, you are one of the great master teachers of mankind, and you must allow your readers to approach you, at least intellectually, in a personal relationship as well. My ideal of truth that strikes down all consideration is certainly nothing less than the most self-evident consequence of your teachings. I am convinced that I am not the only one who, in important decisions, in self-criticism, etc., always asks and has asked himself the question: How would *Freud* relate to this? Under "Freud" I understood his teachings and his personality, fused together in a harmonious unity.
>
> So I am and have been much, much more intimately acquainted with you than you could have imagined. . . .
>
> I must come back again and again to the fact that I am aware of the excessiveness of my demands. But I believe that you underestimate much too much the ennobling power of psychoanalysis if you don't believe that it makes people who have completely grasped its meaning absolutely worthy of trust. . . .
>
> Unfortunately—I can't begin, you have to! After all, you are $\psi\alpha$ in person! (219–20)

The moral of this moving eulogy is not only that it is impossible to separate the intellectual from the personal in psychoanalysis, but also that Ferenczi, as Freud's strongest reader, may indeed have understood the lessons of this "master teacher of mankind" more profoundly than he did himself. No one could have exemplified more steadfastly than Ferenczi the "ennobling power" of the "ideal of truth" in psychoanalysis. Like Groddeck, he had the humility to recognize that his greatest discoveries were inseparable from his mistakes, that his creativity and healing powers sprang from what in a postscript to this letter he did not scruple to call his "infantile weakness and exaggerations" (220). In the spirit of Nietzsche's *Thus Spoke Zarathustra*, Ferenczi bore witness that "one repays a teacher badly if one always remains nothing but a pupil" (Nietzsche 1883, 190) by paying Freud the ultimate tribute of going beyond him and becoming a master in his own right.[17] By doing so, he outgrew the epithet, honorific yet condescending, of "paladin and secret Grand Vizier" (Falzeder and Brabant 2000, 373–74) and proved himself to be what each of us must continually strive to become—"$\psi\alpha$ in person"—and our most trustworthy guide to its future.[18]

17. A longer extract from *Thus Spoke Zarathustra* containing this key sentence was quoted by Jung on March 3, 1912, in a letter to Freud on the eve of their rupture. As I argued in *Freud and Oedipus* (1987, 221–23), had Freud shown greater humility, he would have issued this warning himself, rather than having it flung at him as a reproach by his chosen successor.

18. Freud bestowed the title of "paladin and secret Grand Vizier" in a letter of December 13, 1929, after Ferenczi's initial stirrings of personal and intellectual independence. While implying that Ferenczi was his chief subordinate, as the Grand Vizier was to the Sultan, Freud reinforced his subservience, and even this equivocal sign of favor was kept a "secret." "Paladin" goes back to 1912 and the formation of the Secret Committee, which Jones envisioned in a letter of August 7 as "a united small body, designed, like the Paladins of Charlemagne, to guard the kingdom and policy of their master" (Paskauskas 1993, 149). As Breger remarks, notwithstanding the "romantic aura" of the Committee, it defined psychoanalysis as a "holy war" (2000, 209), with Freud cast as the Emperor.

7

The Analyst's Murder of the Patient

Of the radical and innovative ideas put forward by Ferenczi during his final years none is more startling than the suggestion in his 1932 *Clinical Diary* that although the analyst "may take kindness and relaxation as far as he possibly can, the time will come when he will have to repeat with his own hands the act of murder previously perpetrated against the patient" (1985, 52). In this chapter, I propose to use the *Diary* to explore not only the theoretical and clinical implications of this thesis but also its autobiographical roots and its bearing on Ferenczi's relationship to Freud.

It must be said immediately that the murder of which Ferenczi speaks is not literal, but rather emotional or psychic. As he goes on to explain, "analytic guilt consists of the doctor not being able to offer full maternal care, goodness, self-sacrifice; and consequently he again exposes the people under his care, who just barely managed to save themselves before, to the same danger, by not providing adequate help" (52–53). Once this is understood, it becomes clear that Ferenczi is referring to the way in which the inevitable imperfections and limitations of the analyst trigger the memory of childhood traumas experienced by the patient, which must be relived during analysis in order to be exorcised.[1] This model of

---

1. As Lewis Aron observes, Ferenczi's conception goes "far beyond the simplistic notion that the analyst needs to be a 'good object' or better parent to the patient"

the analytic process proposed by Ferenczi is very similar to that articulated independently by Winnicott in his posthumously published paper "Fear of Breakdown," where he explains that the agony of the patient "experienced in the transference, in relation to the analyst's failures and mistakes," is what enables him or her to recollect "the original failure of the facilitating environment" (1974, 91).

The approach to psychoanalysis exemplified by Ferenczi and Winnicott stresses the need for humility on the analyst's part and the indispensability of emotional repeating as well as intellectual remembering to the therapeutic process. In "Freud's Influence on Medicine," Ferenczi acclaims Freud's fusion of science and humanism in the discovery of psychoanalysis by calling it "utraquistic" (1933b, 147–48).[2] Since utraquism is an ecclesiastical term, used originally of the moderate fifteenth-century followers of Jan Hus who defended the right of the laity to take communion in both kinds, I think it appropriate to label Ferenczi's own approach "utraquistic" in its insistence that, in Peter Lomas's words, "just as man cannot live by bread alone, so he cannot live by taking thought alone: interpretation is not enough" (1987, 5). The analyst, that is, must heal the patient with the wine of sympathy as well as with the bread of insight. As Ferenczi affirms in the *Diary*: "Analysis on its own is intellectual anatomical dissection. . . . Kindness alone would not help much either, but only both together" (1985, 207).

Although Ferenczi employs the notion of the analyst's murder of the patient in a metaphorical sense, this does not make it any less real. Sexual or other forms of abuse in childhood can lead to spiritual death, transcending anything that might be classified as castration anxiety, which makes the analytic process ultimately a quest for rebirth. Like Harry Guntrip (1975), whose extraordinary narrative of his successive analyses with Fairbairn and Winnicott compellingly illustrates this claim, Ferenczi must have experienced a soul murder in childhood, as his *Diary* confirms: "The continuous protests (from the deepest unconscious) that I do not have any real empathy or compassion for the patient, that I am emotionally dead, was in many respects analytically proven, and could

---

(1996, 168). He notes Ferenczi's anticipation of Shengold's (1989) concept of "soul murder."

2. Earlier Ferenczi had employed this term in the introduction to *Thalassa* to describe his own "reciprocal analogizing" between the fields of natural science and psychology (1924, 3).

be traced back to deep infantile traumata" (1985, 85).[3] He proceeds to acknowledge how his "infantile aggressiveness and a refusal of love toward my mother became displaced onto the patients. But, as with my mother, I managed with tremendous effort to develop a compulsive, purely intellectual superkindness" (86). Thus, in a complex dialectic, Ferenczi recreated the failures of nurturing to which he had been subjected at the hands of his mother in his own insincerity toward his patients, a symbolic murder that replicated what they too had suffered in infancy. Analysis for Ferenczi, therefore, is always mutual in that it consists of a "dialogue of unconsciouses" (84) and entails "the finding of that common feature" in the emotional histories of doctor and patient "which repeats itself in every case of infantile trauma" (15).

Ferenczi divulges his childhood traumas in letters to Freud and Groddeck, and he is no less unsparing in the *Clinical Diary*. He traces his wounds back "to excessive demands of genitality on the part of adults, to conflicts with the puritanical spirit within the family, and, not least, possibly to a traumatic event in earliest infancy" (85). "Excessive demands of genitality" alludes to Ferenczi's seduction by a nursemaid, as a result of which he later "masturbated four to five times a day and, using immense concentration and the summation of every erotically stimulating situation, contrived to squirt his semen onto the ceiling, some five or six meters above him" (89).[4] He tags his masturbatory exploits with the Latin

3. For a comprehensive discussion of Guntrip's case, which draws on his unpublished *Psycho-Analytical Autobiography*, see my chapter, "The Two Analyses of Harry Guntrip," in *The Psychoanalytic Vocation* (1991, 115–48).

4. In his letter to Freud of December 26, 1912, Ferenczi recounts a separate but related incident when, at the age of five, a somewhat older playmate "tempted me into allowing him to put his penis into my mouth" (Brabant, Falzeder, Giampieri-Deutsch 1993, 452). It is striking that both Rank and Jung likewise reported being victims of childhood sexual molestation. At the age of twenty, Rank in his diary wrote of an "important occurrence" that "even today after thirteen years, stands as my introduction to erotic experience in my seventh year through one of my friends, for which I still curse him even today" (quoted in Taft 1958, 10). In a letter on October 28, 1907, Jung confided to Freud that "as a boy I was the victim of a sexual assault by a man I once worshipped," leaving him with an "abominable feeling" that fueled his dangerous "'religious' crush" on Freud (McGuire 1974, 95). Although significant in themselves, these sexual traumas should be seen as emblematic of more profound emotional deprivations in the childhoods of Ferenczi, Rank, and Jung. These unresolved problems drew them to Freud in the first place and perhaps contributed also to the tragic endings of their relationships with him. Following Krüll (1979), Vitz (1988, 129–41) has contended that Freud too may have been sexually abused in early childhood, perhaps by his nurse. Even if we do not place too much weight on these conjectures, the emotional unavailability of Freud's mother due to her repeated pregnan-

phrase *ejakulatio usque ad coelum* (15). While engaged in mutual analysis with an unidentified female patient (presumably Elizabeth Severn), he has a fantasy about "the image of a corpse, whose abdomen I was opening up." He links this fantasy to "passionate scenes, which presumably did take place, in the course of which a housemaid probably allowed me to play with her breasts, but then pressed my head between her legs, so that I became frightened and felt I was suffocating. This is the source of my hatred of females" (61).

The housemaid indicted here is apparently the same nursemaid who precociously aroused Ferenczi's genitality, and the memory of having had his head forced between her legs—as if into a corpse—appears to be the mysterious "episode in his infancy" that took place in connection with a nurse "at the age of one year" (13). In describing to Freud the funeral of his mother, Ferenczi says in a letter of July 24, 1921, that he had, while under the influence of medication, the "hypnagogic hallucination" that "the coffin would fall out of the hearse and the corpse would tumble out of the coffin," which he interprets as "an ambivalent fantasy: revenge up to the grave and the wish for her resurrection" (Falzeder and Brabant 2000, 61). He goes on to chronicle his own medical woes, the symptoms of which, though in part psychogenic, he wants his physician, Lajos Levy, to be able to treat organically in order "to take out of my hands the weapons with which I (ucs.) want to commit suicide" (62). As during mutual analysis with Severn, Ferenczi responds to his mother's death with an "ambivalent fantasy" in which murder is inseparable from suicide, and "revenge" from "resurrection." In his magnificent self-analytic letter to Freud of December 26, 1912, he makes it explicit, as we saw in the previous chapter, that his mother's excessive strictness with him as a small boy gave rise to an "impotent rage" (enacted against Freud in the transference by his repressing the German equivalent of *tehetetlen*) and a "fantasy of murder" that was "immediately turned toward my own person" (Brabant, Falzeder, Giampieri-Deutsch 1993, 452).

An important link in Ferenczi's chain of traumas with mother figures is the death of his pupil and analysand, Erzsébet Radó-Révész, the wife of Sándor Radó, in 1923. Whereas the death of Ferenczi's mother took place two months before his first visit to Groddeck's sanatorium, the death of Radó-Révész occurred a year and a half later, after Ferenczi had withdrawn from Freud and turned instead to Groddeck as a source of

---

cies and the sudden disappearance of his nurse were traumas closely analogous to those of his disciples that Freud himself was never able to work through analytically.

emotional support and analytic sounding board. There is thus a highly charged significance to the disparity between the five-line letter to Freud on January 28, 1923, in which Ferenczi perfunctorily reports the facts of the matter—the pregnant woman died of a previously mentioned pernicious anemia, though surgeons tried to save her baby by a caesarian section—and the impassioned account of both the event itself and his upheaval in response to it in Ferenczi's letter to Groddeck.

Writing to Groddeck on February 19, Ferenczi reveals that Radó-Révész contracted her pernicious anemia "after the death of her loved-hated father," and that his analysis of her was conducted without the knowledge of her husband, who was in Berlin for his own analysis (Ferenczi and Groddeck 1982, 58–59). The caesarian section was performed on the woman, whose pregnancy was in the sixth or seventh month, after her blood corpuscles had dropped to a critical level; but she survived the operation by only two, and the baby by eight, days. Immediately before her death, Ferenczi adds, "there sprung up in me new cardiac symptoms (skipping of the pulse) and a recrudescence of the old insomnia, attacks of nocturnal apnoea with chills—in a word, death-longing" (59).

There is an uncanny—what one might call a Groddeckian—irony in the fact that Ferenczi himself would die of pernicious anemia ten years later, and that he seems to have contracted his disease just at the time of Radó-Révész's death.[5] From what we have seen, it seems clear that his "death-longing" and attendant symptoms of anxiety were triggered by the impending operation on a pregnant woman's body in which he identified simultaneously with the mother and baby. As at the death of his mother, Ferenczi has a "fantasy of murder" that was "immediately turned toward my own person." The memory of Radó-Révész's operation appears to underlie his fantasy years later during mutual analysis of "the image of a corpse, whose abdomen I was opening up," recorded in the *Clinical Diary;* and both of these can be traced back to his infantile traumas, including the feeling of suffocation when his head was pressed between the legs of the housemaid.

Strikingly, however, Ferenczi in his letter to Groddeck of February 19, 1923, seems unaware of the maternal component of his anxiety attack, claiming that his self-scrutiny has established "a clear parallel between the condition and my corresponding involvement in the triangle" (Ferenczi and Groddeck 1982, 59), presumably a reference to his analysis of

5. The timing of the onset of Ferenczi's pernicious anemia is noted by the editors of the Ferenczi-Groddeck correspondence (1982, 58). There is thus a foundation to Freud's allegation that Ferenczi had been ill "for many years" before his death. See chapter 6, p. 116 above.

Radó-Révész without her husband's knowledge. As in his letter to Freud of December 26, 1912, Ferenczi's theoretical formulations lag behind his phenomenological experience, though oedipal factors are certainly part of the equation. That Ferenczi kept his analysis of Radó-Révész a secret from her husband lends a twist to his final October 2, 1932, entry in the *Clinical Diary*, in which Ferenczi (in ironic retribution for his own earlier cruelty toward Jung and Rank) bemoans his desertion "by colleagues (Radó, etc.) who are all too afraid of Freud to behave objectively or even sympathetically toward me" (1985, 212).

Ferenczi's own history of childhood sexual abuse subtends his rehabilitation of Freud's pre-1897 seduction theory of neurosis.[6] As he emphasizes in the *Diary*, however, his renewed attention to real events does not mean a corresponding neglect of fantasy: "The fact that infantile sexuality exists obviously remains undisputed, yet much of what appears as passionate in infantile sexuality may be a secondary consequence of the passionate behavior of adults, forcibly imposed on children against their will and, so to speak, artificially implanted in them. . . . Children want no more than to be treated in a friendly, tender, and gentle way" (79). In "The Principle of Relaxation and Neocatharsis," the paper delivered at the 1929 Oxford Congress in which Ferenczi heralds his new outlook, he continues to agree with Freud that "children themselves manifest a readiness to engage in genital eroticism more vehemently and far earlier than we used to suppose," but with the crucial proviso that "the premature forcing of genital sensations has a . . . terrifying effect on children; what they really want, even in their sexual life, is simply play and tenderness, not the violent ebullition of passion" (1930, 121).

That Ferenczi draws self-analytically on his personal history helps to account for the exceptional power and continuing resonance of his texts from 1930 to 1933. Just as analysis is a "dialogue of unconsciouses," so inspired psychoanalytic writing most often occurs when an author's area of private madness is called into play. One of Ferenczi's acutest insights is that a trauma inflicted by an adult in the external world becomes internalized in, and thereby deforms, the psyche of the child. Anticipating

6. For a perceptive discussion of this turning point in Freud's thought, see Holland (1989). As Holland argues, what Freud's new emphasis on fantasy led him to abandon was not his awareness of the reality of childhood sexual abuse, but rather his belief that such experiences were the direct causes of later mental illness. But it remains true that Freud's epistemological shift led him drastically to underestimate the importance of actual events in the formation of neurosis, and Holland goes seriously astray when he belittles "poor Ferenczi's last paper, written in his psychosis" (348).

Anna Freud's (1936) concept of identification with the aggressor, Ferenczi explicates in his final paper, "Confusion of Tongues between Adults and the Child": "Through the identification, or let us say, introjection of the aggressor, he disappears as part of the external reality, and becomes intra- instead of extra-psychic. . . . The most important change, produced in the mind of the child by the anxiety-fear-ridden identification with the adult partner, is *the introjection of the guilt feelings of the adult* which makes hitherto harmless play appear as a punishable offense" (1933a, 162). In "The Principle of Relaxation and Neocatharsis," Ferenczi represents this process of deformation metaphorically as a tumor or "*teratoma* which harbours in a hidden part of its body fragments of a twin-being which has never developed" (1930, 123).

Whereas Rank's theory and practice from 1924 to 1927 align him with the extreme fantasy-based version of object relations theory espoused by Klein, Ferenczi's emphasis on the etiological role of early environmental traumas makes him the precursor rather of the Independent tradition of object relations as well as of attachment theory, both of which have been much more thoroughly vindicated by scientific research. Winnicott's (1960) concept of the True and False Self epitomizes his affinity with Ferenczi. Both analysts distinguish between creativity or spontaneity, seen as the natural tendency of the human organism, and compliance, which supervenes in the event of external impingement or deprivation. Ferenczi affirms in the *Diary* that the willingness to share exhibited by the child reared in "an optimal environmental climate" constitutes a "psychic parallel" to the "unimpeded physical and mental growth" enjoyed by the fetus in the womb (1985, 151).

As he distills the essence of the True Self, so Ferenczi in his last *Diary* entry—written after his final meeting with Freud in Vienna prior to the Wiesbaden Congress, at which Freud responded icily to "Confusion of Tongues" and refused to shake his hand at parting—poignantly captures the False Self. He writes on October 2, 1932: "Is the only possibility for my continued existence the renunciation of the largest part of one's own self, in order to carry out the will of that higher power to the end (as though it were my own)?" (212). Ferenczi's metaphor of the False Self as a teratoma becomes uncannily literal when he equates his subservience to Freud with the disease of pernicious anemia from which he was soon to perish: "And now, just as I must build new red corpuscles, must I (if I can) create a new basis for my personality, if I have to abandon as false and untrustworthy the one I have had up to now?" (212). Like any attempt to postulate a causal connection between Radó-Révész's death from pernicious anemia and Ferenczi's contracting of the same disease, so Ferenczi's own insinuation that Freud is somehow to blame for his affliction is likely to strike us as a Groddeckian exaggeration. Yet Ferenczi's anguished indictment of Freud as an "indifferent power"—an amoral Yahweh—by whom he was "trampled under foot" as soon as he decided to "go my own way and not his" (212) contains a profound psychological truth.[7]

To extend this comparison between Ferenczi and Winnicott, the True Self can be aligned with the tenderness of childhood, and the False Self with a prematurely inflicted passion. Both Ferenczi and Winnicott believe that existence entails a continuity of being, and they therefore define trauma as an interruption of that continuity, which brings about a split in the psyche. Because, in Ferenczi's words, "the childish personality, as yet barely consolidated, does not have the capacity to exist without being supported on all sides by the environment," when that environment has been deficient the aim of analytic treatment must be "to provide for the patient the previously missing favorable milieu for building up the ego" (1985, 210–11).

As empathic analysts attuned to what has traditionally been regarded as the maternal function of nurturing their patients, both Ferenczi and Winnicott postulate the coexistence of male and female elements in the psyche. In the *Diary*, Ferenczi contends that "in the female organism or psyche a specific principle of nature is embodied, which, in contrast to the egoism and self-assertion of the male, could be interpreted as the maternal willingness to suffer and capacity for suffering," though this femininity is "completely independent of sexuality" (1985, 41). And just as Winnicott (1971a, 72–85) regards female "being" as prior to male "doing," so Ferenczi esteems the female principle as the "more intelligent" of the two (1985, 42).[8]

Ferenczi dates his seduction by the nursemaid to "the age of one year," notwithstanding the fact that, as Breger has cautioned, "modern

7. On Jung's *Answer to Job* (1952a) as an allegory of his relationship to Freud, with Freud cast in the role of Yahweh, see Slochower (1981).

8. Ferenczi's respect for the female principle leads him to urge that nature must be seen "not only from the point of view of the principle of egoism but also from the opposite direction . . . of selflessness" (41). In arguing that self-interest is balanced by an equally primary altruism, Ferenczi parts company with both Freud and Klein. Elsewhere in the *Diary* he rejects the ideas of innate envy (151) and the death instinct (200), and warns of the "paranoid atmosphere" (95) produced by excessive reliance on transference interpretations in analysis.

research on memory has shown that it is impossible for an adult to recall events" from that age (2000, 274).[9] Ferenczi's putative memory is thus a reconstruction less important in itself than as a symbol of his disturbed relations to maternal figures and the traumatic quality of his upbringing as a whole. He attributes his difficulty in relaxing to "the terrifyingly rough treatment I received from a nurse in my early childhood after an incident of anal soiling, [which] has given rise to an exaggerated tendency in me to attach too much importance to the wishes, likes, and dislikes of other people" (1985, 36). This "anal" incident compounds "the excessive demands of genitality on the part of adults" and gives rise to Ferenczi's "conflicts with the puritanical spirit within the family." Here he struggles not with the enticing but with the punitive maternal figure. However, in a pattern typical (as I have argued in chapter 1 with respect to Norbert Hanold) of borderline conditions, and exemplified in real life by the case of Harry Guntrip, the imago of the hostile preoedipal mother concealed beneath the oedipal mother herself conceals the depressed mother who left her child "emotionally dead." Ferenczi compensates for his sense of inner lifelessness by "a compulsive desire to help anyone who is suffering, especially women," as well as "a flight from situations in which I would have to be aggressive" (61).

If Ferenczi's mother psychically murdered her son, with the complementarity characteristic of unconscious processes he likewise murdered her. Ferenczi discloses that the "tragic moment" of his childhood occurred when his mother declared: "'You are my murderer'" (1985, 53). He connects this incident to the earlier trauma of having been pressed suffocatingly between his housemaid's legs: "This is why my mother's accusation . . . cut to the heart" (61). On the mythological plane, Ferenczi's crime is the matricide of Orestes, a more primitive transgression than Freud's oedipal patricide. In Winnicott's (1969) terms, Ferenczi's mother could not survive her son's destructive impulses; because she retaliated by accusing him of murder, he never placed her outside the area of his omnipotent control. Ferenczi's lifelong interest in telepathy, as well as his extreme emotional sensitivity to others, comes into focus as a manifestation of this dynamic of failed object use.

9. Breger's caveat refers specifically to Freud's insistence in the case of the Wolf Man that his patient had witnessed the primal scene at the age of one and a half, but it has a wider implication. He provides a useful compendium of the relevant research on infancy and mother-infant interaction (2000, 388).

As a therapist renowned for treating the most difficult cases, Ferenczi attracted a clientele that included individuals who, like himself, had been victims of sexual or emotional abuse. This is true of the two most important patients of his final years, Clara Thompson and Elizabeth Severn, known respectively in the *Diary* by the code names of Dm. and R.N.[10] Ferenczi describes Thompson as having been "grossly abused sexually by her father" (1985, 3), and Severn too apparently experienced a "brutal attack" at the age of one and a half and again at five (8). Intriguingly, Severn had been in therapy with Rank when she sought out Ferenczi, with whom she remained in treatment—culminating in the experiment of mutual analysis—from 1924 until his death nine years later.[11] Thompson was treated by Ferenczi, having gone to him at Sullivan's urging, in the summers of 1928 and 1929, and then continuously from 1931 until his death (Silver 1996, 94). It was Thompson's public boast, "'I can kiss Papa Ferenczi as often as I like'" (Ferenczi 1985, 2), that brought down Freud's well-known recriminations in his letter of December 13, 1931, concerning Ferenczi's "kissing technique."

Murder is a leitmotif in the histories of both these American women. Ferenczi quotes Severn's references to the "'experience of being murdered'" (14) and her "incessant protestations that she is no murderer, although she admits to firing the shots" (17).[12] In her college yearbook, Thompson gave an unusually frank account of the motivations for her decision to pursue a career in medicine: "To murder people in the most

10. On Severn's importance for the history of psychoanalysis, see the papers by Fortune (1993, 1994, 1996). Fortune's groundbreaking work has been extended by Smith (1998), whose reading of Severn's three books shows the emancipation of her spirit in the last, *The Discovery of the Self* (1933), published after Ferenczi's death. On Thompson I have profited from the papers by Shapiro (1993) and Silver (1996).

11. Ferenczi's first recorded allusion to Severn occurs in his Easter 1925 letter to Freud: "I have been treating a patient whom Rank analyzed in America, so that I was now able to catch glimpses of his technique" (Falzeder and Brabant 2000, 211). In the *Diary*, he describes the participants in mutual analysis as "two equally terrified children who compare their experiences, and because of their common fate understand each other instinctively" (1985, 56). For judicious critiques of this "Hansel and Gretel" conception of analysis, see Hoffer (1996) and Aron (1996, 173–79), both of whom argue that, in his desire for mutuality, Ferenczi loses sight of the asymmetry that is also vital to safeguarding the relationship between patient and analyst.

12. Fortune's research has traced the latter statement to Severn's "image of having been forced . . . to participate in the murder of a black man" as a child (1993, 107). In a personal communication, he has told me that the source of this information is an interview he conducted with Severn's daughter.

refined manner possible" (quoted in Shapiro 1993, 165). Ferenczi felt a mystical bond with Severn that both he and she attributed to Severn's "Orpha," that split off part of her psyche that sheltered her and telepathically led her to Ferenczi as "the only person in the world who owing to his special personal fate could and would make amends for the injury that had been done her" (Ferenczi 1985, 121). But in Severn, whose "marble-like rigidity of her facial features" and "sovereign, majestic superiority of a queen, or even the royal imperiousness of a king" (97) initially aroused Ferenczi's antipathy, he found "his mother again, namely the real one, who was hard and energetic and of whom I am afraid" (45). Thus, he could "make amends" to Severn only by reenacting the dialectic of soul murder and symbolically murdering (and being murdered by) Severn as his own mother had murdered (and been murdered by) him.

An even more haunting repetition of Ferenczi's relationship with his mother occurs in his transference to Freud. Proposing that the Latin word *amicus* derives etymologically from *umbilicus*, Ferenczi writes in a letter of June 13, 1917: "the friends become mother and child *to each other*" (Falzeder and Brabant 1996, 219). But Freud, no less than Severn, is "hard and energetic," and Ferenczi is "afraid" of him. Ferenczi behaves toward Freud with the same "infantile aggressiveness" and "refusal of love" that he displaces from his mother onto Severn; he likewise camouflages his anger with hypocritical docility.

These unconscious dynamics become tragic, given that in 1932, at the time Ferenczi wrote the *Clinical Diary*, both he and Freud were mortally ill. The analyst's murder of the patient, used by Ferenczi as a metaphor for the clinical process, becomes, like the teratoma, all too literal when applied to himself and Freud. As in the original mother-child dyad, the soul murder between friends is reciprocal. Ferenczi's mother tells him, "'You are my murderer,'" and shatters her son in the process. Ferenczi kills Freud no less than Freud kills Ferenczi. "The anxiety-provoking idea, perhaps very strong in the unconscious," he writes, "that the father must die when the son grows up, explains [Freud's] fear of allowing any one of his sons to become independent" (1985, 184–85). By seeking independence, Ferenczi confirms Freud's fear. Ferenczi analyzes Freud's pathology using the language of oedipal conflict, but his patricide is simultaneously a matricide. Severn is both a "queen" and a "king," and Freud, like Gizella Pálos, replaces the mother as well as the father in Ferenczi's psyche. The beloved is always a combined parent. As he does with his patients, Ferenczi registers the affinities between Freud's life and his own. His own "tragic moment" finds a parallel in his avowal that Freud "wants to ignore the traumatic moment of his own castration in childhood; he is the only one who does not have to be analyzed" (188). Even while he traces his own "hatred of females" to early experiences with his mother and housemaid, Ferenczi speculates about the biographical sources of Freud's "unilaterally androphile" theory of sexuality: "He recoils from the task of having a sexually demanding mother, and having to satisfy her. At some point his mother's passionate nature may have presented him with such a task" (187–88). Ferenczi differs from Freud, however, in his willingness to acknowledge, and thereby to leave behind, his misogyny.

Ferenczi's quadrille with his patients and Freud reflects what in "The Principle of Relaxation and Neocatharsis" he defines as his "double role" in the psychoanalytic movement that made him "a kind of cross between a pupil and a teacher" (1930, 108–9). Ferenczi's unique role as a mediator between Freud and his followers in turn finds a counterpart in Severn: "My pupils' confidence in me could give me a certain self-assurance; in particular, the confidence of one person who is both a pupil and a teacher" (1985, 212). With both his patients and Freud, Ferenczi experiences the ambivalent emotions of love and hate. "No analysis can succeed if we do not succeed in really loving the patient" (130); yet when Severn demands to be loved, as his mother had done, Ferenczi confesses, "In actual fact and inwardly . . . I did hate the patient, in spite of all the friendliness I displayed" (99). Like Winnicott (1947), Ferenczi broaches the tabooed subject of hate in the countertransference. If love, and not hypocritical politeness, is to prevail in the analytic situation, its opposite must be acknowledged. Quoting Freud's statement that patients are a "'rabble'" and "'only any good for making money out of, and for studying,'" Ferenczi adds the sardonic qualification, "true, but must be admitted to the patients" (1985, 118).

From the agony of his failed relationship with Freud as well as his own interminable struggles as an analyst, Ferenczi learned two indispensable lessons. The first is the need for honesty with patients and a detestation of posturing of any sort. Invoking the cherished names of Groddeck and Thompson, Ferenczi proclaims on the opening page of his *Diary*: "*Natural and sincere behavior* . . . constitutes the most appropriate and most favorable atmosphere in the analytic situation" (1). Later he describes himself as one "impressed ultimately only by the truth" (94). The second lesson is that intellectual honesty is not enough, and can even be a species of brutality if it is not leavened by love.[13] Ferenczi warns of the "explosion on contact between the worlds of emotion and thought" that is sure to take place if a patient is induced to repeat a childhood trauma in analysis without having learned to trust "the real kindness of the analyst" (210).

Since the analyst must in some way fail—that is, murder—the patient, the criterion of a successful termination becomes whether the patient is able to forgive the analyst. "In contrast to the original murder," Ferenczi observes, the analyst "is not allowed to deny his guilt" (52). The childhood trauma must be repeated, but because "there is nevertheless a difference between our honesty and the hypocritical silence of parents," Ferenczi does not despair and counts on "the return of trust in spite of all the disillusionment" (53). Forgiveness, however, cannot be received in the abstract; each sin must be confessed and atoned for separately. "It does not seem to suffice to make a general confession and to receive general absolution; patients want to see all the sufferings that we caused them corrected one by one, to punish us for them, and then to wait until we no longer react with defiance or by taking offense, but with insight, regret, indeed with loving sympathy" (209). Ferenczi notes in his final *Diary* entry: "I released R.N. from her torments by repeating the sins of her father, which I then confessed and for which I obtained forgiveness" (214). He generalizes: "That the first step could be taken toward forgiveness for causing the trauma indicates that [the patient] had attained insight. . . . Finally it is also possible to view and *remember* the trauma with *feelings of forgiveness* and consequently *understanding. The analyst who is forgiven*: enjoys in the analysis what was denied him in life and hardened his heart. MUTUAL FORGIVENESS!!—Final success" (201–2).

As Ferenczi's letters make clear, he shared Freud's conviction that there is no place in psychoanalysis for the false consolations of religion. On March 22, 1910, he criticizes Pfister's failure to comprehend that "the analytical conception *carried through to its conclusion* does away with theology" (Brabant, Falzeder, Giampieri-Deutsch 1993, 153); and on July 14, 1915, he likewise affirms that "psychoanalysis signifies man's convales-

---

13. In *The Leaven of Love*, Izette de Forest writes that "Ferenczi allowed no artificial distance to intervene between himself and his patients, for he thought of them as friends. . . . Psychoanalytic treatment, he thought, should take place as a natural, concerned, personal relationship, a part of life, not something removed from the experience of everyday living" (1954, 8). For a contemporary representative of this tradition, see Peter Lomas's interview with me (Rudnytsky 2000, 51–62).

cence, the emancipation from religion" (Falzeder and Brabant 1996, 70). Despite his endorsement of Freud's atheism, however, Ferenczi's version of psychoanalysis recognizes the existential truth of Christianity. A practitioner of humility, he recasts the opposition between agape and eros into one between tenderness and passion, and holds the former to be no less fundamental to human nature than the latter. Our mothers do not always withstand our murderous attacks; they may retaliate and kill us by dying. But if we are forgiven, if the beloved object we have slain comes back to life, then we ourselves can be reborn. As Brooke Hopkins (1989) has argued in an exegesis of the resurrection story in terms of Winnicott's concept of object use, it is because Christ survives the ultimate destructive attack of crucifixion that he proves to humanity that love is psychically stronger than death.

Ferenczi's *Clinical Diary* teaches that analysis is ultimately a matter of the analyst's murder of the patient, and the patient's learning to forgive this reenactment of the parental crime. Where Freud "hardened his heart," Ferenczi proclaims the need for "mutual forgiveness" in a psychoanalytic New Testament:

> Should it even occur, as it does occasionally to me, that experiencing another's and my own suffering brings a tear to my eye (and one should not conceal this emotion from the patient), then the tears of doctor and patient mingle in a sublimated communion, which perhaps finds its analogy only in the mother-child relationship. And this is the healing agent, which, like a kind of glue, binds together permanently the intellectually assembled fragments, surrounding even the personality thus repaired with a new aura of vitality and optimism. (1985, 65)

As Ferenczi sought and obtained forgiveness from his patients for his trespasses against them, he forgave Freud's trespasses against him. But analysis with Freud could never be mutual; he refused the mother's role and was not given to tears.

8

Groddeck's Gospel

I

There is widespread agreement that 1923 constitutes a turning point in the history of psychoanalysis. Indeed, many commentators would rate this year as second in its momentousness only to 1897 when Freud, in the self-analysis he conducted in letters to Fliess following his father's death, jettisoned the seduction theory and first adumbrated the Oedipus complex. In the words of Ilse Grubrich-Simitis, "the model of the psyche, of its structure and functioning, that [*The Ego and the Id*] introduces is so innovative and formative in its intrinsic potency that the year of publication of the brief text, 1923, [figuratively] marks a watershed in the psychoanalytic literature" (1993, 138). Although I concur with Grubrich-Simitis as to the importance of the date in question, her account reflects an exclusive concern with Freud and a corresponding neglect of the ramifications of this juncture on psychoanalysis as a whole.

Besides *The Ego and the Id*, the years 1923 and 1924 saw the publication of a cluster of works by Freud's leading disciples, all of which can justly be hailed as classics. These include, in 1923, Ferenczi's *Thalassa* and *The Development of Psychoanalysis*, authored jointly with Rank; and, the following year, Rank's own *The Trauma of Birth* as well as Fritz Wittels's

Sigmund Freud: His Personality, His Teaching, and His School, the first biography of the founder of psychoanalysis, which, despite (or because of) the ambivalence in Wittels's motivations, remains an impressive performance and merits closer scholarly attention that it has customarily been accorded.[1] Beyond these textual landmarks, 1923 was also the year that Freud was diagnosed with the cancer of the jaw to which he would finally succumb in 1939.

Thus, in assessing the significance of the years 1923 and 1924 for the history of psychoanalysis, it is imperative to situate *The Ego and the Id* not only in the context of Freud's metapsychology but also as a vector for all the forces—personal and theoretical—that made this brief span so turbulent and decisive. It marks the moment when Freud introduced his structural theory of superego, ego, and id, but it is also one in which psychoanalysis itself reached a crossroads: the choice between Freud's new model of ego psychology and what we can now recognize to be the relational turn, the foundations of which were laid down in the contemporaneous works of Ferenczi and Rank.[2]

Once the crisis of 1923 is understood to involve not simply a turning point in Freud's own thinking but also the birth pangs of rival psychoanalytic paradigms, it becomes clear that yet another text published in that same fateful year must also be taken into account. I refer, of course, to Georg Groddeck's *Book of the It.* At least among English-speakers, Groddeck's life and work are much less familiar in the psychoanalytic world than those of Ferenczi and even Rank.[3] In taking up Groddeck, I shall, for the most part, not be concerned with mapping his influence on subsequent analytic thinking, which in the United States long had its epicenter at Chestnut Lodge, a psychiatric hospital in Rockville, Maryland, where Groddeck's memory was venerated by Frieda Fromm-Reichmann, who

1. On Wittels's relationship to Freud, which was mediated by his ties to both Karl Kraus and Wilhelm Stekel, see his memoirs (1995), the long-lost manuscript of which was rediscovered by Edward Timms.

2. For a discussion of the controversies surrounding *The Trauma of Birth* and *The Development of Psychoanalysis* in terms of competing medical and hermeneutic models of psychoanalysis, see Bókay (1998). Like Grubrich-Simitis, Arlow hails *The Ego and the Id* as affording a "new paradigm" (1975, 512) for psychoanalysis; but, taking for granted the hegemony of ego psychology, he neglects to mention any of the contemporaneous texts that presented an alternative to this mainstream tradition.

3. To my knowledge, there has not been a biography or extended critical study of Groddeck in English since Grossman and Grossman (1965). Key works in other languages include Will (1984), Lewinter (1990), and, most recently, the biography by Martynkewicz (1997).

had known him personally in Germany.[4] But, as I shall argue, of the four works that constitute a collective counterweight to *The Ego and the Id*— *Thalassa*, *The Development of Psychoanalysis*, *The Trauma of Birth*, and *The Book of the It*—Groddeck's is by far the most profound and important; and it is time, therefore, that his eminence as a progenitor of the relational tradition be given its due. As we shall see, the fate of Groddeck's ideas, like those of Rank and Ferenczi, is intertwined with his relationship with Freud. Since the "two-person" paradigm of relational theory has by common consent now supplanted the "one-person" paradigm of ego psychology, which for decades represented the reigning orthodoxy of American psychoanalysis, it is not an overstatement to say that *The Ego and the Id* has become a book of the past, whereas *The Book of the It*—like Ferenczi's *Clinical Diary*—remains a book of the future.[5]

If contemporary students of analysis remember anything about Groddeck, it is likely to be that he furnished the concept of the id (*das Es*), as Freud acknowledged in *The Ego and the Id*, when he wrote that "we shall gain a great deal by following the suggestion of a writer who, from personal motives, vainly asserts that he has nothing to do with the rigors of pure science." Groddeck, Freud continued, "is never tired of insisting that what we call our ego behaves essentially passively in life, and that, as he expresses it, we are 'lived' by unknown and uncontrollable forces." In a footnote, however, Freud immediately minimized his indebtedness to Groddeck by asserting that "Groddeck himself no doubt followed the

4. Even Harold Searles, the leading member of the Chestnut Lodge group in the generation after Fromm-Reichmann, quotes the same passage from *The Book of the It*, having to do with the reversal whereby the patient becomes the therapist of the analyst, in two different papers (1961, 539; 1972, 446); so his use of Groddeck is actually quite cursory. Searles's quotation of Groddeck is in turn quoted by Aron (1996, 131–32), who senses his importance, though Aron does not appear to have studied Groddeck's work closely. Fromm-Reichmann dedicated her *Principles of Intensive Psychotherapy* (1950) "To my teachers: Sigmund Freud, Kurt Goldstein, Georg Groddeck and Harry Stack Sullivan." Lamentably, Chestnut Lodge closed its doors in 2001.

5. As Aron points out (1996, 154–57), Martin Buber's *I and Thou* was also published in 1923. Although grounded in a philosophical and not a psychoanalytic tradition, Buber's opposition between "I-It" (*Ich-Es*) and "I-You" (*Ich-Du*) relationships poses the essential choice between ego psychology (*Das Ich und das Es*) and relational psychoanalysis (*Ich und Du*). Aron documents Buber's influence on recent relational thinking. As Ferenczi recalled in his letter to Freud of January 26, 1917, Buber had visited Freud in 1908 and requested that Freud write a book on the topic *Neurosis as a Social Institution* for his monograph series, *Society* (Falzeder and Brabant 1996, 178–79). Compounding the historical ironies, Italo Svevo's modernist masterpiece, *Zeno's Conscience*, a novel inspired by psychoanalysis, likewise appeared in 1923, one year after James Joyce's *Ulysses*.

example of Nietzsche" in using "this grammatical term for whatever in our nature is impersonal" (1923b, 23).

Freud's assertion that the It derives from Nietzsche has, however, been confuted by scholars of intellectual history, who have been unable to locate this concept in Nietzsche's works. Groddeck's proximate source appears to have been rather Wilhelm Bölsche's 1904 essay, "The Resurrection of Religion through Art," which postulated the It as a creative principle uniting soul and body and likewise espoused Goethe's principle of "Godnature," a term adopted by Groddeck in his pre-psychoanalytic work of 1909, *Towards Godnature*.[6] Bernd Nitzschke (1983) has speculated that Freud credited Nietzsche with paternity of the It in order to conceal his own intellectual debts to Schopenhauer and Eduard von Hartmann. This seems doubtful, however, because Nietzsche posed a graver threat to Freud's originality than did Schopenhauer; and the influence of both these major thinkers on Freud far overshadowed that of the popular but ultimately inconsequential author of *Philosophy of the Unconscious*.[7]

Although Nitzschke's argument is mistaken in its details, he astutely highlights what Harold Bloom (1973) has taught us to recognize as the anxiety of influence in Freud's dealings with Groddeck. Their contacts began when Groddeck, a comparatively obscure author and sanatorium director in the provincial German town of Baden-Baden, sent the internationally renowned Freud a long letter on May 27, 1917. In this letter, Groddeck thanked Freud for his works and apologized for having formerly attacked his ideas in print without first-hand knowledge, but he claimed to have arrived independently at many of the discoveries of psychoanalysis through his own clinical experience with a female patient

6. The case for Bölsche's influence on Groddeck has been proposed by Martynkewicz (1997, 207–8). Lewinter (1990, 15–16), Nitzschke (1983), and Will (1984) all concur that Groddeck did not derive the It from Nietzsche. As Will writes: "the reason why Freud insisted so much on Nietzsche as the father of the id . . . is left up in the air. And the reason why Freud so disgracefully eliminated Groddeck as the father of the id remains equally unsettled" (126). In part 1, section 17 of *Beyond Good and Evil*, however, Nietzsche does insist that "a thought comes when 'it' ['er'] wishes, and not when 'I' ['ich'] wish, so that it is a falsification of the facts of the case to say that the subject 'I' ['ich'] is the condition of the predicate 'think.' It [*Es*] thinks; but that this 'it' ['es'] is precisely the famous old 'ego' ['ich'] is, to put it mildly, only a supposition" (1886, 24). Despite this anticipation of the concept of the It, Nietzsche never elaborated his *aperçu* in a more systematic fashion, as did Bölsche and Groddeck.

7. See my discussion of Freud's relations to these philosophical precursors in *Freud and Oedipus* (1987, 175–223).

beginning in 1909.[8] He also advocated extending psychoanalytic techniques to the treatment of physical illness and outlined his distinctive concept of the It. Of particular interest is Groddeck's avowal that when he finally procured *The Interpretation of Dreams* and *The Psychopathology of Everyday Life* in 1913, "the effect of the books was so shattering that, despite the awareness that I was depriving myself of an extraordinary enrichment of knowledge and life, I read neither of the two books to the end" (Freud and Groddeck 1974, 8).[9]

Groddeck's letter elicited a powerful response from Freud. As he informed Ferenczi on June 3, 1917, it was "the most interesting letter from a German physician that I have ever received" (Falzeder and Brabant 1996, 212). Two days later, Freud wrote to Groddeck in a similar vein, famously assuring him that "anyone who recognizes that transference and resistance are the hubs of treatment belongs irremediably to the savage army," adding that "whether he calls it the 'Ucs.' or the 'It' makes no difference" (Freud and Groddeck 1974, 14). Freud, however, cogently objected that Groddeck went beyond the legitimate insistence that "the ps[ychic] factor has an unsuspectedly great significance also for the inception of organic diseases" (an idea that he noted had been implied in his own 1915 paper "The Unconscious") to insinuate that "it *alone* makes these diseases" and "the difference between the mental and the somatic is thereby somehow infringed" (15). Freud chided Groddeck for having "so little overcome the banal ambition that wants to be original and strives for priority," warning him that "an untamed ambitious man sooner or later pops up and becomes an eccentric to both his own detriment and that of science." "What," Freud demanded, "is the point of striving after priority against an older generation?"

The issue of priority thus surfaces in the first exchange of letters between Groddeck and Freud, and it continues to haunt their entire relationship. Although Carl and Sylva Grossman contend that Freud was

8. Groddeck attacked Freud in *Nasamecu*, the title of which is an acronym formed by the initial letters of *natura sanat, medicus curat* ("Nature heals, the physician cures"). This slogan was taken over by Groddeck from his mentor, the physician Ernst Schweninger. Despite its apparent humility, the phrase connotes the physician's exalted status as Nature's viceroy. Although he advocates "psychic treatment," Groddeck relies in this work on the physician's "power of suggestion" and deprecates psychoanalysis as a form of "soul dismemberment" preoccupied by "sexual episodes" (Martynkewicz 1997, 141, 146). Groddeck's letter dates *Nasamecu* to 1912, but the work was actually published in 1913.

9. All translations from the Freud-Groddeck and Ferenczi-Groddeck correspondences in this chapter are my own, as are those from *The Book of the It* and *The Soul-Seeker*. For Groddeck's other works, I have used the available English editions.

"bored by struggles for priority in scientific discovery" (1965, 110), this is patently untrue. Freud's praise of Groddeck is laced with condescension and a barely veiled threat to curb his originality, a response that suggests the stirring of competitive feelings in Freud. Groddeck's avowal of the anxiety that impeded his ability to read Freud's books, moreover, must have resonated with uncanny familiarity, since Freud had himself confessed in 1908 to the Vienna Psychoanalytic Society that his "occasional attempts at reading" Nietzsche's works "were smothered by an excess of interest" (Nunberg and Federn 1962, 359).

This parallel between Groddeck's inhibition in reading Freud and Freud's inhibition in reading Nietzsche suggests a hypothesis that, although incapable of proof, may help to account for Freud's otherwise puzzling reassignment of credit for the It from Groddeck to Nietzsche. It is not that he used Nietzsche to defend against Schopenhauer and von Hartmann, but rather that he used Groddeck to defend against Nietzsche, and Nietzsche to demote Groddeck. In a two-pronged stratagem, Freud simultaneously counteracted his belatedness vis-à-vis Nietzsche and justified his own appropriation of the It from Groddeck by alleging that Groddeck had borrowed his most original idea from Nietzsche; thus it was Groddeck and not he himself who was guilty of plagiarism. In his last reference to Groddeck, Freud in the *New Introductory Lectures* reduced him to a conduit between himself and Nietzsche: "Following a verbal usage of Nietzsche's and taking up a suggestion by Georg Groddeck, we will in future call [the mental region that is foreign to the ego] the 'id'" (1933a, 72).[10]

However his motives may be interpreted, Freud's assimilation of Groddeck to Nietzsche attests to his respect for Groddeck as a thinker. The same respect, though with a strongly negative charge, informs Freud's association of Groddeck's name with that of Wilhelm Stekel. In a letter of July 29, 1921, Freud thanked Groddeck for having sent him the

10. Even more puzzling than Freud's maneuvers is that Groddeck himself twice, in 1926 and 1929, conceded that he had derived the It from Nietzsche (Will 1984, 126). I would interpret Groddeck's acquiescence in Freud's usurpation of his originality as a symptom of his hero worship, the self-effacing counterpart to his truculent iconoclasm. Groddeck's maternal grandfather, August Koberstein, was director of the elite Pforta school (which Groddeck himself later attended) when Nietzsche was a pupil there. Nietzsche frequented the Koberstein home and probably read Groddeck's father's notorious 1849 medical dissertation, *De morbo democratico*, which diagnosed democracy as a pathological condition. In 1904, Groddeck visited Nietzsche's grave with Nietzsche's anti-Semitic sister, Elizabeth Förster-Nietzsche (Grossman and Grossman 1965, 20–21; Will 1984, 126; Martynkewicz 1997, 22–23).

latest installment of the manuscript of *The Book of the It*, but rebuked him for having perpetrated "a few misdeeds": "As a warning example there rises in the distance a certain all-too-unbridled, and at the same time inconstant, W. Stekel" (Freud and Groddeck 1974, 44). Although now generally forgotten, Stekel, a physician and prolific author whom Freud credited with initiating the Psychological Wednesday Society but who broke ranks with him in 1912 in the wake of Adler's departure, was in the early years of the psychoanalytic movement one of its most distinguished adherents.[11] As late as 1924, Wittels in his biography of Freud hailed Stekel as "Freud's most distinguished pupil" (1924, 17).

More than any other renegade, however, Stekel came to be regarded by Freud with unbridled contempt and loathing. As in the case of Groddeck, Stekel's specter obtruded itself into the heated exchange of letters between Freud and Ferenczi in December 1931 over the alleged improprieties of Ferenczi's "kissing technique." Stung by Freud's accusation that "the inclination toward sexual playfulness was not alien to you in pre-analytic times, so that one could put the new technique into context with the old misdemeanor," Ferenczi insisted that he had worked through his "youthful sins" analytically and would not "turn into another Stekel" (Falzeder and Brabant 2000, 423–24).

Why Freud should have regarded Stekel with such animosity is difficult to determine. From Ferenczi's protestations, it would appear that Stekel had become a byword for sexual transgressions with patients, although this was by no means a rare problem, and I am not aware of any other evidence that supports this accusation. But Freud had other reasons to harbor a grudge against Stekel. A principal one was the *Zentrallblatt für Psychoanalyse*, the journal founded in 1910 to placate Freud's Viennese followers after the Nuremburg Congress at which Jung had been elected President of the newly formed International Psychoanalytic Association. Adler and Stekel were appointed editors of the *Zentrallblatt*, with Freud as its director, and it was agreed that each member of the triumvirate would have a veto power over all submissions. Ironically, Freud exercised his veto power against Stekel's paper, "The Obligation of the Name," and he sought to install Victor Tausk, who had clashed with Stekel at meetings of the Vienna Psychoanalytic Society, as a review editor of the journal. Matters came to a head when, after securing Adler's resignation from the editorship, Freud sought to oust Stekel, only to dis-

11. The most up-to-date research on Stekel has been done by Clark-Lowes (2001). A useful summary of what was previously known is provided by Roazen (1971, 211–22).

cover that Stekel had entered into a secret agreement with the publisher, J. F. Bergmann, providing for Freud's dismissal in the event of a dispute.[12] In his last letter to Jung, dated January 27, 1913, Freud branded Stekel's action "a "pretty piece of treachery" (McGuire 1974, 541), and he never forgot it.[13] Freud's inability to wrest the *Zentrallblatt* from Stekel, who ended the journal with the onset of World War I, led Freud and his allies to launch the *Internationale Zeitschrift für Psychoanalyse* in its stead.

Stekel's thwarting of Freud with respect to the *Zentrallblatt* could not be held against anyone else, but this did not deter Freud from elevating him into a bogeyman in his dealings with Ferenczi and Groddeck. As a theorist, Stekel was famed for his intuitive grasp of sexual symbolism, a talent that earned Freud's admiration but for which he also castigated Stekel for his arbitrariness and crudity.[14] In this respect, Groddeck resembled Stekel, as one of his foremost detractors, Oscar Pfister, recognized. From January to March 1921, Freud and Pfister engaged in an

12. On Stekel's pact with Bergmann, see Clark (1980, 329). In his *Autobiography* (1950, 127–45), Stekel details his clashes with Tausk and Freud, but neglects to mention his devious counterplot, however justified his suspicions of Freud may have been.

13. In *On the History of the Psycho-Analytic Movement*, Freud contented himself with hinting darkly that it was "not easy to publish an account" of Stekel's behavior (1914a, 47). When Stekel, upon learning of Freud's cancer in 1923, sought a reconciliation, Freud brusquely rebuffed him with the reminder that "I broke with you after you deceived me in the most heinous manner (You never even mentioned this occasion—*Zentrallblatt*—in your letters)" (1960, 347–48). To Wittels Freud wrote in the same year that he had ignored Stekel's "lack of self-criticism and truthfulness" until "a certain occasion which revealed his treachery and ugly dishonesty" (346). Even before the conflict over the journal, however, Freud in a letter to Jung of November 11, 1909, branded Stekel "a perfect swine" (McGuire 1974, 259), so Stekel's behavior on this occasion may have been less the cause of than an excuse for Freud's outrage.

14. This ambivalence is reflected in Freud's recurrent use of olfactory metaphors to describe Stekel. At a 1909 meeting of the Vienna Psychoanalytic Society, Freud referred to Stekel as endowed with a "scent" for the unconscious (Nunberg and Federn 1967, 273); and he reiterated this sentiment in writing to Jung on November 11, 1909: "[Stekel] is a slovenly, uncritical fellow who undermines all discipline. . . . Unfortunately, he has the best nose of any of us for the secrets of the unconscious" (McGuire 1974, 259). Stekel's book, *The Language of Dreams*, he noted on March 14, 1911, was "rich in content—the pig finds truffles, but otherwise . . . incredibly sloppy" (404). In a 1925 addendum to *The Interpretation of Dreams*, Freud ambivalently described Stekel as one who "has perhaps damaged psychoanalysis as much as he has benefited it," and compared his intuitive gift for understanding symbols to basing "the diagnosis of infectious diseases upon olfactory impressions received at the patient's bedside—though there have undoubtedly been clinicians who could accomplish more than other people by means of the sense of smell (which is usually atrophied) and were really able to diagnose a case of enteric fever by

epistolary debate over Groddeck's novel *The Soul-Seeker*, which Pfister censured for its licentiousness. When Freud defended Groddeck by comparing him to Rabelais, the Swiss pastor responded that "his interpretations are too Stekelian for me," though he conceded that "the state of mind that leads you to encourage Groddeck is exactly the same as that which made you the discoverer and pioneer of psychoanalysis" (Freud and Pfister 1963, 81).

Beyond the three grounds I have already enumerated—Stekel's presumed sexual transgressions, the dispute over the *Zentrallblatt*, and Stekel's unscientific aptitude for decoding symbols—there is yet another likely reason for Freud's antipathy to Stekel, and it bears directly on Freud's response to Groddeck. Difficult though it may be to take seriously today, one of the chief controversies between Freud and Stekel, thrashed out at meetings of the Vienna Psychoanalytic Society in 1911 and 1912, had to do with whether masturbation and allied sexual practices such as *coitus interruptus* had deleterious physical consequences, or whether any ill effects were solely the result of psychological conflicts. Whereas Freud sought to preserve his pre-1900 distinction between "actual" (i.e., present-day) neurosis and psychoneurosis by positing the category of non-psychological anxiety neurosis, Stekel held that masturbation and other allegedly inferior modes of sexual release produced no somatic toxins and that the meaning of these behaviors could, like those of any other symptom, be explored through psychoanalysis.

Freud's clash with Stekel over masturbation was on the surface a theoretical matter, but it had a personal undercurrent. As one of Freud's earliest disciples, Stekel in 1900 underwent an eight-session analysis; and in a reprehensible breach of confidentiality, Freud wrote in 1924 to Wittels, who had become Stekel's pupil and analysand after falling out of favor with Freud: "One day when I am no more—my discretion will also go with me to my grave—it will become manifest that Stekel's assertion about the harmlessness of masturbation is based on a lie" (1960, 352).[15] In view of Freud's prejudices against masturbation, and that he continued to associate this practice with Stekel a quarter-century after his analysis,

smell" (1900, 350–51). As Clark-Lowes has observed, "these condescending remarks are, of course, backhanded compliments" (2001, 71).

15. As Roazen points out (1971, 212), Ernst Freud makes nonsense of this passage in his edition of Freud's letters by inserting the phrase "my alleged claim of" in square brackets after "Stekel's assertion about." Stekel, not Freud, regarded masturbation as innocuous; and, as he would later do with Ferenczi, Freud casts aspersions on Stekel's sanity as a refutation of his well-founded theoretical position. In addition to specifying the duration of

it is not surprising that he was perturbed by *The Book of the It* and that his reading of Groddeck's manuscript caused him to see the "warning example" of Stekel looming on the horizon.

In *The Book of the It*, Groddeck not only depicts masturbation as the primordial manifestation of human sexuality but also reports his own experiences with astonishing frankness. Indeed, in letter 5, he accords masturbation the centrality that Freud, in *Totem and Taboo* had reserved for the Oedipus complex: "our human world, our culture is in large part built on self-gratification" (Groddeck 1923, 51). Rejecting the conventional assumption that masturbation is a substitute for sexual intercourse, Groddeck claims the reverse to be true: "Self-gratification accompanies the person in one form or another throughout the whole of life; so-called normal sexual activity, however, first makes an appearance at a certain age and often disappears at a time when masturbation once again resumes the childlike form of a conscious play with the sexual parts" (55). On a personal note, Groddeck informs his readers that his mother used to remove his penis from its foreskin to enable him to urinate (64; letter 6); that he wet his bed until he was a teenager (181; letter 20); that at the age of sixteen a friend warned him, "'If you go on masturbating like that, you'll be totally crazy; you're half-crazy already,'" after which he contracted scarlet fever (219–20; letter 25); that his masturbation fantasies were filled "almost exclusively with the love of boys" (229; letter 26), and so forth. Unlike Ferenczi, who confided his masturbatory exploits to the *Clinical Diary*, Groddeck flaunted his in *The Book of the It*; and this breach of decorum must have struck Freud as a "misdeed."[16]

When Freud compared him to Stekel, Groddeck knew that he was being chastised, but not precisely how or why, since he was not privy to what had caused the animosity between the two men. Quite by chance, however, Freud's barb struck Groddeck in his Achilles' heel since, as he admitted—first in general terms in his reply on August 6, 1921, and then

---

his analysis, Stekel himself indicates that he consulted Freud about "some sexual problems" and discloses that he suffered from impotence for two years during his unhappy first marriage (1950, 107, 123). Presumably, Freud attributed Stekel's impotence to masturbation.

16. Freud continued to campaign against masturbation in his 1938 jottings, "Findings, Ideas, Problems": "The ultimate ground of all intellectual inhibitions and all inhibitions of work seems to be the inhibition of masturbation in childhood. But perhaps it goes deeper; perhaps it is not its inhibition by external influences but its unsatisfying nature in itself. There is always something lacking for complete discharge and satisfaction" (1941, 300).

explicitly on May 31, 1923—he "had appropriated various things from Stekel's book on the dream, without having really digested it" (Freud and Groddeck 1974, 65). As Groddeck wrote to Rank on May 7, 1922: "All I know by Stekel is *The Language of Dreams*, but I stole a great deal from it, especially number symbolism. Freud's warning hit me in a sensitive spot, and hence arises the anger expressed in my letters. Why I transferred the resentment meant for father Freud onto you and the Press goes without saying."[17] Notwithstanding this self-analysis, Groddeck did not get over his anger at Freud's rebuke; and he disclosed his true feelings in a letter to his wife, Emmy, of May 15, 1923: "*The Ego and the Id* is nice, but for me entirely inconsequential." Groddeck went on to disparage Freud's work as "fundamentally a composition secretly meant to enhance himself by borrowing from Stekel and me. His Id has thereby only a limited worth for the neuroses. He only makes the step into the organic secretly, with the help of a death- or destruction-drive taken from Stekel and Spielrein" (Freud and Groddeck 1974, 103).

Freud may have missed the mark in accusing Groddeck of having borrowed the It from Nietzsche, but Groddeck had indeed stolen from Stekel; and he retaliated by charging Freud (behind his back) with having committed the same offense. Despite his animus, Groddeck's citing of Spielrein and Stekel as two immediate sources for Freud's concept of the death instinct is historically accurate.[18] What is more, from the standpoint of contemporary relational theory, his dismissal of *The Ego and the Id* as "entirely inconsequential" now seems prescient rather than eccentric. In a 1928 paper, Groddeck states explicitly that in *The Ego and the Id* Freud "does something which is the exact opposite of what I intended with the choice of the word '*Es*'. . . . The consequence is that my

17. I quote this letter from a manuscript in the Groddeck archive, formerly located in Freiburg and now housed with the Schiller archive in Marbach. Groddeck's apology for shifting his resentment from "father Freud" to Rank ironically prefigures Rank's own abject December 20, 1924, *Rundbrief* to members of the Committee abjuring *The Trauma of Birth* and his strivings for independence: "my affective reactions toward the Professor and you, insofar as you represent for me the brothers near to him, stemmed from unconscious conflicts" (quoted in Taft 1958, 110). *The Language of Dreams* was published in 1911.

18. As Kerr (1993, 498–502) has shown, although Freud claims Spielrein as a precursor in *Beyond the Pleasure Principle*, her thesis that the ego fears its destruction through sexuality in fact differs fundamentally from the death instinct. In his *Autobiography*, Stekel protests that "Freud later adopted many of my discoveries without mentioning my name. Even the fact that . . . I had defined anxiety as the reaction of the *life instinct* against the upsurge of the *death instinct* was not mentioned in his later books, and many people believe that the death instinct is Freud's discovery" (1950, 138).

Book of the It is incomprehensible to all those people who adopted the later, Freudian meaning of the word" (212). As Herbert Will has remarked, *The Ego and the Id* "cast the development of psychoanalytic theory into a direction diametrically opposed to Groddeck's thought" (1984, 74). James Strachey's decision to translate Freud's *Ich* and *Es* by the Latin "ego" and "id," instead of the vernacular "I" and "it," thus turns out to have been a masterstroke, since it catches precisely the distinction between Freud's scholastic structural theory and Groddeck's sweeping and unabashedly subjective vision of the power of the It to shape human life. As Freud wrote to him on June 18, 1925, "In your It [*Es*] I naturally cannot recognize my civilized, bourgeois id [*Es*] stripped of mysticism. Still, you know, mine is derived from yours" (Freud and Groddeck 1974, 79).

Freud's pairing of Groddeck with both Nietzsche and Stekel—his most formidable precursor and most scorned disciple—reflects the ambivalence in his attitude toward this brilliant but unruly noncommissioned officer in the "savage army." For others in the psychoanalytic movement, Groddeck, who made his début at the 1920 congress at The Hague with a free associative monologue in which he cheerfully proclaimed himself to be a "wild analyst," functioned as an ideological touchstone. Whereas those of orthodox temperament inevitably regarded him with suspicion and dislike, liberal spirits welcomed his iconoclasm with bemused approbation. Besides Pfister, those ranged against Groddeck were led by Abraham and Jones, the latter going so far as to write to Freud on December 12, 1928, that Groddeck "has very little knowledge of ψα and it is a pity he was admitted to the movement, for he certainly does it more harm than good" (Paskauskas 1993, 655).[19]

On the other side, Groddeck's partisans included Erich Fromm, Frieda Fromm-Reichmann, Karen Horney, and Ernst Simmel. Horney began corresponding with Groddeck after reading *The Book of the It*, and her first shot across the bow of Freud's phallocentrism, "The Genesis of the Castration Complex in Women," was published in the fateful

19. Abraham reported on the Bad Homburg Congress in a letter to Freud of September 8, 1925: "there was only one [paper] which was really bad and that was Groddeck's." In the same letter, Abraham dismisses Ferenczi's paper, "Contra-Indications to the 'Active' Psycho-Analytical Technique," which initiates the turn to empathy, mutuality, and the exploration of the effects of childhood trauma in Ferenczi's final period, as "not as rich as usual in original ideas" (Freud and Abraham 1965, 393). This is likewise the letter (cited in chapter 5, note 4) in which Abraham, with perhaps greater justice, characterizes Rank as "really ill" and in a "manic phase."

year of 1923. Recognizing Groddeck's feminist leanings, Horney cited him both in "The Flight from Womanhood" (1926) and "The Dread of Woman" (1932). In a 1933 letter to Groddeck, Fromm-Reichmann praised him unstintingly: "Nothing psychoanalytic that has ever been published speaks to me with such immediacy—as at once so new and long-familiar—as your books. Scarcely anything has a more bracing effect on me, and nothing makes the picture of what psychoanalysis really is more alive or assured for me than what you say about it" (quoted in Will 1984, 184).[20]

As I have argued in the foregoing chapters, Ferenczi formed a bond of friendship with Groddeck in which each man found in the other the unconditional acceptance that neither had been able to obtain from Freud. Rank's relationship with Groddeck was far more distant. Like the other creators of relational psychoanalysis, he was favorably impressed by Groddeck's improvised performance at The Hague. Reciprocally, Groddeck wrote to Freud on October 17, 1920: "Rank's acquaintance was especially pleasant for me. The few words that he spoke at the Congress said definitively and clearly what he meant, and that is a gift which interests me" (Freud and Groddeck 1974, 33). In his editorial capacity, Rank supplied Groddeck with the perfect title for his 1921 novel, *The Soul-Seeker* (*Der Seelensucher*); and, upon its publication, he seconded Freud's defense of the work against Pfister's carpings. But Groddeck's relationship with Rank soured over *The Book of the It*. Rank once again acted as Freud's surrogate, though now his task was to mandate cuts rather than to be Groddeck's advocate. Groddeck's resentment came to the fore not only in the previously quoted 1922 letter to Rank but also in his letter to Freud of May 31, 1923, in which Groddeck instanced Rank's interference and Freud's comparison of him to Stekel as causes of the "mighty louse" that had troubled his relationship with Freud (Freud and Groddeck 1974, 65). Whatever sympathy may have existed between Rank and

20. Fromm wrote to Groddeck's widow in 1934, "He was so great as a person that one thinks of the psychologist only in the second place; and yet he was scarcely less unique as a psychologist than as a person" (quoted in Will 1994, 721). On Horney and Groddeck, see Quinn (1987, 215–17) and Grossman and Grossman (1965, 132–33). Fromm was first Fromm-Reichmann's husband and later Horney's lover. Simmel, a Berlin analyst of socialist convictions known for taking on intractable cases, hailed Groddeck on his sixtieth birthday in 1926 as "a fanatic in the cause of healing" and a "wild" analyst only in the laudatory sense that "he owes his treatment to no one but himself" (quoted in Grossman and Grossman 1965, 167). In the aftermath of World War I, Simmel's percipient view of war neurosis as a traumatic stress disorder stood in sharp contrast to Freud's doctrinaire attempt to explain shell shock in terms of his sexual theory (Breger 2000, 258–59).

Groddeck evaporated over *The Book of the It*, but the absence of genuine affective ties precluded a violent quarrel.

Like Rank, Lou Andreas-Salomé was initially quite taken with Groddeck, commending especially his "Psychic Conditioning and the Psychoanalytic Treatment of Organic Disorders" (1917), but later came to view him with pronounced reserve. Her critique, however, was considerably more discerning than those of Abraham and Jones. In a letter of September 3, 1924, she chided Freud for describing "the sick man as a criminal to be punished," because he thereby seemed to concur with Groddeck that "the actual form our physical suffering takes is not a matter of chance." Instead of blaming himself for his recently diagnosed cancer, Andreas-Salomé pleaded with Freud to recognize that a human being paradoxically "both is and is not his own body—that his body despite everything is a piece of external reality like any other" (Freud and Andreas-Salomé 1966, 138).

Andreas-Salomé's letter to Freud, protesting against Groddeck, is sandwiched between two others that take up the cudgels against Rank, including that (discussed in chapter 5) of September 21, 1924, in which she trenchantly anatomizes *An Analysis of a Neurosis in Dreams*. In the crisis precipitated by Rank's publication of *The Trauma of Birth* and his ensuing break with Freud, the tumult over *The Book of the It* constituted a sideshow. Still, the loyalists' campaigns against Rank and Groddeck unrolled in tandem, and they exhibit striking parallels. Freud initially greeted *The Trauma of Birth* as a major contribution. As Ferenczi reminded him on March 24, 1924, he had said to him about Rank's thesis, "'I don't know if 33 or 66% of it is true; in any case, this is the most significant advance since the discovery of psychoanalysis. Someone else would have made himself independent with this discovery'" (Falzeder and Brabant 2000, 131). Less familiar is his comment to Pfister in 1923, "Groddeck is surely 4/5 right with his relating of organic suffering to the It, and perhaps even with the other 1/5 he points to the right thing" (quoted in Grossman and Grossman 1965, 129). In both cases, Freud comes down in favor the works in question; indeed, these are the highwater marks of his assessments of *The Trauma of Birth* and *The Book of the It*. But by his very reliance on a calculus of percentages, Freud indicates that his approval is not unqualified and thereby sows the seeds of subsequent discord.

As Freud, spurred on by his conservative lieutenants, became increasingly disenchanted with Rank, he expressed his criticisms of the birth trauma theory in "The Dissolution of the Oedipus Complex" (1924) and

Inhibitions, Symptoms and Anxiety (1926b). Strikingly, Freud's sharpest rebuke of Groddeck likewise occurs in *Inhibitions, Symptoms and Anxiety*, where, as with Rank, he does not mention the latter by name. Acerbically remarking that "many writers have laid much stress on the weakness of the ego in relation to the id and of our rational elements in the face of the daemonic forces within us; and they display a strong tendency to make what I have said into a cornerstone of a psycho-analytic *Weltanschauung*," Freud deplores those who would adopt "such an extreme and one-sided view." He adds, "I am not partial to the fabrication of *Weltanschauungen*. Such activities may be left to the philosophers" (95–96).

In his letter of March 24, 1924, Ferenczi comes to Rank's defense and asks Freud whether "already the title 'Decline of the Oedipus Complex' [perhaps according to Spengler's book title?] is tinged by affect."[21] He seeks to reassure Freud that "no basis for affective reaction exists" in *The Trauma of Birth*; rather, "only the bio-psychological *foundation* for your immortal discoveries is becoming evident everywhere" (Falzeder and Brabant 2000, 132–33). Replying two days later, Freud concedes, "you may be right that the affect-tinged title indicates an agitation in me that has to do with the birth trauma," though he insists that "I didn't mean that the Oedipus complex is succumbing to the Rankian doctrine of birth trauma" (136).

With both Rank and Groddeck, moreover, Freud's antipathy to their theoretical innovations leads him to stoop to *ad hominem* accusations. Again, his attack on Rank is familiar. Freud wrote on July 23, 1924: "The exclusion of the father in your theory seems to me to reveal too much the result of personal influences in your life which I think I recognize, and my suspicion grows that you would not have written this book [*The Trauma of Birth*] had you gone through an analysis yourself" (quoted in Taft 1958, 99). (This reverses Freud's previous attitude, expressed in a *Rundbrief* of December 22, 1922: "In 15 years of consistently intimate working relationship with Rank the idea scarcely occurred to me, that *he* needed an analysis" [quoted in Lieberman 1985, 185].) Similarly, Freud chided Groddeck on Christmas Day 1922—in the same letter in which he first advanced the claim that Groddeck had derived the It from Nietzsche—because of "your placement of my person in the maternal

21. Freud's German word, *Untergang*, was the same as that used by Oswald Spengler in his influential work *Decline of the West* (1922). As Grubrich-Simitis has pointed out (1993, 70), in his manuscript of "The Dissolution of the Oedipus Complex" Freud had described *The Trauma of Birth* as "fascinating," but in the published version of the paper Rank's book was downgraded to merely "interesting." The brackets are Ferenczi's.

sequence—into which I obviously do not fit," noting that this "shows clearly how you want to evade the father transference" (Freud and Groddeck 1974, 59).[22]

Both Rank and Groddeck naturally objected to the aspersions cast by Freud on their motives. Rank denied that he had "excluded the father," claiming simply to have given him "the correct place"; he likewise insisted that Freud's interpretation "says nothing of the truth or value of this insight" since psychoanalysis itself teaches us that "the greatest achievements themselves result from complexes and their overcoming" (quoted in Taft 1958, 100–102). Groddeck's rejoinder came in a letter of May 23, 1923. Like Rank, he admitted the subjective determinants of his thought, but argued that they did not undermine its validity: "I am aware of my own complexes in the father question, but cannot help it for the time being that I operate better with the mother than the father." He appended a proviso: "The investigation of castration can, however, scarcely bypass the act of birth and of sucking and weaning, and I believe for the time being that this anxiety pertains as much to the mother as to the father, and that it finds a third root in evacuations" (Freud and Groddeck 1974, 64).[23] Groddeck thus not only joins Rank in incurring Freud's wrath by challenging his one-sided preoccupation with the father at the expense of the mother, but he anticipates Rank's shift in *The Trauma of Birth* away from the triangular structure of Oedipus complex and toward a concern with dyadic issues of separation and loss.

Although Groddeck's role in founding the relational tradition has been accorded less recognition by psychoanalysts than those of Ferenczi or Rank, he has paradoxically had the greatest influence on American culture at large. Here too, however, Groddeck's ideas have generated

22. H.D. reports Freud's comment during her analysis in 1933, "I do *not* like to be the mother in transference—it always surprises and shocks me a little. I feel so very masculine" (1933, 146–47). As he did with Groddeck and Rank, to say nothing of Ferenczi, Freud resisted the maternal role with H.D.; but at least in her case he did not blame the patient for his own limitations.

23. In a footnote added in 1923 to the case of Little Hans, Freud sought to counter the notion that birth, weaning, and the loss of feces are experienced by the infant as separations on a par with castration, insisting that "the term 'castration complex' ought to be confined to those excitations and consequences which are bound up with the loss of the *penis*" (1909a, 8). Freud omits Groddeck, but the latter's argument complements those of Stärcke, Andreas-Salomé, and Alexander cited in Freud's note. In 1920, Groddeck had written in "On the It" that birth "marks a stage in the process of the child's separation from the mother, which will continue throughout life from that moment" (151).

sharply polarized reactions. On the one hand, in *Illness as Metaphor* Susan Sontag reprehends Groddeck as the epitome of a bad physician who, because he ascribes diseases to internal causes, holds the patient responsible for his or her own suffering. Sontag believes this outlook to be particularly insidious in the case of cancer because Groddeck seeks to connect the disease to the patient's repressed character. "Such preposterous and dangerous views," she writes, "manage to put the onus of the disease on the patient and not only weaken the patient's ability to understand the range of plausible medical treatment but also, implicitly, direct the patient away from such treatment" (1978, 47).

Sontag arraigns Groddeck's defects, but fails to do justice to his considerable virtues. The main thesis of her book, after all, is that "illness is *not* a metaphor, and that the most truthful way of regarding illness—and the healthiest way of being ill—is one most purified of, most resistant to, metaphoric thinking" (1978, 3). From a psychoanalytic standpoint, Sontag's prescription of an exclusively literal-minded approach to illness is no less futile than it is misguided. Her puritanism overlooks that human beings engage in primary process as well as secondary process thinking, and metaphors are endemic to the primary process. Like Andreas-Salomé, Sontag justifiably resists the masochistic view of "the sick man as a criminal to be punished," but she fails to consider that even a physical illness for which one is not responsible will be given unconscious meanings by the person who suffers from it. What is more, how a patient thinks about his or her condition—that is, the metaphors that one fashions—has a demonstrable effect on the efforts of the body's immune system to fight its disease.[24]

A far more judicious (and appreciative) response to Groddeck is furnished by Oliver Sacks. Preemptively rebutting Sontag, Sacks takes as the epigraph to *Migraine* Groddeck's declaration, "Illness does not come from without; man creates it for himself." According to Sacks, "a migraine is a physical event which may also be from the start, or later

24. Sontag's attack on regarding illness as metaphor extends the anti-intellectualism of her essay "Against Interpretation," where she compares criticism to environmental pollution: "Like the fumes of the automobile and of heavy industry, which befoul the urban atmosphere, the effusion of interpretations of art today poisons our sensibilities" (1964, 7). Sontag's romanticism causes her to be no less suspicious of consciousness than of the unconscious, and her notion that one can have an unmediated experience of art—or an unmetaphorical experience of illness—is no less "preposterous and dangerous" than Groddeck's antipathy to science.

become, an emotional or symbolic event. A migraine expresses both physiological and emotional needs: it is the prototype of a psycho-physiological reaction" (1970, 29). Sacks does not take the extreme position that every migraine must have a psychological cause; he grants that it may originate as a physical affliction and only later become a "symbolic event." Nonetheless, the neurologically trained Sacks joins Groddeck in recognizing the inseparability of the somatic from the psychic and endorsing the principle that even a "physical event" can represent unconscious "emotional needs." However an illness arises, Sacks and Groddeck agree that it will be invested with meanings inscribed by the It.

A consummate illustration of the intertwining of psyche and soma is afforded by Freud's own cancer. On November 6, 1917, less than six months after receiving his first letter from Groddeck, he wrote to Ferenczi:

> Yesterday I smoked away my last cigar, and since then I have been grumpy and tired, got heart palpitations and an increase in the painful swelling of my gums (carcinoma? etc.), which has been noticeable since the meager days. Then a patient brought me fifty cigars, I lit one, became cheerful, and the gum irritation rapidly abated! I wouldn't have believed it, if it weren't so striking. Totally Groddeck. (Falzeder and Brabant 1996, 245)

In a macabre inversion of the medical reality, Freud associates a premonition of his cancer of the jaw with a temporary *cessation* of smoking—necessitated by wartime deprivation—and an alleviation of his symptoms with a resumption of his habit. As Freud's conclusion attests, Groddeck's name had already become synonymous with such ostensibly miraculous psychosomatic cures.

The tragic irony of Freud's letter to Ferenczi, however, comes fully into view only if one probes his thoughts about smoking more deeply. Writing to Fliess on December 22, 1897, Freud imparted his latest revelation: "The insight has dawned on me that masturbation is the one major habit, the 'primary addiction,' and it is only as a substitute and replacement for it that the other addictions—to alcohol, morphine, tobacco, and the like—come into existence" (Masson 1985, 287). Freud, as we know, insisted in defiance of both Stekel and logic that masturbation had noxious physical effects, and (unlike Ferenczi and Groddeck) he never admitted in so many words to having engaged in the practice himself.[25] Nonetheless, his description of smoking as a replacement for the "'primary addiction'" carries an implicit self-reference. Fliess, moreover, concurred with Freud that masturbation caused sundry physical ills, which he connected to "genital spots" in the nose; and the topic of operations on noses—on Freud's own as well as Emma Eckstein's—was a recurrent one in their correspondence.[26] Freud wrote on February 19, 1899: "self-punishment is the final substitute for self-gratification, which comes from masturbation" (345). As Max Schur has observed, Freud's linking of masturbation to both smoking and self-punishment makes masturbation not only the "'primal addiction'" but also, in Schur's words, the "original sin" (1972, 193). He quotes Freud's letter to Eitingon of July 13, 1931, thanking him for a gift of cigars, which he continued to smoke despite the lesions in his mouth: "I am again sinning more" (412).

As I have proposed, the year 1923 constitutes a turning point for psychoanalysis, not only because of the convergence between *The Ego and the Id* and the antithetical texts of Rank, Ferenczi, and Groddeck, but also because of the onset of Freud's cancer. In a letter of January 4, 1924, Groddeck renewed a long-standing appeal to Freud to visit him at his sanatorium in Baden-Baden; at the same time he drew Freud's attention to a passage in *The Psychopathology of Everyday Life* that, along with his wife, he believed "permits an entry to the deep layers of your unconscious, access to which might lead to the healing layers of your being"

25. Freud's masturbation fantasies fuel both "Screen Memories" (1899) and his "botanical monograph" dream in *The Interpretation of Dreams* (1900, 169–76, 282–84). Swales (1983, 17–18) cites letters between Jones and Bernfeld discussing how this delicate topic ought to be handled in Jones's biography. Regarding "Screen Memories," Vitz makes the point that, contrary to his own theory, "Freud gave no really clear trauma or decisive event" (1988, 134) that lay concealed behind the ostensibly innocuous childhood memory of his and John's "defloration" of Pauline recounted in the paper; and Vitz nominates either the disappearance of Freud's nursemaid or his own "seduction to masturbation" (Freud 1899, 319) by that same nursemaid as the most likely candidates for the occluded trauma.

26. Webster (1995, 221, 224) has proposed that Fliess's 1893 account of "a recent case in which, in a typical neurasthenic episode associated with ophthalmic migraine caused by onanistic abuse, the nasal membranes were very much swollen," may refer to Freud. As late as the Dora case, Freud affirmed that "gastric pains occur especially often in those who masturbate" and cited a "personal communication" from Fliess (from whom he was by then estranged) that "it is precisely gastralgias of this character which can be interrupted by an application of cocaine to the 'gastric spot' discovered by him in the nose, and which can be cured by cauterization of the same spot" (1905a, 78).

(Freud and Groddeck 1974, 72). Although many of Freud's followers, including Jung and Rank, attempted in the course of their relationships to analyze him to a certain extent, after Freud was struck by cancer, only Groddeck and Ferenczi seriously offered to take him into analytic therapy. As Ferenczi wrote on February 26, 1926, "Perhaps this is the occasion on which I can say to you that I find it actually tragic that you, who endowed the world with psychoanalysis, find it so difficult to be—indeed, are not at all—in a position to entrust yourself to anyone" (Falzeder and Brabant 2000, 250). That this suggestion should have come independently from Ferenczi and Groddeck attests both to their wisdom and to their compassion for Freud. Although it is sometimes assumed to be out of the question that Freud could have turned to anyone else for analysis, surely either Ferenczi or Groddeck could have been of genuine help to him had he been willing to risk exposing his vulnerabilities to them in psychotherapy.

The passage in *The Psychopathology of Everyday Life* to which Groddeck draws Freud's attention concerns the unconscious psychic determinism of numbers chosen apparently at random. It contains an autobiographical example that Freud had originally reported in a letter to Fliess of August 27, 1899, transcribed in his published work of 1901.[27] As Freud had written to Fliess, he was resolved to make no more corrections to *The Interpretation of Dreams*, even if that meant that the book would "contain 2,467 mistakes—which I shall leave in it" (Masson 1985, 368).

The question then becomes, how did Freud happen to arrive at this number? The answer, as he recounts it in the *Psychopathology*, turns on a story that Freud had read in the newspaper in 1899 about a general who had recently retired from his post. Freud had once met the man, in 1880, when he himself was a twenty-four-year-old medical officer in military service. "That gives you the '24' in 2,467," he explains (1901, 243). In 1899, Freud was forty-three. Then, he continues, "take my present age—43—add 24, and you have 67." The entire episode had been triggered by his wife's jest that he, like the general, should already "'be on the retired list.'" Stung by the disparity between the General's distinguished career and his own lack of eminence, but consoled by the

---

27. The postscript containing this analysis is missing from the Freud-Fliess correspondence since Freud had asked Fliess to return the sheet in order to be able to utilize it for *The Psychopathology of Everyday Life*.

thought of his comparative youth, Freud writes, "my wish gave me another twenty-four years' work."[28]

What is uncanny, as Groddeck's wife, Emmy, realized in the course of preparing a Swedish translation of *The Psychopathology of Everyday Life*, and Groddeck in turn imparted to Freud in his letter inviting him to Baden-Baden, is that in 1923, when he contracted his cancer, he was sixty-seven years old, "exactly the age at which the master of ordnance was retired" (Freud and Groddeck 1974, 72). Even more remarkably, though neither Emmy Groddeck nor anyone else appears to have realized it at the time, this was also twenty-four years after 1899, when Freud had read the article about the retired general and made up the unconsciously determined number 2,467. In light of this series of coincidences, the possibility arises that when Freud was stricken by cancer in 1923, the disease fulfilled his wish in 1899 for twenty-four more years of work, and was thus indeed a symbolic expression of his It. Strikingly, Freud himself allowed for such an eventuality in writing to Ferenczi on February 23, 1909: "in some patients, the maturation of the illness is the fulfillment of a forgotten (repressed) wish" (Brabant, Falzeder, and Giampieri-Deutsch 1993, 46).

After Groddeck, the first to explore the ramifications of the number 2,467 was Max Schur, who became Freud's personal physician in his final years. In his biography, Schur opposes the line of speculation that I have here propounded: "Let me reiterate that I in no way believe that Freud developed cancer at 67 because at 43 he wished for 24 more years of productive work" (1972, 197). Despite this disclaimer, however, Schur admits the likelihood that Freud's behavior in 1923, which included taking no action for two months after he noticed a lesion in his mouth, might have been influenced by a fatalism concerning the date of his death that was

28. Freud reverts to this vignette in his letter to Jung of April 16, 1909, in which he seeks to counteract the effects of an incident in which Jung, during a visit to Vienna, had accurately predicted the repetition of a mysterious noise in Freud's bookcase. In a letter of April 2, Jung adduced this feat of prognostication as evidence of a prospective "'psychosynthesis' which creates future events according to the same laws" as those of psychoanalysis (McGuire 1974, 216). In his reply, Freud analyzed his own superstition (focusing on the belief that he would die at the age of sixty-one or sixty-two, not sixty-seven), tracing it back to the "hidden influence" of Fliess, in order to explode Jung's "spook complex," which he proposed to regard as a "charming delusion" (219–20). In addition to demonstrating Freud's continuing preoccupation with the number 2,467, this letter links Jung to both Fliess and Groddeck as proponents of a parapsychological mysticism that, like literature, at once attracted and disconcerted Freud as the uncanny double of psychoanalysis.

reflected in what he had written in 1899. As Schur comments, "the determinants . . . could now, in 1923, be having their effect on the events of his life, 24 years later, when he had reached the age of 67" (356).

As we have seen, Schur not only follows Groddeck in examining the unconscious significance of the number 2,467 in Freud's life, but he also links Freud's cancer to his smoking, and his smoking to the "'primal addiction'" or "original sin" of masturbation, about which Freud plainly harbored a considerable degree of guilt. In this connection, Schur cites Freud's letter to Ferenczi of November 6, 1917, in which he exclaimed, "Totally Groddeck," after the apparent alleviation of the precancerous swelling of his gums when he resumed smoking cigars. In the same letter to Fliess of February 19, 1899, that he called self-punishment "the final substitute for self-gratification, which comes from masturbation," moreover, Freud compared his all-consuming work to "a sort of neoplastic tissue infiltrating the human and finally replacing it." He ominously added, "I have turned completely into a carcinoma" (Masson 1985, 344–45). Even as he highlights the prescience of Freud's metaphor, Schur again strives to preserve a balance between skepticism and faith:

> I am not inclined to believe, as some do, that the unconscious "knows" about a future illness 24 years before it becomes manifest. Nor do I believe that Freud's cancer was a *direct* consequence of guilt feelings about this "original sin" [of masturbation] or any other. I do believe, however, that on some level Freud never forgot this metaphor. . . . Freud eventually did "punish" himself: while he did not develop his cancer out of guilt, he contributed to his recurrences by persisting in his heavy smoking. (1972, 194)

Without blaming Freud for his cancer, Schur recognizes that even a physical disease can be, in Sacks's words, "an emotional or symbolic event." Thus, if we understand Groddeck metaphorically, he is surely right to insist that Freud's cancer is, as it were, pregnant with unconscious meaning and arises out of a necessity of his being. The uncanny coincidences that invite one to interpret Freud's cancer in this Groddeckian fashion, moreover, find an astonishing parallel in Ferenczi's pernicious anemia, which, as I noted in the previous chapter, also commenced in 1923, when his patient, Erzsébet Radó-Révész, who was six months pregnant at the time, perished of the same disease. Groddeck's divination that an analysis of why Freud had alighted on the number 2,467 would lead to "the deep layers of your unconscious," including conflicts over masturbation, and that this might have not only a psychological but also a physical benefit, turns out to have been entirely justified.

There is an epilogue to this story of Groddeck's attempt to minister to Freud's cancer. One of his final texts, written in 1934 and published posthumously, was "On the Psychic Conditioning of Cancer Sickness."[29] Acknowledging receipt of the manuscript, Freud wrote on March 4, 1934, that its topic "lies, unfortunately, much nearer to me" than that of a second essay on Dürer, but added, "what you say about it seems too indefinite to me, and probably also to you" (Freud and Groddeck 1974, 90). Groddeck's thesis in the former essay is that there is an "unconscious identification of the growth of a child and a cancer," and since the male "does not possess the organs required for actual pregnancy," this equation must be "symbolically expressed." Hence cancer most often strikes men in "sites specially connected with intake, nourishment, and expulsion, i.e., the mouth, the stomach, the rectum" (1951b, 162). As Ferenczi identified simultaneously with Radó-Révész and the baby in her womb who could not be saved by caesarian section, and recreated this dynamic of murder-suicide between mother and child in his failed relationship with Freud, so Groddeck avenged his grievances against Freud by consigning him for a final time to the maternal role he loathed, by extension equating himself with the cancer that, like the "embryo of some monstrous changeling" (162), was cannibalistically metastasizing inside Freud's oral cavity.

2

If *The Book of the It* is arguably the greatest masterpiece of psychoanalytic literature, its sublimity originates in Groddeck's decision to cast his work in an epistolary form. By presenting his psychoanalytic primer in the guise of thirty-three letters written by one Patrik Troll, a transparent autobiographical persona, to an unnamed lady friend, Groddeck exploited the theoretical potential of an illustrious literary genre—the epistolary novel—and turned to his creative account the quintessential mode of communication among Freud and his early disciples. Above all, by foregrounding the relationship between author and reader, Groddeck

29. In the last six weeks before his death, on June 11, 1934, in Medard Boss's sanatorium near Zurich, Groddeck suffered a psychotic breakdown, during which he apparently wrote one or more letters to Hitler appealing for support of a psychoanalytic cancer research institute. There are no surviving copies of these letters, which (if indeed they ever existed at all) may never have been mailed.

found an objective correlative for the interplay of transference and countertransference that is the nub of psychoanalytic therapy. He thereby contrived to write a text that dynamically enacts the concepts it propounds and brings unconscious processes to life in a way that remains unsurpassed to this day.

To see how Groddeck practices what he preaches, one can turn to letter 6, in which he descants on transference, repression, and symbolism. He illustrates symbolism by the example of a wedding ring, which—in contrast to those who might suppose that it stands for either eternity or a fetter—he interprets in sexual terms as a symbol of the female genital, while the finger is a symbol of the male genital. Just as the ring is to stay on the finger of the husband or wife, so their genitals are not to unite with those of other people (1923, 59). In letter 7, Patrik Troll points out to his lady friend that she has, in her (imaginary) reply, referred to transference and repression but not to symbolism, though she did happen to report that she had lost a topaz ring that once belonged to her dead sister. "But you see," Groddeck explains, "instead of mentioning the symbol in your letter, you lose it in the form of your topaz ring. Isn't that droll?" (72). He reminds his lady friend that, as a child, she had once injured the eye of that same sister with a pair of scissors, causing a scar. Because she lost the ring on the day that she had received his letter propounding his views on the centrality of masturbation to human life, against which she had protested, he infers that this sister had initiated his correspondent into "the play with the ring of the woman" (71).

The crucial dynamic to which Groddeck draws attention—the symptomatic action of his lady friend's loss of the ring, and then her failure to acknowledge his ideas on symbolism—takes place in the interstices between his letters. In indirectly confirming his theory of symbolism, the lady friend exhibits the workings of repression. She likewise exemplifies transference, notwithstanding her objections, since she reports having just seen a schoolgirl for whom she felt an affection that she found mysterious, until Patrik Troll pointed out that this girl must have reminded his lady friend of her deceased sister not only in the sharpness of her tongue but also in having a scar over her left eye.

Insofar as Groddeck (through Patrik Troll) presents himself as the expositor of psychoanalytic theory and interpreter of his lady friend's words and deeds, he assumes the role of the analyst. But inasmuch as he is the writer of the letters we read and exposes the workings of his own psyche, he also—and in a more primary sense—occupies the role of patient. At bottom, *The Book of the It* is a work of self-analysis in which the lady friend serves as a stand-in for the analyst. The crucial transference is thus Groddeck's onto his reader. He trains his self-scrutiny on his own invest-ment in the writing process and, in letter 16, analyzes the causes of his writer's cramp. Disclosing that he plays with his watch-chain as he writes—a substitute for masturbation as is the lady friend's playing with her ring—he explains: "The pen is the male sexual symbol, the paper is the receptive woman, the ink the semen, which streams out in the rapid up-and-down of writing. In other words, writing is a symbolic sexual act. But it is also simultaneously the symbol of masturbation, of the fantasied sexual act" (1923, 151). Going further, Groddeck equates the inkwell with the mother and compares his insertion of the letter into its envelope and then its opening by the recipient with pregnancy and birth respectively.

As we have seen, Freud proffers his most stringent critique of Grod-deck in *Inhibitions, Symptoms and Anxiety*, though he avoids mentioning Groddeck by name. He remarks in the same work: "As soon as writing, which entails making a liquid flow out of a tube on to a piece of white paper, assumes the significance of copulation, or as soon as walking be-comes a symbolic substitute for treading upon the body of the mother earth, both writing and walking are stopped because they represent the performance of a forbidden sexual act" (1926b, 90). The analogy be-tween writing and sexual intercourse is found not only in *The Book of the It* but also in two of Groddeck's earlier works, both of which were indu-bitably known to Freud.[30] The conclusion therefore seems inescapable that, just as Freud in *The Ego and the Id* appropriated the It from Grod-deck while falsely claiming that Groddeck had derived the concept from Nietzsche, so too in *Inhibitions, Symptoms and Anxiety* he chastised Grod-deck for constructing a *Weltanschauung* while plagiarizing one of his most cherished tropes. What had for Groddeck been a subjectively felt and artistically rendered truth, moreover, Freud flattens out into a gen-eralized and impersonal truism.

Corroboration that the lady friend of *The Book of the It* plays the parts of both analyst and patient is provided by an excavation of her biograph-ical origins. As Wolfgang Martynkewicz has shown (1997, 211–12), Grod-

30. In *The Soul-Seeker*, the protagonist Thomas Weltlein declares: "'The sheet of paper is a woman, the pen the man—'" (1921, 392). Groddeck elaborates in "The Com-pulsion to Use Symbols," published in *Imago*: "Handwriting in its hasty up-and-down, its combination of pen and ink-pot and oozing liquid, betrays its symbolic erotic origin, while the individual forms of writing with their deviations from the straight line up-or-down are symbols of excitement or slackness while gaps in a word indicate a prolongation of lust" (1922, 169).

deck modeled his fictive addressee in the first place on Hanneliese Schumann, a member of the anti-capitalist Dürer League with whom he corresponded from 1909 to 1919. Whether he and Schumann had a sexual relationship is not known, but this inference would appear warranted from letter 27, in which Patrik reminds his lady friend of a "little adventure" that the two of them shared in 1912, in which they settled a quarrel "in another fashion" than by conversation (Groddeck 1923, 235). Not only did Schumann confide her marital travails and ambivalent feelings toward her children to Groddeck, but he reciprocated with intimate disclosures of his own. He averred in 1917, "I always write to you when I need you, exactly as to my mother" (quoted in Martynkewicz 1997, 235).

Although Martynkewicz's identification of the lady friend with Schumann is convincing, it is not the whole story. Groddeck did not begin work on *The Book of the It* until 1921, two years after his correspondence with Schumann had ended. Thus, she would in all likelihood no longer have been an object of libidinal or emotional investment for him. A far more important person in his life by then was Emmy von Voigt, the Swedish widow eight years his junior whom Groddeck met as a patient at his sanatorium in Baden-Baden in 1915 and married in 1923, after the formal dissolution of his first marriage. Groddeck brought Emmy to the 1920 congress at The Hague, incurring the opprobrium of bourgeois analysts who professed to be scandalized by a married man who would attend a scientific meeting with his mistress (Martynkewicz 1997, 239). Groddeck's persona in *The Book of the It* combines "Patrik," his own nickname as a youth, with "Troll," his pet name for Emmy (Freud and Groddeck 1974, 48), though its derivation from Ibsen's *Peer Gynt* associates it in his mind also with "the negative of the mother image" (Groddeck 1927, 167).

In addition to these two women, Hanneliese Schumann and Emmy von Voigt, moreover, there can be no doubt, as François Roustang has argued, that the letters making up *The Book of the It* "are in fact addressed to Freud" (1976, 116). Born in 1866, Groddeck was the youngest of five children in his family to survive infancy. He experienced the death of his father in 1885, of his mother in 1892, and of his last remaining sibling in 1914. In a letter to Freud on August 6, 1921, Groddeck reflected on this series of bereavements: "What is especially remarkable is that, since the death of the last Groddeck, I have fastened myself with all my power of feeling to a person and empowered myself with attributes of his that daily and hourly remind me of one or another member of my family, especially my sister and my mother" (Freud and Groddeck 1974, 46). Although the "person" (*Mensch*) to whom Groddeck clings as a replacement for his deceased relatives is presumably Emmy, she goes unnamed in the letter, and all the pronouns in German are masculine, as the gender of the word *Mensch* requires. This serves, in Roustang's words, to leave "some doubt hanging over the question of who the person was and to keep open the possibility that it might have been Freud" (1976, 126), whom Groddeck finally met in 1920, three years after he had initiated their correspondence.

That Groddeck's fictive addressee, whom he addresses in letter 6 as his "dear and severe female judge" (1923, 58), includes Freud among its prototypes becomes clear when *The Book of the It* is read against the backdrop of the Freud-Groddeck correspondence. As we have seen, Freud voiced misgivings about Groddeck's work-in-progress on July 29, 1921, by saying he had perpetrated "a few misdeeds" that were ominously reminiscent of Stekel. Specifically, Freud objected to Groddeck's interpretation of the creation story in Genesis. In letter 11, Groddeck proposes that the rib from which Eve is formed represents an erect penis, which implies that Adam's primal desire is autoerotic: "the creation of woman, the cutting out of the rib, which gives rise to the wound of woman—this castration is, in the end, punishment for masturbation" (105). Groddeck accepts Freud's phallocentric theory of castration anxiety, but he fuses it with a brilliant feminist critique of how, in one of the founding myths of patriarchy, woman functions as a projection of masculine desire and fantasy. Freud, however, refuses to grant the possibility that the male usurpation of female reproductive power has a psychological meaning. For him the Genesis story has only one latent content—mother-son incest.[31] He admonishes Groddeck that the biblical text "is probably a deliberate, priestly twisting of the old myth and, as a result, also the only known example of the creation of woman from man instead of the opposite (incestuous) relationship" (Freud and Groddeck 1974, 44).

Groddeck's rejoinder to Freud's criticism comes in letter 28 of *The Book of the It*. Here Patrik Troll thanks his lady friend for urging him to publish his letters, but confesses a reluctance to revise them. In an unmistakable reference to his exchanges with Freud and Rank, he states

31. Freud had previously advanced this oedipal interpretation of the creation story in a letter to Jung of December 17, 1911, in which he deemed the Genesis account "a wretched, tendentious distortion devised by an apprentice priest." Freud credited Rank with the suggestion that "the Bible story may quite well have reversed the original myth. Then everything would be clear; Eve would be Adam's mother, and we should be dealing with the well-known motif of mother-incest" (McGuire 1974, 473).

that when, several years ago, he sent a manuscript to a trusted friend, the latter responded "with a charming letter containing many encomiastic words, but saying he thought that the thing was much too long and much too coarse. It looked, he said, like an embryo with uncannily hypertrophied sexual parts. I should cut, cut, cut, and then it would be a handsome child" (1923, 242). The friend advised him to emulate the man who followed his fiancée to the lavatory, telling himself that if what he smelled there reminded him of fresh pastry he would marry her, but that if it stank, he would set her free. Unlike the anxious suitor, however, when Patrik Troll read over what he had written, it smelled to him as fragrant as fresh pastry, and he decided to cross nothing out.

Groddeck then returns to his exegesis of the creation myth: "I confess that priests invented the stories. There you are right" (243). But he insists that his lady friend is mistaken to object that this point invalidates his thesis that, in children's fantasy, "woman arises from the man through castration." As Patrik Troll explains, children have an experiential awareness of the birth process, but "onto this original knowledge, just as occurred in the Old Testament, is then grafted the castration idea of childhood priests, parents, and other wise persons; and as Judeo-Christian humanity has for millennia believed the priestly fairy tales, so the child believes the fairy tale of his own observation and his educators' lies." In this tour de force, Groddeck rebuts Freud's charge that his interpretation relies on a "priestly twisting of the old myth" by implicitly condemning Freud himself as a modern priest who reinforces the distortions in children's understanding of their experience. Groddeck does not dispute that the fantasy of women as castrated has a tenacious hold on the human psyche, but he delves beneath the phallic-oedipal level of the creation story to expose it as an inversion of the reality that women give birth to men.

Whereas Freud comprehends only castration anxiety and the woman's desire to be a man, Groddeck accords equal weight to the man's desire to be a woman. As he sets forth his more balanced view in letter 2, "Perhaps it is also envy that leads me to mock mothers—envy that I myself am not a woman and cannot become a mother. . . . The only thing odd about the idea of the man bearing a child is that it is so stubbornly denied" (21). As I have argued in chapter 2, Freud spells out his theory of sexual difference in the case of Little Hans. Recognizing the importance of this text to his quarrel with Freud, Groddeck in letter 10 details the boy's apprehension at the prospect that his "little tail will be cut off, because from time to time Mama makes red blood instead of bright yellow peepee in the pot" (101). There could be no finer gloss on Little Hans's exclamation, "'But out of my wiwimaker there comes no blood!'" (1909a, 10; translation modified); and Groddeck's use in the immediate vicinity of both the word "*Pipimaker*" and the phrase "*der liebe Gott*" confirms that he has Freud's case on his mind. In letter 28, Groddeck caps his rejoinder to Freud on the meaning of the creation story by noting that Little Hans referred to bowel movements as "lumpf." He satirically proposes that the "earth" out of which divinity created mankind was really a stool, while "the living breath, together with its life-giving fragrance, would then have been blown out of the same hole from which came the turd" (1923, 244).

It is not by chance that Groddeck's dispute with Freud should center on sexual difference and the mother-child bond. As I have documented, Freud attacked Groddeck for seeking to place him "in the maternal sequence," which Freud regarded as proof that Groddeck wanted "to evade the father transference." By amalgamating Freud with Hanneliese Schumann and Emmy von Voigt in the persona of his lady friend, however, Groddeck refutes Freud in the most effective way possible—by imposing on Freud the maternal transference that he so adamantly resisted. That Groddeck saw Freud in fundamentally maternal terms is clear from their correspondence. On October 17, 1920, shortly after their meeting at The Hague, Groddeck wrote to Freud: "I followed you around during the Congress days in a half-twilight state, just like a lover" (Freud and Groddeck 1974, 33). As Roustang observes, Groddeck's description "recalls the picture of a child clinging onto its mother's skirts, no longer aware of anything from the outside world" (1976, 113). In the same vein, he concluded a letter to Freud on November 20, 1920: "I hope that my declarations of love do not suffer from monotony. But at bottom I am calm about it since I have seen your understanding smile, in which the word, 'judge not,' is so well personified" (Freud and Groddeck 1974, 36).

Groddeck's image of Freud as one whose "understanding smile" signifies his adherence to the Christian precept against judgment was, of course, no more than a transferential fantasy, as Groddeck soon realized. But Groddeck's longing for unconditional acceptance was real enough, and it is inextricably tied to his conflicts with the maternal imago. As he elsewhere writes: "Judge not, lest ye be also judged. Leave judgment to the mothers who cannot escape this duty, since they have to prepare their children for life. Their judgments are destined to weave the bonds of mother-love and mother-hate" (1951b, 186).[32] By the time of *The Book of the It*, Groddeck was disabused of his faith in Freud's capacity to be a benevolent nurturer, but this only served to confirm his role as a bad mother in Groddeck's mind. In a letter of September 9, 1927, he cited St. Paul's warning that "the letter killeth, but the spirit giveth life": "you are, moreover, not a reader in the usual meaning of the word, but rather Freud, and as such you might perhaps do better to judge the follies of your admirers leniently. For just as your acknowledgment bestows life, so your criticism kills" (Freud and Groddeck 1974, 84). This revised perception of Freud's maternal role is crystallized in Patrik Troll's denominating the recipient of his letters as his "dear and severe female judge."

Just as *The Book of the It* arises out of Groddeck's letters to Freud, so, too, its reception is imbricated in his correspondence with Ferenczi. As I have shown in chapter 6, Ferenczi's initial visit to Groddeck's sanatorium in Baden-Baden in September 1921—three months after the death of his mother—was a turning point in his life, and its impact was equally profound on Groddeck. Each man became for the other a surrogate for Freud, with the result that both men's relationships with Freud himself cooled markedly. In a postcard to Groddeck cosigned by all six members of the Committee, Freud wrote on September 23, 1921, "Hope you were satisfied with the substitute." To this, Ferenczi, who had just left Baden-Baden, appended the postscript, "Were you?" (Freud and Groddeck 1974, 47).

Not only did Ferenczi and Groddeck turn to each other for what neither was able to obtain from Freud, but their relationships to Freud exhibit striking parallels. Both men responded negatively to their initial encounter with Freud's works or reputation—Groddeck by his ill-informed attack in *Nasamecu* in 1913, and Ferenczi by declining to review *The Interpretation of Dreams* at the time of its publication (Moreau-Ricaud 1990, 46)—but then became converts to his cause. Just as Freud succeeded the physician Ernst Schweninger as an object of Groddeck's paternal transference, so for Ferenczi he took the place of the physician and publisher Miksa Schächter. Noting this resemblance, Will contrasts the "fraternal friendship" of Ferenczi and Groddeck with the "filial friendship" that both men formed with Freud (1994, 720). He adds that Groddeck, Ferenczi's senior by seven years, became effectively an elder brother to the latter.

32. The volume from which I quote this passage, *The World of Man*, is an amalgam of Groddeck's texts from different periods in which it is often impossible to ascertain the exact source.

An indispensable document for understanding Ferenczi's double bond to Freud and Groddeck is his lengthy Christmas Day 1921 letter to Groddeck, which contains the only extant account of the "Palermo incident" that occurred during Freud and Ferenczi's trip to Sicily in September 1910. In the course of his self-analytic meditation, Ferenczi remarks on his penchant for wordplay: "Now I realize that with such crumbs of wit as I scatter in this letter I am copying your *Letters to a Lady Friend*. Are you perhaps the Lady Friend, or is your friendship for me its homosexual substitute[?]" (Ferenczi and Groddeck 1982, 39).[33]

Clearly, Groddeck must have shared the manuscript of *The Book of the It* with Ferenczi during his visit; and the ensuing conflict in Ferenczi's mind between Groddeck and Freud is made manifest by a revealing passage earlier in his letter. Ferenczi confides: "I declare myself conquered [*besigt*] by your naturalness, your natural amiability, and disposition to friendship. Never before have I expressed myself so candidly in the presence of a man, not even of 'Siegmund' (Freud), whose name caused the error in writing the word 'conquered' [*besi(e)gt*]" (36). Ferenczi's "error" consists in his having omitted the second "e" in "*besiegt*." He explains his lapse by his association of this word with Freud's given name "Sigmund," which in its modern spelling lacks the "e" originally found in its first syllable (*Sieg* = victory; *Mund* = mouth). Thus, in spelling "Siegmund" Ferenczi restores the archaic "e" and puts the name in quotation marks, just he puts the missing "e" in parentheses when he spells "*besiegt*" correctly the second time.[34] Ferenczi's slip of the pen reveals his ambivalence toward Freud while conflating him with Groddeck. Ferenczi is "conquered" by Groddeck's kindness, which permits him to vent his pent-up resentment against Freud, by whom he has been "conquered" in a more oppressive way.

Ferenczi then informs Groddeck how, as a child, he received "too little love and too much severity" at the hands of his mother. Affection, he reports, was "something unknown" in his family, and his parents demanded a "fearful respect" (36). Ferenczi links his parents' aloofness to

33. I have supplied the question mark in Ferenczi's sentence.

34. The dynamics of Ferenczi's slip are rendered unintelligible in the German edition of the Ferenczi-Groddeck letters. The editors mistakenly assert that Ferenczi has spelled "*besiegt*" correctly, while adding a superfluous "e" to "*Siegmund*." But Ferenczi's lapse occurs not in the second but in the first use of "*besiegt*," where he has left out the second "e" and subsequently added it above the line. The spelling "*Siegmund*" and the parenthetical "e" in the second reference to "*besi(e)gt*" are both deliberate glosses of his original slip of the pen. I am grateful for this clarification to Christopher Fortune, whose English edition

his disappointment with his brief periods of formal analysis with Freud: "I could not open myself freely to him; he had too much of that 'fearful respect,' he was too great for me, too much of the father" (36–37). By placing the phrase "fearful respect" (*scheue Achtung*) in quotation marks when he uses it for a second time, Ferenczi underscores the transferential nature of his response to Freud's paternal authority. He proceeds to recall, as we have seen in chapter 6, that a "dismissive judgment"—presumably by his mother—of his youthful literary productions had wounded his self-esteem. He connects this blow to the way that a "dismissive utterance" by Freud later induced him to renounce Elma Pálos and marry her mother Gizella instead. Unlike his deliberate repetition of the phrase "fearful respect," Ferenczi appears to be unaware of the recurrence of the word "dismissive" (*abfällige*) in his letter. This suggests that Ferenczi's assimilation of Freud to his mother remains repressed, as opposed to his conscious perception of the paternal dimension of his transference.

The parallels between Ferenczi's and Groddeck's relationships to Freud extend to the psychosomatic symptoms from which they both suffered as a result of their struggles with his influence. The writer's cramp analyzed by Patrik Troll in *The Book of the It* was literally experienced by Ferenczi. As he recounts to Groddeck in his Christmas Day 1921 letter, when he strove to write *Thalassa* during World War I: "*Never* could I decide to commit this valuable—heretofore most considerable—work to paper." His inhibition did not end with the war: "A few weeks ago I developed an arthritic swelling of the right wrist; naturally that likewise prevents me from writing" (Ferenczi and Groddeck 1982, 38). And during their ill-starred 1910 trip to Sicily, when Freud had attempted to turn him into an amanuensis and bizarrely accused him of wanting to take over the Schreber case for himself, Ferenczi tells Groddeck, "the bitterness knotted my throat" (37). By the same token, Groddeck begins "Psychic Conditioning and the Psychoanalytic Treatment of Organic Disorders" by probing the psychological roots of a throat infection that prevented him from swallowing: "my It refused to swallow a piece of knowledge that it found unpleasant. This was the knowledge that certain ideas concerning the interaction between an individual's unconscious and his life were not my own, as I had been telling myself for years, but Sigmund Freud's" (1917, 109). It would be going too far to blame Freud

---

of the Ferenczi-Groddeck correspondence has now (2002) been published by Other Press.

for Groddeck's anxiety of influence, though he does bear responsibility for his browbeating of Ferenczi; but the visceral responses of both men to the threat posed by Freud to their psychic integrity are uncannily similar.

If the origin of *The Book of the It* lies in part in Groddeck's letters to Freud, while Ferenczi's letters to Groddeck provide the prototype for its sympathetic reception, it completes the circle to bring Groddeck's text to bear on an exegesis of the Freud-Ferenczi correspondence. One of the revealing features of these letters, as of all Freud's correspondences, is the salutations used by the two men. Almost from the beginning, the inequality between Freud and Ferenczi is ritualized as Ferenczi deferentially addresses Freud as "Dear Professor," while Freud greets Ferenczi as "Dear Friend." Late in the correspondence, however, the pattern is broken when in his letter of January 17, 1930, Ferenczi commences, "Dear Friend." As Ferenczi's first paragraph makes clear, this was "a parapraxis," in which "instead of the 'Professor,' I suddenly see the friend on the paper, in black and white" (Falzeder and Brabant 2000, 382).

Strikingly, it is in this letter that Ferenczi finally voices his long-suppressed personal and theoretical criticisms of Freud. These include the reproach (against which Freud continued to object in "Analysis Terminable and Interminable") that Freud had failed to analyze his negative transference, his resentments concerning "the strictness which you punished my obstinate behavior in the matter of the Schreber book"—an allusion to the Palermo incident twenty years earlier—as well as his doubts about "the one-sidedness in the development of psychoanalysis" under Freud's leadership, which Ferenczi says that only "considerations for your health kept me for a long time from communicating" (383). All these grievances were reiterated by Ferenczi in his *Clinical Diary*, and the observation about Freud's "strictness" implicitly equates him with Ferenczi's excessively severe mother.

In view of the content of this letter, certainly Ferenczi's slip in addressing Freud as "Dear Friend" is charged with meaning. But whereas Ferenczi himself interprets his parapraxis as "a sign of my real feelings" (382)—that is, an expression of his desire for a relationship of genuine mutuality and equality with Freud—even this confession of his abiding affection for Freud is laced with ambivalence. For not only has Ferenczi turned the tables on Freud—just as he experimented with an analogous role reversal in mutual analysis—but he has recast Freud in the image of Groddeck, the true friend with whom he was on linguistically intimate terms.

The genius of *The Book of the It*, as I have suggested, stems from Groddeck's deployment of the epistolary form, which allows him not merely to expound but to embody psychoanalytic teachings. In letter 10, for instance, as Patrik Troll expatiates on the Freudian doctrine of the castration complex—with, as we have seen, a tacit reliance on the case of Little Hans—he comments self-consciously on his repeated resort to dashes, noting with astonishment how "I think and write with so many interruptions of my sentences" (1923, 100). He leaves it up to his lady friend "to draw from that your own conclusions as to my personal castration complex." A similar self-reflexive moment occurs in Ferenczi's letter to Freud of October 23, 1911, which has to do with an ill-advised letter that Ferenczi had just sent to Emma Jung. Ferenczi acknowledges having misread the word "strike" (*streichen*) as "touch on" (*streifen*) in Freud's intervening letter (Brabant, Falzeder, and Giampieri-Deutsch 1993, 307). Ferenczi introduces this embarrassing theme by drawing a line in his text, to which he calls attention by saying, "At this point I have to draw a line in my letter and report a complication that I am unconsciously guilty of causing." In his reply two days later, Freud analyzes Ferenczi's act as one of "false obedience," since "you drew a line [*Strich*] in the middle of the letter and called it that. I did, after all, ask you to 'strike' both points" (308). Ferenczi, that is, "touched on" the topics to Emma Jung that Freud had asked him to avoid, but attempted to compensate for this parapraxis by belatedly drawing a "strike" in his letter to Freud.

It is a measure of Groddeck's accomplishment in *The Book of the It* that he succeeds in creating a fictional representation of unconscious mental processes no less compelling than those found in the actual correspondences of the early psychoanalysts. Threatened by Groddeck's defiance of the metapsychology of *The Ego and the Id*, however, Freud could not appreciate what Groddeck had wrought, and his enthusiasm for Groddeck's masterpiece—no less than for Rank's *The Trauma of Birth*—quickly evaporated. In a letter to Groddeck on September 7, 1927, Freud depreciated *The Book of the It* for its "unsatisfying monotony" and averred his preference for *The Soul-Seeker* through the initials of their respective authorial personae, Patrik Troll and Thomas Weltlein, "I make no secret of the fact that P.T., although I borrowed something from him, has for a long time been less sympathetic to me than T.W." (Freud and Groddeck 1974, 83).

To *The Soul-Seeker* belongs the distinction of being the first literary work to be written with the express purpose of promoting Freudian ideas. But despite being immensely entertaining, the novel is hobbled by didacticism and Groddeck's nationalist politics.[35] *The Book of the It*, conversely, breaks free of ideological trammels and soars on the wing of creative inspiration. Like Freud's genealogy of the It, his evaluation of the merits of Groddeck's books cannot be taken at face value. It is rather a reaction to the subversion of his authority that he unerringly detected in *The Book of the It*. As Roger Lewinter sums up Freud's blunder, "in connection with *The Soul-Seeker* he had named Cervantes, while *The Book of the It* . . . reminded him of Stekel" (1990, 46).[36]

3

In my reassessment of Rank in chapter 5, I quoted Lewis Aron to the effect that, more than any set of theoretical beliefs, "what many relational theorists have in common seems to be an emphasis on the mutuality between patient and analyst in the psychoanalytic process" (1985, 123). Aron makes the further valid point that "those contributions, focusing on greater mutuality between patient and analyst and acknowledging the intersubjective dimension of treatment, are likely to have been influenced by feminist consciousness and by the feminist emphasis on egalitarianism" (20). Nonetheless, he cautions, "we have been slow to recognize or acknowledge the mother as a subject in her own right" (65); and "it may be that psychoanalytic theorists were unable to conceptualize early development intersubjectively because they were avoiding the recognition of the mother as a separate subject" (75).

Of Groddeck, whose feminist credentials are attested by Horney, it cannot be said that he was slow to recognize maternal subjectivity. In a letter of June 9, 1923, Ferenczi credits him with underscoring "the exor-

35. Groddeck began to conceive *The Soul-Seeker* as early as 1904 (Martynkewicz 1997, 178). Although a bagatelle when measured against *Zeno's Conscience*, Groddeck's fiction was published two years before Svevo's; it is thus *The Soul-Seeker* that should properly be regarded as "the first psychoanalytic novel" (Esman 2001). For a judicious assessment of Groddeck's politics, including the vexed question of his Nazi sympathies, see Will (1995).

36. Freud compared *The Soul-Seeker* to *Don Quixote* in a letter to Groddeck of February 8, 1920, just as he compared its humor to that of Rabelais in defending the novel against Pfister's strictures. In 1926, Groddeck echoed Freud in calling *The Soul-Seeker* his "best achievement" and characterizing it as "a conscious imitation of the novel of Cervantes" (quoted in Will 1984, 65). As with his endorsement of Freud's genealogy of the It, however, Groddeck's acquiescence does not ratify or rectify Freud's misjudgment about his works.

bitant meaning of the mother," adding that he himself intends to review *The Book of the It* (Ferenczi and Groddeck 1982, 61). (For reasons that remain unclear, this review was never published.) On August 5, Ferenczi informs Groddeck that he is committing "the entire Genital Theory" to paper, predicting that his friend will be pleased with it no less than with "a new book by Rank," an allusion to *The Trauma of Birth*. Ferenczi continues: "A technical, scientific-political work (together with Rank) pursues similar purposes of restoration to those you are demanding" (62). Thus, Ferenczi brings together the four texts of 1923 that collectively constitute a counterweight to *The Ego and the Id—The Book of the It, Thalassa, The Trauma of Birth*, and *The Development of Psychoanalysis*—and places them in Groddeck's orbit.

Nor can Groddeck's meditation on motherhood be accused of sentimentality. In writing to his lady friend, modeled in part on Hanneliese Schumann, Groddeck's persona in *The Book of the It* harps on the inescapable conflict in the mother-child relationship. "It is already enough," remarks Patrik Troll in letter 3, "to observe a mother interacting with her child for twenty-four hours in order to see a goodly dose of indifference, weariness, hate. . . . If you know mother love, do you also know mother hate?" (1923, 28–29). Carrying this idea to its ultimate conclusion, Groddeck avers that "I am convinced that the child is born through hatred" (36), since the mother's disgust at the prolonged distension of her body causes her to propel the child into the world. By way of recompense, "no sooner are we reminded that she bore us than we hate her," he rues in letter 21; and in an implicit rebuke of Rank's biological theory of the birth trauma, Groddeck continues: "that is the unconscious memory of the struggle for breath during birth, say our analytic know-it-alls and know-nothings. 'No,' whispers the evil spirit, 'that is your sins against the mother who bore you, the mortal sins of ingratitude, of incest, of bloodshed, of murder'" (189).

But if Groddeck, like Rank, is ahead of his time in espousing "the exorbitant meaning of the mother," he counts as a precursor of contemporary relational thinking above all because of his "emphasis on the mutuality between patient and analyst in the psychoanalytic process." As I contended in chapter 5, Groddeck resembles Ferenczi but differs crucially from Rank (despite Rank's conceptual grasp of the analyst's maternal function) in his affirmation that "it is not the doctor who is the essentially active partner, but the patient. The doctor's chief enemy is Hubris" (1926b, 126). Groddeck stresses that in every healing relationship there will inevitably come "a strange turning point where the patient becomes the doctor and decides himself what he is to do with his servant's services and even whether he wants to accept them at all" (1928, 215). By the same token, "there are always two simultaneous, interacting treatments and therefore two persons who do the treating: the doctor treats the patient, the patient at the same time treats the doctor" (1926j, 225). If the therapeutic process breaks down for any reason, "the doctor will have to tell himself: I have made a mistake; what matters then is to find out what kind of mistake it was and to discuss it honestly with the patient without any embarrassment or attempt at apology" (226).

How Groddeck arrived at this dialectical conception of the analytic relationship—or, at least, how he later believed he had achieved this breakthrough—can be reconstructed from letter 30 of *The Book of the It*, where Patrik Troll recounts to his lady friend "how I came to psychoanalysis" (1923, 264). His story turns on a fourteen-year treatment of a patient, Miss G., which commenced in 1909. In his biography, Martynkewicz casts doubt on the veracity of Groddeck's narrative, saying that it is supported by "no documentation" (1997, 199). But Groddeck mentions this same patient in his introductory letter to Freud of May 27, 1917, citing her case as the one that "compelled me down the same path that I later came to know as that of psychoanalysis" (Freud and Groddeck 1974, 7). Given the consistency between this letter and Groddeck's detailed description of his relationship to Miss G. in *The Book of the It*, I see no reason to question her actual existence, whatever Groddeck's fictional embellishments may have been.

At the time of his initial encounter with Miss G., Groddeck recalls through his fictional persona, he was in the throes of a Hamletesque melancholy—"I seemed old to myself, took no pleasure in either woman or man"—and accepted the diagnosis that he was "hysterical" (1923, 264). In this condition, "I took over the treatment of a severely ill woman, who compelled me to become an analyst." As the two of them labored together, a transformation gradually took place both in their interaction and in Groddeck's self-awareness. The patient, "who saw in me the mother," induced Groddeck to renounce the practice of "authoritative, infallible, fatherly suggestion" that he had learned both from his father and from his mentor Schweninger. Instead, "it was no longer a matter of giving the patient instructions, of prescribing to her what I thought right, but rather of becoming what the patient needed me to be." Whereas formerly he had been an "active, meddling doctor," Groddeck now sought to be "a passive tool" who placed himself at the patient's disposal (266–67).

To his astonishment, Groddeck discovered that he himself was being healed as a result of this reversal: "Then suddenly I stood before the odd fact that I am not treating the patient, but that the patient is instead treating me; or to translate it into my language, that the It of my neighbor seeks so to transform my It, indeed so transforms it, that it becomes serviceable to its purposes" (267).[37] Groddeck's encounter with Miss G. is thus a conversion experience in every sense of the term. It leads him to shift from a paternal to a maternal identification, from an active to a passive posture, and from casting himself exclusively in the role of the doctor to being also the patient. Groddeck permitted Miss G. to use him as the object of a maternal transference, a flexibility conspicuously lacking in Freud, who insisted on remaining "authoritative, infallible, fatherly" in his dealings with Groddeck and everyone else.

From this experience Groddeck draws far-reaching conclusions, which he expresses in biblical language: "It seems that the most difficult thing in life is to let oneself go, to listen to the It-voices of oneself and one's neighbor and to follow them. But it is worth it. One gradually becomes a child again, and you know: Unless ye become as children, ye shall not attain the kingdom of heaven." He appends an anti-phallic corollary: "One should give up the desire to be big at twenty-five; until then, one assuredly needs it, but later on the erection is required only on rare occasions" (267).

Although less well known than Ferenczi's later experiments with Elizabeth Severn, Groddeck's treatment of Miss G. falls into the category of what would today be called mutual analysis. If one were to write a history of mutual analysis, it would probably have to begin with Jung. In what appears to be the first reference to such a procedure, Jung wrote to Freud on May 25, 1908, about his treatment of the drug-addicted psychoanalyst Otto Gross at the Burghölzli Clinic in Zurich: "I have let everything drop and have spent all my available time, day and night, on Gross, pushing on with his analysis. . . . Whenever I got stuck, he analyzed me" (McGuire 1974, 153). Jung is exemplary for future practitioners of mutual analysis in his willingness to dedicate "day and night" to Gross, an expression of therapeutic zeal reminiscent of

37. This is the passage twice cited by Searles, and cited again by Aron. See note 4 above.

Ferenczi's commitment to Severn. Jung's experience with Gross has a striking counterpart also in his relationship with Maria Moltzer, a nurse and the daughter of a wealthy Dutch distiller, whom Jung trained as a psychotherapist. At the time of his rupture with Freud, Jung sought to claim the moral high ground by asserting, in his letter of December 18, 1912, that, unlike the self-analyzed Freud, "I have submitted *lege artis et tout humblement* to analysis and am much the better for it" (McGuire 1974, 535). That it was Moltzer whom Jung regarded as his analyst is clear from Freud's disparaging observation in a letter to Ferenczi five days later, "The master who analyzed him could only have been Fräulein Molzer [*sic*], and he is so foolish to be proud of this work of a woman with whom he is having an affair" (Brabant, Falzeder, and Giampieri-Deutsch 1993, 446).[38]

Given that Maria Moltzer, from being Jung's pupil, became not only his analyst but also his lover, this early venture in mutual analysis proves to be object lesson in the dangers of boundary violation inherent in such an enterprise. But the fact that Jung's example has negative as well as positive facets only enhances its relevance to the careers of Ferenczi and Groddeck, who, like Jung, sought in their own ways to evolve alternatives to strictly Freudian models of therapy and technique. It was, after all, Freud's refusal to enter into a mutual analytic relationship not only with Jung but also with Ferenczi during their transatlantic crossing in 1909 that was the cause of Jung's rift. As Jung reminded Freud three years later, in his letter of December 3, 1912, Freud had broken off the interpretation of one of his own dreams with the notorious remark, "'I could tell you more, but I cannot risk my authority'" (Billinsky 1969, 42).[39]

Consequently, just as Jung provides a prototype for subsequent innovators in his openness to a more egalitarian relationship with his own patients—even though he takes this laudable impulse to the destructive extreme of an actual love affair—he likewise blazes the trail followed severally by Ferenczi, Groddeck, and Rank in daring to confront Freud

38. In an effort to impeach the credibility of Jung's letter of December 18, 1912, Slochower has claimed that "there is no evidence of Jung having been analyzed" (1981, 26); but such corroboration is now furnished by Freud's letter to Ferenczi. Whatever the wisdom of Jung's conduct with Moltzer, there is no doubt that he thought of what took place between them as an analysis.

39. I quote Freud's words as reported by Jung many years later in an interview with the American theologian, John Billinsky; but this account is consistent with his letter of December 3, 1912, as well as with that in *Memories, Dreams, Reflections* (1965, 158). As Jung

with the same demand for reciprocity. As we have seen, after Ferenczi's first visit to Baden-Baden in 1921 cemented his friendship with Grod-deck, the two men found in each other the unconditional acceptance and genuine warmth that neither had obtained from Freud. Shaken by the news of Freud's cancer in 1923, both Ferenczi and Groddeck sought to reach out to him analytically in the same spirit, though Freud rebuffed their overtures. In the light of this history, it is not surprising that the friendship between Groddeck and Ferenczi led to what Will has charac-terized as a "collaborative and reciprocal analytic activity" that "is un-doubtedly the precursor of Ferenczi's later concept of mutual analysis" (1994, 734). Writing on October 11, 1922, Ferenczi urged Groddeck to come to Budapest "to continue your interrupted analysis.—Whether and to what extent that is compatible with the simultaneous analysis of my own person, we shall have to see" (Ferenczi and Groddeck 1982, 46). Conversely, Groddeck informed Freud on May 31, 1923, that Ferenczi had been "in treatment" with him since his visit to Baden-Baden in Sep-tember 1921, and that the following year "Ferenczi was with me again; I treated him again, and was analyzed by him six or seven times. He spoke to me very insistently about my father-complex" (Freud and Groddeck 1974, 66).

Like Groddeck's treatment of Miss G., an important but little-known link between Jung's early experiments in mutual analysis with Gross and Moltzer and Ferenczi's with Severn is Ferenczi's analysis of Eugenia Sokolnicka. Sokolnicka, a Pole who became a member of the Vienna Psychoanalytic Society after undergoing analysis with Freud in 1913–14, saw Ferenczi for a second analysis after World War I. In a let-ter of June 4, 1920, Ferenczi apprised Freud of his progress. Interest-ingly, Sokolnicka, who was herself still married at the time, must have had a romantic involvement of some kind with Rank since, as Ferenczi reports, the latter's wedding in 1918 to Beata Mincer (who, like Sokol-nicka, was Polish) "made [Sokolnicka] fall unhappily in love with him, after the fact, although, where she might still have had an opportunity to do so, she was unable to love him totally" (Falzeder and Brabant 2000, 23). Ferenczi, torn between the active technique that he had taken over from Freud and Rank and his inclination to indulgence, ad-vised Sokolnicka to give up masturbation and at first refused her de-mand that he change the time of her session, though he soon capitu-

---

revealed to Billinsky, he believed that the content of Freud's suppressed dream concerned his relationship with Minna Bernays.

lated. As Ferenczi tells Freud, Sokolnicka, discontented both with his severity and with his laxity, "turned the spear around, began to analyze *me*, called me a severe neurotic, whom her keenness would have paralyzed, counted out my analytic sins to me, my inability to work out my ideas, etc." (25).

At this relatively early date, Ferenczi did not embark with Sokolnicka on a full-fledged mutual analysis, although she did—in a foreshadowing of what was to come with Severn—contrive "a plan *to follow me over the summer and to want to take analytic lessons during the vacation as well!*" (26). It was, rather, only in his correspondence with Freud that Ferenczi worked through the lessons of his struggles with this exceptionally difficult patient. Still, Ferenczi did not shy away from the realization that Sokolnicka had hit the mark with her accusations. As Ferenczi, tormented by the writer's block that prevented him from completing his *magnum opus*, confessed, "the patient has this time diagnosed something correct in the doctor. With her observation sharpened by the neurosis, she has guessed that my 'laziness' in working cannot be explained by the (justified, by the way) tiredness. There is something else neurotic behind it" (26). Ferenczi went on to locate the hidden cause of his woes in the "tragic circumstances" of his marriage—namely, the death of Géza Pálos on the day of Ferenczi's wedding to Gizella, as well as his protracted oscillation between Gizella and her daughter Elma. As Ferenczi acknowledged, this concatenation of events "happened at the expense of my ability to love" and caused him to remain dissatisfied throughout his first year of marriage. What is more, Sokolnicka's reproaches aroused Ferenczi's conflicts with his mother: "the patient seems to have guessed that scolding and bickering out of the mouth of a woman affects me as *extremely* unpleasant. That has to do with the most painful and effective traumas of my childhood: the relationship with my strict mother" (26–27).

Thus, both in their relationships with their most important patients and in their relationships with each other, Ferenczi and Groddeck, like Jung before them, were willing to risk a mutuality that was anathema to Freud himself. Just as Freud had an antipathy to Severn, whom he branded "Ferenczi's evil genius" (quoted in Jones 1957, 407), so too he could not abide Sokolnicka.[40] He responded on June 17, 1920, to Ferenczi's self-analytic report by disparaging her as "a basically disgusting

40. Jones does not identify the person to whom Freud referred as an "evil genius," but his mockery of Ferenczi's susceptibility to his patient's belief in the power of telepathy makes it clear that it must be Severn (Fortune 1993, 103, 115).

person" who "doesn't want to see now that she has already become an old woman" (Falzeder and Brabant 2000, 29). For Ferenczi, as well as for Groddeck, their breakthrough to a relational conception of analysis was made possible by a capacity to survive a maternal transference on the part of their patients and by a concomitant recognition of maternal subjectivity in its traumatic effects on them as sons.

4

The profundity of Groddeck's exploration of the mother-child relationship prompts one to wonder about its roots in his personal experience. Beginning with Freud's self-analysis, as I have argued throughout this book, psychoanalytic theory has advanced to the extent that its practitioners have confronted their areas of acutest emotional vulnerability. Besides being a literary masterpiece, *The Book of the It* bears comparison to *The Interpretation of Dreams* as the preeminent work of self-analysis in the psychoanalytic canon.[41] Like Ferenczi and at least the early Freud, but unlike the reticent Rank, Groddeck makes explicit the subjective dimension of theory-formation in psychoanalysis. As I map the prominent features of Groddeck's psychic landscape, I shall—to borrow Freud's metaphor for condensation in dreams—simultaneously attempt to generate a "composite photograph" (1900, 293) that allows us to discern the configurations that link Groddeck's inner world to those of Freud, on one hand, and Winnicott, on the other.

The essential point to bear in mind is that Groddeck's mother, Caroline, appears to have been seriously depressed during his early childhood. As he wrote in his memoir "White as Snow, Red as Blood, Black as Ebony":

"Black as ebony"—that was my mother. Her hair was shining black, and I never saw her wear any but a black dress. She took to black after the death of her father, for she never became a true Groddeck, but only Frau, or perhaps not even that, but always Fräulein Koberstein. (1925b, 22)

The blackness of Caroline Groddeck's dress, worn in perpetual mourning after the death in 1870 of her father, the distinguished literary histo-

41. For yet another monument of self-analysis, see again (as in chapter 7, note 3, above) my discussion (1991, 115–48) of Harry Guntrip's *Psycho-Analytical Autobiography*, the longer—and, regrettably, still unpublished—version of his paper (1975) on his analyses with Fairbairn and Winnicott.

rian and pedagogue August Koberstein, blazons forth her emotional unresponsiveness to Georg, her youngest child, who was only four at the time. Indeed, Groddeck's title presages André Green's concept of the "dead mother," which turns on a chromatic contrast between red—the color of blood and the bodily wound of castration—and black and white, the colors, respectively, of the bloodless wounds of mourning and anxiety. In Green's formulation, which can be applied to Caroline Groddeck, "a living object, which was a source of vitality for the child," is rendered "a distant figure, toneless, practically inanimate" (1983, 146).[42]

Groddeck concludes his autobiographical sketch by recalling another traumatic memory from the same year of his childhood:

> The black-white-red of the woman very early made me into a solitary, for I saw it clearly enough at four years old, when my mother took me into the bath with her. He who seeth his mother's nakedness shall not surely die, but in a sense the mother dies, for him. That comes to all of us, though for most the experience is unconscious. (1925b, 24–25)

By fusing an allusion to the story of Ham, who "saw the nakedness of his father," Noah (Gen. 9:22), with the serpent's rewording of the divine interdiction on the Tree of Knowledge, "Ye shall not surely die" (Gen. 3:4), Groddeck makes it clear that his mother was psychically dead to him. Although his voyeuristic transgression has a manifestly sexual content, it functions as a screen memory for a diffused sense of emotional abandonment.

To scholars of psychoanalysis, this incident in which Groddeck saw his mother naked in the bath inevitably will recall Freud's own memory of seeing his mother naked during a train trip from Leipzig to Vienna,

---

42. Superimposed on Groddeck's struggle with the depressed mother is his conflict with the punitive preoedipal mother. This bifold relationship with the maternal imago, which underlies the Oedipus complex, as I have tried to demonstrate, is a pattern found also in Ferenczi, Guntrip, and Norbert Hanold. In Grossman and Grossman's words: "Groddeck's attachment to his mother seems a hostile identification, a kind of unity in which there was little room for an identity of his own. His early arrogance and attitudes of omnipotence, as well as his later symptoms of psychic turmoil, can be seen as both an expression of and a defense against awareness of this unity. He persisted in claiming to be his mother's favorite, yet the defensive denial against a feeling of being unloved appears again and again in his formulations" (1965, 204). Freud, too, always depicted himself as his mother's favorite, a self-image that likewise becomes problematic when it is seen as "the defensive denial against a feeling of being unloved."

which he reported using the Latin words *matrem nudam* in his letter to Fliess of October 3, 1897, at the height of his self-analysis (Masson 1985, 268). Although Freud told Fliess he was between two and two and a half at the time, he was actually four years old when his family moved to Vienna. He was, however, two and a half when his mother gave birth to his sister Anna, an event that coincided with the sudden disappearance from his family of his Catholic Czech nanny. As Louis Breger has argued, not only is Freud's account of the train journey a reconstruction rather than a genuine memory, but his incipiently oedipal emphasis on "adultlike sexual desire for his mother" served as a "comforting myth" that shielded him from the "overwhelming emotions" aroused by the "traumatic losses" of his nursemaid as well as of his mother (2000, 18–19), who had been pregnant first with Julius and then with Anna and a series of other siblings throughout Freud's childhood. Groddeck's experience parallels Freud's in that both men saw their mothers naked at approximately the same age, but Groddeck's interpretation brings out the dynamic of maternal depression and unavailability that profoundly affected Freud, though he was unable to formulate this insight for himself.[43]

Symbolizing Groddeck's feeling of abandonment as a result of his mother's depression is the fact that he was not breast-fed by her. In letter 1 of *The Book of the It*, he uses the phrase "alma mater" to organize his investigation of "the first and hardest conflict of my life" (1923, 12). His mother nursed only the eldest of her five children, and because Groddeck was born earlier than anticipated, a wet nurse was not on hand. For three days he had to make do with a woman who came twice daily to feed him. "I was told that it didn't do me any harm," he comments, "but who can judge the feelings of a suckling?"

Groddeck's sense of primary oral primary deprivation was thus exacerbated by his split maternal image, both halves of which he could not

43. As Breger notes, Freud's brother Julius was named after his mother's own younger brother, who died of tuberculosis at the age of twenty, one month before the birth of his namesake. Thus, when her child Julius died, as he did when Freud was not yet two, Amalie Freud suffered a second jolt, and "it is a good guess that the loss of this baby, in the context of the other deaths, created a family atmosphere of mourning and depression" (2000, 12). The "other deaths" to which Breger refers are those of Jacob Freud's first and second wives as well as of his father, Schlomo, who died only six months before Freud's birth. Freud's given names were Sigismund Schlomo; like Julius, he was thus named according to Jewish custom after a deceased relative of whom he then became the replacement.

help hating as well as loving. There was one woman who had kept him inside her body for nine months, but did not suckle him; and another woman whose milk he imbibed every day, but was not his biological mother. Groddeck traces his romantic conviction that science must yield to the power of fantasy to his divided loyalties in early childhood: "The suckling who is fed by a nurse is thrown in doubt, and this doubt he will never lose. . . . The choice between two possibilities is more difficult for him than for other people" (14).

Not only did Groddeck, like Freud, internalize his mother's depression through a screen memory of seeing her naked, but both had two mothers in early childhood. What is more, the separation anxiety induced in Freud by his nurse's mysterious disappearance finds an uncanny counterpart in Groddeck's loss of his surrogate mother, which left him stupefied:

> I can't recall any longer how she looked, know no more than her name: Berta, the shining one. But I have a clear memory of the day on which she went away. She gave me at parting a copper threepenny piece [*Dreier*], and I know for sure that instead of using it to buy a piece of candy, as she wanted, I sat down on the stone staircase of the kitchen and rubbed the threepenny piece on the steps until it shone. The number three has pursued me ever since. (1923, 15)

Strikingly, the departure of the nurses of both Groddeck and Freud is connected with coins. As Freud tells Fliess in his letters of October 3–4 and October 15, 1897, the crux of his relationship to this female caretaker is contained in an ambiguous dream-memory in which either she stole ten-penny coins (*Zehners*) from his mother, or else he stole them from his mother on her behalf, a crime for which she was punished by dismissal from the household and ten months in prison.

Groddeck's meditation on his lost nurse and her gift to him of a coin leads him to recognize the continuity between his preoedipal and oedipal experience. Although this event was a moment of dyadic separation anxiety, the coin was a "*Dreier*," which introduces the motif of triangulation and prompts Groddeck to say that "the number three has pursued me ever since." He connects "the effects of the double relation to mother and nurse" to the way that "whenever my heart spoke, I intruded as a third in an existing relationship of affection between two people, so that I continually separated the one whom I desired from the other, and my ardor cooled as soon as I had accomplished this" (15–16). This is a classic statement of the plight of the oedipal lover, exemplifying Freud's thesis that that such a man's first precondition for loving is that "there should be 'an injured third party'; it stipulates that the person in question shall not choose as his love-object a woman who is disengaged . . . but only one to whom another man can claim right of possession as her husband, fiancée or friend" (1910c, 166). In conformity with these expectations, Groddeck's first wife, Else von der Goltz, whom he married in 1896, was married to someone else and the mother of two children when she met Groddeck two years earlier.

The same continuity between preoedipal and oedipal experience exhibited in Groddeck's memory of his nurse's disappearance also figures in Freud's case. Upon being told by his mother, whom he had asked about the nurse when his memories of her came flooding back in October 1897, that it was she and not he himself who had stolen the coins in question, Freud recollected a scene in which his half-brother Philipp had opened an empty wardrobe (*Kasten*). As Freud realized when he revisited this memory in *The Psychopathology of Everyday Life*, not only was Philipp responsible for his nurse's arrest and hence for her being "boxed up" (*eingekastelt*) in prison, but he had constructed a fantasy in which Philipp was the cause of his mother's pregnancy with his sister Anna.[44] The empty wardrobe condensed Freud's anxieties having to do with the vanishing of his nurse and his mother's pregnant body. Immediately after concluding his second commentary on his nurse's disappearance, in his letter to Fliess of October 15, 1897, Freud begins a new paragraph and offers for the first time his epochal exegeses of *Oedipus Rex* and *Hamlet*, in which he ascribes the "gripping power" of Sophocles' drama to the way that it makes manifest the pattern of the son's love for the mother and jealousy of the father that he believed to be "a universal event in early childhood" (Masson 1985, 272).

Freud's seamless transition from his nurse's disappearance to an interpretation of *Oedipus Rex* demonstrates how his adumbration of the Oedipus complex emerges against a backdrop of preoedipal experience. This connection between Freud's relationships with his mother and his nurse and his discovery of the Oedipus complex has not escaped the notice of psychoanalytic commentators. As Jim Swan wrote in a classic paper:

44. Freud makes this fantasy explicit in a passage added in 1907 and then in a footnote added in 1924 to the chapter on "Childhood and Screen Memories" in *The Psychopathology of Everyday Life* (1901, 49–52), but the connection between his mother's pregnancy and his nurse's disappearance underlies his recollections in October 1897.

Having two such mothers, and the luck of having the "bad," ugly mother banished from his life when he was only two and a half, allows Freud to maintain a secure split between his internalized good and bad mothers. It also allows him to preserve his close relationship with his actual, very idealized mother, who, in turn, idealizes her first-born and only son. (1974, 34)

Freud's nurse, in other words, is seen in this account as the "bad mother" who functions as a precursor to the punitive, castrating father, and her disappearance becomes a fortunate event because it allows Freud to preserve an idealized image of his birth mother, while his resentments against her are displaced onto his father, his rival in the oedipal schema.[45]

From a contemporary perspective, however, this analysis is not so much wrong as it is insufficient. It requires modification in that it gives scant attention to the defensive functions of Freud's oedipal theory. The Oedipus complex can no longer be taken for granted as a universal truth the unveiling of which was made possible by a series of lucky breaks in Freud's early life. Rather, as Madelon Sprengnether has contended, in a line of interpretation that dovetails with Breger's, "in the days and weeks preceding his formulation of the oedipal model, Freud was exploring not his childhood rivalry with his father and desire for his mother, but rather his feelings of being displaced and betrayed in an evolving family dynamic that included a dismissed nanny and a mother whose attention was given elsewhere" (2000, 24–25). Although Freud chose *Oedipus Rex* as his paradigm, it is, as Sprengnether shows, actually *Hamlet* that comes far closer to mirroring the bewildering complexity of his series of traumatic losses. And it is likewise the under-song of mourning and loss accompanying the Oedipus complex that Groddeck brings to the fore in his self-analytic soundings in letter 1 of *The Book of the It*.

A remarkable feature of Groddeck's memory of his lost nurse is the way that he literalized the meaning of her name, Berta ("the shining one"), by rubbing the coin she had given him on the kitchen steps. His relationship to her is thus on one level determined, in Lacanian fashion, by the signifier. Groddeck's play with "Berta" also evokes the name of Zoe Bertgang in *Gradiva*, although Freud's commentary on Jensen's novella concentrates not on the meaning of "Bert-" but rather on the ambulatory connotations of "-gang," which are replicated in the name and gait of "Gradiva." Just as Jensen's text is susceptible to multiple in-

45. I adhered to Swan's view of Freud's two mothers in *Freud and Oedipus* (1987, 87).

terpretations, at once humanist and postmodernist, so too Groddeck's memory simultaneously exemplifies the power of the signifier and shows a Winnicottian transitional object in the making. Instead of using his nurse's gift of a coin to buy candy, as she intended, Groddeck postponed oral gratification and transformed the coin itself into an aesthetic object that took the place of his lost maternal surrogate.

Not only did Groddeck as a child spontaneously resort to a transitional object, but he foreshadows Winnicott's formulation in his writings. On November 12, 1921, in one of his few surviving letters to Ferenczi, he wonders: "So you hold, for example, that the father transference is necessary for the success of the analysis. But why should the mother transference—or that to playmates, or to the milk bottle, or to rhythm, or to the rattle—be any less useful?" (Ferenczi and Groddeck 1982, 53). Even as he takes the decisive step beyond the father to the mother, Groddeck prophetically envisions how the analyst might function for the patient as a transitional object or a transitional phenomenon in the transference.

Groddeck's theoretical affinities with Winnicott are not limited to his anticipation of the concept of the transitional object. Much of Winnicott's thought is condensed in the aphorism, "*There is no such thing as a baby*" (1952, 99). Groddeck similarly urges, "if anything goes wrong with a baby the first question ought to be, 'What is wrong with the mother?'" (1933, 74). For Groddeck no less than for Winnicott, the baby is not an isolate but always exists in a relationship with a primary caregiver. Groddeck points out that the neonate is exceptionally attuned to communications from its mother: "The child's sensitiveness to all that is going on in the It of its mother seems to be extraordinarily acute in earliest infancy, and to diminish by degrees as it grows older" (1926a, 91). Physical or emotional disorders in the infant can thus often be explained as symptoms of illness in the mother. For this reason, he adds, "I have made a practice of studying the mother's unconscious whenever a baby's health is disturbed, and above all in those surprising cases when the baby refuses to take its food" (91). What Groddeck says about the mother-child bond can be applied to the analytic relationship, in which the patient is "extraordinarily acute" concerning "all that is going on in the It" of the analyst, while disturbances in the patient's state of mind can often be traced to countertransferential pressures emanating from the analyst.

In view of how Groddeck's ideas function as a bridge between those of Freud and Winnicott, it becomes interesting to return to my metaphor of the "composite photograph" and explore the parallels between his life and Winnicott's in greater detail. In addition to the disclosures about not being breast-fed by his mother, the delayed arrival of his wet nurse, and the subsequent split of his maternal imago, Groddeck in letter 1 of *The Book of the It* recounts an incident from his third year when he warned his sister Lina—the next-youngest child in the family and the only girl—that her doll would suffocate if she clothed it in a certain dress. He comments: "in the moment I uttered the thought . . . the wish must have been living in me to murder some being or other, whose place was being taken by the doll" (1923, 10). Although he places this incident a year before the death of his maternal grandfather, the reference to the dress suggests that Groddeck may well have been thinking of his mother and her mourning costume. As a child, Winnicott smashed a doll belonging to one of his sisters with a croquet mallet, though he was relieved when his father was able to repair the damage by melting the wax on the doll's face. As Clare Winnicott reported his interpretation of this event: "'This early demonstration of the restitutive and reparative act certainly made an impression on me, and perhaps made me able to accept the fact that I myself, dear innocent child, had actually become violent directly with a doll, but indirectly with my good-tempered father, who was just then entering my conscious life'" (quoted in Rudnytsky 1991, 101).

Whether real or fantasied, the early attacks on a doll by both Groddeck and Winnicott represent displaced acts of violence against a family member. Although Winnicott adheres to the oedipal script by naming his father, I think that, as was true of Groddeck, a more plausible primary target would be his mother, screened behind the figure of his sister.[46] Like Groddeck's fantasy of suffocating Lina's doll, Winnicott's destructive attack on his sister's doll with a croquet mallet may well have been induced by his mother's depression. At the age of sixty-seven, he sent the following poem, "The Tree," to his brother-in-law, James Britton:

> Mother below is weeping
> weeping
> weeping
> Thus I knew her

46. In letter 10 of *The Book of the It*, Groddeck, who suffered from enuresis until adolescence and was a notorious troublemaker at the Pforta school, claims to remember "virtually nothing from the time between twelve and seventeen, which I had to spend separated from my mother" (1923, 97). Even if we make allowances for rhetorical exaggeration, Groddeck's professed amnesia for this prolonged period of separation from his mother underscores the intensity of his conflicts with her.

Once stretched out on her lap
as now on dead tree
I learned to make her smile
to stem her tears
to undo her guilt
to cure her inward death
To enliven her was my living.
(quoted in Phillips 1988, 29)

As Brett Kahr proposes, the depression of Winnicott's mother was an underlying factor in his unhappy marriage to his first wife Alice, who became psychotic and from whom Winnicott separated after twenty-five years:

> It would not be unreasonable to suspect that Winnicott harboured extensive rescue fantasies in relation to his depressed mother, Elisabeth, and he then enacted these wishes in his marriage by looking after a woman with profound vulnerabilities. Eventually, the strain of a partnership based on clinical care-taking became unbearable. (1996, 44)

Uncannily, Groddeck first marriage in 1896 to the beautiful and musical but ultimately tiresome and unstable Else von der Goltz was similarly haunted by unresolved conflicts with his dead mother. He writes in "Coughs and Colds," one of his autobiographically richest communications:

> In my first year of marriage I was seriously ill, and my wife nursed me. I was like my father, perhaps less raging in my anger, but the more morose, oppressive, and terrifying. Yet my wife nursed me, and somewhere a voice says to me, "You have hurt her, and we should not give pain to those who have given us love." (1925a, 139)

Groddeck's grounds for remorse toward Else included his dissolution of their marriage and remarriage to Emmy. After their separation, Else fell into serious and prolonged depressions (Martynkewicz 1997, 160).[47] Else's collapse after being abandoned by Groddeck can be understood in Winnicott's (1969) terms as an instance of failed object use

---

47. Their daughter, Barbara, was born in 1901. She was Groddeck's only child. After a promising youth, Barbara proved unable to live independently and was eventually institutionalized.

in which she, like Groddeck's depressed mother, was unable to withstand his destructive attacks. But if Groddeck, like Winnicott, acted out his anger toward his mother in his first marriage, both men found happiness when afforded a second chance—Groddeck with Emmy von Voigt, and Winnicott with Clare Britton.

According to "Coughs and Colds," Groddeck's father died on September 22, 1885, and his mother died on September 20, 1892, while his marriage to Else took place on September 21, 1896. This date seems singularly inauspicious in light of Groddeck's history and indeed suggests an unconscious act of sabotage on his part. More precisely, Groddeck's wedding date constitutes an anniversary reaction, which, in George Pollock's words, can be a symptom of "unfinished or abnormal mourning, usually from childhood" (1972, 480). Groddeck, that is, introjected his mother's (and perhaps also his father's) depression and expressed his own unresolved grief and anger toward his parents not only by marrying Else on the anniversary of their deaths but also by being "seriously ill" during the first year of marriage. He stood in for his father and made Else into a replica of his mother.

Unlike Freud, who in the 1908 preface to the second edition of *The Interpretation of Dreams* famously declared that the death of a father was "the most important event, the most poignant loss, of a man's life" (1900, xxvi), Groddeck held the death of the mother to be "more potent": "I have never yet met any man who, at the death of his mother, has not had the feeling, 'I, her son, have murdered her'" (1925a, 138). The point, however, is not to have a contest over which loss is worse but to recognize that every child is destined to harbor love and hate toward *both* parents, and that in cases where this ambivalence is particularly acute, the death of either of the primary attachment figures will stir up a storm of emotional conflicts. Just as Freud's insistence on the universality of the Oedipus complex can now be seen to be a defensive formation that conceals his preoedipal anxieties, so too his statement about the superlative importance of the father's death is an unconscious way of diverting attention (his own as well as the reader's) from his aggressive impulses toward his mother who was still very much alive. Both Groddeck and Ferenczi go beyond Freud in their acknowledgment that the mother-child relationship is no less ambivalent than that between father and son. This is a corollary of their acceptance of maternal subjectivity and leads them to reject what Ferenczi in the *Clinical Diary* called Freud's "unilaterally androphile" theory of sexuality (1985, 187).

The relational tradition that extends from Ferenczi and Groddeck through Winnicott and beyond differs from the classical tradition of Freudian psychoanalysis above all in abandoning any pretense to omniscience and adopting an attitude of humility and even reverence toward patients. Winnicott's moving dedication to *Playing and Reality*—"To my patients, who have paid to teach me"—is anticipated when Groddeck writes: "It is our patients who can best teach us the art of psychotherapy and to them we doctors owe our thanks" (1926c, 214). And when Groddeck advises, "if it can be avoided, the doctor should not attempt the interpretation himself" (1928, 219), he foreshadows Winnicott's realization, "I think I interpret mainly to let the patient know the limits of my understanding" (1969, 87). In the *Clinical Diary*, Ferenczi quotes Freud's contemptuous dismissal of patients as "a rabble, good only to support us financially" (1988, 186). To recapitulate, the paradigm shift initiated by Groddeck and Ferenczi has less to do with their reorientation from the father to the mother, or from castration to separation, on the plane of theory than with their espousal of a dialectical rather than a dogmatic conception of therapy. This transformation in practice vindicates Groddeck's insistence that Freud's "id" is antithetical to his own "It," as well as his prophecy that *The Book of the It* will be "incomprehensible to all those people who adopted the later, Freudian meaning of the word" (1928, 212).

5

When in "The Tree" Winnicott says that "Mother below is weeping" and that he was "Once stretched out on her lap / as now on dead tree," he brilliantly fuses an image of himself as Christ on the cross with one of himself as the infant Christ distended across the Virgin's body. Indeed, in conflating the iconography of the crucifixion with that of the Madonna and Child, Winnicott equates the "dead tree" of the cross with the grief-stricken mother whose "inward death" it was his mission as a child to redeem and "cure."

Winnicott's artistic transformation of his personal struggle with a depressed mother into the archetypes of Christianity seals his affinity with Groddeck, in whom precisely the same trajectory can be traced. After Freud's break with Jung, Groddeck, along with Pfister and Jones, was one of the few gentiles in his inner circle. Like Pfister, Groddeck sought to prove that Freud was a Christian despite himself.

Distressed by Freud's self-characterization as a "godless Jew," Pfister in a letter of October 29, 1918, endeavored to persuade him not only that he was "no Jew," but also that he was "not godless," for "he who lives in truth lives in God." "If you raised to your consciousness and fully felt your place in the great design," Pfister added, "I should say of you: A better Christian there never was" (Freud and Pfister 1963, 63).[48]

As Yosef Hayim Yerushalmi has pointed out, Pfister's "good-natured" tribute is "a direct quotation from Lessing's 1779 play *Nathan the Wise*, that glowing testimony to his friendship with Moses Mendelssohn and a singular document of a moment when the future seemed full of promise for German-Jewish brotherhood in a mutual religion of tolerant reason" (1991, 8). In the spirit of the German Enlightenment, Pfister seeks to assimilate Freud to a Christianity that he conceives of as a rational rather than a revealed religion.

Whereas Pfister claims Freud for Christianity by contending that Freud is neither godless nor Jewish, Groddeck does so rather by affirming his Jewishness and daringly likening him to the Son of God. In "Repression and Release," a supplementary "letter 34" to *The Book of the It*, Groddeck hails psychoanalysis as

the road open to all who wish to unlearn hatred and to learn love. It is, notwithstanding its origin, identical with the method of Him who called Himself the Son of Man, perhaps even by virtue of its origin, since however painful it may be for the world's haters, it cannot be denied that Christ was a Jew. (1926i, 219)

Groddeck not only equates Freud's teachings with those of Christ, but he also pairs them as Jewish founders of a religion. Integral to Groddeck's analogy between psychoanalysis and Christianity is the emphasis placed by both systems of belief on childhood as a repository of truth. As he writes in "On the It": "The result of an investigation of the child's It may teach us that the saying 'unless you be as little children, you will not enter the kingdom of heaven' is legitimate, that the aim in life is to become a child again and that we have only one choice—that of becoming childlike or childish" (1920, 136).

48. In the same letter of October 9, 1918, in which he characterizes himself as a "godless Jew," Freud gives vent to his misanthropy: "I have found very little that is 'good' about human beings on the whole. In my experience most of them are trash" (Freud and Pfister 1963, 61).

Groddeck's true kindred spirit in his radical amalgamation of psycho-analysis and Christianity is not the respectable Pfister but the mystical poet H.D. H.D.'s memoirs of her experience on Freud's couch in Vienna in 1933 and 1934, *Advent* (1933) and *Writing on the Wall* (1945)—published together as *Tribute to Freud* (1956)—are at once an incomparable literary representation of the psychoanalytic process and an invaluable historical document for a study of Freud the man and how he worked as an analyst.[49] Uncannily, H.D. appeals to the same passage from Matthew 18:3 (coupling it with a passage from Luke 17:21) cited by Groddeck in "On the It," while she also underscores Jewish identity as a common denominator between Christ and Freud: "There was another Jew who said, *the kingdom of heaven is within you.* He said: *unless you become as little children, you shall not enter the kingdom of heaven*" (1945, 104). One example of H.D.'s dialectical response to Freud must stand for many:

> I had a dream about my little bottle of smelling-salts, the tell-tale transference symbol. In my dream, I am *salting* my typewriter. So I presume I would salt my savorless writing with the salt of the earth, Sigmund Freud's least utterance. (1933, 148)

On the one hand, H.D. dreams that Freud enlivens and preserves her otherwise "savorless writing"; on the other, because "salt of the earth" is a biblical locution—employed by Christ in Matthew 5:13 in addressing the disciples after he has uttered the beatitudes—H.D. remakes Freud in her Christian image even as she pays homage to his "least utterance." Salt becomes a "transference symbol" not merely in a psychoanalytic sense, but as a nodal point for the convergence of sacred and secular discourses.

49. H.D., whose real name was Hilda Doolittle, further metabolized her relationship with Freud in poetic form first in "The Master," probably written in 1934 but only published posthumously; then in *Trilogy* (1944), where he appears as Kaspar, one of the Magi, and she as Mary Magdalene; and again in *Helen in Egypt* (1961), where they are reincarnated as Theseus and Helen. On H.D. and Freud, see the books by Friedman (1981) and Chisolm (1992). Friedman (2002) provides a portrait in letters of H.D.'s analysis with Freud. In her introduction to *Trilogy*, Aliki Barnstone writes that "H.D. creates a poetics combining the salvific forces of Freud and Jesus Christ" (1998, xiii). Spiro (2001) critically reads H.D.'s resistance to Freud's phallocentric construction of female sexuality in terms of H.D.'s own allegiance to "the powerful tradition of Christian supersession, with its grand apparatus for suppressing Jewish self-understanding" (617).

Although H.D. looks upon Freud as a modern Christ, she also wonders, in connection with her dream of Miriam—the half-concealed child who sees the Egyptian princess find Moses in the bulrushes—whether she too does not wish, "in the deepest unconscious or subconscious layers of my being, to be the founder of a new religion" (1945, 37). The same gnostic identification of himself with the deity informs and counterpoises Groddeck's veneration of Freud. Writing in *The Ark*, the periodical he conducted at his sanatorium, Groddeck takes his syncretic fusion of psychoanalysis and Christianity to its limit: "To anyone who makes use of psychoanalysis the Gospels will take on new life: Christ will rise once more, and the Son of Man become the Son of God" (1951b, 268).[50] But psychoanalysis, in Groddeck's view, enables the "Son of Man" to be resurrected as the "Son of God" only because Christ is another name for Everyman:

> If it is true that Christ is the Son of Man—and that in very truth He is—it is equally true that all the sons of men are Christian, in so far as this word signifies a belief in the redemption of man through love and death. . . . One may even go further and say that no man can fail to be the Christ, whatever may be his conscious beliefs, for in the unconscious, Love, Death, and Christ are identical symbols. (1951b, 265)

Groddeck's espousal of Christianity is in no sense literal. In "The It and the Gospels," which Martin Grotjahn has praised as "one of his most original and profound writings" (1966, 315), Groddeck acknowledges that "salvation is not limited to Christianity alone" and "every man is saved after his own fashion" (1926d, 165–66). Because Groddeck belongs to the European tradition, Christianity is central to his thinking, but he insists that all religions are to be revered as expressions of the It: "In very truth the myth is truth, symbolic truth, while reality is error. The man who learns to see the symbol will laugh at talk about a Reality Principle, even if he honours and loves Freud, as I do" (1951b, 268). Or, as he affirms in "On the It": "God is in us, we are God, the It is God, an omnipotent it. . . . We are forced to believe in God because we are ourselves God" (1920, 152).[51]

50. This selection from *The World of Man* is an amalgamation of texts published in 1925 and 1926.

51. Compare "The Master," where H.D. writes of her sessions of dream analysis with Freud: "nothing was lost / for God is all / and the dream is God; / only to us, / to us, / is small wisdom, / but great enough / to know God everywhere" (1983, 451–52).

Because of his veneration of symbol over reality, Groddeck in "The It and the Gospels" dismisses as misguided the quest for the historical Jesus: "the important character is not Jesus but Christ, and Christ is not historically but humanly true" (1926d, 167). He adds, invoking Christ's words in John 8:58, "He is no creature of reality, as we sometimes consider reality, He is the Truth, which is something quite different. 'Before Abraham was, I am,' He said of himself." H.D., whose rearing in the Moravian Church of Bethlehem, Pennsylvania, predisposed her to espouse a heretical version of Christianity, echoes Groddeck's belief that "myth is truth." She quotes an exchange with Freud about the two Bethlehems: "'You were born in Bethlehem? It is inevitable that the Christian myth—' He paused. 'This does not offend you?' 'Offend me?' 'My speaking of your religion in terms of myth,' he said. I said, 'How could I be offended?' 'Bethlehem is the town of Mary,' he said" (1933, 123). In *Trilogy*, where she takes up Freud's hint by casting herself as Mary Magdalene, while depicting Freud as Kaspar the friendly Wise Man, H.D. weaves the same words from John 8:48 quoted by Groddeck into a poem that expresses her ambition to fuse all sacred myths—Egyptian, Judeo-Christian, Freudian—into an indivisible whole:

> plasterer, crude mason
>
> not too well equipped, my thought
> would cover deplorable gaps
>
> in time, reveal the regrettable chasm,
> bridge that before-and-after schism,
>
> (*before Abraham was I am*)
> uncover cankerous growths
>
> in present-day philosophy,
> in an endeavor to make ready,
>
> as it were, the patient for the Healer;
> correlate faith with faith,
>
> recover the secret of Isis,
> which is: there was One

in the beginning, Creator,
Fosterer, Begetter, the Same-forever

in the papyrus-swamp
in the Judean meadow.

(1944, 54–55)

It is characteristic of H.D.'s gnosticism that she should appropriate Christ's claim of divine priority over the merely patriarchal Abraham for her own poetic power. Groddeck likewise extends Christ's proclamation of having existed from eternity to all mankind when he avers: "every man is and was before Abraham was, man is of no age, or he is of every age at one and the same time. . . . Whoever has given serious thought to Christianity knows that it recognizes no differences of age, nor of sex, and certainly none between man and man" (1926e, 49). Both H.D. and Groddeck find a forerunner in Sir Thomas Browne, whose metaphysical prose and paradoxical reconciliation of his identities as a man of science and of faith make his *Religio Medici* (1643) a seventeenth-century counterpart to *The Book of the It*. "*Before Abraham was, I am*, is the saying of Christ; yet it is true in some sense if I say it of my selfe, for I was not only before my selfe, but *Adam*, that is, in the Idea of God, and the decree of that Synod held from all Eternity" (I.59).[52]

Groddeck's identification with Christ informs not only his fictional persona of Thomas Weltlein, the holy fool of *The Soul-Seeker*, but also his earlier literary self-portrait as Gottfried Lange in *The Pastor of Langewiesche* (1909), which concludes with the protagonist in paranoid exaltation literally nailing himself to the cross on which an image of Christ worshipped by his parishioners used to hang. Christ is for Groddeck principally the mythological being in whom the son's ambivalence toward his mother plays itself out most fully. In "The It and the Gospels," he argues that Christ "looses the bond which binds man to his mother, and—perhaps—this may be a way to save mankind" (1926d, 183). Profoundly, however, Groddeck takes "mother" to mean not simply the female parent, but the past as a whole: "The past is the mother of the present: our past character is always close on our heels, trying to direct us. . . . Now we may well regard the past in its entirety as the mother, and then the 'mother-imago' is the picture that we may have of ourselves, after which,

52. My reference to *Religio Medici* is by book and section number.

be it pleasing or ugly, we are always striving" (185). Christ is thus "a man of the present"—or, at least, "He wishes to be"—and to break free from the past amounts to severing his ties to his mother (186).

In Groddeck's revisionist exegesis, the crucifixion becomes the culminating moment in the process by which "Christ gives up His past, and loses himself that He may find himself" (188). Such a consummation is, however, fraught with ambivalence, since the cross itself represents the past—the mother—from which the Son of Man desires to escape: "Christ died upon the cross, death seized Him from behind, from what stood behind Him, from His past. It seized Him in the form of love" (189). The cross, that is—exactly as in Winnicott's poem—with its outstretched wooden beams, is "a false image of love," a "dead thing," to which Christ's arms must first be nailed in order that they can be set free "to draw the whole world into His embrace." The relationship between mother and son (Groddeck says nothing about daughters) begins "as the closest of all love-relations," since for thrice three months "the son lives in the mother," but life soon "separates them more widely than any other two human beings can be separated." As a fitting emblem of this separation-in-union, Groddeck notes that Christ "is crucified with his back turned to his mother" (190).[53]

A basic duality thus structures Groddeck's attitude toward the mother-son relationship as portrayed in the Christian myth. On the one hand, Groddeck celebrates Christ's quest to escape his mother's influence; on the other, he warns against its impossibility and the crushing burden of guilt that follows in its wake. In "The It and the Gospels," Groddeck points out that the German word for pelvis, *Kreuzbein* ("cross-bone"), alludes to the cross, "and that same bone is called in Latin, *os sacrum*, the sacred bone. It is at this bone that the pains of delivery start. The cross, the sacred bone, is the mother; upon her dies the son" (1926d, 189). Following Christ's crucifixion, however, Groddeck affirms in the last sentence, he is "born again" (190) by becoming as a little child for whom there is only a present tense.

53. Groddeck's emphasis on the detail that Christ has his back to the cross is echoed in his comments on several works of art. He remarks of Michelangelo's *Pietà* in St. Peter's that it shows that "even death cannot annul the human commandment which separates mother and son, for it is only with averted face and body, only lying on his back, that the son may rejoice in death on the body of his mother" (1926f, 164). He likewise glosses Memling's painting *Madonna and Child with Angels:* "The Christ-Child turns away from the woman who has been His mother, and towards the world beyond. That is human destiny. Life may indeed be regarded as one long process of getting free from the mother" (1951b, 213–14).

Although this cycle of death and resurrection is meant to lead to emancipation from the mother-imago, it paradoxically does so by reenacting a primordial act of reciprocal murder between mother and son from which there is no escape. Just as, according to letter 21 of *The Book of the It*, "there has never yet been a man who did not kill his mother" (1923, 189), so, conversely, Groddeck laments in letter 20: "It is the disposition of the mother to wound her child in his deepest feelings; this is her fate" (185). Like Ferenczi's clinical concept of the analyst's murder of the patient, Groddeck's psychoanalytic reading of the mother-son relationship in Christian symbolism displaces Freud's emphasis on patricide by defining matricide as the primordial human crime. But whereas Ferenczi holds out hope that the analyst who functions as a maternal object can survive the patient's destructive attacks and thereby put an end to the cycle of violence, Groddeck dwells on the catastrophe of crucifixion and evinces only an exiguous confidence in the prospect of enduring spiritual rebirth.

Groddeck's spin of the Freudian paradigm leads him to equate Christ with Oedipus, who is transmogrified from the slayer of his father to the victim of his mother. Again prefiguring "The Tree," Groddeck writes in letter 14: "Look at the cross with its extended arms. . . . The Son of God hangs and dies thereupon. The cross is the mother, and we all die from our mothers. Oedipus, Oedipus" (1923, 133). Groddeck's coupling of Oedipus and Christ, like his syncretic blending of psychoanalysis and Christianity, is highly original, but it also reflects a broader tendency in modernist thought. Strikingly, H.D., whose own equation of Freud with Christ we have already considered, writes to her intimate companion Bryher (Winnifred Ellerman) on March 1, 1933, about her first meeting with Freud in Vienna: "I was so scared by Oedipus. . . . I am terrified of Oedipus Rex" (Friedman 2002, 34). Likewise, in *A Vision*, Yeats aspires to "proclaim a new divinity" by combining the antithetical heroes of Hellenism and Hebraism: Oedipus, who, at the moment of death, "sank down soul and body into the earth"; and Christ, who, "crucified standing up, went into the abstract sky soul and body" (1937, 27). Yeats and H.D. share with Groddeck the conviction that "religions are creations of the It" (1923, 133), but only Groddeck aligns Oedipus and Christ under the tragic star of matricide, which is indistinguishable from filicide. In the nails used in the crucifixion, he discerns a symbol of the indissoluble agony of mother and son: "If the cross is the mother, then the nails, which fasten him to her, pass also through her flesh; she feels the same pain, the same suffering as her son" (133).

The comparisons of Freud to Christ, and of psychoanalysis to Christianity, put forward by Groddeck and H.D. are by no means aberrations in the early history of the psychoanalytic movement. Such analogies arose naturally in the minds of the small band of true believers at the dawn of the twentieth century for whom the discovery of Freud's works gave new meaning to their lives and constituted a conversion experience. Even Stekel, whom Freud treated with unbridled contempt, wrote nostalgically in his *Autobiography*, "I was the apostle of Freud who was my Christ!" (1950, 106).

Perhaps the most incisive first-hand account of the religious dimension of the psychoanalytic movement is furnished by Max Graf, the father of Little Hans, in the same paper (1942) I have already mined in chapter 3 for what it inadvertently reveals about Freud's subjective involvement in his famous case history. Graf describes the Wednesday-evening meetings in Freud's apartment at Berggasse 19 that led in 1908 to the establishment of the Vienna Psychoanalytic Society: "There was an atmosphere of the foundation of a religion in that room. Freud himself was its new prophet who made the theretofore prevailing methods of psychological investigation appear superficial. Freud's pupils—all inspired and convinced—were his apostles" (471).

But Graf's memoir does not end with the birth of Freudianism. For as he goes on to recount, "after the first dreamy period and the unquestioning faith of the first group of apostles, the time came when the church was founded. Freud began to organize the church with great energy. He was serious and strict in the demands he made of his pupils; he permitted no deviations from his orthodox teaching" (472). As distinguished recruits from Zurich, Budapest, and beyond flocked to the cause, "branches of the Freudian church were founded in all parts of the world" and "the original circle of Viennese apostles began to lose its significance for Freud" (472). When Adler sought to follow an independent path, "Freud would not listen. He insisted that there was but one theory." Graf concludes: "In short, Freud—as the head of a church—banished Adler; he ejected him from the official church. Within the space of a few years, I lived through the whole development of a church history: from the first sermons of a small group of apostles to the strife between Arius and Athanasius" (473).

If, during "the first dreamy period," Freud was worshipped with "unquestioning faith" by "a small group of apostles" for whom he was a "new prophet," Graf's chronicle makes it clear that there soon followed a second stage in which what had originally been experienced as a revelation turned into an "official church" with Freud as its "head." There is, accordingly, an analogy to be drawn between psychoanalysis and Christianity not simply as religions in a spiritual sense but also as temporal institutions, with their rituals of initiation and hierarchies of power. For Freud to prevail as he did, it was not enough for him to be a charismatic leader with revolutionary ideas; he also needed to evolve enduring social structures through which his adherents could forge a new professional identity and earn their livelihoods.[54] But just as with Christianity, this triumph of psychoanalysis (as I put it in chapter 4 with respect to Freud's record of broken friendships) was also its tragedy, for the founding of a visible church inevitably led to its corruption and a loss of the inspiration that had caused it to come into being.

Implicit in the second stage of Graf's narrative of "church history" is a comparison of Freud not to Christ but to the Pope.[55] Graf's reference to "the strife between Arius and Athanasius" is resonant in a psychoanalytic context because, beyond evoking in a general fashion the struggles of the early Christian church to distinguish orthodoxy from heresy—with the attendant threats of excommunication—the conflict between these two fourth-century theologians had to do specifically with Arius's promulgation of the anti-Trinitarian doctrine that the Son was not consubstantial with the Father, an issue with oedipal overtones. In his biography of

54. Fromm provides a classic analysis of how "Freud's own messianic impulses . . . transformed psychoanalysis into the Movement" (1959, 111). As Fromm notes, Freud's "first most loyal disciples"—the six members of the Secret Committee—"were urban intellectuals with a deep yearning to be committed to an ideal, to a leader, to a movement, and yet without having any religious or political or philosophical ideals or convictions. . . . Their religion was the Movement." Rose (1998) usefully situates the early Viennese psychoanalysts' sense of calling in its cultural context. Despite a tendency to go overboard, evidenced by his conclusion that "from Freud's example, one has reason to suspect that behind many an atheist, agnostic, or skeptic of today lies shame, disappointment, or rage directed at the father" (1988, 220), there is a good deal to be gleaned from Vitz's study of Freud's "Christian unconscious."

55. Similarly, in "The Master," H.D. foretells that "they will build a temple / and keep all his sacred writings safe," adding, "only I, / I will escape" because "it was he himself, he who set me free / to prophesy" (1983, 457–58). H.D. exposes the pitfalls of discipleship endangering those on the psychoanalytic quest, but that she as a poet (and woman) is able to elude: "he did not say / 'stay, / my disciple,' / he did not say, / 'write, / each word I say is sacred' / he did not say, 'teach' / he did not say, / 'heal / or seal / documents in my name,' // no, / he was rather casual, / 'we won't argue about that' / (he said) / 'you are a poet'" (458). H.D.'s poem mirrors the passage from *Thus Spoke Zarathustra* quoted by Jung to condemn Freud on the eve of their rupture for demanding idolatry from his disciples, but H.D. received from Freud the gift of freedom to be herself that Jung did not. See chapter 6, note 17 above.

Freud, Wittels independently corroborates Graf's diphasic history of the psychoanalytic movement and likewise dates the founding of the "official church" to the moment when Freud "banished Adler" and Stekel. As Wittels writes, "it was somewhere around 1910 when Freud's pupils began to promote the master to the rank of Pope, and Stekel ran counter to the dogma of infallibility" (1924, 227). And in April 1913, Freud himself quipped to Ludwig Binswanger that the reason Adler and Jung had broken away from him was "precisely because they too wanted to be Popes" (Binswanger 1956, 9).

Multiple factors converge to help account for the resemblances between the organization of what Graf called the "Freudian church" and Roman Catholicism. On a sociological plane, it may well be, as André Haynal has argued, that psychoanalysis was "heavily inspired" by its "archenemy," the counter-Reformation version of Catholicism that Freud had encountered "in its overall dominating influence on the conservative Hapsburg empire." The Austrian Catholic church, Haynal continues, had remained insulated from the groundswell of change unleashed across Europe by the Enlightenment and the French Revolution, and it continued to aim "at the conquest of the world" (1996, 118–19). Considered biographically, Freud's elevation to the "rank of Pope," with the concomitant "dogma of infallibility," is also a manifestation of his inability to permit Jung or any of his other disciples to transform their relationships with him into ones of genuine equality. As Haynal further remarks, "Freud in moments of crisis wanted to make Adler, Jung, Rank, and Ferenczi presidents [of either the Vienna Psychoanalytic Society or the International Psychoanalytic Association], in order to bind them institutionally to the movement" (118). From this standpoint, the establishment of a psychoanalytic church served Freud's interests in that it created a power structure that enabled him to dangle prestigious positions before his would-be rivals as an incentive to keep their strivings for independence in check.

Set in the context of the other writers whom I have adduced, Groddeck's synthesis of psychoanalysis and Christianity comes into view as the crowning expression of an intuition shared by some of the most discerning commentators on the history of psychoanalysis. Groddeck stands out, however, not only by virtue of the depth and breadth of his reflections on this conjunction but also because of his practical efforts to restore psychoanalysis to its roots by once again defining it, as it were, as a vocation rather than a profession.[56] Indeed, Groddeck seeks to bring about nothing less than a Reformation of psychoanalysis.

Although I have emphasized Groddeck's significance as a progenitor of object relations theory, his advocacy of a "return to Freud" no less strikingly prefigures Lacan.[57] As early as 1926, he protests that "since the time Freud made his discoveries a crop of wrong ideas has sprung up about his teaching," which requires the student "to go back to the fountain head, *i.e.* to read Freud's own books" (1926g, 42). For diplomatic reasons, Groddeck refrains from saying so publicly, but it is clear that he does not exempt Freud's recent writings from those that promulgate "wrong ideas" about psychoanalysis. As we have seen, Groddeck dismissed *The Ego and the Id* in a letter to Emmy von Voigt of May 15, 1923, as "entirely inconsequential" (Freud and Groddeck 1974, 103); and he offers a preliminary version of this appraisal in a letter to Ferenczi of November 12, 1922: "The legislative process in our specialized field has, in my opinion, progressed so far that essential things can no longer be discovered by convinced analysts, but rather only by the doubters, among whom I number Freud, you, and me. Freud is inhibited by his unholy belief in the absolute necessity of baptism—of giving names—but he evens the score by his genius" (Ferenczi and Groddeck 1982, 54).[58]

If Groddeck anticipates Lacan in calling for a "return to Freud," he

56. The theme of psychoanalysis as a vocation is addressed not only in my book (1991) but also by Wheelis (1956) and in an excellent paper by Benjamin (1998). Wallerstein devotes the final chapter of his magisterial work on the controversy over lay analysis in the United States (1998a, 443–55) to what it means to have a psychoanalytic identity and to the changing identity of psychoanalysis itself as a discipline.

57. For a Lacanian appreciation of Groddeck, see Mannoni (1979).

58. Groddeck elaborates his view of the history of psychoanalysis in a 1926 article in *The Ark* that chronicles its decline from "the time of Freud's great discoveries, in which a new world appeared" to the era of "scientific psychoanalysis" in which access to the psychoanalytic field "is permitted only with special entrance tickets" and Freud has been made a "schoolmaster" (1926h, 841). Groddeck concocts a "fairy tale" in which one of the pupils in Freud's classroom, aware of his teacher's illness, resolves that "the time has come for cheap fame and writes a book that he calls *The Trauma of Birth*" (843). Convinced that he has rendered the world "a great service," Groddeck continues, Rank did so despite himself because his book "is in some way or another connected to Freud's recovery." Thanks to Rank, Freud's "truth-loving eyes are again able to look fearlessly and without turning to stone on the mother-Medusa; and one can hope that the school too will gradually grasp that the incest wish must precede father-hatred." Freud, Groddeck insists, "is not the property of a school, but rather belongs to everyone." Groddeck's fable attests that Rank's contemporaries regarded his revolt against Freud as a response to Freud's cancer. See chapter 4, note 7 above.

likewise shares Lacan's antipathy to Freud's later view of the ego as the seat of perception and consciousness. Not only does the year 1923 mark a crossroads between the divergent paths of ego psychology and object relations theory, but it also constitutes the moment when Lacan believes that Freud went astray by discarding his original topographical model, which posited a barrier between the conscious and unconscious mental systems. Writing to Freud on May 23, 1923, Groddeck alleges "the concept of the I to be a mirage of the It" and objects to the following sentence from *The Ego and the It*: "Consciousness depends on this I; the I controls access to motility, to the discharge of energy in the external world" (Freud and Groddeck 1974, 64; see Freud 1923b, 17).[59] In proto-Lacanian fashion, he asserts in letter 32 of *The Book of the It* that what distinguishes his practice as a psychoanalyst from the therapeutic techniques he had employed previously "is only the point of attack of the treatment, the symptom that seems to me to be present in every connection, the I" (1923, 289).

Groddeck's desire to effect a Reformation of psychoanalysis prompts him to identify with Luther, whose rejection of the belief in free will parallels his own relentless attacks on the ego. In letter 10 of *The Book of the It*, Patrik Troll exhorts physicians to recognize that it is the dynamics of the patient's transference and not their own healing powers that determine the success or failure of the treatment: "'Not all my worth nor all my pride'—anyone who wishes to live at peace with himself must be reconciled to this saying of Luther's" (1923, 97). Insisting on the supreme value of "the gift of irony" that allows one "to see at the same time many sides of life" (1926d, 172), Groddeck is drawn to the parables of the New Testament as a vehicle to express the essential duality of the It: "Only in the form of irony can the deepest things of life be uttered, for they lie always outside morality; moreover, truth is always ambivalent, both sides are true." He concludes: "the Gospels will only bring good tidings when we give up the strange idea that Christianity is a system of moral instruction, when we allow the Son of Man to indulge in humor" (1951b, 262).

What Groddeck says of Christianity can be applied as well to psychoanalysis. The appeal of Christ, like that of children, in Groddeck's eyes is that both are, in a Nietzschean sense, before or beyond morality. "Who has ever yet seen a child to whom the word 'good' could be applied?"

59. To my knowledge, this is the only occasion on which Groddeck quotes directly from *The Ego and the It*.

(1926d, 169), Groddeck demands in "The It and the Gospels." By the same token, "Christ has the imperishable human qualities; like man, he is neither good nor evil" (167). As an ironist, Groddeck refuses to pass judgment, even upon himself, and he holds that the worst thing imaginable is to be a hypocrite. Of all the parables, none is more vital to his thinking than that of the Pharisee and the publican (Luke 18:10–13), and he uses it to drive home the speciousness of all self-righteousness: "Only now and then for a few moments is man, because of his human nature, permitted to beat his breast in honesty and to cry: 'God be merciful to me a sinner'" (173).

In keeping with his critique of ego psychology, Groddeck equates the It with the humble publican and the I with the haughty Pharisee who is blind to the true conditions of his existence. At the same time, however, Groddeck cautions that it is insufficient simply to identify with the publican and despise the Pharisee, for that would paradoxically be to boast of one's humility and thereby to reassert one's moral superiority. On the contrary, heeding his own dictum that "only in the form of irony can the deepest things of life be uttered," Groddeck confesses that he too—like everyone else—is at once Pharisee and publican.

Beyond his theoretical reorientation from the father to the mother, and beyond even his prescient emphasis on the mutuality of the therapeutic relationship, Groddeck's gospel—his Reformation of psychoanalysis—has to do with his puncturing of its pretensions to be a "system of moral instruction" with a subversive double vision. By permitting his disciples to transform him from an all-too-human Christ into an infallible Pope, Freud became for Groddeck at once the founder and the betrayer of psychoanalysis. As he counsels his lady friend in letter 26 of *The Book of the It*, Christ and Judas are ultimately indistinguishable: "Think of the greatest moment of your life, and then keep looking until you have found the Judas-attitude and the Judas-betrayal" (1923, 225). "Just as treachery invariably enters into and helps form every noble deed of man, so in all that we call evil there is invariably also the essence of Christ or—if you prefer so to call it—the essence of loving, of benevolence" (226–27).

Groddeck arraigns Freud not because he bequeathed a curse as well as a blessing to posterity, but rather because he could not accept this inevitable ambiguity of his legacy. But even as he preaches that man should not judge, Groddeck is confronted by the impossibility of heeding his own admonition: "Let one try as hard as one likes to give up judging," he rues in letter 17 of *The Book of the It*, "one can never succeed.

Ever and always man pronounces value judgments. They belong to him as do his eyes and his nose. Indeed, it is just because man has eyes and a nose that he must ever and always say, 'That's bad'" (1923, 158). In letter 32 he sums up this existential dilemma as it pertains to the supreme fiction of the ego:

I am I. That is a fundamental sentence of our life. My assertion that this sentence, in which the ego-feeling of man expresses itself, is an error will not shatter the world, as it would if one believed the assertion. One will not believe it, cannot believe it; I myself don't believe it, and yet it is true. (279)

Hence Groddeck cannot escape the conclusion that "man's essential quality is vanity and self-overvaluation" (263). He ends letter 33, and with it his masterpiece, on a fittingly self-deconstructive note: "Seemly is he alone who says with the publican: 'God be merciful to me a sinner.' But don't you find that just this last—precisely this last—is pharisaical?" (305).

9

Psychoanalysis and the Dream of Consilience

I

If, as I have argued in the preceding chapter, there exists a consensus that the year 1923 marks a watershed in the history of psychoanalysis, there is no less unanimity that what may justly be called a paradigm shift has taken place in the past two decades in the American scene. The essence of this transformation has been summarized by Robert Wallerstein as

> a shift away from a natural science, positivistic model anchored in a one-person psychology based on the intrapsychic vicissitudes of the patient's instinctual strivings and the defenses ranged against them, all of this authoritatively surveyed by an objective, neutral analyst, the privileged arbiter of the patient's psychic reality, and on the patient's neurosis as projected onto the analyst's blank screen—away from all that to the ramifications of a two-person psychology focused on the always subjective interactions of the transferential internalized object relationships of the patient with the countertransferential (or equally transferential) internalized object relations of the analyst. (1998b, 1021–22)

Despite having been formed in the tradition of ego psychology, Wallerstein chronicles the changes he observes in a sympathetic and open-minded spirit. The same cannot be said of Leo Rangell, whose loyalty to the same tradition leads him to denounce the trends in contemporary psychoanalysis as "a successful negative paradigm" involving "the near-overthrow of an enduring and scientifically viable paradigm, that of gradually evolving psychoanalytic theory tested on the cumulative clinical experience of a century, and its replacement by formulations destined for transience" (1988, 318). Rangell cannot conceive that the versions of psychoanalysis with which he disagrees could offer an explanatory framework no less comprehensive than his own "total composite theory." Rather, in his opinion, all the elements that "have served as nodal points of alternative theories are included in this total unitary theory, whereas the converse is not true" (317). He quotes the dogmatic pronouncement of Otto Fenichel: "There are many ways to treat neuroses, but only one way to understand them" (1945, 554).

Rangell's jeremiad is the logical culmination of his earlier insistence that "indefensible arguments . . . are invariably the glue which binds a new group together" (1982, 31), and that self psychology and allied movements are "pathological developments" reflecting "a negative transference to psychoanalysis itself" (33, 35), the seeds of which are sown during the training analysis.[1] Rangell's protest, however, itself ironically bears out the truth of his conclusion that "the mainstream today is no longer 'main,'" and the "average psychoanalyst" currently espouses "a combination of self psychology and object relations theory, in contrast to traditional or 'Freudian' psychoanalysis" (1988, 316). Indeed, in his overview of reconceptualizations in American psychoanalysis, Wallerstein notes that it "had already occurred elsewhere over a period of many decades (within, for example, the British object relations school) and had had its forerunners just as long ago in America—in Harry Stack Sullivan's interpersonal perspective, which at the time was not accepted within the ego psychological mainstream" (1998b, 1021).

A consensus, by definition, is not controversial, and nothing that I have thus far said can claim to be original. Concurring with Wallerstein, Lewis Aron (1996) has summed up the changes in contemporary psychoanalysis as consisting of a dual, if not quite parallel, movement from drive to relational theory and from an objectivist to a constructivist epistemology (256). The former reorientation has been promulgated most notably in a series of books by the late Stephen Mitchell (Greenberg and

1. See my critique of Rangell's earlier formulations in *The Psychoanalytic Vocation* (1991, 92–93).

Mitchell 1983; Mitchell 1988, 1993, 1997, 2000), while the latter has found its foremost champions in the late Merton Gill (1994) and his erstwhile collaborator, Irwin Hoffman (1998). Drawing a comparison to the history of British psychoanalysis, in which the conflict between the followers of Anna Freud and Melanie Klein during World War II led to the emergence of a Middle Group (or Independents), Charles Spezzano has referred to this broad conglomeration of relationalists and constructivists as "the American Middle School" (1995, 23).

When the present situation is viewed against the backdrop of the crossroads in 1923, in which the psychoanalytic movement faced a choice between the ego psychology promulgated in Freud's *The Ego and the Id* and the countervailing relational orientation set forth in the contemporaneous works of Ferenczi, Rank, and Groddeck, it is clear that what has taken place over the past decades has been the belated revenge and ultimate triumph of the relational paradigm against the ego psychological paradigm that (at least in the United States) seemed for the first half-century to have routed it in the war of psychoanalytic ideas.[2] As Wallerstein has documented in *The Talking Cures* (1995), the definitive statement of the neoclassical Freudian position is Kurt Eissler's 1953 paper, "The Effect of the Structure of the Ego on Psychoanalytic Technique," which famously stigmatized any modification of the reigning austere technique as a "parameter." Eissler's paper, moreover, in Wallerstein's words, "could be, and was, widely read as the establishment response to the major deviations proposed by [Franz] Alexander in understanding the nature of the psychoanalytic enterprise and how it brought about desired changes" (1995, 107). Alexander's "deviation," of course, was the concept of the "corrective emotional experience," to which he gave influential exposition in a treatise (1946) written jointly with Thomas French, a book that Eissler (1950) had already attacked in a fifty-page review for its advocacy of what he branded "magical therapy" as opposed to the "rational therapy" of authentic psychoanalysis.[3]

2. As Carlo Bonomi sums up the reversal, "As is well known, Ferenczi's battle was lost, the authors [of *The Development of Psychoanalysis*] banned and declared insane [by Jones], and the direction taken by psychoanalysis was largely characterized by its medicalization and bureaucratization. Yet, in the long run, it is precisely Ferenczi's and Rank's 1924 perspective that has been successful" (1998a, 182).

3. As Wallerstein points out, the "onslaught" (1995, 55) against Alexander and French was led by Jones, who accused the authors of "describing something other than the technique of psycho-analysis" (1946, 163), even though they had given their book the title *Psychoanalytic Psychotherapy*.

Wallerstein's scholarship establishes in detail what in any case should be intuitively obvious—that Alexander's "corrective emotional experience" was reprehended by his critics for having been "prefigured in Ferenczi's espousal of a more active therapy and greater emotional expressiveness on the part of the analyst in the transference-countertransference interplay, to make up for the emotional deprivations of the patient's past" (1995, 54).[4] For many years, Alexander's innovation was received sympathetically only by such peripheral figures of the American psychoanalytic establishment as Frieda Fromm-Reichmann—who, as we saw in the last chapter, was likewise one of Groddeck's most stalwart champions. The first break in the logjam came with Leo Stone's 1961 monograph, *The Psychoanalytic Situation*, which, ever so gingerly (and, it must be said, turgidly), sought to acknowledge the ineradicable human element in psychoanalysis. In the appendix to his work, Stone singled out Ferenczi and Alexander by name as having been the only analysts who had previously "tried to establish broad and systematic generalizations regarding the purposive utilization of the analyst's affective responses in the analysis of neurotic patients, within the original framework of psychoanalytic theory" (1961, 132).[5]

Ultimately far more influential than Stone's work—important though that surely was—were the papers of Hans Loewald, especially "On The Therapeutic Action of Psychoanalysis" (1960), which, by stressing the role of the analyst as a "new object" through whom the patient could achieve integrative experiences leading to the "resumption of ego development" (221), managed in effect to smuggle the Trojan horse of a rela-

4. Alexander, like Ferenczi, was Hungarian; but, as Gedo points out, he was analyzed by Abraham and "does not appear to have had significant contact with the Ferenczi circle before his departure to Berlin" (1996, 78). Although Alexander was thus not a member of the "Budapest school," Wallerstein (1995, 54) observes that he did acknowledge his indebtedness to Ferenczi and pay tribute to the latter's "healthy experimental spirit" (Alexander 1954, 689).

5. Two decades later, Stone (1981) more clearly differentiated his views from those of Ferenczi, Alexander, and now also Kohut, but he reiterated his critique of Eissler's "neoclassical point of view" (102). The term "neoclassical," which I have echoed above in the previous paragraph, underscores the disparity between Eissler's rigid precepts and Freud's own often freewheeling practice, just as the unities of time and place mandated by neoclassical critics of the sixteenth and seventeenth centuries were far more restrictive than anything called for in Aristotle's *Poetics* or actually found in the works of the ancient Greek dramatists. The most prominent rebuttal to Eissler's depiction of Freud as an analyst is Lipton's (1977) paper on the "advantages" of Freud's technique in the case of the Rat Man.

tional sensibility inside the ramparts of ego psychological theory, thereby undermining its foundations. As Wallerstein puts it, Loewald "has finally implicated the central importance of the analytic relationship ('attachment'), along with insight ('understanding'), in explaining therapeutic change"; and this accomplishment constitutes "the culmination and vindication of a line of thinking that had originated in Ferenczi's restless struggles" (1995, 307).

Although his *Papers on Psychoanalysis* (1980) was published over two decades ago, and Loewald himself died in 1993, Loewald's synthesis of ego psychology and object relations theory has made him one of the most revered figures in contemporary psychoanalysis. He has been the subject of appreciative studies by analysts from Stephen Mitchell (2000, 3–53) to Jonathan Lear (1998, 123–47), and he has likewise been paired with Kohut as one of the instigators of the "partial revolution" (Teicholz 1999, xix) now allegedly brought to completion by the succeeding generation of "postmoderns."

This, then, is where we are today. The legacy of Ferenczi and his relational confreres has emerged from the shadows to amalgamate with—and, indeed, subsume—the tradition of ego psychology derived from Freud's *The Ego and the Id*. This rediscovery of Ferenczi, and concomitant emergence of a reenergized interpersonal school in the United States, has been coupled with the widespread dissemination of the ideas of Winnicott and the entire cast of characters in the Middle Group of the British Psycho-Analytical Society, where—as the accounts of Wallerstein and Spezzano have indicated—the same basic conceptual revolution from drive to attachment or relational theory had been effected in the 1950s and 1960s. So what is there left to argue about?

2

The insuperable stumbling block is the science question. In other words, what sort of a discipline is psychoanalysis? The various possible answers have been laid before us with customary clarity by Wallerstein. There is, he remarks, "the range through the perspectives of psychoanalysis as a natural science (Freud's vision), or as a different social-behavioral science (with different methods of inquiry or not), or as a uniquely 'hermeneutic science' (Gill's coinage), or as no science at all, a totally hermeneutic discipline, historical or linguistic or philosophical." All these, he adds, "have their advocates, and also their fierce opponents" (2001, 733).

In setting sail on these troubled waters, I do so with no pretense of expertise. I am neither a psychoanalyst, a clinical psychologist, a neuroscientist, nor a philosopher of science, but simply that rankest of all amateurs, a literary critic. But a problem in theory that trespasses on the domains of so many specialists perforce attracts the attention of a generalist, so perhaps this liability can also be considered an asset. At the very least, since Frederick Crews, himself a literary scholar by profession, would have us believe that his "loss of intellectual trust in psychoanalysis came about in the most mundane way, through reading" (1995, 8), and his voice has been among the most audible in the latest round of "Freud wars," I venture to hope that my own perspective, which is also shaped by reading, may likewise merit a hearing.[6]

How, then, does the science question link up with the paradigm shift in contemporary psychoanalysis? If we reread Wallerstein's formulation quoted at the outset of this chapter, we see that he describes the transformation not only as that from a "one-person" to a "two-person" theory, but also as that from "a natural science, positivistic model" to a focus on "subjective interactions." I commend the emphasis of relational theory on the interactive dimensions of the analytic situation and agree that it is necessary to reject positivism insofar as the clinical setting is concerned. Where I have a problem, however, is with the corollary that this must entail a repudiation of natural science and its criteria as bench marks for appraising the claims of analytic theory.

Implicit in my objection is the premise that it is necessary to distinguish between the theory and practice of psychoanalysis. But this axiom, to which I shall return below, is itself based on my conviction that the relational turn initiated in the 1923–1924 works of Ferenczi, Rank, and Groddeck should be credited not only with highlighting the experiential and interactive components of the analytic situation, but also with making it possible for the first time to place analytic theory on a sound scientific footing. In a paradox integral to my argument, by showing where Freud went wrong in important respects, object relations theory simultaneously adumbrates the fulfillment of what Patricia Kitcher (1992) calls Freud's "dream" of psychoanalysis as a "a complete interdisciplinary science of mind."

6. For a more thorough reply to Crews's attacks on psychoanalysis, see my "Wrecking Crews" (1999).

The collapse of Freudian metapsychology—that is, the model of mind resting chiefly on his assumptions about drives and his structural theory of id, ego, and superego—is by now beyond dispute in all but the most benighted corners of the psychoanalytic world. The process of demolition can be traced as it unfolds step by step in Robert Holt's collection of papers, *Freud Reappraised* (1989).[7] As Holt writes, the collective project in which he has been a leading participant seeks "to recover and rehabilitate the clinical theory of motivation"—and, I would add, of psychoanalysis generally—"by clearing away the deadwood of metapsychology, which has buried it to a considerable extent" (1976, 174). But in order to clear away the "deadwood," one must first be able to gather it; and that requires the use of empirical methods. As Holt expounds: "The misfortune of psychoanalysis is that Freud never developed any means of generating and testing predictions, mistakenly believing that there was scientific value in spinning out theoretical speculations that could not be falsified by any kind of data" (1981, 318). Indeed, Freud combined a predilection for unprovable speculations with a tendency to put forward concepts—notably those drawn from the field of biology—that *are* empirically testable and have turned out to be mistaken. Besides his notorious endorsement of Lamarck's belief in the inheritance of acquired characteristics and of Haeckel's "biogenetic law" that ontogeny recapitulates phylogeny, examples include the principle of constancy, which, as Holt writes, is "quite without any biological basis" (1965b, 129), and the model of the nervous system as a passive reflex mechanism, which more recent findings "decisively refute and contraindicate" (128). Holt sums up his position as follows: "Psychoanalysis is *not* autonomous, existing in self-sufficient isolation on an island remote from other sciences" (1985, 340). Accordingly, he continues, "we must go to a nonbehavioral realm, such as neurophysiology, to test a great deal of the most distinctive parts of the clinical theory"; and "if psychoanalysts simply continue down their present path, making no effort at fundamental change, psychoanalysis will continue to shrink and wither, and will eventually collapse."

Although I agree with Holt's premises, I do not share his pessimism about the future prospects of psychoanalysis. For the "fundamental

7. Like Merton Gill, Roy Schafer, and George Klein, three of the other prime movers in the dismantling of metapsychology, Holt was at one time a colleague of the Hungarian-born David Rapaport, whose monograph, *The Structure of Psychoanalytic Theory* (1960), secured his reputation as its leading intellectual architect. Holt is deeply indebted to the work of Benjamin B. Rubinstein, of whose collected papers, *Psychoanalysis and the Philosophy of Science* (1997), he is the editor.

change" that he calls for has, in large part, already taken place. As early as the mid-1930s, both Imre Hermann and Ian Suttie anticipated Bowlby by stressing the importance of ethology for psychoanalysis. In *The Origins of Love and Hate*, Suttie sought "to put the conception of altruistic (non-appetitive) love on a scientific footing" (1935, 3) by drawing on research in animal behavior; and he made the point that such findings "are objective and can be checked by several observers, *unlike evidence derived from the analysis of patients*" (8). Hermann, Ferenczi's successor in Budapest, appealed (1933; 1936) to ethological data to support his hypothesis of a "clinging instinct." Bowlby (1969, 211–14) utilized the classic experiments by Harry Harlow (1958) (who had himself been influenced by René Spitz's work on hospitalism) on the preference of infant rhesus monkeys for surrogate mothers made of wire covered with terry cloth to which they could cling as opposed to other "mothers" that dispensed milk but where the cylindrically shaped wire remained exposed. Extrapolated to human beings, these experiments conclusively refute Freud's hydraulic theory of the drives, which led him as late as *An Outline of Psycho-Analysis* to assert that "love has its origins in attachment to the satisfied need for nourishment" (1940a, 188).[8]

Although it is not the end, object relations theory certainly marks a strong beginning to the task of connecting psychoanalysis to the other sciences. The same weaknesses pinpointed by Holt in Freud's biological assumptions—the principle of constancy and the reflex model of the psychical apparatus—are swept away at a stroke by Fairbairn's (1944) elevation of "object seeking" over "pleasure seeking" as a motivation for human behavior. Within the relational camp, however, there is an important divergence between Bowlby and Winnicott. For Winnicott, despite his acceptance of the validity of Fairbairn's theoretical turn, to the end of his life criticized Bowlby for his use of ethology, claiming that "the whole subject of imprinting is irrelevant to the study of the early object-relating of human infants" (1971a, 79). Even today Winnicott's re-

8. My argument in this paragraph recapitulates that in *The Psychoanalytic Vocation* (1991, 5–6). Strikingly, Hermann was one of the first to recognize the importance not only of ethology but also of hermeneutic theory for psychoanalysis (Rubinstein 1976, 328–29). On the cross-fertilization between ethology and psychoanalysis in the work of Spitz, Harlow, and Bowlby, see also my interview with Mary Ainsworth (Rudnytsky 2000, 40). For one of the most promising current developments in the collective effort to think scientifically about psychoanalysis, see Stanley Palombo's (1999) cogent exposition of the wide-ranging ramifications of complexity theory, which conceives the dynamic relationship between analyst and patient as a *co*-evolutionary process analogous to an ecological system.

luctance to subject the "clinical theory" to external testing—whether at the hands of ethology, neurology, or infant observation—continues to be shared by some analysts; but to those who are serious about safeguarding psychoanalysis as a scientific discipline, this is a complete dead-end.[9] Despite Winnicott's own ill-advised retreat from science, he remains the leading representative of the object relations tradition that has sought to rebuild psychoanalysis on a secure foundation. It is therefore no accident that Arnold Modell, whom Wallerstein has described as "the most significant American exponent and interpreter of the concepts of Winnicott, particularly the object-relational perspective" (1995, 212), should be in the forefront (1990; 1993) of the efforts to integrate psychoanalysis and neurology, about which I shall have more to say in due course.

Holt's diagnosis of the problems besetting psychoanalysis is independently corroborated by Patricia Kitcher. Like Holt, Kitcher focuses on Freud's misjudgments in the field of biology, though she also takes him to task for exhibiting precisely analogous failings with respect to anthropology. As Kitcher argues, Freud's downfall was not that his original "biological bets" (1992, 154) turned out to have been misplaced, but rather that he failed to mend his ways when he should have known better. Kitcher elaborates:

When [Freud] decided to back the twin horses of Lamarckianism and [Haeckel's] recapitulationism in the 1890s, they looked like very good bets. . . . It is equally clear, however, that twenty years later both theories had become highly controversial. Freud was reshaping some aspects of psychoanalysis dur-

---

9. A cautionary example of anti-empiricism and its consequences is furnished by Jean Laplanche, who grants that "the biological exists prior to the human" (1987, 22), but nonetheless perversely lauds Freud because "speculation soon acquires more weight than any experimental reasoning," instancing "his famous speculations about the death drive" (13). Not content with the death drive, Laplanche kowtows to the pleasure principle "as a fiction that we simply have to accept" and insists that "the biological model falls apart if it is expanded to include outside intervention, particularly if that intervention is extremely complex and irreducible to being a supplementary element in a so-called autarchic equilibrium" (24). In ordinary language, Laplanche is saying that we must take it on faith that Freud is right; but even if he isn't, life is just too complicated to be understood using a "biological model" that tries to take into account the open-ended relations between an individual and the environment. The same retrograde view is espoused by André Green, who denies that empirical research "can be of relevance, whether direct or indirect, to psychoanalysis" (Green and Stern 2000, 125). Green aligns himself with Wolff (1996), who challenges "the apparently widespread acceptance that infant observations have falsified a major component of Freud's developmental propositions" (375).

ing this period. Why didn't he free himself from such dubious entanglements when he had the chance? (178)

What is more, Freud erred in "reversing the epistemic dependencies of the disciplines comprising psychoanalysis." In other words, as Kitcher explains, "if Lamarck was right and recapitulation true, then it was reasonable to construe childhood and perhaps neurotic behavior in terms of the practices and experiences of primitive humans or even animals. However, support could not run in the other direction" (179). Nothing derived from clinical practice could properly be invoked as bolstering the dubious notions of a "phylogenetic inheritance" or an "archaic heritage," though Freud persisted in drawing such unwarranted inferences.

By the same token, Freud refused to rethink the speculative hypotheses of *Totem and Taboo* when his anthropological sources came under attack from specialists in the discipline. Indeed, he wrote stubbornly in *Moses and Monotheism*: "I had a right to take out of ethnographic literature what I might need for the work of analysis" (1939, 131). But, as Kitcher rejoins, "this was clearly wrong. He had no right to take theories that were no longer considered sound by expert opinion and present them as scientific evidence in favor of his own position" (1992, 210). She concludes, "As with sexual chemistry, he bet his theories on quite specific future discoveries in other disciplines and then ignored the mounting evidence that these discoveries would never be forthcoming" (212).

Just as Kitcher independently endorses Holt's assessment of the troubles besetting psychoanalysis, so too Holt anticipates Kitcher's indictment of Freud for failing to be "appropriately circumspect" (1992, 61). As Holt has written, the "moral crisis" of psychoanalysis reflected in the "clash between the values we profess and those we live out" can be traced back to the tragic flaws in Freud's character: "He was unusually intolerant of outside criticism. . . . I cannot think of a single incident where he really listened to a critic who was not part of the inner circle and considered the critique on its merits" (1985, 341).[10]

This view of Freud as someone incapable of what Holt terms "peri-

10. In "Freud's Cognitive Style" (1965a), Holt quotes from a 1907 letter by Breuer: "Freud is a man given to absolute and excessive formulations: this is a psychical need which, in my opinion, leads to excessive generalization" (50–51). For a study of how Freud's authoritarian tendencies have been reflected in the cultures of four American analytic institutes, see Kirsner (2000). Although Kirsner's book contains much to ponder about how psychoanalysis has functioned as a religion in a negative sense, the story he tells of psychoanalysis is one in which everything has "gone wrong" (12) and nothing

odic conceptual stocktaking" (1965a, 49) is now widely shared even among defenders of psychoanalysis; and it certainly reflects a sea change from the idealized image of Freud that prevailed in an earlier era. Heinz Hartmann, for example, in discussing the role that intuitions may have played in Freud's work, opined that "his striving for scientific discipline, his patient accumulation of observational data, and his search for conceptual tools to account for them have reduced their importance to a stimulus factor in the formation of psychoanalytic theories" (1959, 339).

Although Hartmann's image of Freud as a cautious empiricist now seems blinded by idolatry, this does not mean that his ideal of psychoanalysis as a science has been similarly tarnished. Here I come back to my paradoxical contention that the new conception of psychoanalysis pioneered by Ferenczi, Rank, and Groddeck in 1923 not only heralds the contemporary appreciation of the interactive and experiential aspects of the analytic relationship. It at the same time takes a decisive step toward fulfilling Freud's dream of psychoanalysis as a "complete interdisciplinary science of mind."

In his 1987 presidential address to the International Psychoanalytic Association (IPA), "One Psychoanalysis or Many?" (1988), Wallerstein has credited Melanie Klein and her followers in England with initiating "the gradual transition of psychoanalysis from being—at least in appearance—a thoroughly unified theoretical structure evolved around the creative intellectual corpus of its founding genius, Sigmund Freud . . . into the present-day worldwide theoretical diversity" (7). In pleading for "tolerance of diverse theoretical viewpoints *within* psychoanalysis," he observes, the Kleinians were simultaneously claiming their innovations "to be in a direct and logical developmental line from the overall corpus of Freud's work" (10).

Although it is true that Klein, who settled in London in 1926, mounted the first successful *open* challenge to psychoanalysis as a "unified theoretical structure," Wallerstein's account does not do justice to the even more important achievement of Ferenczi. As I have tried to elucidate in chapters 6 and 7, the reverence and even love with which Ferenczi is widely regarded today are due above all to the way that he incarnates an authentic psychoanalytic identity while being free of Freud's authoritarian tendencies. In contrast to Klein, who struggled to prove that she—and not Anna Freud—was Freud's true heir, Ferenczi recognized that what psychoanalysis urgently needed was not a reincarnation

---

right; and he evinces no awareness either that psychoanalysis could be genuinely scientific or that its scientific and spiritual impulses could exist in a productive tension.

of but an alternative to Freud. Ferenczi's repudiation of Freud's dogmatism introduced a scientific and critical spirit into psychoanalysis, whereas Klein's desire to wrap herself in Freud's mantle beckoned psychoanalysis further down the primrose path of speculation, which, as Holt has warned, must inevitably lead to its demise.

Although making the relational turn entails a willingness not only to throw overboard many of Freud's ideas but also to take his realistic measure as a man, his greatest pupils have understood the double truth that this emancipation from his oppressive influence is at the same time an expression of loyalty to what is noblest in his spirit. Whether it be Ferenczi's demand that Freud practice the honesty that is the fundamental rule of his own teachings or the theoretical modifications introduced by Fairbairn, Winnicott, and Bowlby, the guiding principle remains the same: it is necessary to let go of Freud in order to preserve psychoanalysis. As Kitcher writes, "the metatheoretic directives of Freud's metapsychology were fundamentally sound" (1992, 57), even though the ways that he went about trying to unite psychoanalysis with other fields of knowledge frequently missed the mark.

The future of psychoanalysis, then, depends on not abandoning Freud's—or Hartmann's—vision of psychoanalysis as a science and recasting it as, in Wallerstein's phrase, "a totally hermeneutic discipline." Rather, its hermeneutic superstructure must be firmly grounded on a base of scientific theory. In an interview with me, Mary Salter Ainsworth said that while Bowlby had concluded that Freud's metapsychology was "very outmoded," he was "a great admirer of Freud's, in many ways. Freud's metapsychology really was an attempt to make a science of psychoanalysis, and Bowlby thought it was just too bad that he picked a Helmholtzian model rather than an evolutionary model" (Rudnytsky 2000, 39). By the same token, Clare Winnicott recounted how, as a student at Cambridge, Winnicott had had the epiphany upon discovering the works of Darwin: "'There's a scientific way of working and that's where I am'" (quoted in Rudnytsky 1991, 182). For Winnicott, his widow added, the essence of science was simply the capacity to change one's mind: "Once you're defending your position, you've lost sight of science, he would say" (190). Winnicott may have been unduly generous in imputing such a lack of defensiveness to Freud, but he was right to remain faithful to this ideal. Given the potential for a rapprochement with science, it reflects a profound misconception of the turn taken by Ferenczi and his colleagues in 1923 to align it with postmodernism, although the relational orientation is able to integrate the valid insights of postmodernism into a flexible and capacious humanist framework.[11]

3

Much of the confusion that tends to pervade discussions of the disciplinary status of psychoanalysis stems from a failure to grasp correctly the distinction between its theory and practice, that is, between its metapsychological and psychological dimensions. Even those analysts, such as Merton Gill, who, following George Klein (1976), make this distinction central to their thinking have often not been able to do so in a consistent and coherent fashion.

In a nutshell, my hypothesis is that while psychoanalysis as a mode of therapy is indeed a hermeneutic discipline—and thus not bound by the canons of natural science—this interpretative practice should be based on a theoretical foundation where such restrictive canons are both necessary and appropriate. Problems arise either when positivistically minded analysts import scientific protocols into the consulting room where they do not belong or when devotees of hermeneutics seek to discard metapsychology altogether and thus eviscerate the legitimate scientific ambitions of psychoanalysis.

There is no better illustration of the former tendency than Eissler's paper on parameters, to which I referred at the outset of this chapter. By "parameters" Eissler meant those departures from the reigning neoclassical technique that were held to be tolerable in treating severely disturbed individuals. Within the confines of ego psychology, therefore, Eissler was writing about patients with what would currently be classified as narcissistic or borderline personality disorders for whom interpretation alone is not enough.

Despite this incipiently forward-looking aspect to Eissler's paper, however, it is fatally flawed by its obliviousness to the interactive dimensions of the analytic relationship, as well as by the scientistic—as opposed to scientific—quality of the writing. According to *Webster's New World Dictionary*, a "parameter" in mathematics is "a quantity or constant whose value varies with the circumstances of its application, as the radius line of a group of concentric circles, which varies with the circle

---

11. For Ferenczi as a postmodernist, see Harris and Aron (1997). Flax (1990) incongruously argues that Winnicott is superior to Lacan because his sensibility is more postmodernist, though she ends up by surrendering to indeterminacy: "our theoretical and interpretive choices matter," but "reasons for making them are currently lacking" (131).

under consideration"; and Eissler, with no sense of incongruity, uses the word in this sense in a therapeutic context. Indeed, once one has become aware of the literal meaning of parameter, one begins to notice the reliance on a mathematical discourse throughout Eissler's argument. He avers that "psychoanalytic techniques depend on three variables: the patient's disorder and personality; the patient's present life circumstances; and the psychoanalyst's personality" (1953, 105). Not only is "variables" a quantitative term, but Eissler neglects to include the psychoanalyst's theory among the possible causes of technical vicissitude. This assumes that there is only one correct theory and that it functions as a transparent medium devoid of any effects on how the analyst treats the patient.

As his rhetoric attests, analytic technique for Eissler should resemble a controlled experiment in which anything that interferes with the analyst's objectivity has been removed. Not surprisingly, Eissler's implicit comparison of the analyst to a mathematician is followed by his overt endorsement of Freud's notorious equation of the analyst with the surgeon in that "all accepted rules of asepsis are thrown aside in some emergency situations; nevertheless, when operating under optimal conditions, the surgeon follows these rules faithfully" (105). The word "asepsis" implies that "under optimal conditions" analysis is not only a neutral but a sterile procedure, though Eissler concedes that in an "emergency" the analyst may have no choice but to risk infection by practicing psychotherapy. He proceeds to define a parameter as "the deviation, both quantitative and qualitative, from the basic model technique, that is to say, from a technique which requires interpretation as the exclusive tool. In the basic model technique the parameter is, of course, zero throughout the whole treatment" (110). In those cases where a parameter is necessary, Eissler insists, "the final phase of the treatment must always proceed with a parameter of zero" (111); and in order to remain within the unwidened "scope of psychoanalysis," the "effect of the parameter on the transference relationship must never be such that it cannot be abolished by interpretation" (113).

By repeatedly invoking mathematical terms such as "zero" and "deviation," Eissler seeks to conjure the reader into sharing his delusion that there could be a form of technique uncontaminated by subjectivity or countertransference on the analyst's part. But as John Gedo (1991) has argued, if even the standard technique aims at "assisting analysands to arrive at their own interpretations," then "interpretation is necessary only because the analysand is unable to process his or her own free associations." Properly understood, interpretation is thus "itself one type of intervention intended to overcome a psychological deficit, in this sense no different from parametric interventions" (110–11).[12] According to Eissler, if a personal element is permitted to interfere with the transference relationship, it must be "abolished by interpretation," that is, made to disappear as though it had never happened. This notion parallels Freud's unduly optimistic early view, to which he still adhered in *Delusions and Dreams*, that "the disorder vanishes while being traced back to its origin; analysis, too, brings simultaneous cure" (1907a, 89).

Because the extremism of Eissler's formulations makes him an easy target, it might seem unfair to single him out as I have done. But not only was his paper—published in the first volume of the *Journal of the American Psychoanalytic Association*—enormously influential, it was also representative of mainstream American psychoanalysis after World War II. The crucial feature of what I have called Eissler's scientism is his refusal to acknowledge the interactive dimension of the analytic relationship. In adopting this stance Eissler was by no means alone. Only one year later, Rangell asserted that the difference between psychoanalysis and psychotherapy lay in the fact that in the former the analyst "sits at the margin, like a referee in a tennis match," whereas in the latter he is "on the court with the patient, interacting with him, the two magnetic fields interlocked" (1954, 742). In portraying analysis as a tennis match played by the patient against himself, moreover, the Los Angeles–based Rangell is simply embroidering the orthodox opinion of his intellectual (and geographical) precursor, Fenichel: "In what is called 'handling of the transference,' 'not joining in the game' is the principal task" (1941, 73).

That these statements would be almost universally rejected by ana-

12. Gedo adheres to the sound position that "it is not possible to systematize the clinical data obtained through the psychoanalytic method without articulating one's basic biological assumptions, as Sigmund Freud did in proposing a speculative metapsychology" (1991, ix); and he likewise recognizes that Freud's decision to ground his theory on a metapsychology "lacking in empirical referents was a desperate expedient" (4). But though he emphasizes the importance of neuroscience and criticizes those analysts, including Gill and George Klein, who "chose to abandon the biological pretensions of psychoanalysis altogether" in favor of hermeneutics (5), he himself falls into the antithetical error of believing that "the unfolding breakthrough toward a biology of the mind promises soon to relegate hermeneutics to a secondary position in the analytic scheme of things and to focus primary attention on learning processes" (12). Gedo's contention that "from the viewpoint of therapeutics, the cardinal implication of the new brain science is that treatment should be aimed at improving the information-processing skills available to the patient" (9) overlooks the role of affects in cognition to which neuroscience itself draws renewed attention.

lysts today registers the "shift away from a natural science, positivistic model anchored in a one-person psychology" described by Wallerstein. The decisive innovation introduced by Loewald is reflected in his proposal that the ideal of analytic objectivity "should not be confused with the 'neutral' attitude of the pure scientist towards his subject of study. . . . [T]he analyst may become a scientific observer to the extent to which he is able to observe objectively the patient and himself in interaction. The interaction itself, however, cannot be adequately represented by the model of scientific neutrality" (1960, 226). Although Loewald takes a quantum leap beyond Eissler, his views remain conservative by present standards, since he continues to speak of the analyst as a "scientific observer" capable of "objectively" scrutinizing the interaction in which he is himself a participant. Instead of thus seeking to yoke ill-sorted classical and relational paradigms, most contemporary analysts would agree with Gill that "because analysis takes place in an interpersonal context there is no such thing as non-interaction" (1984, 168). As Owen Renik has put it in a paper on the analyst's "irreducible subjectivity," "If we accept that an analyst's activity . . . is constantly determined by his or her individual psychology of which the analyst can become aware only after the fact, then we acknowledge the necessary subjectivity of even ideal analytic technique" (1993, 559).[13]

As all these more recent critiques go to show, the insurmountable defect in the neoclassical paradigm of Eissler and his allies is its attempt to conceptualize the interactive and intersubjective clinical encounter in terms of an alien model of natural science, where only a hermeneutic model is appropriate. It remains for me now to argue that, despite being immensely more sophisticated and nuanced, Wallerstein's up-to-date version of the ego psychological position does not remedy this problem.

To be more precise, I think that Wallerstein's latest and very influen-

13. The passages quoted in this and the previous paragraph from Rangell, Fenichel, Loewald, Gill, and Renik can all be found seriatim in Wallerstein (1995, 81, 207, 302, 221, 455). Also pertinent are Wallerstein's citations (201) of Nikolaas Treurniet to the effect that "making an interpretation is a transactional act that cannot be separated from the state of relatedness between analyst and patient" (1993, 219), as well as (Wallerstein 1995, 479) of Robert Stolorow's attack on the concept of analytic neutrality from the standpoint of Kohutian intersubjectivity theory: "What the analyst should strive for in his self-reflective efforts is awareness of his own personal organizing principles—including those enshrined in his theories—and of how these principles are unconsciously shaping his analytic understandings and interpretations. . . . [T]he analytic stance is best conceptualized as an attitude of sustained empathic inquiry" (1990, 122–23).

tial writings on the disciplinary status of psychoanalysis have taken the wrong tack, whereas his original views were on far stronger philosophical ground. That is, I find myself largely in agreement with his paper in the memorial *Festschrift* for George Klein, "Psychoanalysis as a Science: Its Present and Future Tasks" (1976), but part company with his restatement a decade later, "Psychoanalysis as a Science: A Response to the New Challenges" (1986b).[14] The difficulties are compounded in "One Psychoanalysis or Many?" (1988) as well as in "Psychoanalysis: The Common Ground" (1990), where Wallerstein follows up on his 1987 IPA presidential address and reflects on the extraordinary response elicited by that paper.

If Wallerstein went astray between 1976 and 1986, the reason seems to be that, like many others, he allowed himself to be unduly impressed by Adolf Grünbaum's *The Foundations of Psychoanalysis: A Philosophical Critique* (1984). The crucial difference between his 1976 and 1986 papers is that, in the latter, he gives up on the endeavor to "reconcile the search for *meaning* and *reasons* through the individual exploration of a *unique* human life with the effort to fit the findings derived from that search into the explanatory construct of a *general* science of the mind as elaborated within a natural science framework" (1986b, 421). In the earlier paper, that is, Wallerstein had argued that "it is the complexity and the special peculiarity of psychoanalysis as a science that it pursues its inquiry in each of the two realms, the general and the individual, the how and the why, and in so doing forges concurrently the logic of their interrelationships" (1976, 225–26). By the time of the later paper, however, Wallerstein retreats from the prospect of a fusion of science and hermeneutics, insisting that "psychoanalysis, despite the hermeneutic claim, is clearly not distinguishable in theory from the other sciences" (1986b, 426); indeed, hermeneutics "has collapsed into itself," and there is accordingly "no longer a real alternative to an empirical approach to psychoanalysis" (430). But whereas the hermeneutic challenge is pronounced a failure, that of Grünbaum is hailed as "incisive"; and Waller-

14. In the earlier paper, despite his defense of science together with hermeneutics, Wallerstein states that he is "not talking about a science modeled on physics or any other of the natural sciences." "To me," he elaborates, "metapsychology is *not*, as it is to some, equivalent to a biological or neurobiological explanatory framework imposed upon the data and the phenomena of psychology" (1976, 224). But the attempt to distinguish "science" from "natural science" is in vain; and it is possible to have an "explanatory framework" that makes sense of the data without being "imposed upon" them.

stein likewise lauds Grünbaum because he "demonstrates conclusively" that Habermas's distinction between modes of explanation in history and the natural sciences "is but a pseudocontrast" (425).

Wallerstein mounts an effective reply to Grünbaum's focus on the "Tally Argument"—Freud's empirically testable claim that psychoanalytic therapy succeeds in removing symptoms by correctly interpreting their precipitating causes—by pointing out that "psychoanalysis has long since [its first decade] ceased to rest on a theory of neurosogenesis based on specific repressions of specific traumatic events or on a concomitant theory of therapy based on uncovering those repressions" (1986b, 439). Today, the analytic process "is much more complexly configured in terms of repetitive interpretive working over of endlessly recurrent themes linked to the infantile pathological resolutions of the individual's preoedipal and oedipal vicissitudes—the process that we call working through." Thus, "in his assault on the Tally Argument, Grünbaum has been pushing through an open door" (439–40).

Apart from his spirited rejoinder in the matter of the Tally Argument, however, Wallerstein capitulates completely to Grünbaum. Thus, to revert to the alleged "pseudocontrast" between explanation in the natural and the human sciences, this is a topic in which I take a considerable interest, since Grünbaum—in the sequel (1993) to his landmark book—does me the honor of coupling my name with those of Habermas and Gadamer for foolishly continuing to believe that there is "an *asymmetry* of context-dependence" between "history in physical laws" and in psychological narratives (15). In other words, there is in Grünbaum's view no essential difference between understanding a particle and a human being, since the "histories" of both are equally tied to their contexts—magnetic fields for particles, societies for human beings. This is precisely the example found in *The Foundations of Psychoanalysis* (1984, 17), moreover, that Wallerstein himself cites to support his contention that Grünbaum has "incisively" refuted Habermas and indeed demolished the entire hermeneutic approach to psychoanalysis.

But surely there is a problem here, and it is not with those who believe that there is only a "pseudocontrast" between studying physics and the Middle Ages. Rather, what Grünbaum—and, following him, Wallerstein—overlooks is that the crucial point is not that there is no history or context governing the "behavior" of even an inorganic particle, but rather that the presence of *consciousness* in human beings fundamentally alters our relationship to the world; and this is the real "asymmetry" between natural and human sciences to which hermeneutics calls attention. Wallerstein's concurrence with Grünbaum leads him to propose further that "the philosophical *coup de grâce* to the designation of psychoanalysis" as a branch of hermeneutics is delivered, paradoxically, by Karl Popper (against whose designation of psychoanalysis as a pseudoscience Grünbaum polemicizes at length) because of "the effective destruction by Popper, on epistemological grounds, of the conception that there is a great and unbridgeable divide between the methods of natural science and those of historical or so-called hermeneutic science" (1986b, 429). It is not necessary to be sidetracked by Popper's specific arguments to see that Wallerstein has overstated the case by assuming that if the methods of science and hermeneutics are not separated by "a great and unbridgeable divide," then they must be identical. For surely it is possible to grant that both science and hermeneutics can be forms of critical thinking, which seek to implement the attitude of undefended openness to new experience to which I alluded earlier in connection with Winnicott, while also recognizing that they differ in consequential ways. Rather than an either/or, the relation between science and hermeneutics is at once one of contrast and continuity, as Wallerstein himself understood in 1976 when he wrote that "for proper explanation, the two realms must be kept conceptually separate, yet at the same time must be seen in their interrelatedness" (223), but which he had been persuaded by Grünbaum to forget a decade later.

Under Grünbaum's influence, therefore, Wallerstein concluded that hermeneutics had been thoroughly discredited and that there was "no longer a real alternative to an empirical approach to psychoanalysis." But in thus seeking to accommodate not only the theory but also the clinical practice of psychoanalysis within an empiricist paradigm, Wallerstein repeats Eissler's epistemological error and turns science into scientism.

The trajectory I have traced between Wallerstein's papers of 1976 and 1986 in turn provides the backdrop for his two subsequent famous papers, "One Psychoanalysis or Many?" and "Psychoanalysis: The Common Ground." Essentially, Wallerstein's strategy for coping with the apparent fragmentation of psychoanalysis in the post-ego psychological era is to argue that, while pluralism may reign on the plane of theory, all analysts in their consulting rooms follow Freud (1914a) in paying careful heed to "the facts of transference and resistance" (16); and it is this common denominator of clinical practice that tenuously holds psychoanalysis together today.

The most obvious objection to Wallerstein's position is its implication that analysts' theories have a negligible effect on their practice. Indeed, Wallerstein expressly avers his conviction that "there is no theoretical warrant or established clinical evidence for asserting that our theory determines or truly constrains our practice" (1990, 11). Notwithstanding this declaration, however, Wallerstein's thesis is both counterintuitive and contradicted by Victoria Hamilton's (1996) empirical investigation of precisely this question, based on oral interviews with sixty-five analysts, who also filled out a written questionnaire.[15] But an even more serious liability to Wallerstein's formulation, in my estimation, is that he has inverted the proper relationship between science and hermeneutics by equating the former with the therapeutic dimension of psychoanalysis and the latter with its metapsychological theory.

For, as it turns out, not only does Wallerstein believe that clinical work is what unifies psychoanalysis, he also holds that it provides the scientific foundation of the discipline. In his view, the "clinical theory" is "sufficiently experience-near, anchored directly enough to observables, to the data of our consulting rooms, that it is amenable to the self-same processes of hypothesis formation, testing, and validation as any other scientific enterprise" (1988, 17). Conversely, when it comes "to our general theory or theories, our metapsychologies . . . our different and distinguishing theoretical positions, ego psychological, Kleinian, object relational, etc., that mark our psychoanalytic pluralism, in regard to all these I see them, at least at this stage of our historic developmental dynamic, as primarily metaphors."

But this cannot be right. To call something metaphorical is to place it in the domain of poetry rather than science, and thus render it impervious to empirical testing. By this logic, all psychoanalytic theories are equally valid, and the choice among them simply depends on one's personal taste. In his follow-up paper on the "common ground," Wallerstein pulls back from such a radically skeptical inference, insisting that "this is . . . *not* to say that all these theoretical perspectives are truly

15. Hamilton classifies the analysts (who were based in New York, Los Angeles, San Francisco, and London) in her research sample into five groups: Self Psychologists, Kleinians, Independents, Classical Freudians, and Developmental Freudians. As an illustration of the consequentiality of theory for practice, Hamilton found (1996, 95) a statistically significant correlation between analysts' attitudes toward observational studies and toward the concepts of the real relationship and, to a lesser extent, the therapeutic alliance. In particular, those analysts—predominantly, Developmental Freudians and Independents—who affirmed the importance of external reality in theory likewise did so in their clinical practice, while those others—predominantly, Classical Freudians and Kleinians—who had no use for observational studies, conducted their analyses without regard to extra-transferential factors.

equal in their ultimate explanatory power and in their capacity to evolve beyond the metaphoric, and therefore scientifically untestable, status that . . . characterizes each of them at this stage in our historical development" (1990, 5). But even if it might ideally be possible to move psychoanalytic theory beyond metaphor to science at some hypothetical future date, Wallerstein holds fast to his conviction that "at least at this stage of our evolution as a discipline and a science we have no empirical or logical warrant for asserting the greater validity or usefulness of any of our major theoretical systems over the others, except via the beliefs and predilections and biases . . . that each of us has come to live by, professionally and intellectually" (6).

Again, however, this is manifestly untrue, as I have already demonstrated at length in this chapter. Once one has accepted the principle that, in Holt's words, "psychoanalysis is *not* autonomous, existing in self-sufficient isolation on an island remote from other sciences," then it is possible for most people to come to an agreement about which parts of Freud's metapsychology need to be thrown out. Given that Freud's Lamarckianism, recapitulationism, principle of constancy, and passive reflex model of the nervous system have all been shown, as Holt wrote as long ago as 1965, to be "quite without any biological basis," then it can safely be said that any analyst who continues to operate with these assumptions is making a serious mistake. Indeed, as I have argued, the widespread paradigm shift from a "one-person" to a "two-person" psychology is in no small measure due to the fact that Freud's "one-person" model relies on faulty science, whereas the turn to object relations and attachment theory effected by analysts from Ferenczi through Bowlby and beyond links the psychoanalytic peninsula to the mainland of sound scientific knowledge.

Perhaps the fundamental choice faced by psychoanalysis, as I have already intimated, is that between Melanie Klein and Ferenczi, that is, between an outlook that seeks, as Wallerstein has put it, "to be in a direct and logical developmental line from the overall corpus of Freud's work," and one that deems it is necessary (despite feeling an enormous debt of gratitude toward Freud) to reject not only many of his specific ideas but his dogmatic and authoritarian "cognitive style" (Holt 1965a) generally. The choice could also be said to come down to: which Klein? Does one cast one's lot with George Klein, who pioneered in clearing the psychoanalytic forest of the "deadwood of metapsychology"? Or is it to be Melanie Klein, who (notwithstanding her incontestable power and brilliance) built her nest in Freud's barest and most ruined choirs?

My central point is simply, as Virginia Demos has also said, that what psychoanalysis has to offer from a clinical perspective "must always be integrated and brought into correspondence with the current scientific understandings of human capacities and functions gained from such other contexts as neurology, brain sciences, and academic psychology" (1996, 652). In particular, it is imperative for psychoanalysis to give due weight to the cognitive aptitudes of the human neonate, which counterpoise its physical helplessness. Contrary to Wallerstein, I do not think that we are obliged to wait another decade—let alone another century—before heeding Demos's excellent advice. The verdict is already in. It mandates that we replace the incompetent, fantasy-drenched infant of Freud and Melanie Klein with the infant of contemporary research who has "a distinctly human brain that is designed to carry out essential human functions," and a unique "set of biologically based social, experiential, and organizational capabilities" (658).

Wallerstein, then, is wrong to depict the various competing psychoanalytic metapsychologies as no more than metaphors that are "scientifically untestable" and to assert that at present there is "no empirical or logical warrant for asserting the greater validity or usefulness of any of our major theoretical systems over the others." But what about his corollary that the "clinical theory" is "amenable to the self-same processes of hypothesis formation, testing, and validation as any other scientific enterprise"? Once again, I think he has it backwards, though there is an ambiguity in the phrase "clinical theory" that needs to be considered.

For if "clinical theory" is used—as I believe Wallerstein intends the term—to mean a theory *about* the clinical practice of psychoanalysis, then I agree with him that it is scientifically testable. But in that case, the clinical theory is no different from the rest of metapsychology; indeed, it is an integral part of that metapsychology. Wallerstein's own Psychotherapy Research Project at the Menninger Foundation, *Forty-Two Lives in Treatment* (1986a), is the classic work in this field. Through carefully controlled studies with this sample of more than usually disturbed patients extending in many instances over thirty years, Wallerstein and his colleagues came to some surprising conclusions unfavorable at least to the traditional assumptions of psychoanalysis. Most notably, they found that supportive factors played a more important role in bringing about therapeutic change than did insight-oriented interpretation, and that the changes brought about by these two treatment modalities proved to be indistinguishable in stability and duration.

Ironically, Wallerstein's own findings disprove his assertion that there is "no empirical or logical warrant" for asserting the "greater validity or usefulness" of one psychoanalytic theory over another. A hallmark of relational theory, going back to Rank and Ferenczi's *Development of Psychoanalysis*, has been (as I put it in chapter 7) the awareness that psychic healing requires the wine of sympathy as well as the bread of interpretation; and Wallerstein's research empirically corroborates the truth of this proposition.

When Wallerstein uses the phrase "clinical theory," therefore, it signifies a body of abstract and generalized principles that can be deduced using the scientific method. Paradoxically, however, as I remarked a moment ago, the clinical theory so defined is actually *extraclinical* since the perspective it affords on what takes place in the clinical encounter is ultimately that of a detached observer, rather than an involved participant.[16] Thus, although Wallerstein's theory is scientific, it is not truly clinical. For, as I shall go on to argue more fully, in the always unique and never repeatable meetings between two human beings who call themselves analyst and patient, the ground rules are not those of scientific hypothesis-testing but rather of literary hermeneutics.

Before leaving Wallerstein, however, I would like to signal a final problem with his argument. In giving a triad of examples to illustrate his contention that practice and not theory constitutes the "common ground" of psychoanalysis, Wallerstein states about a vignette from Max Hernandez, a Latin American analyst trained in the Independent group of the British Society, that "one would be hard put to distinguish this specimen of clinical work from that of those trained within other theoretical, cultural, or linguistic perspectives" (1990, 15). But in Hernandez's clinical material, which Wallerstein himself summarizes, Hernandez had pointed to his patient's "pleasure that he [the analyst] had indeed survived her violent impulses" (13), a textbook example of Winnicott's (1969) notion of the "use" of an object, a signature of the Middle Group.

16. The same can be said of Lester Luborsky's extremely useful empirically based investigations into motivated forgetting (1996) and transference (Luborsky and Crits-Christoph 1990). Although Luborsky succeeds in proving that these psychoanalytic postulates can be scientifically supported through controlled studies utilizing clinical data, the price he pays for seeking to identify a single "core conflictual relational theme" in each patient is inevitably to reduce the tangled web of a human life to operationalized variables that cannot possibly do justice to its complexities. To his credit, however, Luborsky concedes that "there are crucial parts of narratives that cannot be judged with agreement," citing as examples Hamlet's madness and Lear's last words (Luborsky and Crits-Christoph 1990, 278–79), thus acknowledging the hermeneutic dimension of the analytic enterprise.

By the same token, the vignette from Michael Feldman, a British Kleinian, to which Wallerstein (1990) then directs his attention, opens with a patient's "dream material expressing the fear that the analyst might be a murderer, trying to destroy her," and portraying her elderly father as "disabled and helpless" (15). Feldman interprets to the patient that her "focus on the bad analyst also defensively protected . . . against the frightening view of her aging parents as damaged and vulnerable" (16). While conceding that Feldman's technique exhibits "a decidedly Kleinian cast," Wallerstein claims that it does not materially differ from either that of Hernandez or Anton Kris, an American ego psychologist and the last member of his triumvirate. But as an outrider of the relational caravan, I cannot help wondering whether the patient's perception of Feldman as a "murderer" and a "bad analyst" might not be iatrogenically induced and a perfectly appropriate response to his Kleinian insistence on interpreting her concerns exclusively as projective fantasies, rather than as an expression of a legitimate concern about her father's fragility compounded by anger at Feldman for refusing to consider that he might be culpable as an analyst in some way.[17]

The overarching aim of my extended discussions of Eissler and Wallerstein has been to show, on the one hand, that a natural science model is not appropriate to understanding the existential dynamics of the analytic situation and, on the other, that metapsychologies are not mere metaphors but potentially testable theories, some of which are clearly superior to others. I now propose to turn the tables by taking up several prominent advocates of the hermeneutic version of psychoanalysis. In brief, my argument will be that while hermeneutics indeed pro-

17. In "One Psychoanalysis or Many?" (1988), Wallerstein cites a similar example, reported by Kohut (1984) in his last book, of an exchange with a Kleinian analyst from Latin America. To Kohut's surprise, when this analyst interpreted a patient's silence at being notified of the cancellation of a session as an inhibition of "biting words" directed against the "bad breast" (92), this elicited a positive response despite being couched in what Kohut believed to be a misguided theoretical vocabulary. Contrary to Wallerstein, for whom this incident proves the irrelevance of theory to practice, I believe that the key point is Kohut's observation that the analyst addressed the patient in a "warmly understanding tone of voice." Thus, although the analyst's Kleinian theory was indeed wide of the mark, this handicap was more than compensated for by the analyst's supportive demeanor. The lesson to be drawn once again is not that all theories are interchangeable and equally approximate metaphors, but rather that (as in Wallerstein's own Psychotherapy Research Project) there is empirical justification for the emphasis on the affective dimension of the analyst-patient relationship common to both object relations theory and self psychology.

vides the best framework for comprehending the analytic dialogue, it should not lead us to reject metapsychology altogether or to renounce Freud's dream of placing psychoanalytic theory on a truly scientific foundation.

The central claim advanced by hermeneutic philosophers is—as I have already intimated in my rejoinder to Grünbaum's equation of people and particles—that it is imperative to make a distinction between the human and the natural sciences. In "Psychoanalysis and Hermeneutics" (1979), Robert Steele quotes one G. Radnitzky (no relation to the present author) who defines this antinomy as one between methods investigating "entities with which the inquirer can establish communication and may at least in principle enter into a dialogue and those with which it is not possible" (390). In an earlier and still more influential paper, "The Concept of Mind" (1966), H. J. Home phrases the contrast as one between "how" and "why" questions and their respective answers in terms of "causes" and "reasons": "science asks the question how does a thing occur and receives an answer in terms of causes, whereas a humanistic study asks the question why and receives an answer in terms of reasons" (44).[18] As Home elaborates, if entities "are seen as dead their behavior has to be accounted for in terms of causes; if they are seen as alive they have to be accounted for in terms of a spontaneous subject."

The impact of Home's formulations can be seen in Wallerstein's 1976 paper, where (as he later put it in retracting these views) he urged that psychoanalysis should "reconcile the search for *meaning* and *reasons* through the individual exploration of a *unique* human life with the effort to fit the findings derived from that search into the explanatory construct of a *general* science of the mind as elaborated within a natural science framework" (1986b, 421). With this fundamental proposition I am in complete agreement. Because hypothesis testing is by definition impossible with single cases, a different method of inquiry must be used when trying to make sense of an individual human life or cultural artifact. I thus regret, as I have said, Wallerstein's retreat from his original position that "for proper explanation, the two realms must be kept conceptually separate, yet at the same time must be seen in their interrelatedness" (1976, 223), in favor of an exclusively "empirical approach" (1986b, 430).

18. For an account of how the icy response to Home's paper led to Charles Rycroft's withdrawal from the British Psycho-Analytical Society, see my interview (2000, 74–76) with Rycroft.

The problem with the hermeneutic perspective, however, comes when its incontrovertibly valid insights are taken to extremes no less indefensible than Eissler's attempt to eradicate subjectivity from the "basic model technique" of psychoanalysis. These extremes can, paradoxically, take the form either of seeking to exaggerate the genuine differences between science and hermeneutics into "a great and unbridgeable divide" (to borrow Wallerstein's Popperian phrase) or of seeking to abolish them completely by alleging that psychoanalysis—or even science as a whole—is simply a branch of hermeneutics.

The former tendency is exemplified by Home, who asserts that "the logic and method of the humanities is radically different from that of science" (1966, 43). How one defines "radically different" is, of course, itself a matter of interpretation. For Home, the contrast "is expressed in the canons of scientific method which demand that a clear distinction always be maintained between observation and inference, whereas in a humanistic study a clear distinction is demanded only in respect of who is saying what" (43–44). But the insinuation that the humanities can dispense with the distinction between observation and inference is justly derided by Holt: "Try to sell *that* to any good historian!" (1981, 311). Home only makes matters worse with his assertion that, unlike a scientific theory, which "takes its original point of departure from a demonstrable fact and must eventually return to it, . . . neither history nor the mind, conscious or unconscious, is a fact or event such as scientific method can investigate" (1966, 45). This is again a statement likely to perplex both historians, who (whatever may be said about "history" in the abstract) make it their business to study facts and events, and also a neuroscientist such as Gerald Edelman who (as we shall see) has indeed shown that not only the brain but also the mind is something that the "scientific method can investigate."

Home, then, opens himself to criticism by his penchant for overstatement, though, as I have argued, this does not mean that the opposition between science and hermeneutics can be dismissed entirely. If, as Holt points out, "a reason is one kind of cause, a *psychological* cause, and . . . various types of causes can be handled in the same study without confusion" (1981, 313), it is still important to try to distinguish what makes a "psychological cause" different from other kinds of causes; and to the extent that reasons are unique to human beings, a hermeneutic approach to their understanding is warranted.

Whereas Home represents the tendency to exaggerate the split between science and hermeneutics, the opposite tendency to collapse psychoanalysis into hermeneutics is epitomized by Steele and, even more, by Gill. Although Steele's exposition of their commonalities is very useful, he simply takes it for granted that "psychoanalysis like hermeneutics recognizes that human activities and cultural products can be more rigorously investigated by a method growing out of the study of the human order rather by a method based on the study of the natural order" (1979, 389), instead of presenting this as a controversial thesis that needs to be defended. Toward the end of the paper, Steele asserts that "Freud's biology, like his history, has its origins in the verbal exchanges between analyst and analysand" (406). There can be no doubt that Freud's biology is seriously inadequate, and the Lamarckian notion of inheritance of acquired characteristics applies much better to transmission in the realm of culture than it does to transmission in the realm of nature. But Freud's blunders have not themselves been inherited by most subsequent psychoanalysts; it is thus incorrect for Steele to say that "psychoanalytic biology is quasi-biology because instead of describing causal connections between material bodies it serves the purpose of providing a frame of reference for the creation of psychoanalytic case histories" (407). Psychoanalytic biology is simply biology, deployed to advance psychoanalytic knowledge in theory or practice. Asking in conclusion whether psychoanalysis is an art or a science, Steele tries to cut the Gordian knot, but in so doing merely begs the question: "The answer is that it is both, and the only way it can be both is as a form of hermeneutics."

Steele's incoherent suggestion that psychoanalysis can only be a science by avowing itself a "form of hermeneutics" is taken to an even more radical length by Gill, who, in his last book, strives to convince the reader that "all science is constructivist" (1994, 5). Hence, Gill proposes, "while hermeneutic studies in the humanities may not be a science, psychoanalysis as hermeneutics can be." This line of reasoning leads Gill to define psychoanalysis oxymoronically as a "hermeneutic science" (4).

There are two major steps in this argument, both of which are missteps. The first—the general claim about the constructivist nature of science—erases any distinction between science and other forms of knowledge, thereby providing a mirror image of Eissler's denial of the interactive dimension to the analytic relationship. Whereas for Eissler the aim of the analyst should be to achieve a "parameter of zero," Gill thinks that because "the contribution of the observer can never be reduced to zero" (5), both the natural and the human sciences are essentially hermeneutic endeavors.

Although Gill is right that even in natural science the role of the observer can never be expunged completely—the influence of operations of measurement on the phenomena under observation (at the level of subatomic particles) being the gist of Heisenberg's uncertainty principle—there remains a critical difference between those disciplines that seek to keep the observer's subjectivity as unobtrusive as possible and those that cultivate it as a primary tool of knowledge. To borrow Home's terminology, in answering "how" questions, "it is essential that observation shall not be interfered with or confused by impulsive acts of interpretation based on identification" (1966, 45); however, in answering "why" questions—though impulsiveness and confusion are surely to be eschewed—empathic identification is indispensable. Neither type of knowledge can supplant the other; each lacks something that the other has to offer. Oscar Wilde captures this interdependence of scientific and hermeneutic truth with his customary epigrammatic wit: "The advantage of the emotions is that they lead us astray, and the advantage of Science is that it is not emotional" (1891, 47).

Since I mentioned Heisenberg's uncertainty principle, I would like to seize this moment to make a larger point about twentieth-century science. It is frequently argued by postmodernists that the radical changes in contemporary scientific thought associated with the names of Einstein and Heisenberg have, in Lewis Aron's words, forced us to renounce "the search for general, universal laws and all-encompassing principles" that are a legacy of Freud's outmoded adherence to "nineteenth-century scientific and scholarly thinking" (1996, 24). But this is too simple. As Holt has noted, Einstein actually preferred the term "invariance theory" to the more popular term "relativity"; and though his revolution in physics did entail "giving up Newton's absolute framework of a fixed reference system of space and time," he did so paradoxically in order to vindicate the traditional scientific belief that "the basic physical laws will always be the same, regardless of the circumstances under which observations are made" (1984, 357). Gerald Edelman—whose work I shall examine in greater depth in the following section—likewise emphasizes that, even now, "the goal of physics remains Galilean: to describe laws that are invariant. . . . This is because Einsteinian and Heisenbergian observers, while embedded in their own measurements, are still psychologically transparent. Their consciousness and motives . . . do not *have* to be taken into account to practice physics" (1992, 11). Such a separation of mind from nature is, however, impossible when mind itself becomes the object of investigation.

Gill's premise that "all science is constructivist," despite its superficial plausibility, is thus a mandate for dispensing with science altogether. Although Gill does concede in principle that there is such a thing as external reality about which one can have knowledge—thus distinguishing his own position from what he calls "*radical* constructivism" (1994, 2)—he becomes so carried away by the idea that "what we understand of reality is not reality as such but the construction we make of reality" that he fails seriously to ponder what it might mean that the "constraints of reality" indeed place limits on our "constructions," refuting some (Lamarckianism), while confirming others (Darwinism). All constructions are not created equal, and it is the task of science to find ever closer approximations of the "invariant laws" of nature. As Holt has articulated this understanding of constructions from a genuinely scientific standpoint, "outside all vantage points of the individual observers, there is a constant and asymptotically approachable framework of reality. We cannot always—perhaps never—see it directly, but we can construct it" (1984, 359).

The perplexity into which Gill wanders in his exposition of the philosophy of science leads him still further astray when he takes up the epistemology of psychoanalysis. Echoing the title of his paper in the memorial volume for George Klein, "Metapsychology Is Not Psychology" (1976), Gill proposes to banish metapsychology from psychoanalysis altogether while retaining only a clinical psychology: "Freudian metapsychology is in a natural science framework; its natural scientific terms are force, energy, substance, and space. Freud's clinical theory, his psychology, is in a hermeneutic metapsychology; it deals with human meanings. Freud's metapsychology and his psychology are confusingly intertwined" (1994, 6). For Gill the notion of natural science invariably carries a pejorative taint. It does not occur to him, as it did not occur to Steele, that the "natural science framework" proposed by Freud might be faulty in certain respects, but that his mistakes could be rectified by future generations. Rather, Gill vaults to the conclusion that "psychoanalysis can and should be a purely psychological discipline" (9), and that the only possible theoretical discourse is a "hermeneutic metapsychology."

Having expelled science by the front door, Gill then tries to smuggle it in at the back by coining the oxymoron of "hermeneutic science." It is true that in German the word *Wissenschaft* is used interchangeably for natural and humanistic disciplines, and it is therefore customary to refer in English to both the natural and the human "sciences." But *Wissenschaft* is a substantive formed from the verb *wissen*, meaning "to know," and it is misleading to give *Wissenschaft* the connotation of "hard science," when it should have the much broader meaning of any "field of knowledge." Gill trips over the definition of science when he writes that "the scientific method of a hermeneutic science is, or will be, different from the scientific method of the natural sciences" (7). The preoccupations of hermeneutics are indeed different not only in degree but also in kind from those of the natural sciences, but that is exactly why it makes no sense for Gill to try to dignify the humanistic discipline of interpretation practiced by clinical analysts by dressing it up and calling it a science.

The last straw for a literary scholar is Gill's second claim that "while hermeneutic studies in the humanities may not be science, psychoanalysis as hermeneutics can be" (5). In other words, unlike psychoanalysis, which can boast of being a "hermeneutic science"—meaningless though we have seen this phrase to be—the hermeneutics employed by humanists is of an inferior grade, regular rather than premium, as it were. Gill justifies this assertion on the grounds that "a crucial difference between a literary text and the human being as a text in the psychotherapeutic situation is that the human text answers back. The psychotherapeutic interpretation is met by a response; a poem does not reply to an interpretation of its meaning" (4). Once again, Gill joins one weak link to another. By his logic, because the psychoanalytic situation is interactive, whereas reading is not, that makes the interpretation of a "human text" *more* scientific than the interpretation of a "literary text." But he has it backwards. If anything, an intersubjective encounter between two minds should be *less* amenable to scientific study than an encounter between a single mind and a literary text considered as a reified object. Thus, the fact that "the human text answers back," rather than proving Gill's point, actually undercuts it.

To make matters worse, Gill's assumption that "a poem does not reply to an interpretation" is itself contradicted by hermeneutic teachings. As Steele points out, not only another person but also a text can be a "partner in dialogue"; and in dealing with a text, the established procedure for checking an interpretation "is the test of the part against the whole; that is, seeing that each new interpretation of a part fits with an emerging conception of the whole" (1979, 392). In addition, the interpreter has an obligation to hearken to what can be gleaned from "investigating parallel texts by the same author, texts from the same tradition, and the historical period of the text's creation" (393), as well as from the history of the reception of the text. In all these ways, the written text, like a person, "answers back" to the interpreter; and it is only the prejudice of the clinician against "applied analysis" that causes Gill to overlook that the interpretations of scholars in the humanities are no less interactive—and no more scientific—than his own.

Like Eissler, Gill was one of the giants of twentieth-century American psychoanalysis, and quintessentially representative of his era of "a world without consensus," as Wallerstein (1995) defines it, just as Eissler was of the preceding era of the "majority consensus." If Eissler may be compared to Brezhnev, trying from his position as Director of the Freud Archives to hold the empire of ego psychology together by authoritarian fiat, Gill is like Gorbachev, presiding (at least intellectually) over its restructuring and irreversible collapse.

In a classic statement of the hermeneutic position, Habermas reprehended "the scientific self-misunderstanding of psychoanalysis inaugurated by Freud himself" when he took his discovery of "the only tangible example of a science [i.e., field of knowledge] incorporating methodical self-reflection" (1968, 214) and sought to confine it in a theoretical discourse derived from the natural sciences. Eissler's paper on parameters attests that there is at least a measure of truth to this accusation. But if the "scientific self-misunderstanding of psychoanalysis" occurs whenever the clinical encounter is viewed through the diminishing lens of positivism, so too there can be a "hermeneutic self-misunderstanding of psychoanalysis," and it is exemplified by Gill's reductive credo that "psychoanalysis can and should be a purely psychological discipline," without a scientific metapsychology.[19]

As I have argued throughout this chapter, what psychoanalysis needs to do is to take Eissler's science—the thesis—and Gill's hermeneutics—the antithesis—and combine them into a dialectical synthesis. Although

---

19. Within the hermeneutic camp, there is a pronounced difference between the extremists represented by Donald Spence, according to whom "interpretations are persuasive . . . not because of their evidential value but because of their rhetorical appeal; conviction emerges because the fit is good, not because we have made contact with the past" (1976, 32), and the moderates, such as Paul Ricoeur (1977), who see no inherent contradiction between "coherence" and "correspondence" theories of truth. Indeed, for the moderates, among whom I number myself, it is when an analyst's interpretation succeeds in making "contact with the past" of the patient that it is most likely to offer a "good fit" in the present relationship. Thus, even in the clinical setting the analyst should preserve a binocular focus on the external as well as the inner worlds; and this entails functioning as a scientist as well as an interpreter of the "human text." For a judicious weighing of the antimony of "coherence" and "correspondence" theories in Freud's thought, see Bass (1998).

I have not seen his views quoted by any of the major protagonists in what Wallerstein has aptly characterized as "The Great Metapsychology Debate" (1986b, 417), I know of no sager counsel on this score than that offered by Bowlby in his papers, "Psychoanalysis as Art and Science" (1979) and "Psychoanalysis as a Natural Science" (1980). As the title of the former suggests, Bowlby seeks to draw attention to the "two very different aspects of our discipline—the art of psychoanalytic therapy and the science of psychoanalytic psychology—and in doing so to emphasize, on the one hand, the distinctive value of each and, on the other, the gulf that divides them—in regard both to the contrasting criteria by which each should be judged and the very different mental outlook that each demands" (1979, 39).

At the end of "Psychoanalysis as a Natural Science," Bowlby expatiates on this tension between psychoanalysis as an art and a science, stressing not only what science can do but—even more importantly—what it cannot. As Bowlby writes, science *deals in generalities but has little to say about specific events*" (1980, 78). Whereas engineers or physicists "have no interest in the future of any particular atom or particle," he continues—choosing by uncanny coincidence an example that bears directly on my debate with Grünbaum—in the realm of history "the individual example is the very essence of the case." Thus, "the distinction between the natural sciences and the historical sciences is not that they use a different method of obtaining knowledge but that the problems that they strive to understand and the criteria they adopt are quite different. One is concerned to formulate general laws in terms of probabilities, the other to understand singular specific events in as much detail as possible."[20] In short, as a set of interconnected theories about the development and functioning of the human mind, psychoanalysis is a "natural science" that, like any other, must conform to "statistical probabilities" (76), whereas "the art of psychoanalytic therapy" is a "historical science" in which the fate of the individual patient "is the very essence of the case," and the subjectivity of the analyst is likewise an indispensable component.

By a far-reaching historical irony, Bowlby's vision of a possible synthe-

---

20. As I have argued, since hypothesis testing is impossible in single cases, the methods used in the natural and the historical sciences are not in fact identical, though they do have common elements, as a psychological reason can be one type of cause. I return to Bowlby's insufficient appreciation of the distinctiveness of hermeneutics in the following section.

sis of science and hermeneutics is closely akin to that of Heinz Hartmann. Like Bowlby, although less magnanimously, Hartmann, too, sought to address the challenge of hermeneutics and to incorporate its legitimate insights into a broader conception of psychoanalysis as a science. Strikingly, his seminal paper on this topic, "Understanding and Explanation," comes from a book written in 1927, and is the earliest piece to be included in his collected papers. Hartmann's thesis, implied by his title, is that the mode of "understanding" advocated by Dilthey as requisite in hermeneutics is insufficient for psychoanalysis and needs to be supplemented by the more abstract mode of "explanation" generated by hypotheses in the natural sciences. But though Hartmann asserts that "psychoanalysis opposes Dilthey when he says that the construction of hypotheses is basically inappropriate to psychology," Hartmann nonetheless allows that "psychoanalysis claims that phenomenological research is only one condition, *though an essential one*, for the fulfillment of its task" (1927, 374; italics added).[21] Consequently, hermeneutics is necessary but not sufficient for psychoanalysis; but if that is so, then the same holds true also for science. As Hartmann writes in the concluding sentences of his paper:

> No psychology of the more complex aspects of the mind can fully dispense with understanding. But as long as it is a science, it must not use understanding without having established the limits of its reliability. To ascertain these limits and thereby to determine the sphere within which understanding and causal connections coincide is one of the essential tasks of psychoanalysis. (403)

These words are as true today as they were when Hartmann wrote them seventy-five years ago. What is more, the convergence between his outlook and Bowlby's suggests that the triumph of the relational orientation has not been absolute. Like Freud, the ego psychologists went wrong in their metapsychology, and they tended to be dogmatic in their cognitive styles, but they were right in their core belief that psycho-

---

21. This crucial proviso means that it is inadequate to say, as Holt does, that "Hartmann explicitly aligned psychoanalysis with the natural sciences, as do many conservative analysts today" (1981, 307). Hartmann's is actually a mixed position very similar to Holt's own position. Like Holt, Hartmann makes the point that a meaning (or reason) can also be a cause: "If . . . a symptom is, in Freud's terminology, considered to be 'meaningful,' this simply refers to the possibility of assigning it a place in the (causal) relationships of the mind" (1927, 400).

analysis could be a general psychology.[22] If psychoanalysis is to move beyond the era of fragmentation to a "new majority consensus," it can only be by fusing the scientific ethos of ego psychology with the predominantly hermeneutic leanings of the relational tradition. "To determine the sphere within which understanding and causal connections coincide" is still "one of the essential tasks of psychoanalysis." That such a synthesis may now be within reach is the wish that inspires the dream of consilience.

4

In the postmodernist version of psychoanalysis that still enjoys widespread popularity in the humanities today, there is no more fundamental principle than that the study of literature should be entirely text-based and forego biography altogether. The *locus classicus* of this approach is Lacan's "Seminar on 'The Purloined Letter'" (1956), in which, as Shoshana Felman has observed, "the analysis of the signifier implies a theory of textuality for which Poe's biography . . . become[s] irrelevant" (1980, 150). In the same vein, Peter Brooks advocates a "textual and rhetorical" model of psychoanalytic reading, while disparaging study of the author's life as "the most discredited" alternative, since the author, like literary characters, has been "deconstructed into an effect of textual codes, a kind of thematic mirage" (1987, 334–35).

22. The idea of psychoanalysis as a general psychology has been dismissed as "grandiose and infertile" by Edelson (1988, xxiii), who likewise pays Hartmann the compliment that "the example set by his theoretical essays may have had a pernicious if not devastating effect on the development of psychoanalysis as a science" (121). But Edelson, the epitome of a conservative analyst devoted to a view of psychoanalysis exclusively as a natural science, despite making in principle the allowance that "the findings of another discipline may constrain to some extent what is possible and what is impossible for psychoanalysis to postulate about the mind" (62), in practice not only disregards neuroscience but also asserts that in psychoanalytic explanations "the vicissitudes of psychosexual phases . . . play a causal role more important than memories of traumatic events or disturbed object-relations" (163). He thus simply takes for granted the truth of Freud's drive theory. In a classic meeting of extremes, Gill's definition of psychoanalysis as a "hermeneutic science" is mirrored by Edelson's definition of it as a "science of imagination" (xxiv). Sharing Grünbaum's disdain for hermeneutics, Edelson scientistically holds that "we do not try to understand a person. We try to understand something *about* a person" (319), and contends that "the case study method," rather than being an intrinsically literary mode of knowledge, has "evidential value" that confers "scientific credibility on psychoanalytic explanations" (321).

Despite the valuable stimulation afforded by Lacan's ideas, these quotations from two eminent critics show why, like Melanie Klein, he leads psychoanalysis in what I believe to be the wrong direction, away from the emerging synthesis between science and hermeneutics, ego psychology and object relations theory—which is where its future lies. In part, my objection is simply to the dogmatism with which Felman and Brooks pronounce approaches that differ from their own to be "irrelevant" and "discredited." Beyond this defect of cognitive style, however, there is a problem with their argument. Although it is, of course, possible to interpret a text without connecting it to the author's life, the assumption that the study of literature can only be "textual and rhetorical" leaves out what Yeats called the "foul rag-and-bone-shop of the heart"—the often sordid reality of human experience that is where the ladder of art begins, and the desire to fathom the mystery of which is surely what motivates most readers and writers to turn to literature in the first place.

If the attitudes toward literature expressed by Felman and Brooks are symptomatic of the dehumanized outlook of postmodernism generally, then another way of making my objection is to say that their rejection of biography is also by extension a rejection of biology. And, as Gerald Edelman has argued, "ignoring the origin of things is always a risky matter" (1992, 33). On the personal level, the origin of a work of art lies in the mind of the artist; but since the artist is himself or herself a member of the human species, the conditions of possibility governing the work of art are laid down by what we know to be true of human beings and their evolution. As Edelman writes, "the practice of ignoring biology when thinking about the mind and how knowledge is acquired . . . has a distinguished history" (34); but while such a neglect may have been understandable in philosophers and psychologists prior to the nineteenth century, it is no longer pardonable in the wake of Darwin. As Edelman sums up the inescapable conclusion of this line of reasoning, "the phenomena of psychology depend on the species in which they are seen, and the properties of species depend on natural selection" (40).

In the remainder of this chapter, I shall seek to develop the implications of this realization for psychoanalysis, concentrating on the increasingly close ties being formed between psychoanalysis and neuroscience.[23] At the same time, in keeping with my governing theme, I shall

23. For the most important work in the emerging field of "neuro-psychoanalysis," see Kaplan-Solms and Solms (2000) and Solms and Turnbull (2002). Demos (2001), too, provides an excellent conspectus of the convergence of psychoanalysis and neuroscience. Un-

seek to demonstrate that this rapprochement between psychoanalysis and science, far from diminishing the importance of hermeneutics, makes it possible to accord the humanistic mode of knowledge its true dignity. Indeed, psychoanalysis comes into its own when it is regarded as a discipline at the crossroads of the natural and the human sciences in which the dream of consilience or the "jumping together" of all fields of knowledge into a unified whole—the origins of which date back to the Enlightenment—finds its fulfillment. My use of the term "consilience" is taken from Edward O. Wilson's (1998) book of that title, and it will be by outlining the congruence between the panoramic visions of Wilson and Edelman that I hope to articulate my own conception of psychoanalysis.

In view of the widespread decline in the cultural prestige of psychoanalysis, it is a remarkable fact that Edelman should have chosen to dedicate his magisterial exposition of neuroscience for the lay reader, *Bright Air, Brilliant Fire: On the Matter of Mind* (1992), "To the memory of two intellectual pioneers, Charles Darwin and Sigmund Freud." Far better known is Frederick Crews's quotation of what he hails as the "stunning pronouncement" of P. B. Medawar that "'psychoanalytic theory is the most stupendous confidence trick of the twentieth century'" (Crews 1986, 25), a denunciation repeated by his fellow Freud-bashers, Robert Wilcocks (1994, 15) and Allen Esterson (1993, 254), in their respective books. Edelman, however, like Medawar, is a recipient of the Nobel Prize for Physiology or Medicine—Edelman in 1972, and Medawar in 1975. Thus, if the Freud wars are to be settled by an appeal to scientific authorities, the outcome is at least a standoff, since a Nobel laureate can also be enlisted as a champion on behalf of psychoanalysis. (That Eric Kandel, whose work I take up in the following section, was also awarded the Nobel Prize for Medicine in 2000 now tips the balance in favor of psychoanalysis.)

One of the most valuable aspects of Edelman's book is the way that he combines a rigorously scientific *Weltanschauung*, including an extension of the principles of natural selection to neurology through his theory of neuronal group selection, with an unblinking recognition of the limits of science. Strikingly, in endorsing the hermeneutic distinction between

---

like Demos, however, I see attachment theory not as an inferior alternative but rather as a valuable complement to neuroscience. The essential point was recognized by Rubinstein as early as 1965: "If we want an empirical theory but do not intend to disregard the mind-body problem, psychoanalytic theory must be formulated in such a way that it will function both as a psychological theory and as a neurophysiological model" (63).

the natural and the human sciences, Edelman invokes the concept of intentionality introduced by Freud's teacher, Franz Brentano, to make the case that "beings with minds can refer to other beings or things; [whereas] things without minds do not refer to beings or other things" (1992, 5). This leads him to maintain, as I (and Habermas and Gadamer) have done in taking issue with Grünbaum, that "methods of doing science on inanimate objects, while fundamental, are not adequate to doing science on animals that have brains and possess intentionality" (7–8). Just as Bowlby defines the contrast between the natural and historical sciences by pointing out that whereas physicists do not take an interest in "any particular atom or particle," in the realm of history "the individual example is the very essence of the case," so Edelman observes that "biological objects under evolution have functional properties that differ from, say, those of molecules. One does not speak of the 'abnormal' function of a molecule as a chemical object. But a biological object has a proper function that depends on its evolutionary history" (240). In an eloquent phrase reminiscent of Bowlby's contention that psychoanalysis must be both an art and a science, Edelman concludes, "so science fails for individual histories even though it may succeed in discerning what is common among twenty chronicles" (138).

The ramifications of Edelman's themes proliferate throughout his book, and the language is sometimes unavoidably technical, but his main points come through with great clarity. To begin with, he takes it as axiomatic that "the description of the world by modern physics is an adequate but not completely sufficient basis for a theory of consciousness" (113). In other words, "physics proper does not deal with recognition systems, which are by their nature biological and historical systems. But all the laws of physics nevertheless apply to recognition systems" (79). And given that "the mind was put back into nature by nineteenth-century studies of physiology and psychology" (67), a science that seeks to encompass beings possessing consciousness—that is, intentionality—as well as "things without minds" must recognize that "there is no qualia-free scientific observer" (115). "Qualia" is a philosophical term for everything "personal or subjective" that can be "experienced directly only by a single observer," the scientific study of which faces the impediment that *"we cannot construct a phenomenological psychology that can be directly shared in the same way as a physics can be shared"* (114). "It is," Edelman adds, exclusively "our ability to report and correlate while individually experiencing qualia that opens up the possibility of a scientific investigation of consciousness" (115).

Having taken this series of steps, each of which is eminently justified and leads ineluctably to the next, Edelman addresses the epistemological questions that are likewise my focus in the present discussion. In a declaration that extends the relation of physics to biology (and psychology) to a paradigm governing the relation of the sciences as a whole to the humanities as a whole, he writes: "Just as different sciences are compatible with each other but are not fully reducible to one another—one being necessary but not sufficient for the next—so a description of the matter of the mind provides a basis for the analysis of relational and symbolic matters" (175). It follows from the irreducibility of discrete forms of knowledge that the expressions of human consciousness "realized in works of art are not susceptible to the methods of scientific analysis. . . . No external, objective analysis, even if possible, supplants the individual responses and intersubjective exchange that takes place within a given tradition and culture" (176). But though there are "methodological differences between *Geisteswissenschaften* and *Naturwissenschaften*"—Edelman relies on Dilthey's categories to uphold this core tenet of hermeneutics—we must not think that "psychology falls outside evolutionary biology, that there is a separate *Geist* and a separate *Natur*" (177). On the contrary—and here Edelman speaks in his capacity as a scientist—"psychology can no longer declare its autonomy from biology, and it must always yield to biology's findings."

Compelling as these statements are in their own right, each of them holds true also for psychoanalysis. The analyst's obligation to rely on hermeneutics in the clinical encounter is affirmed when Edelman contends that "the individual responses and intersubjective exchange" inherent in the exegesis "of relational and symbolic matters" cannot be supplanted by "external, objective analysis," even if such a scientific method has a limited contribution to make, as in the research studies by Wallerstein and others that utilize clinical data as the raw material. On the other hand, the individual mind that is the subject of psychoanalysis is perforce embodied, both locally in the brain and more generally in the body. Thus, every psychoanalytic investigation, though not reducible to biology, is not autonomous from it either; and in the domain of metapsychology, as I have argued, psychoanalysis "must always yield to biology's findings."

Edelman titles the final section of his book "Harmonies," and he does so "to underscore the fruitful interactions that a science of mind must have with philosophy, medicine, and physics" (153). With neuroscience as the nexus, Edelman traverses the length and breadth of knowledge, from the "nonselective material systems" to which only the laws of physics apply to those "living and mental systems" (160) capable of the highest forms of symbolic expression. In sum, Edelman dares to contemplate "a single evolutionarily based theory, one that connects embryology, morphology, physiology, and psychology," insisting that "only such a physically based theory is open to disconfirmation by scientific means" (147). Although he retains fealty to science, Edelman, as we have seen, dialectically recognizes its limits, cautioning that "after a certain point, in its individual creations at least, the mind lies beyond scientific reach" for the reason that "the forms of embodiment that lead to consciousness are unique in each individual, unique to his or her body and individual history" (136).

Although conceived independently, Edelman's proposal of "a single evolutionarily based theory" that not only unites each of the sciences with one another but also bridges the sciences as a whole with the humanities dovetails with Wilson's grand design in *Consilience*. (His most recent book is now *The Future of Life* [2002].) The parallels obtain on multiple levels, beginning with the shape of their scientific careers. Wilson, after making his reputation as an entomologist and the world's foremost expert on ants, widened his horizons in 1975 with the publication of his controversial work, *Sociobiology: A New Synthesis*, which launched a new discipline—subsequently renamed evolutionary psychology—that sought to apply the biological principles used successfully in the study of animals to the social sciences. Edelman, whose Nobel Prize was for his research as an immunologist specializing in the chemical structure of antibodies, also turned only in mid-career to neuroscience, the first fruits of this new departure being gathered in *Neural Darwinism* (1987). After *Sociobiology*, Wilson published *On Human Nature* (1978), and then, twenty years later, cast his net even more broadly in *Consilience*. Like Wilson, Edelman wrote a trilogy by following *Neural Darwinism* with *Topobiology* (1988) and then *The Remembered Present* (1989). Rather than being the completion of his trilogy, *Bright Air, Brilliant Fire* is a distillation of Edelman's foregoing books; but like *Consilience*, it too is a masterpiece in which one of the most eminent scientists of our time synthesizes a lifetime of work to reflect on questions of ultimate importance for human beings.

Beyond the outward parallels between the trajectories of their careers, Wilson and Edelman agree on matters of substance in almost every major respect. First, just as Edelman dedicates *Bright Air, Brilliant Fire* to Darwin and Freud, so, too, Darwin is central to Wilson's sociobiological project. (I shall come back to Wilson's attitude toward Freud presently.) Edelman's conviction that "the phenomena of psychology depend on the species in which they are seen, and the properties of species depend on natural selection," leads him to oppose the functionalist or computational doctrine that "representations have meaning independent of their physical instantiation" (1992, 226).[24] In identical fashion, sociobiology is founded on the hypothesis that "human social behavior rests on a genetic foundation," and this tenet prompts Wilson to reject the so-called Standard Social Science Model—the name derives from its long-unchallenged hegemony in the social sciences—which holds that "mankind has escaped its own genes to the extent of being entirely culture-bound" (1978, 32).

That Darwin is as pivotal to the thought of Wilson as he is to that of Edelman is reinforced by Wilson's concurrence in Edelman's scientific ethos. In part, this entails the recognition, as Wilson writes in *On Human Nature*, that "the heart of the scientific method is the reduction of perceived phenomena to fundamental, testable principles" (1978, 11). But the concept of "reduction" carries a far-reaching corollary, namely, that disciplines are arranged in an intrinsic hierarchy of pairs, consisting of a parent discipline and an anti-discipline, in which "the laws of a subject are necessary to the discipline above it; they challenge and force a mentally more efficient restructuring, but they are not sufficient for the purposes of the discipline" (13). For Edelman, too, as shown by his (already quoted) discussion of the relation of physics to biology, "different sciences are compatible with each other but are not fully reducible to one another—one being necessary but not sufficient for the next."

Finally, the shared veneration of Darwin and common allegiance to the scientific ethos, including the shibboleth of reductionism, culminates in Wilson's joining Edelman in extending this principle to encompass not only the relations of the individual sciences to one another but also the relation of the sciences as a whole to the humanities. Indeed, just as Edelman titles the last section of *Bright Air, Brilliant Fire* "Harmonies," so Wilson even more grandly titles his great book *Consilience*, precisely to convey his vision that the truths of an objectively existing re-

---

24. It is symptomatic of the problems with Edelson's outlook that he regards psychoanalysis as "a representational and computational psychology of mind" (1988, xxiv), thus exemplifying Edelman's prime fallacy "of ignoring biology when thinking about the mind."

ality discovered by science can and will "jump together" with the truths found in the humanities to reveal the unity of all knowledge.[25] Wilson presents his project as a revival and continuation of "the dream of intellectual unity" that "first came to full flower in the original Enlightenment" of the seventeenth and eighteenth centuries (1998, 14). He takes his epigraph from Sir Francis Bacon and singles out Condorcet's *Sketch for a Historical Picture of the Progress of the Human Mind*, written in hiding in 1794 during the French Revolution at the height of the Reign of Terror, as a forerunner of his own testament to the power of human reason and the possibility of continued spiritual as well as material progress. Edelman, while critical of the "mechanistic physics" of the original Enlightenment, as well as its lack of a "body of data or ideas with which to link the world, the mind, and society in the style of scientific reason to which it aspired" (1992, 166), nonetheless shares Wilson's faith in its ideals. "We may well hope," he affirms, "that if sufficiently general ideas synthesizing the discoveries that emerge from neuroscience are put forth, they may contribute to a second Enlightenment. If such a second coming occurs, its major scientific underpinning will be neuroscience, not physics" (171).

I think that the parallels I have traced between Edelman and Wilson are remarkable in their specificity. Both use the phrase "necessary but not sufficient" to explain the idea of reductionism. And just as Edelman grounds his belief in the unity of knowledge in "a single evolutionarily based theory," so, too, Wilson proclaims that "the core of scientific materialism is the evolutionary epic" (1978, 201); and for Wilson the naturalist no less than Edelman the neuroscientist, "every epic needs a hero: the mind will do" (203).

Although I find this "consilience" between Wilson and Edelman to be intrinsically beautiful, I adduce it here because it provides an intellectual context for contemporary psychoanalysis. We may begin to draw together the threads of this discussion by coming back to the question of Wilson's attitude toward Freud. Not only does Edelman dedicate *Bright Air, Brilliant Fire* to the memory of Freud as well as Darwin, but he declares that Freud's "basic theses about the action of the unconscious were essentially correct," from which it follows—against Descartes—that "conclusions reached by acts of conscious introspection may be sub-

25. Wilson includes *Bright Air, Bright Fire* in a list of books on the brain cited in a footnote (1998, 304), but he does not address or acknowledge any of the connections between his thought and that of Edelman, his most formidable intellectual precursor. A Bloomian dynamic of the anxiety of influence appears to be at work.

ject to grave error" (1992, 145–46). Edelman likewise endorses (182) Arnold Modell's attempt to apply the theory of neuronal group selection to a psychoanalytic model of memory in *Other Times, Other Realities* (1990), a topic to which I will return when I examine the uses made of neurology by several psychoanalytic writers in the next (and last) section of this chapter.[26]

Whereas Edelman's opinion of Freud and psychoanalysis remains consistently positive, it is one of his few differences from Wilson that Wilson's outlook undergoes a subtle but decisive shift between *Sociobiology* and *Consilience*. In "Biology and the Social Sciences" (1977), an essay published two years after *Sociobiology*, he wrote: "Psychoanalytic theory appears to be exceptionally compatible with sociobiological theory. . . . If the essence of the Freudian revolution was that it gave structure to the unconscious, the logical role of sociobiology is to reconstruct the evolutionary history of that structure. When Freud speculated in *Totem and Taboo* on the primal father, primal horde, and the origins of the incest taboo, he created a sociobiological hypothesis, but a poor one" (135–36).

Although Wilson faults some of Freud's specific hypotheses, he nonetheless regards him here as an ally and a kindred spirit whose intellectual ambition is "exceptionally compatible" with his own. And in *On Human Nature*, dating from the same period, despite justly taking Freud to task for his drive-discharge theory of aggression, proposing that aggression should be understood instead as "an ill-defined array of different responses with separate controls in the nervous system" (1978, 101), Wilson refers respectfully to Freud as a figure of cultural authority, and he even invokes Ernest Jones in support of the idea that people show "resistance" to a dissection of the "unconscious order and resolve of their daily lives" (176).

By the time of *Consilience*, however, Wilson strikes a more dissonant chord. Freud, whom he now considers to be "as much a literary stylist as a scientist"—the phrase "literary stylist" instead of "writer" is itself disparaging—is placed in the company of other modernists who, according to Wilson, "had by the middle of the twentieth century all but erased hope for the unification of knowledge with the aid of science" (1998,

26. Edelman, however, is no expert on psychoanalysis. He confuses Breuer and Freud in referring to the challenges "that faced Freud in the early days of psychoanalysis when he confronted his patient Anna O." (1992, 186); and, even more surprisingly, he describes *On Dreams*, rather than *The Interpretation of Dreams*, as Freud's "chef d'oeuvre . . . the work he considered to be his greatest" (258).

40). This is, of course, a complete reversal of his earlier assessment. Freud's conception of the unconscious, despite being "a fundamental contribution to culture," is deemed in *Consilience* to be "mostly wrong"; and Wilson recasts his equivocal but on balance favorable judgment in "Biology and the Social Sciences" to accentuate Freud's failures: "Freud's fatal error was his abiding reluctance to test his own theories— to stand them up against competing explanations—then revise them to accommodate contravening facts. He also suffered from the luck of the draw" (74).

The evolution in Wilson's view of Freud over the past quarter century is symptomatic of the declining fortunes of psychoanalysis in American culture during that time. In large measure, I think Wilson's criticism must be conceded to be just. His diagnosis of Freud's "fatal error" as his "abiding reluctance to test his own theories," as the scientific method requires, is, as we have seen, widely shared by untendentious critics of psychoanalysis such as Patricia Kitcher and even its most thoughtful defenders, such as Robert Holt. Indeed, Wilson's observation that Freud suffered not only from the defects of his temperament but also from "the luck of the draw"—that is, his inclination to align psychoanalysis with theories that initially seemed plausible in his day but have since been discredited by the advances of science—is echoed by Kitcher's observation concerning the unfortunate fate of Freud's "biological bets" when he "decided to back the twin horses of Lamarckianism and recapitulationism." Uncannily, although *Freud's Dream* appeared in 1992, six years before *Consilience*, Kitcher titles the second part, containing her anatomy of Freud's downfall, "The Consilience That Failed," thus vividly illustrating how closely the concerns of her book anticipate those of Wilson's.

But if Kitcher's indictment of Freud bears out the validity of Wilson's perspective in one respect, in another it shows why he is off the mark. For despite Freud's bad bets and deviations from the scientific path, Wilson is mistaken to categorize him with those who "erased hope for the unification of knowledge with the aid of science." Freud's own version of psychoanalysis was a "consilience that failed," but it was undeniably a quest for consilience; and it exhibits Wilson's lack of familiarity with current developments in psychoanalysis that he should lump it together with "postmodernist solipsism" as a school of interpretation that ignores "the material processes of the human mind" (1998, 216), and has therefore become obsolete.

The unduly negative cast to Wilson's verdict on psychoanalysis in

Consilience reflects what I believe to be a greater imbalance in the book. Ostensibly, his vision is one in which the sciences and the humanities possess equal dignity. At the outset of the book, he avers: "If the world really works in a way so as to encourage the consilience of knowledge, I believe the enterprises of culture will eventually fall out into science, by which I mean the natural sciences, and the humanities, particularly the creative arts. These domains will be the great branches of learning in the twenty-first century" (1998, 12). Later, in a representative passage, he states that if "an enduring theory of the arts" is to be created as part of charting the brain, "it will be by stepwise and consilient contributions from the brain sciences, psychology, and evolutionary biology. And if during this process the creative mind is to be understood, it will need collaboration between scientists and humanities scholars" (216).

Although there is nothing wrong on the face of it with either of these declarations, it should be noted that having a "theory of the arts" or understanding the "creative mind" in general is very different from engaging with and interpreting a specific work of art, just as the articulation of a theory of therapy must be distinguished from negotiating an actual clinical encounter. The limitations of Wilson's proposals for the "reinvigoration of interpretation with the knowledge of science and its proprietary sense of the future" (211) come sharply into view when he strives to implement them in practice by expounding the beautiful lines in book 4 of *Paradise Lost* ("Not that fair field / Of Enna . . .") in which, as Wilson puts it, Milton "tries to capture the mythic core of paradise" and "summons archetypes that have descended undiminished from ancient Greece and Rome to his own time, and thereafter to ours" (212). This, I am afraid, will not do as a piece of literary criticism, notwithstanding Wilson's assurance that these archetypes are "innate to the human mental process." Even if we are prepared to grant Wilson's premises, which have a decidedly Jungian cast, they do not account for the distinctive poetic quality of the passage, beginning with the word "Not" by which Milton simultaneously negates and affirms the resemblance between his biblical garden—and Eve—to the classical analogues that are paradoxically at once their prototypes and descendants. Valuable though it is for the literary scholar, like the psychoanalyst, to be informed about "brain sciences, psychology, and evolutionary biology," there is simply no way that the "stepwise and consilient contributions" of these disciplines can serve as anything more than handmaidens to the essentially hermeneutic task of interpreting *Paradise Lost* or any other work of art; and it is the beginning of scientific wisdom to come to terms with this humbling realization.

The difficulties Wilson encounters in his foray into practical criticism are manifestations of a diminished view of the humanities that belies his assertions that they are separate from but equal to the sciences. This subordination of the humanities to the sciences is the legacy of the Enlightenment to which Wilson acknowledges his allegiance. In explaining the importance of Francis Bacon, Wilson writes that he "argued for the full employment of the humanities, including art and fiction, as the best means of developing and expressing science" (1998, 27). This accurately summarizes Bacon's views, but it makes clear that for Bacon the arts and letters were instruments to be used in the advancement of learning, not wellsprings of knowledge in their own right.

Thus, upon careful examination, Wilson's dream of consilience, although admirable in principle and compatible with psychoanalysis, falls short in practice because of its one-sided tilt toward the sciences and away from the humanities. In this regard, Edelman, whose appreciation of psychoanalysis is far greater than Wilson's, likewise proves more scrupulous in recognizing the limitations of science and the need to safeguard the autonomy of the humanities and the hermeneutic methods uniquely appropriate to their study.

Within the field of psychoanalysis, the contradiction between Wilson's theoretically even-handed appreciation of art and science and actual devaluation of the former in favor of the latter finds a close parallel in Bowlby. Bowlby, too, as we have seen, wishes to affirm the "two very different aspects of our discipline—the art of psychoanalytic therapy and the science of psychoanalytic psychology—and in doing so to emphasize, on the one hand, the distinctive value of each and, on the other, the gulf that divides them" (1979, 39). This seems perfectly balanced, and indeed it is as a statement of principle. But he goes on to say, as we have also seen, that the natural sciences and the historical sciences do not "use a different method of obtaining knowledge" (1980, 78), even though one is concerned with "statistical probabilities," while in the other the individual example "is the very essence of the case" (76). This, as I have argued, goes too far, since the methods of hypothesis testing used in statistics are inapplicable to single cases. Similarly, in the headnote to "Psychoanalysis as a Natural Science," Bowlby writes: "To accept that psychoanalysis should abandon its aim of becoming a natural science and instead should regard itself as a hermeneutic discipline has seemed to me to be not only a result of obsolete ideas about science but also a counsel of despair; because, in a hermeneutic discipline, there are no criteria by the application of which it is ever possible to resolve disagreement" (58). Once again, this is an overstatement, since it is one thing to say that psychoanalysis should not regard itself *exclusively* as a hermeneutic discipline, and quite another to say that it should abjure hermeneutics altogether, which would be just as futile as the "counsel of despair" of those hostile to science that Bowlby rightly decries.

Despite my sense that both Bowlby and Wilson end up tipping the delicate balance that needs to be maintained between science and art (or hermeneutics) too much in the direction of science, it would be unjust for me to conclude my assessment of their work on a negative note. For both of these great and profound thinkers have, like Edelman, emphasized not only the desirability but also the possibility of integrating the hemispheres of the natural and the human sciences into a single world of knowledge, just as the left and the right hemispheres are joined in the human brain. If Wilson and Bowlby have, at times, strayed too far in the direction of natural science, that is a pardonable error in an age where the predominant tendency in many quarters has been to cast out the baby of science with the bathwater of scientism and to be seduced by the siren songs of postmodernism.

Just as the principle of reduction implies a hierarchy of sciences—with the laws of physics, for example, being necessary but not sufficient for the purposes of biology—so, too, by the same principle, the humanities in general are constrained by the sciences, but not the other way around. The error of scientism is to extend the scientific method beyond the point it can legitimately go—to claim that it is adequate to the study of what Edelman calls the "individual creations" of the mind. But the error of extreme postmodernism is to deny that the laws of science apply at all, simply because there is a higher linguistic or hermeneutic domain for which they are indeed insufficient. This is far more serious. Carried to its logical conclusion, it could be catastrophic.

In the final pages of *Consilience*, Wilson recalls the two-year experiment in the early 1990s with Biosphere 2, a closed ecosystem in the Arizona desert designed to test against reality "the dream of man freed from the natural environment of Earth" (1998, 279). As Wilson reports the dismal results, many species on which the ecosystem depended "declined to extinction," while a handful of others—cockroaches, katydids, and ants—"multiplied extensively." He quotes the conclusion of two senior biologists who reviewed the data: "'No one yet knows how to engineer systems that provide humans with the life-supporting services that natural ecosystems provide for free,'" and "'despite its mysteries and hazards, Earth remains the only known home that can sustain life'" (280).

Thus, there is ultimately an ethical imperative behind the injunction that we must not lose sight of science, since that would also be to lose sight of the reality of nature by which human life, like all other life, is ultimately constrained. The postmodernist doctrine that there is nothing outside the text imprisons humanity in a conceptual equivalent to Biosphere 2—what Fredric Jameson (1972) has called "the prison-house of language"—with no less ominous consequences. There is, however, an equally compelling ethical imperative behind hermeneutics since, as Kant raised to the level of a philosophical principle, human beings should try to treat one another as ends in themselves and not as means to any other end. From an existential perspective, the individual example is *always* "the very essence of the case," and this is the reality of the interpretative arts that must be counterpoised against the reality of nature and the scientific method.

Psychoanalysis, as I have argued throughout this chapter, at its best gives due weight to each of these complementary, and not competing, injunctions. As a psychological theory, it respects the claims of science, while as a therapeutic practice, it respects those of the individual. Nowhere has this ethical dimension of psychoanalysis been recognized more eloquently than by Robert Holt in his "declaration of faith and hope," in which he expresses the resilient conviction

> that metaphysics does matter, that huge benefits will accrue if satisfactory philosophical foundations can be laid for a true concert of the disciplines—the arts and humane letters along with the sciences. Psychoanalysis will be an indispensable component, with many of Freud's ideas and discoveries finding a permanent place in any scheme to get all the resources of the human mind and heart to work together. So grounded, a new morality for human survival may take root and prosper, filling a gap that now seems to be dangerously widening. (1984, 361)

Holt calls this vision of psychoanalysis a new "world hypothesis." I call it the dream of consilience.

5

To speak in a psychoanalytic context of a "dream" of consilience is to employ a highly charged metaphor. Ever since Freud proclaimed the interpretation of dreams to be *"the royal road to a knowledge of the uncon-*

scious activities of the mind" (1900, 608), dreams have been considered by the proponents and detractors of psychoanalysis alike to be its quintessential phenomenon. Yet, in recent years, Freud's view of dreams has come under sharp attack. In indicting Freud's combination of bad luck and shoddy science, Wilson singles out his theory of dreams, to which Wilson contrasts Darwin's theory of natural selection. Although Darwin did not know that heredity was transmitted by genes, Wilson observes in *Consilience*, his intuitive insight was subsequently borne out by modern genetics. Freud, by contrast, "guessed wrong" when he proposed that dreaming was "the result of savage emotions and hidden memories that slip past the brain's censor" (1998, 75). Instead, dreaming is now believed to be "arbitrary in content" and "a side-effect of the reorganization and editing of memory banks in the brain." For this reason, Wilson concludes, "psychoanalytic theories related to dreaming, as well as parallel supernatural interpretations arising in myth and religion, are at one and the same time emotionally convincing and factually incorrect."

This is indeed a sobering assessment and, if true, it would cast grave doubt on any attempt to place psychoanalytic theory on a firm scientific foundation. A review of the current debate over the psychoanalytic theory of dreams thus provides a fitting point of departure for a broader examination of the conceptual synapses that are, as it were, coming into being between psychoanalysis and neuroscience. By showing how the breakthroughs in neuroscience, far from undermining psychoanalysis as a therapeutic enterprise, are providing it with a more secure grounding, I shall bring to a close my extended argument that Freud's dream of psychoanalysis as a discipline uniquely capable of bridging science and hermeneutics is now becoming a reality.

Wilson bases his critique of psychoanalytic theory on the work of the preeminent neurophysiologist and sleep researcher, J. Allan Hobson, who is assuredly no friend to psychoanalysis. But even Hobson, although he asserts that "it would be more appropriate to compare psychoanalysis to astrology than to astronomy" (1988a, 55), at least credits Freud with having effected "a conceptual advance over biblical prophecy in doing away with the notion of external agency and placing the communicator [in dreams] deep within the self" (11), thus effectively rebutting Wilson's accusation that "psychoanalytic theories related to dreaming" are no better than "supernatural interpretations."

The critical issue, however, is Hobson's attack on what he labels Freud's "disguise-censorship" (12) hypothesis of dreams and urging of its replacement by his own "activation-synthesis" (15) hypothesis. The linchpin of Hobson's theory is that dreams are byproducts of the well-known stage of rapid-eye-movement (REM) sleep, and that there is consequently "a specific brain mechanism that is both necessary and sufficient for dreaming to occur" (15). This empirical finding, and the more sophisticated view of neural activity in the brain that underlies it, is held by Hobson to explode Freud's theory not only of the construction but also of the interpretation of dreams.

In what follows, I shall bring forward evidence, discovered after the publication of Hobson's book, that casts doubt even on the physiological component of his theory of dreaming. But the heart of the matter is that, even if Hobson were completely right in his explanation of how dreams are formed—as he must be to some degree—this would not logically justify the conclusions he draws about how dreams should be interpreted. On this most fundamental level, therefore, Hobson is wrong in his attack on psychoanalysis and grievously misunderstands the epistemological issues at stake.

Wilson actually overstates Hobson's position in claiming that the activation-synthesis hypothesis shows dreams to be "arbitrary in content." What Hobson does say is that he differs from Freud in thinking that "most dreams are neither obscure nor bowdlerized, but rather that they are transparent and unedited" (1988a, 12). But although Hobson agrees with Freud that dreams are "meaningful" and often reveal "highly conflictual themes," he claims that they are "undisguised." Strikingly, while taking aim at Freud, Hobson sides enthusiastically with Jung, affirming that his own position "echoes Jung's notion of dreams as transparently meaningful and does away with any distinction between manifest and latent content."

Whereas my argument in this chapter imputes to psychoanalysis the potential to fulfill a dream of consilience, Hobson's vision is rather a nightmare in which it falls, as it were, between two schools. With some justice, he attributes "the current sterility of psychoanalysis"—or what I would rather call the wrong turn taken until recently by many in the psychoanalytic establishment—to "Freud's distinctive leadership style," an infelicitous but accurate way of accounting for the "undue reliance" placed by psychoanalysis "upon speculative philosophy to develop its ideas and . . . a political organization to promote them" (1988a, 53). Because of the historic isolation of psychoanalysis from medical science, combined with its worship of Freud as a heroic genius, Hobson maintains that the field today finds itself polarized between the "antibiological revisions of the hermeneuticians" (another deplorable locution), on one hand, and the "obscurantist and pseudo-scientific" technocrats, on the other.[27]

This diagnosis of the condition of psychoanalysis is quite close to my own, except that I think that Ferenczi and the entire tradition of object relations theory has since the turning point of 1923 provided an alternative to Freud's example, which now enables contemporary psychoanalysis to reconcile the antitheses of science and hermeneutics into a philosophically viable and intellectually generative whole. Thus, when Hobson proposes that the findings of his neurologically informed dream theory should be welcomed by both the defenders of "orthodoxy" who wish to "maintain their allegiance to Freud and his scientific style" and the "radicals" to whom his theory gives "the interpretive license they seek while offering a safe return to the safe harbor of classical science" (1988a, 215), I can only agree that such a conceptual synthesis is exactly what psychoanalysis requires.

Unfortunately, this consummation, however devoutly to be wished for, will not be brought about by Hobson. Among the warning signs on the horizon is his devotion to Jung. Commenting on the incident during a 1909 visit to Vienna in which Jung predicted to Freud the repetition of a mysterious noise coming from a bookcase in his study, Hobson writes: "Jung was open to the possibility that a noise that both [men] had heard but could not identify was caused by a cabinet moving mysteriously, perhaps even prophetically" (1988a, 67). I am surprised that a scientist of Hobson's caliber would deem an openness to prophetic bookcases to be an asset on Jung's part.[28] No less curious is his assertion that Jung's view of dream symbols is "more literary" (65) than Freud's, especially since he justly observes that Freud's interpretative technique "more closely resembles speculative literary criticism than it does scientific reasoning" (57). And when Hobson says that "Freud never considered the possibility that the symbolic function of the brain-mind is open-ended, allowing a multiplicity of meanings to be suggested by a single object," one has to wonder

27. By this latter group, Hobson seems to mean Lacanians, since he describes them as responsible for "a profusion of quasi-technical linguistic elaborations" (1988a, 53). But while I agree with his characterization of Lacanian linguistics as "pseudo-scientific," I would extend this epithet to Eissler, Rangell, and all the other representatives of the mainstream tradition of ego psychology who deny the inherently interactive nature of the analytic situation.

28. On this incident, which prompted Freud to refer bemusedly to Jung's "spook complex," see chapter 8, note 28 above.

if he has heard of overdetermination, a concept introduced by Freud precisely to account for the way that a "single object," whether in a dream or waking life, can (and indeed must) possess "a multiplicity of meanings."

Although Hobson claims to have given the theories of Freud and Jung "extensive and detailed treatment" (1988a, 53) in *The Dreaming Brain*, his discussion of psychoanalysis is in fact perfunctory and superficial. The notion of dream-work, for example, including its two main forms of condensation and displacement, is nowhere taken up in the book, apparently because Hobson thinks that it has been rendered superfluous as a consequence of his having erased the distinction between latent and manifest content. But it is not necessary to insist on preserving Freud's categories of latent and manifest content—just as it is not necessary to defend his theory that dreams must be wish-fulfillments—to think that Freud was right to insist not only that dreams are profoundly meaningful psychic phenomena but also that their meaning is often veiled or obscure to the dreamer.[29]

Indeed, it might well be argued, as Louis Sass (1998) has done from a hermeneutic standpoint, that the real problem with Freud's theory of the mind is that he underplays the utter strangeness of the unconscious because he regards it as a realm not essentially different from consciousness except that it happens temporarily not to be conscious. As Sass notes, the distinction between the latent and manifest content of dreams presumes that truth must be "a mere uncovering or simple mirroring of a prior reality," which implies that "obscurity is really only superficial, a reflection not of an ambiguity or mystery inherent in human existence but of dynamic forces that, on principle at least, could always be uncovered and overcome" (285).

But Hobson, rather than chastising Freud for underestimating the obscurity of dreams, faults him for failing to appreciate, in Jungian fashion, that they are "transparently meaningful." In a paper that forms a pendant to his major book, Hobson contrasts his view of dreaming and Freud's by noting that whereas the "disguise-censorship" hypothesis sees the task of interpretation as "complex and arbitrary," his own "activation-synthesis" hypothesis has the advantage of making interpretation "simple and unambiguous" (1988b, 289).

29. On whether dreams are wish-fulfillments, see my interview with Charles Rycroft, who agreed with my suggestion that they might be better regarded as "problem-solving activities" (Rudnytsky 2000, 70).

This, as I have already indicated, is where Hobson goes badly astray. The question of how dreams are formed in the brain is of a qualitatively different order from the question of what they may mean to the dreamer, and no criticism that Hobson can offer of the physiological basis of Freud's model of dreaming suffices to bridge the conceptual chasm between science and hermeneutics, or "how" and "why" questions. Beyond this insurmountable logical fallacy, the idea that the meaning of dreams is "simple and unambiguous" will, I think, strike almost anyone who has emulated Freud and seriously tried to interpret a dream as self-evidently unconvincing.

Intriguingly, Hobson provides one of his own dreams as a test case to illustrate the differences between his theory and that of psychoanalysis. He calls it "Mozart at the Museum." The dream concerns a concert at the Museum of Fine Arts in Boston, such as the ones in a program that his wife, Joan, directs in real life. The concert, in the large Remus auditorium, is a Mozart piano concerto. But he then decides "to explore and go down to the smaller, older theater (near the Egyptian sarcophagi)" (1988a, 220). This theater is now used only for lectures, but, twenty years ago, he and his wife had attended programs there similar to those now held in Remus under her direction. "Opening the door a crack" in a "bustle of excitement," Hobson is "amazed to realize that Mozart himself is on stage, playing the same concerto . . . on an antique harpsichord," though "not the Mozart pianoforte." In addition to Mozart's period costume, Hobson notices that he "has gotten a bit overweight." The report ends, "I close the door with a shhh!, and try to figure out how to tell Joan of my discovery."

Hobson boasts that his activation-synthesis hypothesis renders it superfluous "to resort to interpretation via the technique of free association to find dream meanings" (1988a, 219). As we have seen, he also castigates psychoanalytic interpretations for being "arbitrary," thus overlooking the likelihood that eliciting the dreamer's own thoughts may actually be the best way to *diminish* the arbitrariness of an interpretation.[30] Given Hobson's aversion to free associations, any attempt on my part to interpret his dream of "Mozart at the Museum" must per-

---

30. As Grünbaum has cogently insisted (1984, 186), it is a fallacy to assume that a dreamer's associations to a dream necessarily lead back to the thoughts that caused the dream to arise in the first place. All that can be said is that the free associations provide a context that fosters the understanding of the dream after it has been reported. Ironically, Hobson's claim that there is a logical connection between the physiological origin and the psychological meaning of dreams simply repeats this genetic fallacy on a grand scale. As I argued in my interview with Frank Sulloway (Rudnytsky 2000, 182–83), it is when Freud interprets the dreams of patients by means of his own associations that his exegeses be-

force be a piece of "wild" analysis; but I shall give it a whirl just the same.

Hobson's own discussion of his dream takes the form of a table consisting of three columns, the first consisting of a series of questions about the dream, and the latter two containing what he believes to be the answers that would be proposed, respectively, by "Psychoanalysis" and "Activation Synthesis." The content of these columns is surprising. Indeed, given that they constitute Hobson's suggestions of possible interpretations of his dream—disavowed, in the one case, and accepted in the other—I think it is warranted to take all of this material together as Hobson's "free associations" and see what, if anything, can be made of it.

The most surprising thing is that Hobson's "psychoanalytic" interpretation is along the most hackneyed—indeed, "arbitrary"—oedipal lines. If this interpretation had come from anyone else, it could be dismissed out of hand; but coming from Hobson himself, it piques the reader's curiosity. Apart from a desire to show the banality of psychoanalysis, what might be motivating these ideas? In answer to his own question about the cause of the bizarreness of the dream, including the detail of the corpulence of Mozart, Hobson offers the following "Freudian" explanation: "Mozart is an obvious symbol of a powerful, venerated but unapproachable male—that is, my father. The fact that he is overweight clinches the argument (but my father is not overweight!)" (1988a, 221). He goes on to offer a seemingly parodic psychoanalytic account of the role of conflict in the dream: "I want my mother, but my father is in the way. I have to knock him off, but that's not nice." He concludes with a précis of the alleged psychoanalytic meaning: "Opaque: You hate your father and you want to kill him! But you can't face that base wish, so you turn him into a great man and laud him" (222).

Admittedly, it is not easy to see immediately where Hobson gets the idea that the dream is about his desire to "knock off" his father, but it is just this seeming oddity that causes one to suspect that his energetic denials of the relevance of this train of thought cannot be taken at face value. Certainly, in view of the frequency with which Hobson likens Mozart to his father, and the fact that no one except himself has pointed to Mozart's being overweight in the dream as what supposedly "clinches the argument," Hobson's aside that his father is "not overweight" in real

_____

come tortured, whereas his interpretations of his own dreams—embedded as they are in the fabric of his own life—are generally far more compelling.

life by no means proves—as he seems to think it does—that the figure of Mozart does not represent his father. On the contrary—though this cannot, of course, be demonstrated with mathematical certainty, but only offered as a highly plausible hermeneutic inference—what I think we are dealing with here is a classic case of Freudian negation, where Hobson's reiterated insistence, "it's *not* my father," means, unconsciously, "yes, it *is* my father."[31]

The same holds true for the oedipal interpretation of the dream as a whole that Hobson introduces only to disavow it. I do not mean to insinuate, of course, that this is the only level of significance to the dream, but it must be present—and prominent—in Hobson's psyche, although he himself is unable to entertain this possibility except as an object of ridicule.[32] In the "Activation-Synthesis" column, Hobson informs us that "Mozart is Mozart," and his appearance in the dream is due to the fact that Hobson had seen the film *Amadeus* at the Fine Arts Museum, "although in the dream it was not a film" (1988a, 221). What is more, "the body-type file has been opened," and Mozart's corpulence somehow connects to the realization that Hobson's own "belly has begun to bulge" in real life. As opposed to the "opaque" psychoanalytic interpretation, in which the repressed "base wish" to kill his father causes Hobson to "turn him into a great man and laud him," he gives a "transparent" activation-synthesis interpretation: "I would love to see Mozart, to have my wife 'score' by attracting him to the museum, and to discover him there so that I could report her coup to others" (222).

There is much that must remain speculative in my analysis of Hobson's dream. But from what Hobson himself has said, his own identification with Mozart is indisputable. As he admits in his concluding com-

31. See the opening paragraph of Freud's "Negation" (1925b, 235).

32. A similar oedipal interpretation—based on the fact that he had dreamed of talking to a colleague named Van in Williamstown, Massachusetts, where Hobson's father actually lives—is introduced only to be retracted in Hobson's interpretation of another autobiographical dream he records in the book (1988a, 233–34). Strikingly, this dream also includes a woman, Mary, married to Bart, another friend of Hobson's living in Williamstown. By Hobson's own admission, the dream expresses his feeling of having been "left in the lurch" by Van and his uncertainty whether Van is a "friend or foe," while it enables him to "get revenge" on Van by accusing him of "mercenary motives." One could scarcely ask for a more "transparent" depiction of the son's ambivalence toward the father (various aspects of whom are represented by both Bart and Van) in the Oedipus complex. Hobson, who dances with Van in the dream, even raises the possibility that doing so could reflect "a thinly veiled homosexual desire," though he does not consider this idea seriously.

ments, "I *am* ambitious. I *do* admire Mozart. I *would*, consciously, like to be Mozart. Some of my most devoted friends have even called me 'Mozart'" (222). Thus, notwithstanding his protestation that "Mozart is Mozart," Mozart is, at the very least, also J. Allan Hobson. And if Mozart bears one metaphorical meaning, why cannot he bear several? Hobson does not notice the oddity of the fact that, by his own account, he himself appears twice in the dream as the spectator and "Mozart himself . . . on stage." Hobson, it will be recalled, rebuked Freud because he "never considered the possibility that the symbolic function of the brain-mind is open-ended, allowing a multiplicity of meanings to be suggested by a single object." In actuality, it is rather Hobson who betrays a numbing literal-mindedness.

If one trusts the dream and not the dreamer, the evidence is overwhelming that the figure of Mozart represents not only Hobson but also his father. Fusing the corpulence and ambitiousness of the son with the attributes of the "venerated but unapproachable" father, the image of Mozart goes beyond Freudian condensation to exemplify a veritable Joycean consubstantiality of the son and the father. And beyond simply expressing the son's ambivalent feelings of love and hate toward his father, Hobson's identification with Mozart shows that his deepest desire is to break out of the cycle of generation altogether and, like the supreme artist, to achieve immortality through his work.[33]

What I have said so far simply the scratches the surface, as it were, of Hobson's dream. But even these interpretations, made with the help of Hobson's own "free associations," are more than sufficient to impugn his premise that dreams are "transparent" and possess a "simple and unambiguous" meaning. Psychoanalysis may not always be right, but Hobson is almost certainly wrong. In a Groddeckian spirit, I will venture some further conjectures about what else I think is going on in "Mozart at the Museum."

As already quoted, Hobson sums up the "transparent" meaning of his dream from an activation-synthesis standpoint by stating that he "would love . . . to have my wife 'score' by attracting [Mozart] to the museum." *Score?* As when Little Hans's father casually mentions that Freud gave his son the gift of a rocking horse, the psychoanalytic reader is surely en-

33. I am indebted for this formulation to Jean Kimball's excellent commentary on the "fugue of fatherhood" in Stephen Dedalus's theory of *Hamlet*, as set forth by Joyce in the "Scylla and Charybdis" of *Ulysses*, in light of "patterns of the family romance described by Freud and the myth of the hero interpreted by Rank." See Kimball's forthcoming study, *Joyce and the Early Freudians*.

titled here to "prick" up his third ear and wonder about the *double entendre* that Hobson at once highlights (with quotation marks) and ignores. It needs no ghost of Freud come from the grave to tell us that Hobson's ostensible wish that his wife might "score" by "attracting" Mozart carries a sexual connotation. In the very sentence with which Hobson seeks to dispatch psychoanalysis by asserting the "transparency" of his dream, that is, he unconsciously employs a series of "switch words" that confirms the presence of a second track of meaning consisting of precisely those forbidden desires for incest and patricide that he has admitted under the sign of negation in the second column of his table.

Let us press on with this "wild" analysis. Can it really be a coincidence that the manifest content of Hobson's dream refers to a "bustle of excitement," his "opening the door a crack," though "it is open only for an instant," and even a "blissful smile" on Mozart's face as Hobson hears "the arpeggios stream through the door into my ear" (1988a, 220). The narrative concludes, it will be recalled, with the sentence, "I close the door with a shhh!, and try to figure out how to tell Joan of my discovery."[34]

The sexual interpretations I have offered are corroborated, if only indirectly, by Hobson's own words and vehement denials. To suggest that his dream contains an infantile or childhood memory of a primal scene can be no more than speculation. But the Wolf Man himself could not have done a better job of vindicating Freudian theory. Everything in the dream, including Hobson's antithetical statements that he "had seen the film *Amadeus* at a special museum showing" but "in the dream it was not a film," as well as his beholding Mozart "on stage," points to motifs of seeing. This is combined with the overheard sounds, and it is all described in language suggestive of sexual excitement—perhaps that of masturbation—culminating in the "beatific smile" of orgasm, which may also be that of the sated infant at the breast. In the opening scene of the dream, however, Hobson describes himself as "feeling like the third wheel on Joan's business bicycle" (1988a, 220), where the affective tone is rather one of resentment at being excluded from the parental couple.

All this, to repeat, is speculative, and I place no weight on it as evidence of anything except the incalculable depth of dreams and the insufficiency of Hobson's own interpretative soundings. But it bears emphasizing how much of his dream Hobson simply leaves out in his sketchy efforts to

---

34. There is a slight but perhaps significant discrepancy between Hobson's statement in the dream that he wanted to "tell Joan" about Mozart and the activation-synthesis interpretation that he hoped he "could report her coup to others."

make sense of it. One of the features that he passes over in silence is that the central scene in which Hobson sees a man playing a keyboard instrument occurs twice in the dream—first, upstairs in the Remus auditorium where someone is playing a Mozart concerto on a "large Steinway"; and second, downstairs in the "smaller, older theater (near the Egyptian sarcophagi)," where Hobson and his wife had actually heard concerts twenty years ago and where, in the dream, it is Mozart himself "playing the same concerto . . . on an antique harpsichord."

The occurrence of repetition is of itself highly suggestive. Combined with Hobson's descent from a higher to a lower level, the dream seems to enact a regression both temporally from the present to the past and, in Freudian parlance, topographically from the conscious to the unconscious stratum of the mind. If that is so, it would bear out my suggestion that the latter part of the dream taps into memories from Hobson's childhood. The form of Hobson's dream strikingly parallels a dream of Jung's in his autobiography, *Memories, Dreams, Reflections*, a book where Jung promulgates the view that dreams are "a part of nature, which harbors no intention to deceive" (1965, 162), and cited by Hobson in his bibliography.

Jung's dream, which he recounted to Freud while the two men sailed with Ferenczi to America in 1909, concerns a two-story house with a cellar. As Jung descended in the dream first from the upper to the lower floor, and then to the cellar, the construction and furnishings changed from rococo to medieval to Roman. Finally, in the cellar, Jung saw a stone slab with a ring that, when he lifted it, revealed a stairway leading to a subterranean cave. Here, among "scattered bones and broken pottery" that resembled the "remains of a primitive culture," Jung discovered "two human skulls, very old and half disintegrated" (159).

There is much that could be said about this dream of the two skulls, which Freud wanted to interpret as proof of Jung's death-wishes toward him, but which Jung himself (possibly to insinuate his secret knowledge of Freud's affair with his sister-in-law Minna Bernays) associated to "'My wife and my sister-in-law,'" since he "had to name someone whose death was worth the wishing!" (160). But that is the subject of another book. Suffice it to note here that Jung reports the dream in the context of discussing his rift with Freud, and highlights their different theoretical approaches to dreams.

Thus, if one of the sources of Hobson's dream is his reading of *Memories, Dreams, Reflections*, and his own descent to the realm of "Egyptian sarcophagi" bears more than an archetypal resemblance to Jung's subterranean excavation of "the remains of a primitive culture," this would lend an additional level of symbolic meaning to Hobson's dream. Like Jung, Hobson is at war with Freud, and he girds himself for battle by unconsciously identifying with his precursor in the heroic quest to expurgate and demystify dreams.

I have directed my critique of Hobson, first, at his belief that his activation-synthesis hypothesis of how dreams are formed could, under any circumstances, guide us in the interpretation of dreams and hence serve as a basis for the refutation of Freudian theory. Second, I have striven to show that Hobson's efforts to interpret his own dreams are inadequate, and thus his contention that dreams are "simple and unambiguous" is subverted by the very examples he uses to try to make his case. This argument is purely hermeneutic in that it has to do only with how we are to understand the meaning of dreams, and not with how we are to explain them in neurological terms. The upshot of this discussion is that Hobson's choice—the activation-synthesis hypothesis or none—turns out to be a false dichotomy, since it would be perfectly possible to agree with Hobson about the biology of dreams and with Freud about their subjective meanings.

In point of fact, however, as I have indicated, it is not at all clear that Hobson is right even about the biology of dreaming. The key issue is whether, as he claims, REM sleep constitutes the outward sign of "a specific brain mechanism that is both necessary and sufficient for dreaming to occur." The new evidence against Hobson's view is resumed by Mark Solms, the leading contemporary neuroscientist with psychoanalytic training, in an essay (2001) written as the introduction to a reprint of the first edition of *The Interpretation of Dreams*. First, it turns out, contrary to what was once believed, that reports of dreaming occur not only during REM sleep but also during non-REM sleep; thus, "whatever the explanation may be for the strong correlation that exists between dreaming and REM sleep, it is no longer accepted that dreaming is caused exclusively by the REM state" (82). What is more, although the pons—an area of the brain located in the brainstem, near the nape of the neck—is responsible for REM sleep, only one of the twenty-six cases reported in the neurological literature concerning individuals who have suffered destruction of the pons makes mention of a cessation of dreaming. On the other hand, of the 110 cases in which loss of dreaming has occurred, two entirely unrelated parts of the brain—both in the cerebral hemispheres—have been involved. As Solms concludes, "this dissociation between cessation of REM and cessation of dreaming seriously undermines the doctrine that the REM state is the physiological equivalent of the dream state" (83). To the extent that REM sleep causes dreaming, it is only through the mediation of a process by which dopamine is transmitted in a higher brain pathway, and "a variety of other triggers, which act independently of REM, have exactly the same effect" (84). This explains the correlation between REM sleep and dreaming initially noticed by researchers, but directly refutes Hobson's premise that REM sleep is "both necessary and sufficient for dreaming to occur." Since one function of the pathway that gives rise to dreams is to instigate goal-seeking and appetitive behaviors, Solms notes, this "gives us every reason to take seriously the radical hypothesis . . . to the effect that dreams are motivated phenomena, driven by our wishes" (84). Freud's account of the dream-work as a process of regression by which abstract thoughts are reduced to perceptual form is, according to Solms, likewise compatible with the current scientific evidence. Even Fechner's famous statement that "*the scene of action of dreams is different from that of waking life*," which Freud cited as "the only hypothesis that makes the special peculiarities of dream-life intelligible" (1900, 536), turns out to be not merely metaphorically but literally true since, as Solms explains, the "scene of action" in waking life "is concentrated in the dorsolateral region at the front of the brain," whereas "in dreams it is concentrated in the occipito-temporo-parietal region at the back of the brain, in the memory and perceptual systems" (2001, 87).

It is not necessary to my argument that Freud should turn out to have been right in every particular concerning the neurology of dreaming, just as I have no interest in defending any other portion of his theory for its own sake. But at a time when criticism both just and unjust has rained down on Freud, it helps to put things in perspective to realize that, rather than having "guessed wrong" in almost every respect, many of his essential insights, like those of Darwin, have actually been vindicated by the advances of science.

What Solms has done to rehabilitate the viability of Freud's theory of dreams has been accomplished, in an equally condensed essay, with respect to neurology as a whole by Oliver Sacks (1998). Sacks, whose extraordinary gifts as both a scientist and literary artist can justly be compared to those of Freud himself, and who—as we have seen with respect to Groddeck—always contrives to put psychoanalysis in the best possible light, hearkens back to Freud's 1891 monograph, *On Aphasia*, in order to retrace the "other road" of neurology that led him to the "royal road" in *The Interpretation of Dreams*.

As Sacks shows, *On Aphasia* is above all a polemic against the reigning theory of localization in neurology, which, by attributing disturbances in cognitive functioning to damage to specific parts of the brain—as Broca had done in 1861 with respect to aphasia—had, in Freud's view, "a mechanical quality, treating the brain, the nervous system, as a sort of ingenious but idiotic machine, with a one-to-one matching of elementary components and functions, denying it organization—and evolution and history" (Sacks 1998, 13). Against this precursor of present-day computational theories of mind, Freud from his earliest histological researches under Brücke's tutelage took the position that "it was not the cellular elements which were different in primitive or advanced animals, but their *organization*," a conviction that gave his work "a sense of a Darwinian evolution whereby, using the most conservative means (the same basic anatomical cellular elements), more and more complex nervous systems could be built" (12).

The greatest influence on Freud's thought in *On Aphasia* was exerted by the English neurologist Hughlings Jackson, twenty years Freud's senior, who, himself under the influence of Darwin and Herbert Spencer, was, in Sacks's words, "developing an evolutionary view of the nervous system, unmoved by the localizationist frenzy all around him" (13). Citing Jackson's declaration, "'I do not trouble myself about the mode of connection between mind and matter. It is enough to assume a parallelism,'" Sacks (16) draws attention to the following crucial passage from *On Aphasia* where Freud writes:

> The relationship between the chain of physiological events in the nervous system and the mental processes is not one of cause and effect. The former do not cease when the latter set in; they tend to continue, but, from a certain moment, a mental phenomenon corresponds to each part of the chain, or to several parts. The psychic is, therefore, a process parallel to the physiological, a "dependent concomitant." (1891, 55)

The concept of the "dependent concomitant" has an extremely useful double-edged quality. On the one hand, as Sacks stresses, it allows Freud to argue that "psychological processes have their own laws, principles, autonomies, coherences; and these must be examined independently, irrespective of whatever physiological processes may be going on in parallel" (1998, 16). On the other, because Freud continues to envision these psychological processes as being "dependent" on the physiological, he does not sever the connection between mind and brain, even if it cannot be understood in terms of a simple "cause and effect."

Sacks's mapping of Freud's abbreviated career as a neurologist has the virtue of situating him within a broadly Darwinian context, as opposed to the more narrowly Lamarckian and Haeckelian impulses to which he gave free rein in his later metapsychology. As with Solms's rehabilitation of Freud's theory of dreams, Freud emerges from Sacks's appraisal as a scientist and thinker whose key ideas have been borne out by subsequent researchers. His concept of "contact barriers" in the *Project for a Scientific Psychology* (1895)—the working title of which, as Sacks reminds us, was "A Psychology for Neurologists"—anticipates by a decade Sherrington's naming of synapses; and Freud's view of contact barriers as "capable of selective facilitation or inhibition, thus allowing permanent neuronal changes which corresponded to the acquisition of new information and new memories," is "a theory of learning basically similar to that which Donald Hebb was to propose in the 1940s, and which is now supported by empirical findings" (Sacks 1998, 19). On a more abstract level, Freud's de-emphasis of specific sites within the brain in favor of complex systems that can be greatly affected by the individual's experiences was, as Sacks says, "a striking anticipation of the notion of 'functional systems,' developed by A. R. Luria, the founder of neuropsychology, fifty years later" (15).

Sacks concludes his essay by recalling that Ernest Jones paid tribute to Freud as "the Darwin of the mind," and—in a convergence with my concerns in the present chapter—notes that Gerald Edelman dedicated *Bright Air, Brilliant Fire* to the memory of Darwin and Freud. Indeed, highlighting the "attunement" between Freud's views and Edelman's, Sacks reveals himself to be among the apostles of consilience: "here, at least, one has the sense that psychoanalysis and neurobiology can be fully at home with one another, congruent and mutually supportive" (21). Sacks's vision, moreover, is not simply of a reconciliation between psychoanalysis and neurobiology but between the sciences and the humanities as a whole: "it may be that . . . we see a hint of how these two seemingly disparate universes—the universes of human meaning and natural science—may come together."

Sacks suspends his bridge between the universes of science and hermeneutics on the cables of memory, and specifically on the use made by Arnold Modell of Edelman's work to redefine Freud's concept of *Nachträglichkeit* in more up-to-date terms as "recategorization." I shall return to this important conjunction between psychoanalysis and neuroscience presently. But if Solms has resuscitated parts of Freud's theory of dreams by showing them to be compatible with sound science, and Sacks has done the same for his standing as a neurologist, the next step in the argument is to consider the clinical implications of the neuroscientific revolution.

Still a seminal work on this subject is Morton F. Reiser's *Mind, Brain, Body: Toward a Convergence of Psychoanalysis and Neurobiology* (1984), the title of which signals its relevance to the concerns of this chapter.[35] Indeed, Reiser displays exemplary awareness both of the need to reground psychoanalytic theory on a solid scientific foundation and of the limits of what science can accomplish. As he states on the opening page of his introduction, "clinical practice is always pragmatic, obliged to be humanistic as it deals with the pain and discomfort of the human organism" (3). Yet, he continues, "metapsychological theory, while useful, perhaps even necessary for certain purposes, has led psychoanalysis into a virtual *cul de sac* that is isolated from empirical and conceptual articulation with biological sciences" (7). In dealing with an emotion such as anger, the neurological correlative of which is the firing of hypothalmic cells, Reiser observes, "it is possible to describe the phenomenon in either mind language or brain language, each language being valid at its own level. . . . Mistakes and confusion result from attempts to locate the causes at one level with respect to consequences at the other level. Rather, it is necessary to map events at one level onto events at the other, each described in its own terms" (17).

Although Reiser does not use the term "dependent concomitant," he follows Freud in recognizing the need to avoid conceiving the relation between brain and mind as one of cause and effect while nonetheless insisting that "the realm of mind, which deals with meanings, and the realm of brain-body, which deals with matter and energy" (5), cannot be

35. Susan C. Vaughan's self-described "neurological romp through the brain and mind" (1997, 158) goes over much the same ground as Reiser's book in breezier and less rigorous fashion. She invokes (9) Hobson's work on dreaming, for example, without informing the reader that Hobson is actually a detractor of psychoanalysis, and wishes that she could "tuck some free samples" of Prozac in Freud's pocket (22). Despite its limitations, Vaughan's book offers a useful introduction to "the science behind psychotherapy." As Vaughn popularizes Reiser, so Antonio Damasio (1999) offers a perhaps more accessible, but in my view less profound, counterpart to Edelman. Like Edelman, Damasio cites Darwin and Freud (as well as William James) as precursors of his own work on the neurobiology of emotions (38–39), and he aligns himself with both Freud and Jung in contending that "the evidence for unconscious processing has not ceased to accumulate" (297).

understood in isolation from one another.[36] In the two main sections of *Mind, Brain, Body*, Reiser approaches his search for what he calls an "intermediate conceptual template" or "conceptual Rosetta stone" that "would be isomorphic with both the biological and psychological realms, which are not themselves isomorphic with each other" (17–18), first from the side of mind (or psychoanalysis) and then from that of brain (or neurobiology), while the final section, "Body," opens up to consider the broader implications of his argument for clinical medicine and psychiatry.

Perhaps the most fascinating aspect of Reiser's book is his extended case history—unfolding in a series of chapters—of Carol, a woman whose mother died in childbirth (when Carol was four and a half) the day after an argument in which Carol had kicked her in the belly. Carol's neurotic conflicts resemble Hamlet's in more ways than one, and there is no better antidote to Hobson's crude forays in dream analysis than to accompany Reiser as he reveals, through a dissection of several of Carol's dreams and phobic symptoms, the intricacy of a single psychic landscape.[37] He shows, for example, how a "switch word" such as "tan" from a dream Carol had at the age of thirty-eight links up with a repressed memory of the name of an emergency medication (tannic acid) that she had been sent to fetch from the drugstore twenty-five years earlier after her brother (the child born at the time her mother's death) had been scalded due to Carol's negligence. Rather than impose any preconceptions on his material, Reiser endeavors to "go back to a phenomenological study of the process, method, and primary clinical data, as independent of theory and metapsychological constructs as possible" (26). The value of psychoanalysis lies in the "crude ore" of its subjective data; how-

36. Edelson (1988) rebukes Reiser on the grounds that when "he explores the relation between psychoanalysis and neuroscientific knowledge, he writes not only about psychoanalysis but about a general psychology of mind, or he writes about psychoanalysis as a general psychology of mind" (149). This is true; but rather than being, as Edelson supposes, a liability, it is Reiser's supreme virtue; and it places his vision of psychoanalysis squarely in the tradition of Hartmann. Declining to see the relation of mind to brain as one of dependent concomitance, Edelson rejects the ideal of consilience: "Instead of the vision of a unity of science that depends on deriving the theories of every special science from the theories of physics and chemistry, let us put instead the vision of autonomous disciplines" (156).

37. Inasmuch as Reiser's case history, like those of Freud, does succeed in capturing with literary artistry the true complexity of a human life, it also points up the limitations of Luborsky's attempt to study the dynamics of psychotherapy scientifically in terms of discrete "core conflict relational themes." See note 16 above.

ever, if it is to be scientifically viable, "methods must be developed to extract and refine it" (22). Thus, Reiser concludes his first main section, "Mind," by posing the following question: "Can the raw data of the clinical psychoanalytic process directly or even indirectly generate questions that can be investigated within the psychoanalytic context or within the context of other disciplines by investigators using more conventional experimental and statistical methods?" (95).

When Reiser turns from "Mind" to "Brain," he is no longer able to rely on his own clinical experience as a psychoanalyst. Instead he draws on the research of others, above all that of the cellular neurobiologist Eric R. Kandel. Trained as a psychiatrist but not a psychoanalyst, Kandel has probably gone farther than anyone else in explaining scientifically just how it is that the talking cure brings about its beneficial effects.

Kandel's thesis, set forth in two intriguingly titled papers, "Psychotherapy and the Single Synapse: The Impact of Psychiatric Thought on Neurobiologic Research" (1979) and "From Metapsychology to Molecular Biology: Explorations into the Nature of Anxiety" (1983), may initially seem surprising, but upon closer acquaintance takes on an air of inevitability. It is that "the ultimate level of resolution for understanding how psychotherapeutic intervention works is identical with the level at which we are currently seeking to understand how psychopharmacologic intervention works—the level of individual nerve cells and their synaptic connections" (1979, 1028).

As with the research of Solms on dreams, the neurobiological research of Kandel has the dividend of placing psychoanalysis in what is today an unusually favorable light. Kandel notes that "the exploration of psychoanalytic theories has been hampered by a lack of opportunities for experimental verification. Nevertheless," he continues, "psychoanalytic thought has been particularly valuable for its recognition of the diversity and complexity of human mental experiences, for discerning the importance both of genetic and learned (social) factors in determining the mental representation of the world, and for its view of behavior as being based on that representation" (1983, 1282). Psychoanalysis is thus for Kandel "a source of modern cognitive psychology"; and just as "the vigor now evident in cognitive psychology will be strengthened by its contact with the cellular neurobiology of invertebrates," so also in turn "the emergence of an empirical neuropsychology of cognition based on cellular neurobiology can produce a renascence of scientific psychoanalysis." As Reiser's practice exemplifies, the form of psychoanalysis envisioned by Kandel "may be founded on theoretical hypotheses that are more modest than those applied previously but that are more testable because they will be closer to experimental inquiry."

Kandel's neurobiological perspective permits a synthesis of psycho-analysis with both cognitive psychology and behaviorism. On the theoretical plane, he is critical of the "extreme behaviorist view" that "observable behavior is synonymous with mental life" because it "defines a larger reality, psychic life, in terms of the scientific techniques for studying it. By so doing, this approach denies the existence both of conscious and unconscious mentation, feelings, and motivation merely because they cannot be studied objectively" (1983, 1281). Despite his agreement with cognitive psychology (and psychoanalysis) on the importance of doing justice to "the richness of the internal representations that intervene between stimuli and response," however, Kandel fully recognizes the contributions of behaviorism in advancing the understanding of the various forms of learning.

Indeed, Kandel's argument in "Psychotherapy and the Single Synapse" hinges on showing the links between "two paradigms that psychology and psychiatry have defined for neurobiology and that are now being addressed on the cellular level: the effects on later development of certain types of social and sensory deprivation in early life, and the mechanisms of learning" (1979, 1029). The former, strikingly, leads Kandel to retrace the work of maternal deprivation of René Spitz (on infants raised in foundling homes) and Harry Harlow (on primates), thus integrating the tradition of attachment theory with contemporary neurobiology. The evidence gathered by these pioneer researchers into the effects of social deprivation was exclusively behavioral. More recently, however, the new technology permitting a mapping of the connections among neurons has, when used in conjunction with experiments such as the suturing closed of a monkey's eye from birth to three months, "provided direct evidence that sensory deprivation can alter the structure of the cerebral cortex" (1031). These studies enforce the realization that "we are just beginning to explore the structural organization of the brain and the alterations that may be caused by experience and by disease," and likewise open up the horizon of a heretofore unimaginable understanding "of the biologic basis of most forms of mental illness."

If even sensory functioning is affected by deprivations during infancy, the first psychological paradigm for neurobiology—the effects on later development of early experiences—is inextricably bound up with the

second paradigm—that of learning—which Kandel defines as "a prolonged or even relatively permanent change in behavior that results
from repeated exposure to a pattern of stimulation" (1031–32). As he
justly points out, "insofar as psychotherapeutic intervention is successful
in treating mental disorders, it presumably succeeds by creating an experience that allows people to change" (1032); and thus it, too, is a form of
learning or relearning.

The paradigm of learning is, of course, of paramount concern to behaviorism; and in "Psychotherapy and the Single Synapse" Kandel
takes up "two simple forms of nonassociative learning: habituation and
sensitization," each of which "is evident in human beings but can also
be explored effectively in a variety of simple animal models" (1033). Habituation is "a decrease in a behavioral response resulting from repeated
presentation of the initiating stimulus"—as one can gradually become
accustomed to working in a noisy environment—and thus involves
"learning to recognize and to ignore stimuli that have lost novelty or
meaning." Sensitization, conversely, "is the process whereby an animal
learns to increase a given reflex response as a result of a noxious or
novel stimulus. Thus, sensitization requires the animal to attend to
stimuli that potentially produce painful or dangerous consequences"
(1035).

Confirming a hypothesis put forward in 1906 by Sherrington, Kandel's most brilliant achievement is to have proven, through studies of
the neuronal circuits in the marine snail *Aplysia*, that the effects of habituation and sensitization can be empirically measured in the changes
in synaptic transmission between sensory and motor neurons. Whereas
habituation involves a "decrease in synaptic efficacy" (1034), sensitization involves "presynaptic facilitation" that enhances the "ability to release transmitter" on the part of the sensory neurons (1035). These
changes persist for only minutes or hours after a single training session
involving exposure to ten stimuli, but they persist for more than three
weeks after four training sessions. What is more, sensitization was
found to restore the effectiveness of synapses that had been "function-
ally disconnected" (1036) through habituation. The effects of these
most basic forms of learning can be detected not simply in the outward
behavior of the organism but in "specific alteration in neuronal and
synaptic function." Thus, since all learned behavior, including neurotic
illness in human beings, is registered in the brain, it no longer makes
sense to distinguish between biological and nonbiological mental disorders. Rather, "it might make more sense to ask, in each type of mental

illness, to what degree is the biologic process determined by genetic and developmental factors, to what degree is it due to infectious or toxic agents, and to what degree is it socially determined?" As Kandel recognizes, the upshot is that psychotherapy, too, must ultimately work "by acting on brain functions, not on single synapses, but on synapses nevertheless." Aligning himself with Freud's stance in *On Aphasia*, he writes: "Clearly, a shift is needed from a neuropathology . . . based only on structure to one based on function." "Indeed," he concludes, "I would argue that it is only insofar as our words produce changes in each other's brains that psychotherapeutic intervention produces changes in patients' minds" (1037).

Kandel's focus in "Psychotherapy and the Single Synapse" is on the two most elementary forms of nonassociative learning. In "From Metapsychology to Molecular Biology," in addition to developing the theoretical implications of his argument, he turns his attention to the processes of associative learning, specifically to the conditioned reflexes made famous by the experiments of Pavlov. As we have seen, Kandel departs from extreme behaviorism in laying stress on the internal states that even in the simplest organisms must mediate between stimulus and response. But Kandel uses the empirical findings of behaviorism to investigate the similarities between two types of anxiety that can be studied in animal models—anticipatory anxiety and chronic anxiety—and their counterparts in human beings. Anxiety is a particularly useful object of study because, "unlike schizophrenia, which does not exaggerate a normal adaptive process and is therefore a characteristically human mental illness, fear or anxiety is a general adaptive mechanism found in simple as well as complex animals" (1983, 1291). Again, the sea snail *Aplysia* is the star of Kandel's show because the same sorts of conditioning experiments routinely performed on higher animals can be replicated on *Aplysia*, an herbivore for which shrimp extract serves as a neutral stimulus; and the behavioral manifestations of a conditioned reflex (escape locomotion following presentation of the shrimp extract paired with head shock) can be also be measured biochemically on both the cellular and molecular levels.

Essentially, Kandel proposes that whereas anticipatory (or signal) anxiety depends on the existence of a predictable relation between a neutral cue stimulus and a traumatic event—such as there is in classical aversive conditioning—chronic anxiety ensues when (as in sensitization experiments) there is no specific and reliable signal that warns the organism of imminent danger. Danger is thus felt to be ever-present, and the organism is never able to relax in a state of safety.[38] Anticipatory anxiety is adaptive and enhances the chances of survival, whereas chronic anxiety is incapacitating; but both, in Kandel's words, "represent a motivational (defensive) state in preparation for expected danger, a preparation that is not necessarily expressed in motor activity." They produce not merely "a single response," but an entire "repertory," in which "defensive responses are enhanced and appetitive responses suppressed" (1283).

This line of argument will, of course, sound very familiar to psychoanalysts; and Kandel invokes (1279) *Inhibitions, Symptoms and Anxiety*, the 1926 monograph in which Freud discarded his original (and untenable) theory of anxiety as repressed libido in favor of his revised theory of it as a danger signal. Inspired by Kandel's work, Reiser devotes a chapter of *Mind, Brain, Body* to "a detailed recasting of Freud's centrally important theory of signal anxiety into the Pavlovian paradigm, with the heuristic aim of bringing it into meaningful—perhaps even empirical—articulation with current neurobiologic data and thinking" (1984, 127). As in "Psychotherapy and the Single Synapse," Kandel concludes "From Metapsychology to Molecular Biology" by considering the implications of his research into anxiety for psychotherapy. He draws a key distinction between disorders due primarily to alterations in *gene structure*, which are inherited and thus fundamentally unresponsive to talking cures, and those due to changes in *gene expression*, which are the results of experience and thus can be aided by psychotherapy. The former are the major psychoses—schizophrenia and the mood disorders—while the latter are the manifold varieties of neurotic illness and personality disorders. (This distinction corresponds broadly to that between Axis I and Axis II classifications in the *Diagnostic and Statistical Manual of Mental Disorders*.) Even the psychoses, insofar as they secondarily involve disturbances in gene expression, may derive limited benefit from nonpharmacological interventions. But given that "psychotherapy works and produces long-term learned changes in behavior . . . by producing changes in gene expression" (1288–89), its resources are unlikely to prevail against a congenital mutation in an individual's genetic alphabet.

From all that I have said about Kandel's work, it should be clear why I

---

38. The proposal by Weiss and Sampson (1986) that therapy depends on a process in which patients repeatedly test the safety of the setting by consciously and unconsciously recreating situations of danger, thereby gradually disconfirming their pathogenic beliefs, can be understood in Kandel's terms as a means of transforming the overwhelming condition of chronic anxiety into an efficacious form of anticipatory anxiety.

would in all seriousness maintain that contemporary psychoanalysts may well have more to learn from reading his two papers—in conjunction with Harlow's "The Nature of Love" (1958) on the effects of maternal deprivation in primates—than from the collected works of Lacan and Melanie Klein combined. For my purposes in this chapter, what is most remarkable is that Kandel—followed by Reiser (1984, 25)—bases his conception of the hierarchy of scientific disciplines in "Psychotherapy and the Single Synapse" on the model set forth by E. O. Wilson in "Biology and the Social Sciences" and *On Human Nature*, and then deployed most ambitiously as the linchpin of *Consilience*.

Simply put, as I have already indicated, Wilson's model of "reduction" arranges all the scientific disciplines into a series of pairs consisting of a parent discipline and an anti-discipline. In each pair, the parent discipline is broader in scope than its anti-discipline; but the anti-discipline is, in dialectical fashion, the parent discipline to a still more fundamental anti-discipline. Thus, Kandel's own parent discipline of cellular biology has as its anti-discipline molecular biology, while the anti-discipline of molecular biology is physical chemistry. "In this context," Kandel writes, "it is clear that neurobiology is the new anti-discipline for which psychology in general and psychiatry in particular are the parent disciplines" (1979, 1028).

In arranging fields of knowledge hierarchically, Kandel and Wilson do not mean to imply that any one discipline can take the place of another. Rather, there is always a symbiotic relation between "higher" and "lower" disciplines, in which each has what the other lacks. The parent discipline poses the questions, while the anti-discipline furnishes ways of finding the answers and, in the process, challenges the assumptions of the parent discipline. Thus, "although neuropsychology can provide key insights into the human mind, psychology and psychoanalysis are potentially deeper in content. The hard-nosed propositions of neurobiology, although scientifically more satisfying, have less existential meaning than do the soft-nosed propositions of psychiatry" (Kandel 1979, 1029). There is, finally, no need to choose between science and meaning, or biology and psychology. Like Freud's model of the mind as the "dependent concomitant" of the brain, the theory of "reduction" proposed by Wilson and taken over by Edelman as well as Kandel recognizes that both "hard-nosed" and "soft-nosed" approaches to psychiatry are valid on their own level, but knowledge can advance only if they are not dualistically split from one another.

The productive interaction between the work of Reiser and Kandel is

a concrete illustration of the potential for mutually beneficial cooperation between contemporary psychoanalysis and neuroscience. Another
such example is the cross-fertilization between the work of Edelman and
Arnold Modell, to which I have already alluded several times in this
chapter, and which was cited as exemplary in this regard by Oliver Sacks
in "The Other Road." The sequence of reciprocal moves begins with
Modell's reliance on Edelman's *Neural Darwinism* (1987) in his own 1990
book, *Other Times, Other Realities*, to formulate a scientifically cogent
psychoanalytic model of memory. This effort, as I noted, received Edelman's endorsement in *Bright Air, Brilliant Fire* (1992). Finally, in *The Private Self* (1993), completed after he had met Edelman and to whom he
showed his manuscript, Modell in turn drew on *Bright Air, Brilliant Fire*,
as well as *The Remembered Present* (1989), in essaying a comprehensive
psychoanalytic theory of selfhood.

Although I sympathize with a great deal of Modell's project, he never
says something once when five times will do.[39] Despite my agreement
with his premise that "the psychology of the self is rooted in biology"
(1993, 5), moreover, I am puzzled by Modell's assertion that "the tendency to minimize the importance of the private self can be traced to a
conviction held by some authors that the self is essentially disembodied"
(42). Surely the notion that the self is "essentially disembodied" finds its
apotheosis in Descartes, who is likewise the supreme philosopher of the
"private self." A truly biological and neurological theory of the self, as
Susan Vaughan (1997) has argued, leads rather to the realization that
"one person can function as a regulator of another's brain chemistry and
structure," and thus calls into question the belief, to which Modell also
subscribes, that "we are all alone in our own skins" and must "live and
die so fundamentally separated from one another" (191).

Neither Modell's ponderousness nor the occasional imprecision in his
thinking should, however, be permitted to detract from his positive contributions. To circle back to my historical sketch at the outset of this
chapter, he makes it clear that "contemporary psychoanalytic theory has
lost its central organizing principle"; and he attributes this crisis to the
fact that "Freud's instinct theory, the foundation stone of the psychoanalytic edifice, is incongruent with contemporary biology" (1993, 186–87).
Modell stresses that the paradigm of Freud's drive theory needs to be re-

39. In *Other Times, Other Realities*, he informs the reader that, according to Edelman,
memory is not "isomorphic" with experience twice on page 3, and again on pages 18, 60,
and 64; and this does not purport to be a complete inventory.

placed by a "psychology of the self" that "encompasses emergent motivations of a very different conceptual order" (187). Among those who "recognize the self as a superordinate agent," however, he notes that there is a division "as to whether that agent, the self, is embodied or disembodied"; and Modell, like Edelman, of course, casts his lot with embodiment. Kohut, Lacan, and Schafer, despite their differences, are all justifiably reproached for advocating a disembodied theory of selfhood (188). Modell contrasts this triumvirate with that of Hartmann, Gedo, and Reiser, each of whom affirms the ties between psychoanalysis and biology (198). In place of Freud's superseded drive theory, Modell proposes that "the continuity and coherence of the self is a homeostatic requirement of the psyche-soma" (48), an eminently cogent thesis the implications of which are incompatible with postmodernism.[40]

None of these ideas, however admirable, is especially novel. Modell's most seminal insight, as I have remarked, is that Freud's early concept of *Nachträglichkeit*—usually translated, following Strachey, as "deferred action"—gains support from Edelman's theory that "past experiences are not recorded in the brain in a fashion that is isomorphic with those events; rather, what is stored is the potential to activate *categories* of experience" (Modell 1990, 3). Bolstered by Edelman's view of memory as a continuous process of literally cerebral recategorization, Modell proposes that "it is now possible to modify Freud's antiquated repetition compulsion, derived from his theory of the death instinct, in a way that is consistent with the findings of modern neuroscience" (3–4).

I think that Modell makes too much of the flaws in Strachey's translation. His own proposals (for which he is indebted to an unpublished paper by Helmut Thomä) of "retranscription of memory" or "retrospective attribution" (9) undoubtedly add something to the English-speaking reader's understanding of *Nachträglickeit*. But to say, as Thomä does, that "the primary difference between *nachtragen* and defer consists in the fact that they express exactly opposite relations to time" (quoted in Modell 1990, 153*n*2), is simply incorrect. The noun *Nachtrag* means "supplement" or "appendix," and the literal definition of the verb *nachtragen* is "to carry after" or "append"; a common figurative meaning is

40. In support of his thesis that human beings are motivated above all by a quest for self-actualization, Modell (1993, 44–45) cites the work of Kurt Goldstein, the holistic neuropathologist who, with Freud, Groddeck, and Sullivan, was one of the four men to whom Frieda Fromm-Reichmann dedicated her *Principles of Intensive Psychotherapy*. See chapter 8, note 4 above.

"to bear a grudge" (toward someone) or "to resent" (something). The constellation of meanings that attends *Nachträglichkeit* thus centers on the idea of something not being over when it appears to be over, which is well conveyed by "deferred action," just as it is by the customary French translation *après-coup*. An accurate yet resonant Derridean rendering would be "supplementarity."

Thomä draws attention to the etymological connection between *nachtragen* and *Übertragung*, the German word for transference. This is useful, as is his further reminder that both contain the Latin root *ferre*, meaning "to carry." As Thomä elaborates, *Übertragung* is a counterpart to "*metaferein*, the Greek word related to the noun metaphor, whose original meaning was to carry something from here to there and to transfer or extend to another place or later time" (quoted in Modell 1990, 153*n*2). But having made these excellent points, Thomä stumbles when he proceeds to criticize Strachey because "the metaphorical meaning of *nachtragen* (to hold a grudge) is still associated with the word *Nachträglichkeit*. This is lost in English where the verb to grudge is not associated with the verb carry."

In fact, however, "to grudge" *is* associated in English with the verb "bear," which is a synonym of "carry," thereby overruling Thomä's objection. What is more, Strachey's term "deferred action" preserves the root *fer* also found in transference, thus paralleling the German *Nachträglichkeit* and *Übertragung*. Thomä's contention that *nachtragen* and defer "express exactly opposite relations to time" turns out to be a figment of his imagination; and Modell's uncritical reliance on Thomä's linguistic fancies does nothing to strengthen the case that he is trying to make.

Neither the psychological nor the neurological validity of Freud's concept of *Nachträglichkeit* depends on how it is translated into English. The difference between "retrospective attribution" and "deferred action" is, in any case, simply a matter of the point of view. Deferred action takes, as it were, the perspective of the original event and stresses how its meaning continues to unfold in time; retrospective attribution takes the perspective of the later memory and stresses how it has transmuted the meaning of the prior experience. There is, however, no contradiction here. The same holds true of Modell's attributing to Freud the idea that "memory is retranscribed in accordance with later experience" (1990, 3). What Freud actually says in the *Project* is that deferred action obtains whenever there is "an instance of a memory exciting an affect which it had not excited as an experience" (1895, 413). Rather than memory being retranscribed in accordance with later experience, Freud emphasizes how experience takes on an emotional significance in memory that it did not possess at the time of its original occurrence. Again, Modell's paraphrase is compatible with Freud's more paradoxical formulation, though it loses something of the lingering effect of the past that inheres in *Nachträglichkeit*.

Following out the logic (if not the terminology) of Modell's argument, the conclusion emerges that the aim of analytic therapy is to turn *Nachträglichkeit* into *Übertragung*, or deferred action into transference. The patient enters treatment "bearing grudges" stemming from past traumas, the effect of which is to cause him or her "to generalize or refind the category or class of which the event is a member" (Modell 1990, 64). (This tendency of traumas to become generalized provides a psychoanalytic explanation for what Hobson terms the opening of "the body-type file" in his dream of "Mozart at the Museum.") The treatment setting, however, "*is designed to accentuate multiple levels of reality, which in turn enlarges the potential for both old perceptions and retranscriptions of new perceptions*" (65). What is more, the categories in question are not simply perceptual but affective, and thus are constantly seeking motoric expression. The patient's tendency to repeat the past as well as remember it inevitably implicates the analyst, because "to the extent that a given affect category represents unassimilated trauma, or a central pathogenic fantasy, there will be pressure to evoke a corresponding countertransferen[tial] affective response in the other person that will be self-confirming." But though the patient is in the grip of a compulsion to repeat, "there is also a wish by the patient to have her perception disconfirmed," as happens when the analyst interprets the patient's demand instead of yielding to it; and "the process of *disconfirmation* is essentially a process of *retranscription*" (67–68).[41]

The significance of Modell's work, as of Reiser's, is that it integrates the enduringly valuable components of psychoanalytic theory with recent advances in neuroscience. Since, as he has learned from Edelman, "cognitive repetition through the recreation of categorical memory is also a fundamental biological principle" (Modell 1990, 63), he can point out to others that it is no longer necessary to buttress Freud's profound insight into repetition as a clinical phenomenon by postulating a purely hypothetical and tautological instinct in order to explain it. That Modell

41. Modell here implicitly concurs with Weiss and Sampson's (1986) thesis that therapy proceeds by disconfirming patients' pathogenic beliefs, and he makes this endorsement explicit later in his book (1990, 137). See note 38 above.

should be in the forefront of those dedicated to putting psychoanalysis on a sound scientific foundation is a natural extension of his role as a leading American representative of the ideas of Winnicott and the British Independent tradition generally. Like his fellow dreamers of consilience, Modell concludes *The Private Self* by giving voice to the "hope that contemporary neuroscience will help reestablish the Freudian vision of the unity of psyche and soma, of the unity of mind and brain" (1993, 207).

Throughout this chapter, I have argued that the conception of psychoanalysis as a discipline that unites science and hermeneutics originates with Freud himself, however imperfectly he exemplified it in practice. But this dialectical reading of Freud has been contested by those, most conspicuously Adolf Grünbaum, who see him as wholly on the side of natural science. As Grünbaum writes at the outset of *The Foundations of Psychoanalysis*:

> Throughout his long career, Freud insisted that the psychoanalytic enterprise has the status of a natural science. As he told us at the very end of his life, the explanatory gains from positing unconscious mental processes "enabled psychology to take its place as a natural science like any other." Then he went on to declare: "Psychoanalysis is a part of the mental science of psychology. . . . Psychology, too, is a natural science. What else can it be?" (1984, 2)

Of Grünbaum's two Freud quotations in this passage, the first is from *An Outline of Psycho-Analysis* (1940a), while the second is from "Some Elementary Lessons in Psycho-Analysis" (1940b). If one were to trust Grünbaum, Freud's question in the latter quotation would appear to be purely rhetorical.[42] But Grünbaum neglects to quote the ensuing sentence, which places the matter in an altered light:

> Psychology, too, is a natural science. What else can it be? But its case is different. Not everyone is bold enough to make judgments about questions of physics; but everyone—the philosopher and the man in the street alike—has

42. Coming from an antithetical standpoint, Gill (1994), like Grünbaum, too quickly assumes that "Freud unequivocally regarded psychoanalysis as a natural science," and quotes Freud's question, "'What else can it be?'" as though it ended the discussion (4).

his opinion on psychological questions and behaves as if he were at least an amateur psychologist. (1940b, 282)

Freud's continuation, far from corroborating the identity between psychology and physics, radically qualifies it because the attitude of the ordinary person to the two disciplines is entirely different. This crucial point, suppressed by Grünbaum, is the same one that he fails to comprehend when, as we have seen, he asserts that it is possible to speak of the "histories" of a person and a particle as though these were equivalent. A similar abridgement distorts Grünbaum's quotation from *An Outline of Psycho-Analysis*, where Freud continues in the following paragraph: "Every science is based on observations and experiences arrived at through the medium of our psychical apparatus. But since *our* science has as its subject that apparatus itself, the analogy ends here" (1940a, 158–59. As John Forrester elucidates, in both passages Freud first "asserts that psychoanalysis is a natural science, and then gives a clinching reason for distinguishing it from other natural sciences"; and Grünbaum "twice omits the second step in what is quite literally a dialectical argument that asserts a thesis and then presents the reader with an antithesis which must irreversibly transform the thesis" (1997, 242). In view of his own playing fast and loose with the evidence, that Grünbaum should feel entitled to berate Habermas because he "cites tendentiously" (1984, 32) from Freud's work is unwittingly ironic to say the least.

In 1991, the same year in which I published *The Psychoanalytic Vocation*, Carlo Strenger published his *Between Hermeneutics and Science: An Essay on the Epistemology of Psychoanalysis*. No less than Reiser's augury of a "convergence" between psychoanalysis and neuroscience, Strenger's title succinctly encapsulates my central preoccupation in this chapter. Most uncannily, just as I took the epigraph to my first chapter in *The Psychoanalytic Vocation* from Aristotle's *Nicomachean Ethics*, Strenger independently cited the identical passage to sum up the proper attitude to adopt toward psychoanalytic interpretations. As Aristotle wrote, "It is the mark of a trained mind never to expect more precision in the treatment of any subject than the nature of that subject permits; for demanding logical demonstrations from a teacher of rhetoric is clearly about as reasonable as accepting mere plausibility from a mathematician" (quoted in Strenger 1991, 152; see also Rudnytsky 1991, 1).

Although Strenger does not address neuroscience, his argument in its essential aspects concurs with that which I have presented here. For

Strenger, "psychoanalysis is a *Weltanschauung* no less than an empirical theory" (1991, 186); and this Janus-like quality, at once hermeneutic and scientific, requires that one recognize that "there are purely empirical questions mainly to be settled by research, but there are also many questions which are of a more fundamental, philosophical nature, and they cannot be settled on purely empirical grounds" (146). Exactly as I have done, Strenger insists that psychoanalytic theory must respect the constraint of "*external coherence*" in that it "should be *consistent with accepted background knowledge embodied in other disciplines, and cohere with it*" (188). Freud's failure to observe this principle, as Holt and Kitcher have shown, with respect to the neighboring disciplines of biology and anthropology impeded the progress of psychoanalysis for decades. As examples of beliefs cherished by Freud but now largely rejected by the psychoanalytic community on these grounds, Strenger rounds up (191) the usual suspects—the death drive and Lamarck's doctrine of the inheritance of acquired characteristics.

Thus, as far as its theory is concerned, Strenger holds that psychoanalysis should be regarded as a natural science and judged according to empirical criteria. But though "psychoanalysis is in desperate need of thorough, controlled research to find out the truth about its own subject domain," it is, he admonishes, crucial to realize that "rationality is wider than the scientific method" (27). Thus, as an interpreter of meanings, the psychoanalyst is essentially in the position of a historian or literary critic; and in the human sciences, "a good explanation should take into account all the relevant evidence available, and it should be contradicted by as little evidence as possible" (60). This means, of course, obeying the principle of "external coherence" and not ignoring established knowledge in other domains. But it also means being as scrupulous as possible in proposing interpretations to patients as well as in presenting case histories to the public. In contrast to what Strenger brands the "*stereotyped approach*," which "legitimizes clinical inference on the basis of little evidence by using certain theoretical propositions *as if* they were well-established laws of strong predictive and retrodictive power" (133), the "*undogmatic*" clinician acts and writes in such a way that "even someone knowing very little of psychoanalysis could come to the conclusion that the psychoanalytic history given in the account is plausible" (135).[43] The

43. As an example of the "stereotyped approach," Strenger (1991, 133) cites a notorious case in which Hanna Segal leaps in the first session to a "deep" interpretation of the patient's material on the basis of her Kleinian preconceptions. He adduces (135) the Little

criteria of rationality that guide the humanistic scholar are compatible with, but not reducible to, the methods of the natural scientist. In short, the perspectives of science and hermeneutics are for Strenger "incommensurable," but they "need not contradict each other" (186). Not surprisingly, Strenger shares my admiration for Bowlby, whose "monumental work" he hails as a model of research consistent with scientific knowledge that "has produced one of the most impressive confirmations of some of the central tenets of psychoanalytic object relations theory" (197–98).

If, as Strenger has observed, "the conviction the great texts of psychoanalysis engender is closer to the experience of great works of literature than to that of reading careful scientific publications" (212), then it is fitting that Freud's concept of *Nachträglichkeit* should not only be corroborated by contemporary neuroscience but also have a venerable hermeneutic ancestry. For "deferred action" or "retrospective attribution" is precisely the principle of typological exegesis employed by Christians in the Middle Ages to describe how everything contained in the Old Testament foreshadowed the incarnation of Christ set forth in the New Testament, through whom the true meaning of these unwitting prophecies was revealed, though it was believed that Christ himself would come once again at the end of time to give even the events of the New Testament their ultimate eschatological fulfillment. As Erich Auerbach has expounded this principle of figural interpretation, it "establishes a connection between two events or persons, the first of which signifies not only itself but also the second, while the second encompasses or fulfills the first. The two poles of the figure are separate in time, but both, being real events or figures, are within time, within the stream of historical life" (1944, 53). Similarly, the essence of deferred action, in Jean Laplanche's words, is that two events are "linked by associative chains, but also clearly separated from each other by *a temporal barrier which inscribes them in two different orders of meaning*" (1970, 40), thus synergistically producing a psychic effect that neither could achieve separately.

The literary masterpiece used by Auerbach to exemplify the principles of figural exegesis is Dante's *Divine Comedy*. I would like to suggest

---

Hans case as paradigmatic of an "undogmatic" account, a judgment with which I disagree, though, as I have argued in chapters 2 and 3, it is to Freud's credit that he furnishes the observational data that permit the reader to see how inflexible he is in imposing his theoretical biases.

in conclusion that Dante's work illustrates how *Nachträglichkeit* not only has both a scientific and a hermeneutic truth, but also serves to define the proper relations between these two great hemispheres of knowledge. Just as within the hierarchy of sciences there is a continuous sequence of parent disciplines and anti-disciplines, the former in each case posing the existential questions to which the latter provides the empirical answers, so, at the most general level, the humanities as a whole are the "soft-nosed" parent discipline to which the sciences as a whole are the "hard-nosed" anti-discipline. Without the sciences, the humanities would lack a foundation; but without the humanities, the sciences would lack a purpose.

Exactly the same relation obtains between classical and Christian culture, as personified by the characters of Vergil and Beatrice, in *The Divine Comedy*. Vergil, who represents reason and is for Dante the supreme poet of ancient world, leads the pilgrim to the Earthly Paradise near the summit of the Mount of Purgatory. There he must give way to Beatrice, Dante's deceased beloved and the embodiment of Christian revelation. But if the pilgrim could not reach Beatrice without the aid of Vergil, and reason must thus in a sense precede faith, it is only with the eyes of faith that the pilgrim can retrospectively see the true meaning of what he had partially understood in the light of reason. Thus does Dante's dream of consilience depend on the principle of *Nachträglichkeit*. If the same principle also makes it possible dialectically to unite science and hermeneutics on the "common ground" of psychoanalysis—we must follow the former as far as it can go, though the latter brings us to our destination—then let me end by affirming with Robert Wallerstein: "We can, I am convinced, ultimately fulfill Freud's dream and enlarge it with our own dream for the theoretical structure of the discipline and the science of psychoanalysis" (1990, 19).

References

Abraham, Karl. 1909. *Dreams and Myths: A Study in Folk-Psychology*. In *Clinical Papers and Essays on Psycho-Analysis*. Ed. Hilda Abraham. Trans. Hilda Abraham and D. R. Ellison. New York: Basic Books, 1955, pp. 153–209.

Adler, Alfred. 1908. The Child's Need for Affection. In *The Individual Psychology of Alfred Adler: A Systematic Presentation in Selections from His Writings*. Ed. Heinz L. Ansbacher and Rowena R. Ansbacher. New York: Harper Torchbooks, 1956, pp. 38–43.

Alexander, Franz. 1954. Some Quantitative Aspects of Psychoanalytic Technique. *Journal of the American Psychoanalytic Association*, 2:685–701.

Alexander, Franz, and Thomas M. French. 1946. *Psychoanalytic Therapy: Principles and Applications*. New York: Ronald Press.

Arlow, Jacob A. 1975. The Structural Hypothesis: Theoretical Considerations. *Psychoanalytic Quarterly*, 44:509–25.

Aron, Lewis. 1996. *A Meeting of Minds: Mutuality in Psychoanalysis*. Hillsdale, N.J.: Analytic Press.

Aron, Lewis, and Adrienne Harris, eds. 1993. *The Legacy of Sándor Ferenczi*. Hillsdale, N.J.: Analytic Press.

Auerbach, Erich. 1944. Figura. In *Scenes from the Drama of European Literature*. Trans. Ralph Manheim. New York: Meridian Books, 1959, pp. 11–76.

Balint, Michael. 1932. Character Analysis and New Beginning. In *Primary Love and Psycho-Analytic Technique*. London: Maresfield Library, 1985, pp. 159–73.

———. 1968. *The Basic Fault: Therapeutic Aspects of Regression*. London: Tavistock.

Balmary, Marie. 1979. *Psychoanalyzing Psychoanalysis: Freud and the Hidden Fault of the Father*. Trans. Ned Lukacher. Baltimore: Johns Hopkins University Press, 1982.

Barnstone, Aliki. 1998. Introduction to H.D. 1944, pp. vii–xviii.

Bass, Alan. 1998. Sigmund Freud: The Question of a Weltanschauung and of Defense. In Marcus and Rosenberg 1998, pp. 412–46.

Benjamin, Jessica. 1997. Psychoanalysis as a Vocation. *Psychoanalytic Dialogues*, 7:781–802.

Bernfeld, Suzanne Cassirer. 1951. Freud and Archeology. *American Imago*, 8:107–28.

Bernheimer, Charles, and Claire Kahane, eds. 1985. *In Dora's Case: Freud—Hysteria—Feminism*. New York: Columbia University Press.

Bertrand, Michèle, Thierry Bokanowski, Monique Dechaud-Ferbus, Anouk Driant, Madeleine Ferminne, and Nagib Khouri. 1994. *Ferenczi, patient et psychanalyste*. Paris: Harmattan.

Billinsky, John M. 1969. Jung and Freud (The End of a Romance). *Andover Newton Quarterly*, 10:39–43.

Binswanger, Ludwig. 1956. *Sigmund Freud: Reminiscences of a Friendship*. Trans. Norbert Guterman. New York: Grune and Stratton, 1957.

Bloom, Harold. 1973. *The Anxiety of Influence: A Theory of Poetry*. New York: Oxford University Press.

Bokanowski, Thierry. 1994. Sándor Ferenczi: Negative Transference and Transference Depression. Trans. David Alcorn. In Rudnytsky, Bókay, and Giampieri-Deutsch 1996, pp. 120–44.

Bókay, Antal. 1998. Turn of Fortune in Psychoanalysis: The 1924 Rank Debates and the Origins of Hermeneutic Psychoanalysis. In Bonomi 1998b, pp. 189–99.

Bollas, Christopher. 1987. *The Shadow of the Object: Psychoanalysis of the Unthought Known*. New York: Columbia University Press.

Bonomi, Carlo. 1998a. Ferenczi and Contemporary Psychoanalysis. In Bonomi 1998b, pp. 181–85.

——, ed. 1998b. *Sándor Ferenczi: Psychoanalysis and the Confusion of Tongues*. *International Forum of Psychoanalysis*, vol. 7, no. 4.

Bowlby, John. 1961. Childhood Mourning and Its Implications for Psychiatry. In *The Making and Breaking of Affectional Bonds*. London: Tavistock, 1989, pp. 44–66.

——. 1969. *Attachment*. London: Hogarth Press, 1982.

——. 1973. *Separation: Anxiety and Anger*. London: Hogarth Press, 1985.

——. 1979. Psychoanalysis as Art and Science. In Bowlby 1989, pp. 39–57.

——. 1980. Psychoanalysis as a Natural Science. In Bowlby 1989, pp. 58–76.

——. 1982. The Origins of Attachment Theory. In Bowlby 1989, pp. 20–38.

——. 1985. On Knowing What You Are Not Supposed to Know and Feeling What You Are Not Supposed to Feel. In Bowlby 1989, pp. 99–118.

——. 1989. *A Secure Base: Clinical Applications of Attachment Theory*. London: Tavistock.

Brabant, Eva, Ernst Falzeder, and Patrizia Giampieri-Deutsch, eds. 1993. *The Correspondence of Sigmund Freud and Sándor Ferenczi. Volume 1, 1908–1914*. Trans. Peter T. Hoffer. Cambridge, Mass.: Harvard University Press.

Bray, Jodi. 1992. Young Lover or Reluctant Oedipus?: The Identified Patient in the Case of Little Hans. Unpublished manuscript.

Breger, Louis. 2000. *Freud: Darkness in the Midst of Vision*. New York: Wiley.

Brooks, Peter. 1987. The Idea of a Psychoanalytic Literary Criticism. *Critical Inquiry*, 13:334–48.

Browne, Sir Thomas. 1643. *Religio Medici*. In *Selected Writings*. Ed. Geoffrey Keynes. London: Faber and Faber, 1968, pp. 5–89.

Buber, Martin. 1923. *I and Thou*. Trans. Walter Kaufmann. New York: Scribners, 1970.

Chasseguet-Smirgel, Janine. 1975. Freud and Female Sexuality. The Consideration of Some Blind Spots in the Exploration of the "Dark Continent." In *Sexuality and Mind: The Role of the Father and the Mother in the Psyche*. New York: New York University Press, 1986, pp. 9–28.

Chisolm, Dianne. 1992. *H.D.'s Freudian Poetics: Psychoanalysis in Translation.* Ithaca: Cornell University Press.

Cixous, Hélène, and Catherine Clément. 1975. *The Newly Born Woman.* Trans. Betsy Wing. Minneapolis: University of Minnesota Press, 1988.

Clark, Ronald W. 1980. *Freud: The Man and the Cause.* New York: Random House.

Clark-Lowes, Francis. 2001. Freud, Stekel, and the Interpretation of Dreams: The Affinities with Existential Analysis. *Psychoanalysis and History,* 3:69–78.

Crews, Frederick. 1986. *Skeptical Engagements.* New York: Oxford University Press.

——. 1995. *The Memory Wars: Freud's Legacy in Dispute.* New York: New York Review of Books.

Dachet, François. 1993. Introduction to Herbert Graf, *Mémoirs d'un Homme Invisible,* trans. and ed. Dachet. *L'une bévue.* Supplement to vol. 3, pp. 5–18.

Damasio, Antonio. 1999. *The Feeling of What Happens: Body and Emotion in the Making of Consciousness.* New York: Harcourt Brace.

Davis, Douglas A. 1990. Freud's Unwritten Case. *Psychoanalytic Psychology,* 7:185–209.

de Forest, Izette. 1954. *The Leaven of Love: A Development of the Psychoanalytic Theory and Technique of Sándor Ferenczi.* New York: Da Capo Press, 1984.

Demos, E. Virginia. 1996. Expanding the Interpersonal Perspective. Review of *The Handbook of Interpersonal Psychoanalysis,* ed. Marylou Lionells et al. *Contemporary Psychoanalysis,* 32:649–63.

——. 2001. Psychoanalysis and the Human Sciences: The Limitations of Cut-and-Paste Theorizing. *American Imago,* 58:649–84.

Doolittle, Hilda [H.D.]. 1933. *Advent.* In H.D. 1956, pp. 115–87.

——. 1944. *Trilogy.* New York: New Directions, 1998.

——. 1945. *Writing on the Wall.* In H.D. 1956, pp. 3–111.

——. 1956. *Tribute to Freud.* New York: New Directions, 1974.

——. 1961. *Helen in Egypt.* New York: New Directions.

——. 1983. *Collected Poems, 1912–1944.* Ed. Louis L. Martz. New York: New Directions.

Dupont, Judith. 1982. Introduction to Ferenczi and Groddeck 1982, pp. 8–24.

Edelman, Gerald M. 1987. *Neural Darwinism: The Theory of Neuronal Group Selection.* New York: Basic Books.

——. 1988. *Topobiology: An Introduction to Molecular Embryology.* New York: Basic Books.

——. 1989. *The Remembered Present: A Biological Theory of Consciousness.* New York: Basic Books.

——. 1992. *Bright Air, Brilliant Fire: On the Matter of Mind.* New York: Basic Books.

Edelson, Marshall. 1988. *Psychoanalysis: A Theory in Crisis.* Chicago: University of Chicago Press.

Edmunds, Lavinia. 1988. His Master's Choice. *The Johns Hopkins Magazine,* 40-2:41–49.

Eissler, Kurt R. 1950. The Chicago Institute of Psychoanalysis and the Sixth Period of the Development of Psychoanalytic Technique. *Journal of General Psychology,* 42:103–57.

——. 1953. The Effect of the Structure of the Ego on Psychoanalytic Technique. *Journal of the American Psychoanalytic Association,* 1:104–43.

Esman, Aaron. 2001. Italo Svevo and the First Psychoanalytic Novel. *International Journal of Psychoanalysis,* 82:1225–34.

Esterson, Allen. 1993. *Seductive Mirage: An Exploration of the Work of Sigmund Freud.* Chicago: Open Court.

Fairbairn, W. R. D. 1944. Endopsychic Structures Considered in Terms of Object-Relationships. In Fairbairn 1952, pp. 82–136.

———. 1952. *Psychoanalytic Studies of the Personality*. London: Routledge and Kegan Paul, 1968.

Falzeder, Ernst, and Eva Brabant, eds. 1996. *The Correspondence of Sigmund Freud and Sándor Ferenczi. Volume 2, 1914–1919*. Trans. Peter T. Hoffer. Cambridge, Mass.: Harvard University Press.

———, eds. 2000. *The Correspondence of Sigmund Freud and Sándor Ferenczi. Volume 3, 1920–1933*. Trans. Peter T. Hoffer. Cambridge, Mass.: Harvard University Press.

Felman, Shoshana. 1980. On Reading Poetry: Reflections on the Limits and Possibilities of Psychoanalytical Approaches. In Muller and Richardson 1988, pp. 133–56.

Fenichel, Otto. 1941. *Problems of Psychoanalytic Technique*. Albany: Psychoanalytic Quarterly.

———. 1945. *The Psychoanalytic Theory of Neurosis*. New York: Norton.

Ferenczi, Sándor. 1919. On the Technique of Psychoanalysis. In Ferenczi 1926, pp. 177–89.

———. 1924. *Thalassa: A Theory of Genitality*. Trans. Henry A. Bunker. New York: Norton, 1968.

———. 1925. Contra-Indications to the "Active" Psycho-Analytical Technique. In Ferenczi 1926, pp. 217–30.

———. 1926. *Further Contributions to the Theory and Practice of Psychoanalysis*. Ed. John Rickman. Trans. Jane Isabel Suttie. New York: Brunner/Mazel, 1980.

———. 1930. The Principle of Relaxation and Neocatharsis. In Ferenczi 1955, pp. 108–25.

———. 1933a. Confusion of Tongues between Adults and the Child. In Ferenczi 1955, pp. 156–67.

———. 1933b. Freud's Influence on Medicine. In Ferenczi, 1955, pp. 143–55.

———. 1955. *Final Contributions to the Problems and Methods of Psycho-Analysis*. Ed. Michael Balint. Trans. Eric Mosbacher et al. New York: Brunner/Mazel, 1980.

———. 1985. *The Clinical Diary of Sándor Ferenczi*. Ed. Judith Dupont. Trans. Michael Balint and Nicola Zarday Jackson. Cambridge, Mass.: Harvard University Press, 1988.

Ferenczi, Sándor, and Georg Groddeck. 1982. *Briefwechsel 1921–1933*. Ed. Pierre Sabourin et al. Frankfurt: Fischer, 1986.

Flax, Jane. 1990. *Thinking Fragments: Psychoanalysis, Feminism, and Postmodernism in the Contemporary West*. Berkeley: University of California Press.

Fliess, Robert. 1956. Phylogenetic vs. Ontogenetic Experience: Notes on a Passage of Dialogue between "Little Hans" and His Father. *International Journal of Psycho-Analysis*, 37:46–60.

Fogel, Gerald I. 1993. A Transitional Phase in our Understanding of the Psychoanalytic Process: A New Look at Ferenczi and Rank. *Journal of the American Psychoanalytic Association*, 41:585–602.

Forrester, John. 1980. *Language and the Origins of Psychoanalysis*. New York: Columbia University Press.

———. 1997. *Dispatches from the Freud Wars: Psychoanalysis and Its Passions*. Cambridge, Mass.: Harvard University Press.

Fortune, Christopher. 1993. The Case of "RN." Sándor Ferenczi's Radical Experiment in Psychoanalysis. In Aron and Harris 1993, pp. 101–20.

———. 1994. A Difficult Ending: Ferenczi, "R.N.," and the Experiment in Mutual Analysis. In André E. Haynal and Ernst Falzeder, eds., *100 Years of Psychoanalysis: Contributions to the History of Psychoanalysis*. Geneva: Cahiers Psychiatriques Genevois, pp. 217–23.

———. 1996. Mutual Analysis: A Logical Outcome of Sándor Ferenczi's Experiments in Psychoanalysis. In Rudnytsky, Bókay, and Giampieri-Deutsch 1996, pp. 170–86.

———, ed. 2002. *The Ferenczi-Groddeck Correspondence, 1921–1933*. Trans. Norbert Ruebsaat, Elisabeth Petersdorf, and Jeannie Cohen. New York: Other Press.

Frankiel, Rita V. 1992. Analysed and Unanalysed Themes in the Treatment of Little Hans. *International Review of Psycho-Analysis*, 19:323–33.

Freud, Anna. 1936. *The Ego and the Mechanisms of Defense*. Trans. Cecil Barnes. Rev. ed. New York: International Universities Press, 1966.

———. 1980. Foreword to *Analysis of a Phobia in a Five-Year-Old Boy*. In *The Writings of Anna Freud*. 10 vols. New York: International Universities Press, 8:277–82.

Freud, Sigmund. 1886. Observation of a Severe Case of Hemianaesthesia in a Hysterical Male. In *The Standard Edition of the Complete Psychological Works* [or *S.E.*]. Ed. and trans. James Strachey et al. 24 vols. London: Hogarth Press, 1953–74, 1:25–31.

———. 1891. *On Aphasia: A Critical Study*. Trans. E. Stengel. London: Imago, 1953.

———. 1895. *Project for a Scientific Psychology*. In Marie Bonaparte, Anna Freud, and Ernst Kris, eds., *The Origins of Psychoanalysis: Letters to Wilhelm Fliess, Drafts and Notes: 1887–1902*. Trans. Eric Mosbacher and James Strachey. New York: Basic Books, 1971, pp. 355–445.

———. 1898. Sexuality in the Aetiology of the Neuroses. *S.E.*, 3:263–85.

———. 1899. Screen Memories. *S.E.*, 3:303–22.

———. 1900. *The Interpretation of Dreams*. *S.E.* Vols. 4 and 5.

———. 1901. *The Psychopathology of Everyday Life*. *S.E.* Vol. 6.

———. 1905a. *Fragment of an Analysis of a Case of Hysteria*. *S.E.* 7:7–122.

———. 1905b. *Three Essays on the Theory of Sexuality*. *S.E.* 7:125–245.

———. 1907a. *Delusions and Dreams in Jensen's "Gradiva."* *S.E.* 9:7–95. *Der Wahn und die Träume in W. Jensens "Gradiva."* In *Gesammelte Werke* [or *G.W.*]. Ed. Anna Freud et al. 18 vols. London: Imago, 1941–68. 7:31–125.

———. 1907b. The Sexual Enlightenment of Children. *S.E.* 9:131–39. Zur sexuellen Aufklärung der Kinder. *G.W.*, 7:19–27.

———. 1908a. Creative Writers and Day-Dreaming. *S.E.*, 9:143–53.

———. 1908b. On the Sexual Theories of Children. *S.E.*, 9:209–26.

———. 1909a. *Analysis of a Phobia in a Five-Year-Old-Boy*. *S.E.*, 10:5–149. *Analyse der Phobia eines fünfjährigen Knaben*. *G.W.*, 7:243–377.

———. 1909b. *Notes upon a Case of Obsessional Neurosis*.*S.E.*, 10:155–249. *Bemerkungen über einen Fall von Zwangsneurose*. *G.W.*, 7:381–463.

———. 1910a. *Leonardo da Vinci and a Memory of His Childhood*. *S.E.*, 11:63–137. *Eine Kindheitserinnerung des Leonardo da Vinci*. *G.W.*, 8:128–211.

———. 1910b. The Future Prospects of Psycho-Analytic Therapy. *S.E.*, 11:141–51.

———. 1910c. A Special Type of Choice of Object Made by Men. *S.E.*, 11:165–75.

———. 1911. *Psycho-Analytic Notes on an Autobiographical Account of a Case of Paranoia*. *S.E.*, 12:9–82.

———. 1912. Recommendations to Physicians Practising Psycho-Analysis. *S.E.*, 12:111–20.

———. 1912–13. *Totem and Taboo*. *S.E.*, 13:1–161.

———. 1914a. *On the History of the Psycho-Analytic Movement*. *S.E.*, 14:7–66.

———. 1914b. On Narcissism: An Introduction. *S.E.*, 14:73–102.

———. 1915. Repression. *S.E.*, 14:146–58.

———. 1916. Some Character Types Met with in Psycho-Analytic Work. *S.E.*, 14:311–33.

———. 1916–17. *Introductory Lectures on Psycho-Analysis*. *S.E.*, Vols. 16 and 17.

———. 1918. *From the History of an Infantile Neurosis*. *S.E.*, 17:7–122.

———. 1919a. Introduction to *Psycho-Analysis and the War Neuroses*. *S.E.*, 17:207–15.

———. 1919b. The Uncanny. *S.E.*, 17:219–56. Das Unheimliche. *G.W.*, 12:229–68.

——. 1923a. Dr. Sándor Ferenczi (On His 50th Birthday). *S.E.*, 19:267–69.

——. 1923b. *The Ego and the Id. S.E.*, 19:12–66.

——. 1923c. The Infantile Genital Organization. *S.E.*, 19:141–45.

——. 1924. The Dissolution of the Oedipus Complex. *S.E.*, 19:173–79.

——. 1925a. *An Autobiographical Study. S.E.*, 20:7–74.

——. 1925b. Negation. *S.E.*, 19:235–39.

——. 1926a. Address to the Society of B'nai B'rith. *S.E.*, 20:273–74.

——. 1926b. *Inhibitions, Symptoms and Anxiety. S.E.*, 20:87–172.

——. 1926c. *The Question of Lay Analysis. S.E.*, 20:183–258.

——. 1927a. Fetishism. *S.E.*, 22:152–57.

——. 1927b. *The Future of an Illusion. S.E.*, 21:5–56.

——. 1931. Female Sexuality. *S.E.*, 21:225–42.

——. 1933a. *New Introductory Lectures on Psycho-Analysis. S.E.*, 22:5–182.

——. 1933b. Sándor Ferenczi. *S.E.*, 22:227–29.

——. 1937. Analysis Terminable and Interminable. *S.E.*, 23:216–53.

——. 1939. *Moses and Monotheism: Three Essays. S.E.*, 23:7–137.

——. 1940a. *An Outline of Psycho-Analysis. S.E.*, 23:144–207.

——. 1940b. Some Elementary Lessons in Psycho-Analysis. *S.E.*, 23:281–86.

——. 1941. Findings, Ideas, Problems. *S.E.*, 23:299–300.

——. 1960. *The Letters of Sigmund Freud.* Ed. Ernst L. Freud. Trans. Tania and James Stern. New York: Basic Books.

——. 1985. *A Phylogenetic Fantasy: Overview of the Transference Neuroses.* Ed. Ilse Grubrich-Simitis. Trans. Axel Hoffer and Peter T. Hoffer. Cambridge, Mass.: Harvard University Press, 1987.

Freud, Sigmund, and Karl Abraham. 1965. *A Psycho-Analytic Dialogue: The Letters of Sigmund Freud and Karl Abraham.* Ed. Hilda C. Abraham and Ernst L. Freud. Trans. Bernard Marsh and Hilda C. Abraham. London: Hogarth Press.

Freud, Sigmund, and Lou Andreas-Salomé. 1966. *Letters.* Ed. Ernst Pfeiffer. Trans. William and Elaine Robson-Scott. New York: Harcourt Brace Jovanovich, 1972.

Freud, Sigmund, and Josef Breuer. 1895. *Studies on Hysteria. S.E.*, Vol. 2. *Studien über Hysterie. G.W.*, 1:77–312.

Freud, Sigmund, and Georg Groddeck. 1974. *Briefe über das Es.* Ed. Margaretha Honnegger. Frankfurt: Fischer, 1988.

Freud, Sigmund, and Oskar Pfister. 1963. *Psychoanalysis and Faith. Dialogues with the Reverend Oskar Pfister.* Ed. Heinrich Meng and Ernst L. Freud. Trans. Eric Mosbacher. New York: Basic Books.

Friedman, Susan Stanford. 1981. *Psyche Reborn: The Emergence of H.D.* Bloomington: Indiana University Press.

——, ed. 2002. *Analyzing Freud: The Letters of H.D., Bryher, and Their Circle.* New York: New Directions.

Fromm, Erich. 1959. *Sigmund Freud's Mission: An Analysis of His Personality and Influence.* New York: Grove Press, 1963.

——. 1968. The Oedipus Complex: Comments on the Case of Little Hans. In *The Crisis of Psychoanalysis: Essays on Freud, Marx, and Social Psychology.* Greenwich, Conn.: Fawcett, 1970, pp. 90–100.

Fromm-Reichmann, Frieda. 1950. *Principles of Intensive Psychotherapy.* Chicago: University of Chicago Press.

Garrison, Marsha. 1978. A New Look at Little Hans. *Psychoanalytic Review*, 65:523–32.

Gay, Peter. 1988. *Freud: A Life for Our Time.* New York: Norton.

Gedo, John E. 1991. *The Biology of Clinical Encounters: Psychoanalysis as a Science of Mind*. Hillsdale, N.J.: Analytic Press.

——. 1996. O, Patria Mia. In Rudnytsky, Bókay, and Giampieri-Deutsch 1996, pp. 77–88.

Geller, Jay. 1999. The Godfather of Psychoanalysis: Circmcision, Antisemitism, Homosexuality, and Freud's "Fighting Jew." *Journal of the American Academy of Religion*, 67:355–85.

Gill, Merton M. 1976. Metapsychology Is Not Psychology. In Gill and Holtzman 1976, pp. 71–105.

——. 1984. Psychoanalysis and Psychotherapy: A Revision. *International Review of Psycho-Analysis*, 11:161–79.

——. 1994. *Psychoanalysis in Transition: A Personal View*. Hillsdale, N.J.: Analytic Press.

Gill, Merton M., and Philip S. Holtzman, eds. 1976. *Psychology Versus Metapsychology: Psychoanalytic Essays in Memory of George S. Klein*. *Psychological Issues*, Monograph No. 36. New York: International Universities Press.

Gilman, Sander L. 1993a. *The Case of Sigmund Freud: Medicine and Identity at the Fin de Siècle*. Baltimore: Johns Hopkins University Press.

——. 1993b. *Freud, Race, and Gender*. Princeton: Princeton University Press.

Glenn, Jules. 1980. Freud's Advice to Hans's Father. The First Supervisory Sessions. In Kanzer and Glenn 1980, pp. 121–27.

Graf, Herbert. 1972. Memoirs of an Invisible Man: A Dialogue with Francis Rizzo. *Opera News*. February 5, pp. 25–28; February 12, pp. 26–29; February 19, pp. 26–29; Februrary 26, pp. 26–29.

Graf, Max. 1942. Reminiscences of Professor Sigmund Freud. *Psychoanalytic Quarterly*, 11:465–76.

——. 1952. Interview mit Kurt Eissler. Unpublished manuscript. 57 pp.

Green, André. 1983. The Dead Mother. Trans. K. Aubertin. In *On Private Madness*. London: Hogarth Press, 1986, pp. 142–73.

Green, André, and Daniel Stern. 2000. *Clinical and Observational Psychoanalytic Research: Roots of a Controversy*. Ed. Joseph Sandler, Anne-Marie Sandler, and Rosemary Davies. London: Karnac Books.

Greenberg, Jay, and Stephen A. Mitchell. 1983. *Object Relations in Psychoanalytic Theory*. Cambridge, Mass.: Harvard University Press.

Groddeck, Georg. 1909. *Der Pfarrer von Langewiesche*. Basel: Stroemfeld, 1981.

——. 1917. Psychic Conditioning and Psychoanalytic Treatment of Organic Disorders. In Groddeck 1977, pp. 109–31.

——. 1920. On the It. In Groddeck 1977, pp. 132–57.

——. 1921. *Der Seelensucher: Ein psychoanalytischer Roman*. Wien: Internationaler Psychoanalytischer Verlag, 1922.

——. 1922. The Compulsion to Use Symbols. In Groddeck 1977, pp. 158–71.

——. 1923. *Das Buch vom Es: Psychoanalytische Briefe an eine Freundin*. Frankfurt: Ullstein Sachbuch, 1978.

——. 1925a. Coughs and Colds. In Groddeck 1951a, pp. 131–40.

——. 1925b. "White as Snow, Red as Blood, Black as Ebony." In Groddeck 1949, pp. 20–25.

——. 1926a. Bowel Function. In Groddeck 1949, pp. 81–110.

——. 1926b. Headaches. In Groddeck 1951a, pp. 119–30.

——. 1926c. The "It" and Freudian Theory. In Groddeck 1949, pp. 208–14.

——. 1926d. The It and the Gospels. In Groddeck 1951a, pp. 165–90.

——. 1926e. The It in Everyday Life. In Groddeck 1951a, pp. 47–65.

——. 1926f. The It in Science, Art and Industry. In Groddeck 1951a, pp. 147–64.

——. 1926g. Life's Unknown Ruler, the It. In Groddeck 1951a, pp. 33–46.

——. 1926h. Rank in Freud's School. Trans. Peter L. Rudnytsky. *American Imago, 58* (2001):841–45.

——. 1926i. Repression and Release. In Groddeck 1949, pp. 214–24.

——. 1926j. Treatment. In Groddeck 1977, pp. 222–34.

——. 1927. *Peer Gynt.* In Groddeck 1949, pp. 153–79.

——. 1928. Some Fundamental Thoughts on Psychotherapy. In Groddeck 1977, pp. 211–21.

——. 1933. The Body's Middleman. In Groddeck 1949, pp. 53–81.

——. 1949. *Exploring the Unconscious.* Trans. V. M. E. Collins. London: Vision Press, 1989.

——. 1951a. *The Unknown Self.* Trans. V. M. E. Collins. London: Vision Press, 1989.

——. 1951b. *The World of Man.* Trans. V. M. E. Collins. London: Vision Press, 1967.

——. 1977. *The Meaning of Illness: Selected Psychoanalytic Writings.* Ed. Lore Schacht. Trans. Gertrud Mander. London: Maresfield Library, 1988.

Grosskurth, Phyllis. 1986. *Melanie Klein: Her World and Her Work.* Cambridge, Mass.: Harvard University Press, 1987.

Grossman, Carl M., and Sylva Grossman. 1965. *The Wild Analyst: The Life and Work of Georg Groddeck.* New York: Braziller.

Grotjahn, Martin. 1966. Georg Groddeck: The Untamed Analyst. In Franz Alexander, Samuel Eisenstein, and Martin Grotjahn, eds., *Psychoanalytic Pioneers.* New York: Basic Books, pp. 308–20.

Grubrich-Simitis, Ilse. 1993. *Back to Freud's Texts: Making Silent Documents Speak.* Trans. Philip Slotkin. New Haven: Yale University Press, 1996.

Grünbaum, Adolf. 1984. *The Foundations of Psychoanalysis: A Philosophical Critique.* Berkeley: University of California Press.

——. 1993. *Validation in the Clinical Theory of Psychoanalysis: A Study in the Philosophy of Psychoanalysis.* Madison, Conn.: International Universities Press.

Guntrip, Harry. 1968. *Schizoid Phenomena, Object Relations and the Self.* London: Hogarth Press, 1986.

——. 1975. My Experience of Analysis with Fairbairn and Winnicott—(How Complete a Result Does Psycho-Analytic Therapy Achieve?). *International Review of Psycho-Analysis, 2:*145–56.

H.D. *See* Doolittle, Hilda.

Habermas, Jürgen. 1968. *Knowledge and Human Interests.* Trans. Jeremy J. Shapiro. Boston: Beacon Press, 1971.

Hamilton, James W. 1973. Jensen's *Gradiva*: A Further Interpretation. *American Imago,* 30:380–412.

Hamilton, Victoria. 1996. *The Analyst's Preconscious.* Hillsdale, N.J.: Analytic Press.

Harlow, Harry. 1958. The Nature of Love. *American Psychologist,* 13:673–85.

Harmat, Paul. 1988. *Freud, Ferenczi und die ungarische Psychoanalyse.* Tübingen: Diskord.

Harris, Adrienne, and Lewis Aron. 1997. Ferenczi's Semiotic Theory: Previews of Postmodernism. *Psychoanalytic Inquiry,* 17:522–34.

Hartmann, Heinz. 1927. Understanding and Explanation. In Hartmann 1964, pp. 369–403.

——. 1959. Psychoanalysis as a Scientific Theory. In Hartmann 1964, pp. 318–50.

——. 1964. *Essays on Ego Psychology: Selected Problems in Psychoanalytic Theory.* New York: International Universities Press, 1964.

Haynal, André. 1988. *The Technique at Issue: Controversies in Psychoanalytic Method from Freud and Ferenczi to Michael Balint.* Trans. Elizabeth Holder. London: Karnac, 1989.

———. 1996. What Correspondence between Freud and Ferenczi? In Patrick J. Mahony, Carlo Bonomi, and Jan Stensson, eds., *Behind the Scenes: Freud in Correspondence.* Oslo: Scandinavian University Press, pp. 111–22.

Herman, Judith Lewis, with Lisa Hirschmann. 1981. *Father-Daughter Incest.* Cambridge, Mass.: Harvard University Press.

Hermann, Imre. 1933. Zum Triebleben der Primaten. *Imago,* 19:113–25.

———. 1936. Clinging—Going-in-Search: A Contrasting Pair of Instincts and Their Relation to Sadism and Masochism. Trans. H. Nunberg and F. R. Hartman. *Psychoanalytic Quarterly,* 45(1976):5–36.

Hertz, Neil. 1983. Dora's Secrets, Freud's Techniques. In Bernheimer and Kahane 1985, pp. 221–42.

Hobson, J. Allan. 1988a. *The Dreaming Brain.* New York: Basic Books.

———. 1988b. Psychoanalytic Dream Theory: A Critique Based Upon Modern Neurophysiology. In Peter Clark and Crispin Wright, eds., *Mind, Psychoanalysis and Science.* Oxford: Blackwell, pp. 277–308.

Hoffer, Axel. 1996. Asymmetry and Mutuality in the Analytic Relationship. Contemporary Lessons from the Freud-Ferenczi Dialogue. In Rudnytsky, Bókay, and Giampieri-Deutsch 1996, pp. 107–19.

Hoffman, Irwin Z. 1998. *Ritual and Spontaneity in the Psychoanalytic Process.* Hillsdale, N.J.: Analytic Press.

Hoffmann, E. T. A. 1816. The Sand-Man. In *The Best Tales of Hoffmann.* Ed. E. F. Bleiler. Trans. J. T. Bealby. New York: Dover, 1967, pp. 183–214.

Holland, Norman N. 1989. Massonic Wrongs. *American Imago,* 46:329–52.

Holt, Robert R. 1965a. Freud's Cognitive Style. In Holt 1989, pp. 34–68.

———. 1965b. A Review of Some of Freud's Biological Assumptions and Their Influence on His Theories. In Holt 1989, pp. 114–40.

———. 1976. Drive or Wish?: A Reconsideration of the Psychoanalytic Theory of Motivation. In Holt 1989, pp. 171–96.

———. 1981. The Death and Transfiguration of Metapsychology. In Holt 1989, pp. 305–23.

———. 1984. Freud and the Emergence of a New World Hypothesis. In Holt 1989, pp. 347–62.

———. 1985. The Current Status of Psychoanalytic Theory. In Holt 1989, pp. 324–344.

———. 1989. *Freud Reappraised: A Fresh Look at Psychoanalytic Theory.* New York: Guilford.

Home, H. J. 1966. The Concept of Mind. *International Journal of Psycho-Analysis,* 47:42–49.

Hopkins, Brooke. 1989. Jesus and Object-Use. A Winnicottian Account of the Resurrection Myth. In Rudnytsky 1993b, pp. 249–60.

Horney, Karen. 1923. On the Genesis of the Castration Complex in Women. In Horney 1967, pp. 37–53.

———. 1926. The Flight from Womanhood: The Masculinity Complex in Women as Viewed by Men and Women. In Horney 1967, pp. 54–70.

———. 1932. The Dread of Woman: Observations on a Specific Difference in the Dread Felt by Men and by Women Respectively for the Opposite Sex. In Horney 1967, pp. 133–46.

———. 1933. The Denial of the Vagina: A Contribution to the Problem of the Genital Anxieties Specific to Women. In Horney 1967, pp. 147–61.

———. 1967. *Feminine Psychology.* Ed. Harold Kelman. New York: Norton, 1973.

Irigaray, Luce. 1974. *Speculum of the Other Woman*. Trans. Gillian C. Gill. Ithaca: Cornell University Press, 1987.

Jacobus, Mary. 1982. Is There a Woman in This Text? In *Reading Woman: Essays in Feminist Criticism*. New York: Columbia University Press, 1986, pp. 83–109.

——. 1995. " 'Cos of the Horse": The Origin of Questions. In *First Things: The Maternal Imaginary in Literature, Art, and Psychoanalysis*. New York: Routledge, pp. 153–72.

Jameson, Fredric. 1972. *The Prison-House of Language: A Critical Account of Structuralism and Russian Formalism*. Princeton: Princeton University Press, 1974.

Jamison, Kay Redfield. 1993. *Touched With Fire: Manic-Depressive Illness and the Artistic Temperament*. New York: Free Press.

Jensen, Wilhelm. 1903. *Gradiva: A Pompeiian Fancy*. Trans. Helen M. Downey. New York: Moffat, Yard, 1918.

Jones, Ernest. 1911. *Das Problem des Hamlet und der Oedipus-Komplex*. Trans. Paul Tausig. Leipzig: Deuticke.

——. 1946. Review of *Psychoanalytic Therapy* by Franz Alexander and Thomas Morton French. *International Journal of Psycho-Analysis*, 27:162–63.

——. 1949. *Hamlet and Oedipus*. Garden City, N.Y.: Doubleday, 1954.

——. 1955. *The Life and Work of Sigmund Freud*. Vol. 2. New York: Basic Books.

——. 1957. *The Life and Work of Sigmund Freud*. Vol. 3. New York: Basic Books.

——. 1973. Freud's Early Travels. In Hendrik M. Ruitenbeck, ed., *Freud as We Knew Him*. Detroit: Wayne State University Press, pp. 275–82.

Jung, Carl G. 1912. *Psychology of the Unconscious [Transformations and Symbols of the Libido]*. Trans. Beatrice Hinkle. New York: Dodd, Mead, 1947.

——. 1952a. *Answer to Job*. Trans. R. F. C. Hull. Princeton: Princeton University Press, 1973.

——. 1952b. *Symbols of Transformation*. Trans. R. F. C. Hull. Princeton: Princeton University Press.

——. 1965. *Memories, Dreams, Reflections*. Ed. Aniela Jaffé. Trans. Richard and Clara Winston. Rev. ed. New York: Vintage, 1973.

Kahr, Brett. 1996. *D. W. Winnicott: A Biographical Portrait*. London: Karnac Books.

Kandel, Eric R. 1979. Psychotherapy and the Single Synapse: The Impact of Psychiatric Thought on Neurobiologic Research. *New England Journal of Medicine*, 301:1028–37.

——. 1983. From Metapsychology to Molecular Biology: Explorations into the Nature of Anxiety. *American Journal of Psychiatry*, 140:1277–93.

Kanzer, Mark, and Jules Glenn, eds. 1980. *Freud and His Patients*. New York: Aronson.

Kaplan-Solms, Karen, and Mark Solms. 2000. *Clinical Studies in Neuro-Psychoanalysis: Introduction to a Depth Neuropsychology*. London: Karnac Books, 2002.

Kerr, John. 1988. *The Devil's Elixirs*, Jung's "Theology," and the Dissolution of Freud's "Poisoning Complex." In Peter L. Rudnytsky, ed., *The Persistence of Myth: Psychoanalytic and Structuralist Perspectives*. New York: Guilford, pp. 1–33.

——. 1993. *A Most Dangerous Method: The Story of Jung, Freud, and Sabina Spielrein*. New York: Knopf.

Kimball, Jean. 2003. *Joyce and the Early Freudians*. Gainesville: University Press of Florida.

Kirsner, Douglas. 2000. *Unfree Associations: Inside Psychoanalytic Institutes*. London: Process Press.

Kitcher, Patricia. 1992. *Freud's Dream: A Complete Interdisciplinary Science of Mind*. Cambridge, Mass.: MIT Press, 1995.

Klein, George S. 1976. *Psychoanalytic Theory: An Exploration of Essentials*. New York: International Universities Press.

Klein, Melanie. 1930. The Importance of Symbol-Formation in the Development of the Ego. In *The Writings of Melanie Klein* [*Writings*]. 4 vols. Ed. Roger E. Money-Kyrle et al. New York: Free Press, 1975, 1:219–32.

———. 1961. *Narrative of a Child Analysis: The Conduct of the Psycho-Analysis of Children as Seen in the Treatment of a Ten-year-old Boy. Writings*, Vol. 4.

Kofman, Sarah. 1972. Summarize, Interpret. In *Freud and Fiction*. Trans. Sarah Wykes. London: Polity Press, 1991, 85–117.

———. 1980. *The Enigma of Woman: Woman in Freud's Writings*. Trans. Catherine Porter. Ithaca: Cornell University Press, 1985.

Kohut, Heinz. 1984. *How Does Analysis Cure?* Chicago: University of Chicago Press.

Krüll, Marianne. 1979. *Freud and His Father*. Trans. Arnold J. Pomerans. New York: Norton, 1986.

Lacan, Jacques. 1956. Seminar on "The Purloined Letter." Trans. Jeffrey Mehlman. In Muller and Richardson 1988, pp. 28–54.

La Grange, Henry-Louis de. 1983. *Gustav Mahler. Vol. 2. Vienna: Years of Challenge (1897–1904)*. Oxford: Oxford University Press, 1995.

Laplanche, Jean. 1970. *Life and Death in Psychoanalysis*. Trans. Jeffrey Mehlman. Baltimore: Johns Hopkins University Press, 1976.

———. 1987. *New Foundations for Psychoanalysis*. Trans. David Macey. London: Blackwell, 1989.

Lear, Jonathan. 1998. *Open Minded: Working Out the Logic of the Soul*. Cambridge, Mass.: Harvard University Press.

Leitner, Marina. 1997. Too Rankian for the Freudians, or Too Freudian for the Rankians: Otto Rank's Contributions to Psychoanalysis in the 1920s. *Journal of the American Academy of Psychoanalysis*, 25:37–70.

Lewinter, Roger. 1990. *Georg Groddeck: Studien zu Leben und Werk*. Frankfurt: Fischer. Translated from the French.

Lieberman, E. James. 1985. *Acts of Will: The Life and Work of Otto Rank*. New York: Free Press.

———. 1993. Introduction to Rank 1924f, pp. ix–xv.

Lindon, John A. 1992. A Reassessment of Little Hans, His Parents, and His Castration Complex. *Journal of the American Academy of Psychoanalysis*, 20:375–94.

Lipton, Samuel D. 1977. The Advantages of Freud's Technique as Shown in His Analysis of the Rat Man. *Journal of the American Psychoanalytic Association*, 58:255–73.

Loewald, Hans W. 1960. On the Therapeutic Action of Psychoanalysis. In *Papers on Psychoanalysis*. New Haven: Yale University Press, 1980, pp. 221–56.

Lomas, Peter. 1987. *The Limits of Interpretation: What's Wrong with Psychoanalysis?*. Harmondsworth: Penguin.

Luborsky, Lester. 1996. *The Symptom-Context Method: Symptoms as Opportunities in Psychotherapy*. Washington, D.C.: American Psychological Association.

Luborsky, Lester, and Paul Crits-Christoph. 1990. *Understanding Transference: The Core Conflictual Relationship Theme Method*. New York: Basic Books.

Lupton, Mary Jo. 1993. *Menstruation and Psychoanalysis*. Urbana: University of Illinois Press.

Mahony, Patrick J. 1986. *Freud and the Rat Man*. New Haven: Yale University Press.

———. 1989. *On Defining Freud's Discourse*. New Haven: Yale University Press.

———. 1992. Freud as Family Therapist: Reflections. In Toby Gelfand and John Kerr, eds., *Freud and the History of Psychoanalysis*. Hillsdale, N.J.: Analytic Press, pp. 307–17.

——. 1993. The Dictator and His Cure. *International Journal of Psycho-Analysis*, 74:1245–51.

——. 1996. *Freud's Dora: A Psychoanalytic, Historical, and Textual Study*. New Haven: Yale University Press.

Mannoni, Maud. 1967. *The Child, His "Illness," and the Others*. New York: Pantheon, 1976. Translated from the French.

——. 1979. *La théorie comme fiction: Freud, Groddeck, Winnicott, Lacan*. Paris: Seuil.

Marcus, Paul, and Alan Rosenberg, eds. 1998. *Psychoanalytic Versions of the Human Condition: Philosophies of Life and Their Impact on Practice*. New York: New York University Press.

Marcus, Steven. 1974. Freud and Dora: Story, History, Case History. In *Freud and the Culture of Psychoanalysis: Studies in the Transition from Victorian Humanism to Modernity*. Boston: Allen and Unwin, 1984, pp. 42–86.

Martynkewicz, Wolfgang. 1997. *Georg Groddeck: Eine Biographie*. Frankfurt: Fischer.

Masson, Jeffrey M. 1984. *The Assault on Truth: Freud's Suppression of the Seduction Theory*. New York: Farrar, Straus and Giroux.

——, ed. and trans. 1985. *The Complete Letters of Sigmund Freud to Wilhelm Fliess 1887–1904*. Cambridge, Mass.: Harvard University Press.

McGuire, William, ed. 1974. *The Freud/Jung Letters: The Correspondence between Sigmund Freud and C. G. Jung*. Trans. Ralph Manheim and R. F. C. Hull. Princeton: Princeton University Press.

Meltzer, Donald. 1978. *The Kleinian Development. Part I. Freud's Clinical Development*. Reading, Eng.: Clunie Press, 1985.

Mereschkowski [Merezhkovsky], Dimitri S. 1903. *Leonardo da Vinci: Ein biographisches Roman aus der Wende des 15 Jahrhunderts*. Leipzig: Verlagsbuchhandlung Schulze. Translated from the Russian.

Mitchell, Stephen A. 1988. *Relational Concepts in Psychoanalysis: An Integration*. Cambridge, Mass.: Harvard University Press.

——. 1993. *Hope and Dread in Psychoanalysis*. New York: Basic Books.

——. 1997. *Influence and Autonomy in Psychoanalysis*. Hillsdale, N.J.: Analytic Press.

——. 2000. *Relationality: From Attachment to Intersubjectivity*. Hillsdale, N.J.: Analytic Press.

Mitchell, Stephen A., and Lewis Aron, eds. 1999. *Relational Psychoanalysis: The Emergence of a Tradition*. Hillsdale, N.J.: Analytic Press.

Modell, Arnold H. 1990. *Other Times, Other Realities: Toward a Theory of Psychoanalytic Treatment*. Cambridge, Mass.: Harvard University Press.

——. 1993. *The Private Self*. Cambridge, Mass.: Harvard University Press.

Moi, Toril. 1981. Representation of Patriarchy: Sexuality and Epistemology in Freud's Dora. In Bernheimer and Kahane 1985, pp. 181–99.

Møller, Lis. 1991. *The Freudian Reading: Analytical and Fictional Constructions*. Philadelphia: University of Pennsylvania Press.

Moreau-Ricaud, Michelle. 1990. The Founding of the Budapest School. In Rudnytsky, Bókay, and Giampieri-Deutsch 1996, pp. 41–59.

Muller, John P., and William J. Richardson, eds. 1988. *The Purloined Poe: Lacan, Derrida, and Psychoanalytic Reading*. Baltimore: Johns Hopkins University Press.

Nietzsche, Friedrich. 1883. *Thus Spoke Zarathustra*. In Walter Kaufmann ed. and trans., *The Portable Nietzsche*. New York: Viking, 1967, pp. 115–439.

——. 1886. *Beyond Good and Evil: Prelude to a Philosophy of the Future*. Trans. Walter Kaufmann. New York: Vintage Books, 1966.

Nin, Anaïs. 1992. *Incest: The Unexpurgated Diary of Anaïs Nin, 1932–1934.* Ed. Gunther Stuhlmann. San Diego: Harcourt Brace.

———. 1995. *Fire: The Unexpurgated Diary of Anaïs Nin, 1934–1937.* Ed. Gunther Stuhlmann. New York: Harcourt Brace.

Nitzschke, Bernd. 1983. Zur Herkunft des "Es": Freud, Groddeck, Nietzsche, Schopenhauer und E. von Hartmann. *Psyche,* 37:769–804.

Nunberg, Herman, and Ernst Federn, eds. 1962. *Minutes of the Vienna Psychoanalytic Society, 1906–1908.* Vol. 1. Trans. M. Nunberg. New York: International Universities Press.

———. 1967. *Minutes of the Vienna Psychoanalytic Society. 1908–1910.* Vol. 2. Trans. M. Nunberg. New York: International Universities Press.

———. 1976. *Protokolle der Wiener Psychoanalytischen Vereinigung, 1906–1908.* Vol. 1. Frankfurt: Fischer.

Palombo, Stanley R. 1999. *The Emergent Ego: Complexity and Coevolution in the Psychoanalytic Process.* Madison, Conn.: International Universities Press.

Paskauskas, R. Andrew, ed. 1993. *The Complete Correspondence of Sigmund Freud and Ernest Jones 1908–1939.* Cambridge, Mass.: Harvard University Press.

Phillips, Adam. 1988. *Winnicott.* London: Fontana Press.

Pollock, George H. 1972. Bertha Pappenheim's Pathological Mourning: Possible Effects of Childhood Sibling Loss. *Journal of the American Psychoanalytic Association,* 20:478–93.

Quinn, Susan. 1987. *A Mind of Her Own: The Life of Karen Horney.* New York: Summit Books.

Rand, Nicholas, and Maria Torok. 1997. *Questions for Freud: The Secret History of Psychoanalysis.* Cambridge, Mass.: Harvard University Press.

Rangell, Leo. 1954. Similarities and Differences between Psychoanalysis and Dynamic Psychotherapy. *Journal of the American Psychoanalytic Association,* 2:734–44.

———. 1982. Transference to Theory: The Relationship of Psychoanalytic Education to the Analyst's Relationship to Psychoanalysis. *Annual of Psychoanalysis,* 10:29–56.

———. 1988. The Future of Psychoanalysis: The Scientific Crossroads. *Psychoanalytic Quarterly,* 57:313–40.

Rank, Otto. 1907. *Der Künstler: Ansätze zu einer Sexual-Psychologie.* Vienna: Heller.

———. 1909. *The Myth of the Birth of the Hero.* Trans. F. Robbins and Smith Ely Jelliffe. New York: Journal of Nervous and Mental Disease Publishing Co., 1914.

———. 1910. Ein Traum, der sich selbst deutet. *Jahrbuch für psychoanalytische und psychopathologische Forschungen,* 2:465–540.

———. 1911. *Die Lohengrin Sage.* Vienna: Deuticke.

———. 1912. *Das Incest-Motiv in Dichtung und Sage: Grundzüge einer Psychologie des dichterischen Schaffens.* Leipzig: Deuticke.

———. 1924a. *The Don Juan Legend.* Trans. David G. Winter. Princeton: Princeton University Press, 1975.

———. 1924b. *Eine Neurosenanalyse in Träumen.* Leipzig: Internationaler Psychoanalytischer Verlag.

———. 1924c. Psychoanalysis as General Psychology. In Rank 1996, pp. 51–65.

———. 1924d. The Therapeutic Application of Psychoanalysis. In Rank 1996, pp. 66–77.

———. 1924e. *Das Trauma der Geburt und seine Bedeutung für die Psychoanalyse.* Frankfurt: Fischer, 1988.

———. 1924f. *The Trauma of Birth.* New York: Dover, 1993. Translated from the German.

———. 1924g. The Trauma of Birth and Its Importance for Psychoanalytic Therapy. In Rank 1996, pp. 78–84.

———. 1926a. *Das Incest-Motiv in Dichtung und Sage: Grundzüge einer Psychologie des dichterischen Schaffens.* 2d ed. Leipzig: Deuticke.

———. 1926b. *Sexualität und Schuldgefühl: Psychoanalytische Studien.* Leipzig: Internationaler Psychoanalytischer Verlag.

———. 1926c. *Technik der Psychoanalyse. Die analytische Situation illustriert an der Traumdeutungstechnik.* Leipzig: Deuticke.

———. 1927a. *Grundzüge einer genetischen Psychologie auf Grund der Psychoanalyse der Ichstruktur.* Leipzig: Deuticke.

———. 1927b. Review of Sigmund Freud, *Hemmung, Symptom und Angst. Mental Hygiene,* 11:181–86.

———. 1927c. The Significance of the Love Life. In Rank 1996, pp. 177–88.

———. 1927d. Social Adaptation and Creativity. In Rank 1996, pp. 189–200.

———. 1929. *Truth and Reality.* Trans. Jessie Taft. New York: Norton, 1978.

———. 1929–31. *Will Therapy.* Trans. Jessie Taft. New York: Norton, 1978.

———. 1930a. *Psychology and the Soul.* Trans. W. D. Turner. New York: Barnes, 1961.

———. 1930b. Speech at First International Congress on Mental Hygiene. In Rank 1996, pp. 221–27.

———. 1932. *Art and Artist.* New York: Knopf.

———. 1992. *The Incest Theme in Literature and Legend: Fundamentals of a Psychology of Literary Creation.* Trans. Gregory C. Richter. Baltimore: Johns Hopkins University Press.

———. 1996. *A Psychology of Difference: The American Lectures of Otto Rank.* Ed. Robert Kramer. Princeton: Princeton University Press.

Rank, Otto, and Sándor Ferenczi. 1923. *The Development of Psychoanalysis.* Trans. Caroline Newton. New York: Dover, 1956.

Rapaport, David. 1960. *The Structure of Psychoanalytic Theory: A Systematizing Attempt. Psychological Issues,* Monograph No. 10. New York: International Universities Press.

Reiser, Morton F. 1984. *Mind, Brain, Body: Toward a Convergence of Psychoanalysis and Neuroscience.* New York: Basic Books.

Renik, Owen. 1993. Analytic Interaction: Conceptualizing Technique in Light of the Analyst's Irreducible Subjectivity. *Psychoanalytic Quarterly,* 62:553–71.

Ricoeur, Paul. 1970. *Freud and Philosophy: An Essay on Interpretation.* Trans. Denis Savage. New Haven: Yale University Press.

———. 1977. The Question of Proof in Freud's Psychoanalytic Writings. *Journal of the American Psychoanalytic Association,* 25:835–71.

Roazen, Paul. 1971. *Freud and His Followers.* New York: Meridian, 1976.

Roith, Estelle. 1987. *The Riddle of Freud: Jewish Influences on His Theory of Female Sexuality.* London: Tavistock.

Rose, Louis. 1998. *The Freudian Calling: Early Viennese Psychoanalysis and the Pursuit of Cultural Science.* Detroit: Wayne State University Press.

Roustang, François. 1976. *Dire Mastery: Discipleship from Freud to Lacan.* Trans. Ned Lukacher. Baltimore: Johns Hopkins University Press, 1982.

Rubinstein, Benjamin B. 1965. Psychoanalytic Theory and the Mind-Body Problem. In Rubinstein 1997, pp. 43–66.

———. 1976. On the Possibility of a Strictly Clinical Psychoanalytic Theory: An Essay in the Philosophy of Psychoanalysis. In Rubinstein 1997, pp. 325–59.

———. 1997. *Psychoanalysis and the Philosophy of Science: Collected Papers.* Ed. Robert R. Holt. *Psychological Issues,* Monograph No. 62/63. Madison, Conn.: International Universities Press.

Rudnytsky, Peter L. 1987. *Freud and Oedipus*. New York: Columbia University Press.

———. 1991. *The Psychoanalytic Vocation: Rank, Winnicott, and the Legacy of Freud*. New Haven: Yale University Press.

———. 1993a. Introduction to Rudnytsky 1993b, pp. xi–xxii.

———, ed. 1993b. *Transitional Objects and Potential Spaces: Literary Uses of D. W. Winnicott*. New York: Columbia University Press.

———. 1999. Wrecking Crews. *American Imago*, 56:285–98.

———. 2000. *Psychoanalytic Conversations: Interviews with Clinicians, Commentators, and Critics*. Hillsdale, N.J.: Analytic Press.

Rudnytsky, Peter L., Antal Bókay, and Patrizia Giampieri-Deutsch, eds. 1996. *Ferenczi's Turn in Psychoanalysis*. New York: New York University Press.

Sabourin, Pierre. 1985. *Ferenczi, paladin et grand vizir secret*. Paris: Éditions Universitaires.

Sacks, Oliver W. 1970. *Migraine: The Evolution of a Common Disorder*. Berkeley: University of California Press, 1972.

———. 1998. Sigmund Freud: The Other Road. In Gieselher Guttmann and Inge Scholz-Strasser, eds., *Freud and the Neurosciences: From Brain Research to the Unconscious*. Vienna: Verlag der Österreichischen Akademie der Wissenschaften, pp. 11–22.

Sadger, Isidor. 1908. *Conrad Ferdinand Meyer. Eine pathographisch-psychologische Studie*. Wiesbaden: Bergmann.

———. 1909. *Aus dem Liebesleben Nicolaus Lenaus*. Leipzig: Deuticke.

———. 1910. *Heinrich von Kleist: Eine pathographisch-psychologische Studie*. Wiesbaden: Bergmann.

Sass, Louis A. 1994. *The Paradoxes of Delusion: Wittgenstein, Schreber, and the Schizophrenic Mind*. Ithaca: Cornell University Press.

———. 1998. Ambiguity Is of the Essence: The Relevance of Hermeneutics for Psychoanalysis. In Marcus and Rosenberg 1998, pp. 257–305.

Schafer, Roy. 1988. The Sense of an Answer: Clinical and Applied Psychoanalysis Compared. In *Retelling a Life: Narration and Dialogue in Psychoanalysis*. New York: Basic Books, 1992, pp. 165–86.

———. 1994. The Evolution of My Views on Nonnormative Sexual Practices. In *Tradition and Change in Psychoanalysis*. Madison, Conn.: International Universities Press, 1997, pp. 237–52.

Schreber, Daniel Paul. 1903. *Denkwürdigkeiten eines Nervenkranken*. Leipzig: Oswald Muße.

Schur, Max. 1972. *Freud: Living and Dying*. New York: International Universities Press.

Searles, Harold F. 1961. Phases of Patient-Therapist Interaction in the Psychotherapy of Chronic Schizophrenia. In *Collected Papers on Schizophrenia and Related Subjects*. New York: International Universities Press, 1965, pp. 521–59.

———. 1972. The Patient as Therapist to His Analyst. In *Countertransference and Related Subjects: Selected Papers*. New York: International Universities Press, 1979, pp. 380–459.

Severn, Elizabeth. 1933. *The Discovery of the Self: A Study in Psychological Cure*. Philadelphia: McKay.

Shapiro, Sue A. 1993. Clara Thompson: Ferenczi's Messenger with Half a Message. In Aron and Harris 1993, pp. 159–74.

Shengold, Leonard. 1989. *Soul Murder: The Effects of Childhood Abuse and Deprivation*. New Haven: Yale University Press.

Silver, Ann-Louise S. 1996. Ferenczi's Early Impact on Washington, D.C. In Rudnytsky, Bókay, and Giampieri-Deutsch 1996, pp. 89–104.

Silverman, Martin A. 1980. A Fresh Look at the Case of Little Hans. In Kanzer and Glenn 1980, pp. 95–127.

Slochower, Harry. 1981. Freud as Yahweh in Jung's *Answer to Job. American Imago*, 38:3–39.

Smith, Nancy A. 1998. Orpha Reviving: Toward an Honorable Recognition of Elizabeth Severn. In Bonomi 1998b, pp. 241–46.

Solms, Mark. 2001. The Interpretation of Dreams and the Neurosciences. *Psychoanalysis and History*, 3:79–91.

Solms, Mark, and Oliver Turnbull. 2002. *The Brain and the Inner World.* New York: Other Press.

Sontag, Susan. 1964. Against Interpretation. In *Against Interpretation and Other Essays.* New York: Farrar, Straus and Giroux, 1966, pp. 3–14.

———. 1978. *Illness as Metaphor.* New York: Farrar, Straus and Giroux.

Spence, Donald P. 1976. *Narrative Truth and Historical Truth: Meaning and Interpretation in Psychoanalysis.* New York: Norton.

Spezzano, Charles. 1995. "Classical" vs. "Contemporary" Theory. *Contemporary Psychoanalysis*, 31:20–46.

Spiro, Joanna. 2001. Weighed in the Balance: H.D.'s Resistance to Freud in *Writing on the Wall. American Imago*, 58:597–621.

Spitz, Ellen Handler. 1985. *Art and Psyche: A Study of Psychoanalysis and Aesthetics.* New Haven: Yale University Press.

———. 1989. Conflict and Creativity: Reflections on Otto Rank's Psychology of Art. In *Image and Insight: Essays in Psychoanalysis and the Arts.* New York: Columbia University Press, pp. 235–49.

Sprengnether, Madelon. 1985. Enforcing Oedipus: Freud and Dora. In Bernheimer and Kahane 1985, pp. 254–75.

———. 1990. *The Spectral Mother: Freud, Feminism, and Psychoanalysis.* Ithaca: Cornell University Press.

———. 2000. Mourning Freud. In Peter L Rudnytsky and Andrew M. Gordon, eds., *Psychoanalyses/Feminisms.* Albany: State University of New York Press, pp. 11–37.

Stanton, Martin. 1991. *Sandor Ferenczi: Reconsidering Active Intervention.* New York: Aronson.

Steele, Robert S. 1979. Psychoanalysis and Hermeneutics. *International Review of Psycho-Analysis*, 6:389–411.

Stekel, Wilhelm. 1912. *Die Träume der Dichter. Eine vergleichende Untersuchung der unbewussten Triebkräfte bei Dichtern, Neurotikern und Verbrechern.* Wiesbaden: J. F. Bergmann.

———. 1950. *The Autobiography of Wilhelm Stekel: The Life Story of a Pioneer Psychoanalyst.* Ed. Emil A. Gutheil. New York: Liveright.

Stepansky, Paul E. 1983. *In Freud's Shadow: Adler in Context.* Hillsdale, N.J.: Analytic Press.

———. 1999. *Freud, Surgery, and the Surgeons.* Hillsdale, N.J.: Analytic Press.

Stone, Leo. 1961. *The Psychoanalytic Situation: An Examination of Its Development and Essential Nature.* New York: International Universities Press.

———. 1981. Notes on the Noninterpretive Elements in the Psychoanalytic Situation and Process. *Journal of the American Psychoanalytic Association*, 29:89–118.

Stolorow, Robert D. 1990. Converting Psychotherapy to Psychoanalysis: A Critique of the Underlying Assumptions. *Psychoanalytic Inquiry*, 10:119–30.

Strean, Herbert S. 1967. A Family Therapist Looks at "Little Hans." *Family Process*, 6:227–33.

Strenger, Carlo. 1991. *Between Hermeneutics and Science: An Essay on the Epistemology of Psychoanalysis.* Madison, Conn.: International Universities Press.

Sulloway, Frank J. 1996. *Born to Rebel: Birth Order, Family Dynamics, and Creative Lives.* New York: Vintage Books, 1997.

Suttie, Ian. 1935. *The Origins of Love and Hate.* London: Free Association Books, 1988.

Svevo, Italo. 1923. *Zeno's Conscience.* Trans. William Weaver. New York: Everyman's Library, 2001.

Swales, Peter J. 1982. Freud, Minna Bernays, and the Conquest of Rome: New Light on the Origins of Psychoanalysis. *New American Review*, Spring/Summer, pp. 1–23.

—— 1983. Freud, Martha Bernays, and the Language of Flowers. Privately published by the author.

Swan, Jim. 1974. *Mater* and Nannie: Freud's Two Mothers and the Discovery of the Oedipus Complex. *American Imago*, 31:1–64.

Taft, Jessie. 1958. *Otto Rank: A Biographical Study.* New York: Julian Press.

Teicholz, Judith Guss. 1999. *Kohut, Loewald, and the Postmoderns: A Comparative Study of Self and Relationship.* Hillsdale, N.J.: Analytic Press.

This, Bernard. 1982. "Schrei nach dem Kinde": Le cri de Ferenczi. *Le Coq-Héron*, 85:23–30.

Timms, Edward. 1988. Freud's Library and His Private Reading. In Edward Timms and Naomi Segal, eds., *Freud in Exile: Psychoanalysis and Its Vicissitudes.* New Haven: Yale University Press, pp. 65–79.

Traub, Valerie. 1992. *Desire and Anxiety: Circulations of Sexuality in Shakespearean Drama.* New York: Routledge.

Treurniet, Nikolaas. 1993. Support of the Analytical Process and Structural Change. In Mardi J. Horowitz, Otto F. Kernberg, and Edward M. Weinshel, eds., *Psychic Structure and Psychic Change: Essays in Honor of Robert S. Wallerstein, M.D.* Madison, Conn.: International Universities Press, pp. 191–232.

Urban, Brend, and Johannes Cremerius, eds. 1973. Sigmund Freud, *Der Wahn und die Träume in W. Jensens "Gradiva" mit dem Text der Erzählung von Wilhelm Jensen.* Frankfurt am Main: Fischer, 1981.

Vaughan, Susan C. 1997. *The Talking Cure: The Science behind Psychotherapy.* New York: Putnam's.

Vitz, Paul C. 1988. *Sigmund Freud's Christian Unconscious.* New York: Guilford.

Wallerstein, Robert S. 1976. Psychoanalysis as a Science: Its Present Status and Its Future Tasks. In Gill and Holtzman 1976, pp. 198–228.

——. 1986a. *Forty-Two Lives in Treatment: A Study of Psychoanalysis and Psychotherapy.* New York: Other Press, 2000.

——. 1986b. Psychoanalysis as a Science: A Response to the New Challenges. *Psychoanalytic Quarterly*, 55:414–51.

——. 1988. One Psychoanalysis or Many? *International Journal of Psycho-Analysis*, 69:5–21.

——. 1990. Psychoanalysis: The Common Ground. *International Journal of Psycho-Analysis*, 71:3–30.

——. 1995. *The Talking Cures: The Psychoanalyses and the Psychotherapies.* New Haven: Yale University Press.

——. 1998a. *Lay Analysis: Life Inside the Controversy.* Hillsdale, N.J.: Analytic Press.

——. 1998b. The New American Psychoanalysis: A Commentary. *Journal of the American Psychoanalytic Association*, 46:1021–43.

——. 2001. Review of Joseph Schwartz, *Cassandra's Daughter: A History of Psychoanalysis. American Imago*, 58:723–37.

Webster, Richard. 1995. *Why Freud Was Wrong: Sin, Science, and Psychoanalysis*. New York: Basic Books.

Weininger, Otto. 1903. *Sex and Character*. London: Heinemann, 1906. Translated from the German.

Weiss, Joseph, and Harold Sampson. 1986. *The Psychoanalytic Process: Theory, Clinical Observation, and Empirical Research*. New York: Guilford.

Wellek, René, and Austin Warren. 1942. *Theory of Literature*. Harmondsworth: Penguin, 1970.

Wheelis, Allen. 1956. The Vocational Hazards of Psychoanalysis. *International Journal of Psycho-Analysis*, 37:171–84.

Wilcocks, Robert. 1994. *Maelzel's Chess Player: Sigmund Freud and the Rhetoric of Deceit*. Lanham, Md.: Rowman and Littlefield.

Wilde, Oscar. 1891. *The Picture of Dorian Gray*. London: Penguin Classics, 1985.

Will, Herbert. 1984. *Georg Groddeck: Die Geburt der Psychosomatik*. Munich: Deutscher Taschenbuch Verlag, 1987.

——. 1994. Ferenczi und Groddeck: Eine Freundschaft. *Psyche*, 48:720–37.

——. 1995. War Groddeck ein Nazi? Ein Beitrag zum Verhältnis von Psychoanalyse und Politik. *Luzifer-Amor*, 16:7–21.

Wilson, Edward O. 1975. *Sociobiology: The New Synthesis*. Cambridge, Mass.: Harvard University Press.

——. 1977. Biology and the Social Sciences. *Daedalus*, 106:127–40.

——. 1978. *On Human Nature*. Cambridge, Mass.: Harvard University Press.

——. 1998. *Consilience: The Unity of Knowledge*. New York: Knopf.

——. 2002. *The Future of Life*. New York: Knopf.

Winnicott, D. W. 1947. Hate in the Countertransference. In Winnicott 1958, pp. 194–203.

——. 1952. Anxiety Associated with Insecurity. In Winnicott 1958, pp. 97–100.

——. 1958. *Through Paediatrics to Psycho-Analysis*. New York: Basic Books, 1975.

——. 1960. Ego Distortion in Terms of True and False Self. In *The Maturational Processes and the Facilitating Environment: Studies in the Theory of Emotional Development*. New York: International Universities Press, 1966, pp. 140–52.

——. 1969. The Use of an Object and Relating Through Identifications. In Winnicott 1971b, pp. 86–94.

——. 1971a. Creativity and Its Origins. In Winnicott 1971b, pp. 65–85.

——. 1971b. *Playing and Reality*. London: Tavistock, 1985.

——. 1974. Fear of Breakdown. In *Psycho-Analytic Explorations*. Ed. Clare Winnicott, Ray Shepherd, and Madeleine Davis. Cambridge, Mass.: Harvard University Press, 1989, pp. 87–95.

Wittels, Fritz. 1924. *Sigmund Freud: His Personality, His Teaching, and His School*. Trans. Eden and Cedar Paul. London: Allen and Unwin.

——. 1995. *Freud and the Child Woman: The Memoirs of Fritz Wittels*. Ed. Edward Timms. New Haven: Yale University Press.

Wolff, Peter H. 1996. The Irrelevance of Infant Observations for Psychoanalysis. *Journal of the American Psychoanalytic Association*, 44:369–92.

Wolpe, Joseph, and Stanley Rachman. 1960. Psychoanalytic "Evidence": A Critique Based on Freud's Case of Little Hans. *Journal of Nervous and Mental Diseases*, 130:135–48.

Worbs, Michael. 1983. *Nervenkunst: Literatur und Psychoanalyse im Wien der Jahrhundertwende*. Frankfurt: Europäische Verlagsanstalt.

Yeats, W. B. 1937. *A Vision*. New York: Collier Books, 1966.

Yerushalmi, Yosef Hayim. 1991. *Freud's Moses: Judaism Terminable and Interminable*. New Haven: Yale University Press.

Index

Abraham, Karl, 68, 70, 74n12, 89n4, 109–10, 112, 152, 154, 210n4

Active technique, 94, 100, 180

"Address to the Society of B'nai B'rith" (Freud), 56

Adler, Alfred, 17, 42, 66–69, 70n8, 101, 105, 113, 147, 200, 202

Aeschylus, 73n11

Aggression, 13, 248

Ainsworth, Mary Salter, 92n6, 214n8, 218

Alexander, Franz, 156n23, 209–10

American Psychoanalytic Association, 110n4

American Psychological Association, 110n4

Analysis of a Neurosis in Dreams, An (Rank), 96–98, 105, 154

Analysis of a Phobia in a Five-Year-Old Boy, An (Freud), 22–34, 35– 57, 59, 60, 115, 156n23, 168–69, 174, 261, 282n43. *See also* Oedipus complex

"Analysis Terminable and Interminable" (Freud), 116–21, 173

Andreas-Salomé, Lou, 42n12, 97, 154, 156n23, 157

Anthropology, 215–16, 282

Anxiety, 40, 93, 156, 273–74

Archeology, 13, 19, 55

Aristotle, 71–72, 76, 81, 210n5, 281

Arlow, Jacob A., 142n2

Aron, Lewis, 92n6, 93, 94n9, 109n2, 109n3, 127n1, 136n11, 143n4, 144n4, 175, 178n37, 208, 219n11, 234

Attachment theory, 41, 84, 92n6, 95, 98, 100, 133, 191, 211, 227, 242n23, 271

Auerbach, Erich, 283

Autobiographical Study, An (Freud), 20, 38n7, 60

Bacon, Sir Francis, 247, 251

Bahr, Hermann, 71n10

Balint, Michael, 14, 98, 110, 114

Balmary, Marie, 56

Barnstone, Aliki, 194n49

Bass, Alan, 237n19

Beethoven, Ludwig van, 42

Behaviorism, 40, 271–73

Benjamin, Jessica, 203n58

Berger, Baron Alfred von, 71

Bergmann, J. F., 148

Bernays, Jacob, 71

Bernays, Martha, 8n9, 48, 71n

Bernays, Minna, 18n15, 123n16, 180n39, 263

Bernfeld, Siegfried, 159n25

Bernfeld, Suzanne C., 13n11

Bertrand, Michèle, 109n2

Bible, 78, 167–69, 178, 183, 193–98, 204–6

Billinsky, John M., 179

Binswanger, Ludwig, 202

Biology, 213–15, 227–28, 233, 241, 244, 246,
272–73, 276, 282
Biosphere 2, 252–53
Bleuler, Eugen, 42n12
Bloom, Harold, 144, 247n25
Bölsche, Wilhelm, 144
Bokanowski, Thierry, 116n8, 121n14
Bókay, Antal, 109n2, 142n2
Bollas, Christopher, 11
Bonaparte, Marie, 119n12
Bonomi, Carlo, 209n2
Book of the It, The (Groddeck), 114, 142–43,
147, 149, 152–54, 163– 75, 176–77, 192,
193, 199, 205–6; addressed to Freud,
166–67, 173; disparaged by Freud, 147,
167, 174–75; epistolary form of, 163,
174; and Ferenczi, 171; and Freud-Fer-
enczi correspondence, 173; as master-
piece, 24n4, 36n3, 163, 174–75, 182, 206;
transference in, 164, 169
Boss, Medard, 169n20
Boundary violations, 19, 179
Bowlby, John, 13, 40, 83, 100–101, 105, 214,
218, 238–39, 243, 251– 52, 283. See also
Attachment theory
Bray, Jodi, 29
Breger, Louis, 13n11, 18n14, 38n7, 68n7, 89,
105n18, 111n5, 112, 113, 114, 116, 119n11,
119n12, 126n18, 134–35, 153n20, 184, 187
Brentano, Franz, 243
Breuer, Josef, 19, 48, 69, 111n5, 216n10,
248n26. See also Studies on Hysteria
Brezhnev, Leonid, 237
British Psycho-Analytical Society, 209, 211,
229, 231n18
Britton, James, 189
Broca, Pierre Paul, 266
Brooks, Peter, 240–41
Browne, Sir Thomas, 197
Brücke, Ernst, 18, 266
Buber, Martin, 143n5
Byron, Lord, 67, 78

Castration complex, 23n4, 27–28, 52, 54, 64,
128, 156, 167–68, 174, 192
Cervantes, 175
Charcot, Jean-Martin, 19
Chasseguet-Smirgel, Janine, 23n4
Chaucer, Geoffrey, 78
Chestnut Lodge, 142, 143n4
Chisolm, Dianne, 194n49
Christianity, 78, 128, 140, 168–70, 178,
192–206, 283–84
Cixous, Hélène, and Catherine Clément,
23n4
Clark, Ronald, 148n12

Clark-Lowes, Francis, 147n11, 149n14
Clinical Diary (Ferenczi), 93, 105n19, 110,
112, 114, 115, 122, 127–40, 143, 150, 173,
191
Committee, the, 109, 126n18, 151n17, 170,
201n54
Computational psychology, 246, 266
Condorcet, Marquis de, 247
"Confusion of Tongues between Adults and
the Child" (Ferenczi), 101, 133
Consilience, 242, 245–53, 267, 269n36, 280,
284
Constructivism, 208–9, 233, 235
Countertransference, 23n3, 35–36, 41–42,
46–47, 50, 53, 57, 118, 138, 188, 207, 220,
279
"Creative Writers and Day-Dreaming"
(Freud), 70, 71, 84
Crews, Frederick, 212, 242

Dachet, François, 53n24
Damasio, Antonio, 268n35
Dante, 283–84
Darwin, Charles, 218, 235, 241–42, 246–47,
254, 265–67, 268n35
Davis, Douglas A., 37n5
Death drive, 118, 134n8, 151, 215n9, 277, 282
Deferred action, 27, 62, 267, 277–79, 283–84
de Forest, Izette, 101, 139n13
Delusions and Dreams in Jensen's "Gradiva"
(Freud), 1–21, 36n2, 38, 70, 124, 135,
183n42, 187, 221
Demos, E. Virginia, 228, 241n23
Dependent concomitant, 266–68, 269n36, 275
Derrida, Jacques, 14, 278
Descartes, René, 247, 276
Development of Psychoanalysis, The (Rank and
Ferenczi), 87n2, 109, 141, 143, 176,
209n2, 229
Diagnostic and Statistical Manual of Mental
Disorders, 274
Dilthey, Wilhelm, 71, 239, 244
"Dissolution of the Oedipus Complex, The"
(Freud), 154–55
"Dr. Sándor Ferenczi (On His Fiftieth
Birthday)" (Freud), 112–13
Doolittle, Hilda, 156n22, 194–97, 201n55
Dora case. See Fragment of an Analysis of a
Case of Hysteria
Dreams, 253–65, 269
Drive theory. See Libido theory
Dupont, Judith, 112n6

Eckstein, Emma, 119, 124, 159
Edelman, Gerald, 232, 234, 241–48, 252, 267,
268n35, 275–77, 279

Edelson, Marshall, 240n22, 246n24, 269n36
Edmunds, Lavinia, 39n8
Ego and the Id, The (Freud), 36, 141–43,
    151–52, 159, 165, 174, 176, 203–4, 211
Ego psychology, 142–43, 152, 204–5, 207–8,
    210–11, 213, 219, 222, 225–26, 237, 239–41,
    257n27
Einstein, Albert, 234
Eissler, Kurt R., 43–44, 209, 210n5, 219–22,
    225, 230, 232–33, 237, 256n27
Eitingon, Max, 114, 159
Enlightenment, the, 193, 202, 242, 247, 251
Esman, Aaron, 175
Esterson, Allen, 242
Ethology, 214–15, 275
Euripides, 74

Fairbairn, W. R. D., 14n12, 128, 182n41, 214,
    218
Family romance, 122, 261n33
Family therapy, 23, 44
Fechner, G. T., 265
Feldman, Michael, 230
Fellner, Oscar ("Herr E."), 37, 45–46, 48n18
Felman, Shoshana, 240–41
Female sexuality, 23, 26, 29, 31, 34, 50, 54, 55,
    108, 134n8, 168
Feminism, 16n13, 23, 33–34, 41, 55, 70,
    78–80, 86, 105–6, 115
Fenichel, Otto, 208, 221
Ferenczi, Sándor, 2n2, 17, 45, 59, 68, 69n7,
    89, 91, 98, 156, 183n42, 202, 210–12, 214,
    263
    and Franz Alexander, 210
    on analyst's need for humility, 95, 125, 128,
        140, 192;
    and approval, need for, 111–12, 120n13, 124,
        132, 137
    atheism of, 139–40
    "brother complex" of, 112–13, 117
    childhood traumas of, 115, 116n8, 121– 23,
        128–29, 131, 134–35, 137–38, 171–73, 181
    and Christianity, 140
    father, death of, 113
    as feminist, 105n19, 115, 134n8, 138, 191;
    and Freud: as alternative to, 109–10, 179,
        191, 217–18, 227, 256; correspondence
        with, 110, 112–13, 120, 129, 131, 145, 158,
        161–62, 173, 179–81; conflict with, 110,
        113, 120, 123, 130, 137, 163, 170–73; offers
        to analyze, 160, 180; takes Freud to task,
        112, 115–16, 121, 124, 134, 137–38, 173, 191,
        218; analyzed by, 116–18, 121, 137–38, 173;
    as "Grand Vizier," 126
    and Groddeck: correspondence with,
        120–22, 129, 131, 171, 176, 188, 203; friend-

ship with, 122, 124, 138, 153, 170–71, 173;
    visits to, 120, 130, 170–71, 180
imitates *Book of the It*, 171
infidelities of, 117
"kissing technique" of, 116, 136, 147
medical symptoms of, 120n13, 121–22,
    130–31, 172, 181
misogyny of, 130, 138
mother, death of, 120, 130–31, 170
openness, desire for, 124–25, 138, 171, 218
"Palermo incident," 107n1, 120, 124,
    171–73
and Géza Pálos, death of, 117, 181
and Gizella and Elma Pálos, 44, 117–24,
    137, 172, 181
pernicious anemia of, 116, 131, 133–34, 137,
    162
as postmodernist, 218–19
and Erzsébet Radó-Révész, death of,
    130–32, 134, 162–63
and seduction theory, revival of, 132,
    152n19
self-analysis of, 121–22, 124, 130, 132, 171–72
and Eugenia Sokolnicka, 180–81
and telepathy, 135, 181n40
transforms surgical metaphor, 94
and "utraquism," 128
and Winnicott, 95, 128, 133–34, 138
See also Clinical Diary; "Confusion of
    Tongues between Adults and the
    Child"; *Development of
    Psychoanalysis*; Freud, Sigmund;
    Groddeck, Georg; Mutual analysis;
    Rank, Otto; Severn, Elizabeth; *Tha-
    lassa*
Fetishism, 16, 24
Fielding, Henry, 45
"Findings, Observations, Problems"
    (Freud), 150
Flaubert, Gustave, 48, 70n8
Flax, Jane, 219n11
Fleischl-Marxow, Ernst von, 18
Fliess, Robert, 40n9
Fliess, Wilhelm, 3, 17, 18n16, 36, 37, 41, 45,
    48, 55, 60, 69, 75, 107n1, 119, 124,
    158–60, 161n28, 162, 185
Fluss, Gisela, 47n17
Förster-Nietzsche, Elizabeth, 146n10
Fogel, Gerald I., 87n2
Forrester, John, 59–60, 62, 85, 117n9, 281
Fortune, Christopher, 136n10, 136n11,
    171n34, 181n40
Fragment of an Analysis of a Case of Hysteria
    (Freud), 3, 5, 19, 22, 32, 34, 35, 36n3, 40,
    61, 159n26
Frankiel, Rita V., 43n13

Free associations, 220, 258–59, 261
French Revolution, 202, 247
French, Thomas M., 209
Freud, Anna, 23, 40, 44, 132–33, 209, 217
Freud, Ernst L., 149n15
Freud, Julius. See Freud, Sigmund
Freud, Mathilde, 18
Freud Museum (London), 5
Freud, Sigmund
  and archeology, 13n11, 19, 55
  atheism of, 139–40, 193
  and authority, refusal to surrender, 45,
    48n18, 160, 179–81, 202, 217
  cancer of, 68, 111n5, 116, 119n12, 137, 142,
    148n13, 154, 158–63
  and Christ, 193–95, 199–200, 205
  and death and loss, 13n11, 18n14, 20,
    49n20, 113, 129n4, 184–87
  and dissent, intolerance of, 67–69, 105n18,
    111, 118, 126n17, 133, 148, 200, 202, 216,
    218, 227, 239, 255
  dream of consilience of, 212, 217, 231, 240,
    280, 284
  on dreams, 254– 57, 258n30, 261, 264–65,
    267–68
  and environmental factors, neglect of, by,
    41, 118, 228
  family constellation of, 36, 46–47, 187
  on Ferenczi, 101, 109, 111–20, 133, 136, 147,
    172, 174
  genius of, 57, 108, 124, 203, 218, 255
  on Groddeck, 143, 145–47, 150, 154–55,
    158, 165, 167, 169, 174–75
  heterosexism of, 34
  hyperbole of, 6, 38, 62, 95, 216n10
  on hysteria, 19
  Jewish identity of, 41–42, 51– 56, 193
  and Julius, death of, 16–18, 184n41
  and masturbation, 84–85, 149–50, 158–59,
    162–63
  misanthropy of, 138, 192, 193n48
  and mother-child relationship, 45, 48n18,
    54, 93, 113, 138, 140, 155–56, 163, 169–70,
    178, 183n42, 187
  nanny of, 47, 49, 129n4, 184–87
  as neurologist, 266–68
  analyzes Elma Pálos, 122n15
  phallocentrism of, 24–33, 41, 50, 93, 105,
    115, 118, 138, 152, 167, 191, 194n49
  as Pope, 201– 2, 205
  and Rank: criticizes Rank, 62–63, 65, 69,
    97n12, 102n16, 119n12, 154–56; praises
    Rank, 67, 69, 76, 154–55
  repetition compulsion of, 17, 69, 201
  on science and poetry, 3, 128, 161n28
  scientific limitations of, 37–38, 114, 213–18,

    221n12, 227, 233, 235, 239, 248–49,
    254–55, 267, 282
  scientific validity of, 247, 253, 265, 267–68
  self-analysis of, 24, 57, 60, 113, 119n12, 141,
    160, 179, 182, 184–87
  Elizabeth Severn and Eugenia Sokol-
    nicka, antipathy to, 181–82
  and smoking, 158–59, 161–62
  surgical metaphor of, 93–94, 220
  technique of, 194, 210n5
  travel anxiety of, 47–48
  on war neuroses, 119n11, 153n20
  as writer, 5, 22–23, 248, 265
  See also Ferenczi, Sándor; Groddeck,
    Georg; titles of works
Friedman, Susan Stanford, 194n49
Frink, Horace, 39n8, 44
From the History of an Infantile Neurosis
  (Freud), 40, 47n17, 94, 96, 101–2,
  119n12, 135n9, 262
Fromm, Erich, 40, 152, 153n20, 201n54
Fromm-Reichmann, Frieda, 110n4, 142–43,
  152–53, 210, 277n40
Future of an Illusion, The (Freud), 3
"Future Prospects of Psycho-Analytic Ther-
  apy, The" (Freud), 36n4, 56

Gadamer, Hans-Georg, 224, 243
Garrison, Martha, 40n
Gay, Peter, 69
Gedo, John E., 210n4, 220–21, 277
Geller, Jay, 53n24
Giampieri-Deutsch, Patrizia, 109n2
Gill, Merton M., 209, 211, 213n7, 219, 221n12,
  222, 233–37, 240n22, 280n41
Gilman, Sander L., 41–42, 52–55, 56n26
Glenn, Jules, 28
Goethe, Johann Wolfgang von, 78
Goldstein, Kurt, 143n4, 277n40
Goltz, Else von der. See Groddeck,
  Georg
Gorbachev, Mikhail, 237
Graf, Max, 22–24, 26, 28, 30, 35n2, 42–44,
  51, 53n24, 200–202, 261
Graf, Herbert. See Analysis of a Phobia in a
  Five-Year-Old Boy
Green, André, 183, 215n9
Grillparzer, Franz, 75–76, 78
Grillparzer, Karl, 76
Griselda legend, 78
Groddeck, Barbara. See Groddeck, Georg
Groddeck, Georg, 91, 93, 98, 209–10, 261,
  265, 277n40
  on analytic relationship, 95, 125, 176–78,
    188, 192, 204–5
  anxiety of influence of, 145–46, 151, 172–73

attends Congress in The Hague, 120,
152–53, 166, 169
breakdown of, 163n20
on cancer, 162–63
childhood traumas of, 150, 182–85, 189
and Christianity, 169–70, 178, 192–99,
202–6
contemporary relevance of, 92, 156, 176,
188, 192, 203, 205, 212, 217
cultural influence of, 156–58
daughter Barbara, 190n47
and father, 146n10, 166, 177, 180, 190–91
as feminist, 153, 167–68, 175–76, 191
Ferenczi, mutual analysis with, 180
and Freud: contacts Freud, 120, 144, 167;
correspondence with, 145–47, 150–52,
167, 169; criticizes Freud, 144, 145n8,
151, 153, 156, 163, 168–70, 175, 192, 203,
205; dismisses *The Ego and the Id* by,
151–52, 203–4; interprets Freud's *Psychopathology of Everyday Life*, 159–61; invites Freud to Baden-Baden, 159, 161,
180; sends manuscript of *Book of the It*
to, 147, 150;
and Else von der Goltz, 122, 166, 186,
190–91
id, as source of concept of, 143–44, 146,
155, 165, 175
interprets Genesis, 167–69
as ironist, 205–6
and Lacan, 202–4
longing for acceptance of, 169
on masturbation, 149–50, 158, 164–65, 167
and Miss G., 144, 177–78, 180
on mother-child bond, 166, 169–70, 176,
182–85, 188–89, 191, 197–99
oedipal and preoedipal experiences of,
185–88
persona of, 164, 166, 176–77, 204
psychosomatic symptoms of, 172, 191
on poisoning complex, 61n2
politics of, 175
and Rank, 69n7, 151, 153–56, 167, 176
and reformation of psychoanalysis, 203–5
and Hanneliese Schumann, 166, 169, 176
self-analysis of, 151, 164–65, 174, 182–85,
187, 190
and siblings, 166, 184, 189
as touchstone, 152, 157, 166
and Emmy von Voigt, 122, 151, 159, 161,
166–67, 190–91, 203
warmth of, 122, 171, 180
and Winnicott, 182, 188–92, 198–99
See also Book of the It; Ferenczi, Sándor;
Freud, Sigmund; *Soul-Seeker*
Gross, Otto, 178

Grossman, Carl M., and Sylva Grossman,
142n3, 145–46, 153n20, 183n42
Grotjahn, Martin, 195
Grubrich-Simitis, Ilse, 141, 142n2, 155n21
Grünbaum, Adolf, 223–25, 231, 238, 240n22,
258n30, 280–1
Günderode, Karoline von, 80
Guntrip, Harry, 12, 14n12, 128, 136, 182n41,
183n42

Habermas, Jürgen, 224, 237, 243, 281
Haeckel, Ernst, 213, 215, 267
Hamilton, James W., 13, 21
Hamilton, Victoria, 226
Harlow, Harry, 214, 270, 275
Harmat, Paul, 109n2
Harris, Adrienne, 109n2, 219n11
Hartmann, Eduard von, 144, 146
Hartmann, Heinz, 217–18, 239–40, 269n36,
277
Haütler, Adolf, 81
Haynal, André E., 43n14, 109n2, 202
Hebb, Donald, 267
Heidegger, Martin, 37
Heisenberg, Werner, 234
Heller, Hugo, 7n8
Helmholtz, Hermann von, 218
Herman, Judith Lewis, 79n14
Hermann, Imre, 214
Hermeneutics, 37, 46, 56, 71, 107n1, 211,
214n8, 217, 219, 221n12, 222–25, 229–40,
244, 250–52, 257, 260, 264. *See also* Psy-
choanalysis
Hernandez, Max, 229
Hertz, Neil, 35n1
Hesiod, 73
Hitschmann, Eduard, 67
Hobson, J. Allan, 254–65, 268n35, 269, 279
Hoffer, Axel, 136n11
Hoffmann, E. T. A., 11, 12, 15
Hoffman, Irwin Z., 209
Holland, Norman N., 132n6
Holt, Robert R., 213–15, 218, 227, 232,
234–35, 239n21, 249, 253, 282
Home, H. J., 231–32, 234
Homosexuality, 26, 33–34, 106, 107n1, 125,
150
Hopkins, Brooke, 140
Horney, Karen, 32–33, 115, 152, 165
Human sciences. *See* Hermeneutics
Hus, Jan, 128

Ibsen, Henrik, 79, 166
Imago, 165n30
Incest Theme in Literature and Legend, The
(Rank), 58–85, 97n12, 124

"Infantile Genital Organization, The"
    (Freud), 24, 26n8, 29
Inhibitions, Symptoms and Anxiety (Freud),
    93, 155, 165, 274
International Psychoanalytic Association,
    59, 67, 147, 202, 223
Internationale Zeitschrift für Psychoanalyse,
    148
Interpersonal analysis, 110, 208, 211
Interpretation of Dreams, The (Freud), 2, 3, 18,
    27n8, 38, 41n10, 46, 50n21, 59–62, 73,
    74n12, 75–76, 96n10, 97, 145, 148n14,
    159n25, 160, 170, 182, 191, 248n26,
    253–54, 264, 266
Introductory Lectures on Psycho-Analysis
    (Freud), 38n7
Irigaray, Luce, 23, 28n10, 28n11, 33n17

Jackson, Hughlings, 266
Jacobus, Mary, 15, 40n9
James, William, 268n35
Jameson, Fredric, 253
Jamison, Kay Redfield, 90
Janet, Pierre, 19
Jensen, Wilhelm, 1–21, 124, 135, 187–88. See
    also Delusions and Dreams in Jensen's
    "Gradiva"
Jentsch, Ernst, 11, 16
Jones, Ernest, 2n2, 68, 70, 74, 109–10, 114,
    126n17, 152, 154, 159n25, 181, 192, 209n2,
    209n3, 267; on Rank, 65, 88–90, 209n2,
    247
Journal of the American Psychoanalytic Associa-
    tion, 221
Joyce, James, 143n5, 261
Jung, C. G., 2, 20, 23n3, 45, 59, 60, 68, 109,
    111, 113, 132, 134n7, 147–48, 178–79, 192,
    201n55, 250, 255–57, 263–64, 268n35;
    and Rank, 63–66, 69, 73, 77, 83–84, 90,
    101, 122, 126n17, 129n4, 160, 161n28, 202
Jung, Emma, 174

Kahr, Brett, 190
Kandel, Eric R., 242, 270–75
Kant, Immanuel, 107n1, 253
Kaplan-Solms, Karen, 241n23
Kardiner, Abram, 99n14, 100
Kerr, John, 60, 62, 151n18
Kimball, Jean, 261n61
Kirsner, Douglas, 216n10
Kitcher, Patricia, 212, 215–16, 218, 249, 282
Klein, George S., 213n7, 219, 221n12, 223, 227
Klein, Melanie, 23n4, 55, 84, 96, 98, 100,
    133, 134n8, 209, 217–18, 226–28, 230, 241,
    275, 282n43
Koberstein, August, 146n10, 183

Kofman, Sarah, 1n1, 23n4
Kohut, Heinz, 210n5, 211, 222n13, 230n17, 277
Kramer, Robert, 66n6, 86n1
Kraus, Karl, 142n1
Kris, Anton, 230
Krüll, Marianne, 129n4

Lacan, Jacques, 14, 25, 40n9, 43, 51, 70, 187,
    202–4, 219n11, 240– 41, 256n27, 275,
    277
Lamarck, Jean Baptiste, 213, 215–16, 227, 233,
    235, 267, 282
Laplanche, Jean, 215n9, 283
Lear, Jonathan, 211
Leitner, Marina, 87n2, 92
Leonardo da Vinci and a Memory of His Child-
    hood (Freud), 5–8, 70
Lessing, Gotthold Ephraim, 193
Levy, Lajos, 130
Lewin, Kurt, 105
Lewinter, Roger, 142n3, 144n6, 175
Libido theory, 24, 40–41, 69, 84–85, 86, 93,
    99–100, 108–9, 213–14, 215n9, 240n22,
    247, 276–77
Lieberman, E. James, 65n5, 88, 96, 105
Lindon, John A., 27n9, 40n9
Lipton, Samuel D., 210n5
Little Hans case. See Analysis of a Phobia in a
    Five-Year-Old Boy
Loewald, Hans W., 210–11, 222
Lomas, Peter, 128, 139n13
Luborsky, Lester, 229n16, 269n37
Lupton, Mary Jo, 32n16
Luria, A. R., 267
Luther, Martin, 204

Mahler, Gustav, 53n24
Mahler, Margaret, 92n6
Mahony, Patrick J., 23, 25n7, 35n1, 35n2,
    36n3, 47n17, 49n19, 54n25, 119n12
Mannoni, Maud, 14, 203n57
Marcus, Steven, 22n1
Martynkewicz, Wolfgang, 142n3, 144n6,
    145n8, 146n10, 165–66, 177
Masson, Jeffrey M., 119n12
Matricide, 73n11, 123, 130, 135, 137, 140, 163,
    199
McGuire, William, 2n2
Medawar, P. B., 242
Memling, Hans, 198n53
Meltzer, Donald, 23n4
Mendelssohn, Moses, 193
Menstruation, 32n16, 169
Merezhkovsky, Dmitry Sergeyevich, 7–8
Metapsychology, 213, 218–19, 221n12, 223n14,
    226–28, 230–31, 235, 237–39, 244, 267–68

Michelangelo, 198n53
Milton, John, 81, 250
Mitchell, Stephen A., 109n3, 110n4, 208–9, 211
Modell, Arnold H., 215, 248, 276–80
Moi, Toril, 35n1
Møller, Lis, 15, 19n17
Moltzer, Maria, 179–80
Morgann, Maurice, 4
Moses and Monotheism (Freud), 4, 54, 216
Mozart, Wolfgang Amadeus, 258–63
Mutual analysis, 111, 122, 129–31, 136, 140, 173, 178–82

Nachträglichkeit. See Deferred action
"Negation" (Freud), 260n31
Neuroscience, 213, 215, 221n12, 228, 231, 241–45, 247, 254, 264–81
New Introductory Lectures on Psycho-Analysis (Freud), 23, 27–28, 65, 69, 146
Nietzsche, Friedrich, 71, 125–26, 144, 146, 151, 155, 165, 201n55, 204
Nin, Anaïs, 65, 66n6, 89
Nitzschke, Bernd, 144
Nobel Prize, 242, 245
Notes upon a Case of Obsessional Neurosis (Freud), 6n6, 35–36, 40, 47n17, 54, 61, 210n5
Nuclear complex, 6–7, 59–60, 62–64, 77, 124
Nuremberg Congress, 59, 67, 147

Object relations theory, 13, 41, 55–56, 70, 85, 86–87, 93, 95, 98, 100, 109–10, 133, 142, 151, 153, 156, 165, 182, 192, 203–4, 207–12, 214–15, 218, 226–27, 230n17, 240–41, 256, 280, 283
Oedipus complex, 36, 48, 59–61, 73–74, 76, 121–24, 132, 135, 137, 141, 150, 155–56, 185–86, 189, 205, 259–60, 262; as defensive formation, 54–55, 60, 183n42, 184, 187, 191; in Little Hans case, 38–39, 41, 61; and relational theory, 85. *See also* Nuclear complex
Oedipus myth, 27n8, 36, 56, 61, 74n12, 75–77, 83, 199, 201. *See also* Sophocles; Sphinx's riddle
On Aphasia (Freud), 265–67, 273
On Dreams (Freud), 248n26
On the History of the Psycho-Analytic Movement (Freud), 69, 109, 148n13, 225
"On Narcissism: An Introduction" (Freud), 70
"On the Sexual Theories of Children" (Freud), 27n9
Outline of Psycho-Analysis, An (Freud), 214, 280–81

Palombo, Stanley R., 214n8
Pálos, Elma. *See* Ferenczi, Sándor; Freud, Sigmund
Pálos, Géza. *See* Ferenczi, Sándor
Pálos, Gizella. *See* Ferenczi, Sándor
Parameters, 219–21
Paskauskas, R. Andrew, 89
Paul, St., 170
Pavlov, Ivan Petrovich, 273–74
Pfeiffer, Ernst, 97n12
Pfister, Oscar, 139, 148–49, 152–53, 175n36, 192–94
Phylogenetic Fantasy, A (Freud), 114
Plato, 81
Poe, Edgar Allan, 240
Pollock, George H., 191
Popper, Karl, 225, 232
Postmodernism, 1, 15, 19n17, 70, 82, 188, 211, 218–19, 234, 240–41, 249, 252–53, 277
Primal scene, 47, 101, 104, 135n9, 262
Project for a Scientific Psychology (Freud), 3, 267, 278
Psychoanalysis
    1923 as turning point in, 141– 42, 176, 204, 207, 209, 212, 217–18, 256
    clinical and applied, 5–6, 237
    and cognitive psychology, 221n12, 270–71
    distinction between theory and practice in, 212, 219, 226, 228–30, 235, 238, 253
    ennobling power of, 125, 218
    fusion of science and hermeneutics in, 218–19, 223, 225, 231, 237–43, 249, 251–54, 256, 268, 280, 282, 284
    history of, 62, 107–8, 110, 200–202
    as means of emancipation, 34
    neoclassicism in, 209, 210n5, 219, 222
    paradigm shift in, 109–10, 142–43, 192, 207, 209, 211–12, 222, 227
    personal roots of, 32, 46, 90, 108, 125, 127, 132, 156, 182
    and psychotherapy, 209, 220–21, 228, 270, 273–74, 279
    as religion, 200–206, 216n10
    See also Dreams; Hermeneutics; Neuroscience; Science
Psycho-Analytic Notes on an Autobiographical Account of a Case of Paranoia (Freud), 5, 6, 7, 40, 54, 68, 107n1, 120n13, 172, 173
Psychological Wednesday Society. *See* Vienna Psychoanalytic Society
"Psychopathic Characters on the Stage" (Freud), 42
Psychopathology of Everyday Life, The (Freud), 49n20, 145, 159–62, 186

Qualia, 243
Question of Lay Analysis, The (Freud),
38*n*7
Quinn, Susan, 153*n*20

Rabelais, François, 149, 175*n*36
Racine, Jean, 74
Radnitzky, G., 231
Radó, Sándor, 112, 130–32
Radó-Révész, Erzsébet. *See* Ferenczi, Sándor
Rand, Nicholas, and Maria Torok, 13*n*11
Rangell, Leo, 208, 221, 256*n*27
Rank, Otto
   analytic situation, conception of, 93–104,
      106
   androcentrism of, 79–80, 97, 105
   anni mirabiles of, 64, 86–106, 110, 133
   autobiography, covert, in, 90–91
   childhood trauma of, 129*n*4
   dreams, interest in, 96
   enduring achievements of, 92–93, 98–99
   environmental factors, neglect of,
      99–100, 105–6
   on family romance, 261*n*33
   and Ferenczi, 89, 92–93, 100–101, 104,
      105*n*19, 111, 132, 142, 155, 209*n*2, 212, 217
   and Freud: criticizes Freud, 93, 98, 101–2,
      104, 156; as heir to Freud, 68, 90–91,
      97; reaction to Freud's cancer, 69*n*7,
      89*n*4, 203*n*58;
   on homosexuality, 106
   on incest plots, 75–76
   and Klein, 98–100, 133
   manic-depressive tendencies of, 65,
      88–90, 102, 152*n*19
   marriage of, 87, 180
   as first object relations psychoanalyst, 86,
      92
   oedipal paradigm, rejects, 64, 69*n*7,
      91–92, 155
   productivity of, 65, 87
   as Romantic, 82
   science, rejection of, 104
   self-contradictions of, 88, 103–4
   and Elizabeth Severn, 136
   and Eugenia Sokolnicka, 180
   Trauma of Birth, abjures, 151*n*17
   unconscious and genetic outlook, repudiates, 86, 101–2
   Vienna Psychoanalytic Society, as Secretary of, 58
   weaknesses of final period, 66, 86, 93*n*8,
      104–6
   writings on art and literature, 70
   See also Analysis of a Neurosis in Dreams;

Development of Psychoanalysis; Freud,
   Sigmund; Groddeck, Georg; *Incest
   Theme in Literature and Legend*; Jung,
   C. G.; *Trauma of Birth*
Rapaport, David, 213*n*7
Rat Man case. *See Notes upon a Case of Obsessional Neurosis*
Reader-response criticism, 70, 72
"Recommendations to Physicians Practicing
   Psycho-Analysis" (Freud), 56
Reduction, principle of, 246–47, 252, 275
Regression, 263, 265
Reiser, Morton F., 268–70, 274–75, 277, 279,
   283
Relational theory. *See* Object relations theory
Renik, Owen, 222
Repetition, 277, 279
"Repression" (Freud), 11
Repression, concept of, 6, 16, 73–74, 76,
   79–81, 164
Resistance, 225, 248
Richter, Gregory C., 58*n*1
Ricoeur, Paul, 8, 237*n*19
Roazen, Paul, 147*n*11, 149*n*15
Roith, Estelle, 32
Rose, Louis, 7*n*8, 42*n*11, 70*n*8, 201*n*54
Roustang, François, 166–67, 169
Rubinstein, Benjamin B., 213*n*7, 214*n*8,
   242*n*23
Rudnytsky, Peter L., 16, 37, 56, 60, 66, 76,
   85*n*17, 86, 88, 92*n*6, 93*n*7, 98*n*12, 108*n*1,
   109*n*2, 110*n*4, 126*n*17, 129*n*3, 139*n*13,
   144*n*7, 182*n*41, 187*n*45, 203*n*56, 208*n*1,
   212*n*6, 214*n*8, 218, 224, 231*n*18; 257*n*29,
   258*n*30, 281
Rycroft, Charles, 231*n*18; 257*n*29

Sabourin, Pierre, 109*n*2
Sacks, Oliver, 157–58, 161, 265–68, 276
Sadger, Isidor, 42*n*11, 70
"Sándor Ferenczi" (Freud), 109, 113–16
Sass, Louis A., 107*n*1, 257
Schächter, Miksa, 170
Schafer, Roy, 5, 33, 213*n*7, 277
Schiller, Christophine, 79
Schiller, Friedrich, 67, 72–75, 78–79
Schizophrenia, 273
Schopenhauer, Arthur, 144, 146
Schreber case. *See Psycho-Analytic Notes on
   an Autobiographical Account of a Case of
   Paranoia*
Schumann, Hanneliese. *See* Groddeck,
   Georg
Schur, Max, 8*n*9, 159, 161–62
Schweninger, Ernst, 145*n*8, 170, 177

Science, 104, 133, 137, 185, 197, 211–19,
    222–30, 242, 246, 251, 280–81; and sci-
    entism, 219, 221, 225, 240*n*22, 252. *See
    also* Freud, Sigmund; Psychoanalysis
"Screen Memories" (Freud), 159*n*25
Searles, Harold F., 143*n*4, 178*n*37
Seduction theory, 60, 62, 103–4, 114, 119,
    132, 141
Segal, Hanna, 282*n*43
Self psychology, 208, 230*n*17
Separation anxiety, 24, 64, 100, 103, 156*n*23,
    185, 189*n*46, 192, 198
Severn, Elizabeth, 115, 130, 136–39, 178–79,
    181
"Sexual Enlightenment of Children, The"
    (Freud), 25*n*7, 49*n*19
"Sexuality in the Aetiology of the Neuroses"
    (Freud), 38*n*7
Shakespeare, William, 4, 10–11, 19, 33*n*18,
    36, 73–75, 78, 90, 186– 87, 229*n*16,
    261*n*33, 269
Shapiro, Sue A., 136*n*10, 137
Shelley, Percy Bysshe, 67
Shengold, Leonard, 128*n*1
Sherrington, Sir Charles Scott, 267, 272
Siblings, 31–32, 44, 49, 67, 74–75, 78, 91–92,
    102, 112–13, 122, 164, 166, 184, 189
Silver, Ann-Louise S., 136
Silverman, Martin A., 29*n*12
Simmel, Ernst, 152, 153*n*20
Slochower, Harry, 134*n*7, 179*n*38
Smith, Nancy A., 136*n*11
Sociobiology, 245–46, 248
Sokolnicka, Eugenia, 180–81
Solms, Mark, 241*n*23, 264–65, 270
"Some Elementary Lessons of Psycho-
    Analysis" (Freud), 280–81
Sontag, Susan, 157
Sophocles, 74–75, 81, 186–87. *See also* Oedi-
    pus complex; Oedipus myth
Soul-Seeker, The (Groddeck), 149, 153,
    165*n*30, 174–75, 197
"Special Type of Choice of Object Made by
    Men, A" (Freud), 36*n*4, 59, 186
Spence, Donald P., 237*n*19
Spencer, Herbert, 266
Spengler, Oswald, 155
Spezzano, Charles, 209, 211
Sphinx's riddle, 49–50
Spielrein, Sabina, 151
Spiro, Joanna, 194*n*49
Spitz, Ellen Handler, 83*n*16
Spitz, René, 214, 270
Sprengnether, Madelon, 32, 35*n*1, 187
Stanton, Martin, 109*n*2
Stärke, August, 156*n*23

Steele, Robert S., 231, 233, 235–36
Stekel, Wilhelm, 2, 17, 42*n*11, 65, 67, 80, 111*n*5,
    142*n*1, 146–51, 153, 167, 175, 200, 202
Stepansky, Paul E., 66–68, 93–94
Stolorow, Robert D., 222*n*13
Stone, Leo, 210
Strachey, James, 24*n*5, 24*n*6, 27*n*9, 49*n*19,
    152, 277–78
Strean, Herbert S., 25*n*3
Strenger, Carlo, 281–83
Structural theory. *See* Ego psychology;
    Metapsychology
Studies on Hysteria (Breuer and Freud), 3, 4,
    5, 6, 38, 71
Sullivan, Harry Stack, 136, 143*n*4, 208,
    277*n*40
Sulloway, Frank J., 91–92, 112*n*6, 258*n*30
Suttie, Ian, 214
Svevo, Italo, 143*n*5, 175*n*35
Swales, Peter J., 3*n*3, 18*n*15, 18*n*16, 37*n*5,
    123*n*16, 159*n*25
Swan, Jim, 186–87
Swoboda, Hermann, 3*n*3

Taft, Jessie, 111*n*5
Tausk, Victor, 147
Teicholz, Judith Guss, 211
Thalassa (Ferenczi), 92, 105*n*19, 112, 114,
    128*n*2, 141, 143, 172, 176
This, Bernard, 122
Thomä, Helmut, 277–78
Thompson, Clara, 110, 136, 138
Three Essays on the Theory of Sexuality
    (Freud), 38, 40, 46, 55, 60–61
Timms, Edward, 6*n*5, 142*n*1
Totem and Taboo (Freud), 6, 36, 38, 60, 62,
    92, 123–24, 150, 216, 248
Transference, 1–3, 5, 19–21, 97–98, 103, 108,
    116, 118, 121–23, 130, 134*n*8, 137, 145, 151,
    156, 164–65, 169–70, 172, 178, 182, 188,
    194, 204, 208, 210, 220–21, 225, 229*n*16,
    278–79. *See also* Countertransference
Transitional objects, 84, 188
Trauma of Birth, The (Rank), 64, 66, 68–69,
    89–92, 94*n*9, 96–99, 102–5, 110, 114, 141,
    143, 151*n*17, 154–56, 174, 176, 203*n*58
Traub, Valerie, 33*n*18
Treuerniet, Nikolaas, 222*n*13
Trilling, Lionel, 81
Turnbull, Oliver, 241*n*23
Typology, 283–84

"Uncanny, The" (Freud), 10–11, 16, 17, 56*n*26
"Unconscious, The" (Freud), 145
Unconscious, concept of, 86, 102, 157,
    247–48, 257, 268*n*35

Vaughan, Susan C., 268n35, 276
Vienna Psychoanalytic Society, 2, 22, 42,
    58–59, 62–63, 66–68, 70, 74–75, 81, 145,
    147, 148n14, 149, 180, 200, 202
Vitz, Paul C., 10n10, 53n24, 129n4, 159n25,
    201n54
Voigt, Emmy von. *See* Groddeck, Georg

Wagner, Richard, 42, 53n24
Wallerstein, Robert S., 109n3, 203n56, 207–12,
    215, 217–18, 222–32, 237–38, 244, 284
Webster, Richard, 159n26
Weininger, Otto, 3n3, 52
Weiss, Joseph, and Harold Sampson,
    274n38, 279n41
Wellek, René, and Austin Warren, 71, 75
Wheelis, Allen, 203n56
Wilcocks, Robert, 18n16, 242
Wilde, Oscar, 234
Will, Herbert, 120, 142n3, 144n6, 146n10,
    152, 170, 175n35, 180

Wilson, Edmund, 81
Wilson, Edward O., 242, 245–55, 275
Winnicott, Alice, 190
Winnicott, Clare, 189, 191, 218
Winnicott, D. W., 84, 85n17, 95, 98, 100,
    128, 133–35, 138, 182, 188–92, 198–99,
    208, 211, 214–15, 218, 219n11, 225, 229,
    280
Winnicott, Elisabeth, 190
Wittels, Fritz, 45n15, 141–42, 147, 149, 202
Wittgenstein, Ludwig, 107n1
Wolf Man case. *See From the History of an
    Infantile Neurosis*
Wolff, Peter H., 215n9
Wolpe, Joseph, 40
Worbs, Michael, 71n10

Yeats, William Butler, 199, 241
Yerushalmi, Yosef Hayim, 193

Zentrallblatt für Psychoanalyse, 147–49

Cornell Studies in the History of Psychiatry

A Series Edited by

SANDER L. GILMAN
GEORGE J. MAKARI